Trying kangaroo meat in Northern Territory, Australia

Many Great Barrier Reef fish sport surreal colouring

ADVENTURE TRAVELLERS

AUSTRALIA
& NEW ZEALAND

AA World Travel Guides

ADVENTURE TRAVELLERS

AUSTRALIA
& NEW ZEALAND

Produced by AA Publishing
© Automobile Association Developments Ltd 2001
Maps © Automobile Association Developments Ltd 2001
Coloured maps produced by the Cartographic Department,
The Automobile Association
Black and white maps produced by Advanced Illustration,
Congleton, Cheshire
A CIP catalogue record for this book is available from
the British Library
ISBN 0-7495-2357-3

The contents of this publication are believed correct at the time of
printing. Nevertheless, the publishers cannot be held responsible for any
errors or omissions or for changes in the details given in this guide or for
the consequences of any reliance on the information provided by the
same. Assessments of sights, accommodation, restaurants and so forth are
based upon the authors' own experience and, therefore, descriptions
given in this guide necessarily contain an element of subjective opinion
which may not reflect the publisher's opinion or dictate a reader's own
experience on another occasion.
We have tried to ensure accuracy in this guide, but things do change
and we would be grateful if readers would advise us of any inaccuracies
they may encounter.
The areas covered in this guide can be subject to political, economic,
and climatic upheaval, readers should consult tour operators, embassies
and consulates, airlines, etc. for current requirements and advice before
travelling. The publishers and authors cannot accept responsibility for any
loss, injury, or inconvenience, however caused.

Published by AA Publishing, a trading name of Automobile Association
Developments Limited, whose registered office is Norfolk House, Priestley
Road, Basingstoke, Hampshire RG24 9NY.
Registered number 1878835.

Visit our website at www.theAA.com

Colour separation by Chroma Graphics, Singapore
Printed and bound by G Canale & C. s.p.a., Torino, Italy
Previous page: *Canoeing in Diamond Gorge, Western Australia*
Inset: *Rainforest trek, Queensland*

CONTENTS

INTRODUCTION

Geographically, Australia and New Zealand are vastly different but both countries are renowned for their adventure potential, so you are sure to find something to quicken your pulse in this part of the world. Australia is simply enormous, so plan on coming back to do it justice. With the pristine rainforest wilderness regions of Tasmania, Queensland and the Northern Territory, the sparsely populated deserts of South Australia and the centre, the glorious coastline of Western Australia and the mountains of New South Wales and Victoria, there is a bewildering choice of top class adventure locations. You can bike, hike, dive, climb, surf, drive and ride horses and camels to your heart's content, learn about the incredible Aboriginal people and their culture or visit remote cattle stations. Australia has it all. In comparison, New Zealand is tiny but still manages to pack in an extraordinary variation of terrain, from the rugged, glacial peaks of the New Zealand Alps to the rainforests and lakeland region in the south. Whether you want to travel by bike, horse, raft, jet boat or on foot there are places to visit that rival anywhere else on Earth for beauty. *En route*, you can meet the magnificent Maori people; spot whales or perhaps soak in hot springs. It may be a little nation but New Zealand is certainly in the big league of adventure destinations.

Lake Wakatipu, New Zealand
Inset: *Fox Glacier*

About the Authors

STEVE WATKINS

Photographer and writer Steve Watkins specializes in covering adventure travel, extreme sports and cultural issues, especially in his favourite destinations Latin America and Australia.

His work has featured in numerous publications, including *No Limits World*, *Traveller*, *Global Adventure*, *Wanderlust*, *Mountain Biking UK*, *Sunday Express* and various BBC publications, and his photographs have been widely exhibited, including at London's Barbican Gallery. Now based in south Wales, he has recently finished writing *Adventure Sports Europe* (Queensgate Publishing).

SIMON RICHMOND

Simon Richmond's first brush with adventure was on the Big Dipper roller-coaster in his home-town of Blackpool, England. He's been in search of the same adrenalin rush ever since. Now based in Sydney, Australia, he's worked as a journalist in London and Tokyo. His features have been published in many U.K. newspapers, the *Sydney Morning Herald*, and *The Australian*. He now spends most of his time travelling and writing guidebooks for the AA, Lonely Planet and Rough Guides.

MATT CAWOOD

Matt Cawood is an independent journalist and travel writer. He has written for many magazines and newspapers including the *Sunday Times*. He lives in the Outback in New South Wales.

LEE KAREN STOW

Lee Karen Stow is a full-time travel journalist and photographer, based in Yorkshire, England. A member of the British Guild of Travel Writers, Lee's work has appeared

in a number of publications including *The Times*; the *Sunday Express*; *In Britain*; *Wanderlust*; *Travel Weekly* among others. Born with a wandering spirit, Lee travels whenever possible perhaps scuba diving, scrubbing floors, sailing a yacht or teaching English to schoolchildren.

CHRISTOPHER KNOWLES

Christopher Knowles used to travel the world as a tour guide, specializing in journeys by train across Europe, the Soviet

Union, the Silk Road, Mongolia and China. The author of books on Shanghai, China, Japan, Moscow and St Petersburg, Tuscany, and the English Cotswolds, he also runs a company specializing in walking holidays.

ANNA CARTER

Anna Carter is a full-time writer at what others describe as the wrong end of her forties but which she describes as the best age yet. She is happily ensconced in her homeland, New Zealand, after much wandering, including a lengthy stint in Britain. She was one of the first New Zealand women to qualify as a hot

air balloon pilot and enjoys stepping outside her comfort zone whenever possible.

VERONIKA MEDUNA & ANDY REISINGER

Veronika Meduna has worked for *The Press* in Christchurch, New Zealand, for a number of years and has written several books. She is best known for her international best-seller *Teach your children well*, but has

also written many travel features. Andy Reisinger is a well-known outdoor photographer who works for Hedgehog, New Zealand's leading photographic agency.

REBECCA FORD

Rebecca Ford is a full-time travel writer and photographer. Her travels

have taken her all over the world—from walking the Great Bear's Trail in Finland to whale watching in Canada's Hudson Bay.

How to Use this Book

The book is divided into three distinct sections:

◢ SECTION 1 · PAGES 6–17

This comprises the introductory material and some general practical advice to guide you on your travels. We have included an introduction to the writing team. Our authors come from all walks of life and cover a wide age range. What they do have in common, though, is a spirit of adventure and a wealth of travel experience.

The map on pages 10–11 shows the areas covered, and is colour-coded to highlight the regional divides. The 25 adventures are numbered for reference; the contents page will guide you straight to the relevant page numbers.

Pages 12–17 offer practical advice from experienced travellers, complementing information given later.

The seasonal calendar inside the cover gives a guide to the optimum time to visit the areas covered in the adventures. However, there are many factors affecting when you might like to go, and greater details of climate patterns and their effect on activities are given at the end of each chapter. When arranging your trip always seek advice about the conditions you are likely to encounter from a tour operator or country tourist information office.

◢ SECTION 2 · PAGES 18–256

The main section of the book contains 25 adventures, chosen to give you a taste of a wide range of activities in a variety of places—some familiar, others not. The first page of each adventure carries a practical information box that gives you an idea of what to expect, plus a grade, numbered according to the relative difficulty of the activity or the level of skill required.

Going it Alone—Each adventure ends with a page of dedicated practical advice for planning that specific adventure yourself. This information should be used in conjunction with the "Blue Pages" at the end of the book (see below).

Any prices mentioned in the book are given in U.S. dollars and were the approximate prices current at the time of the trip. Due to variations in inflation and exchange rates these are only meant as guidelines to give an idea of comparative cost.

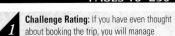

 Challenge Rating: If you have even thought about booking the trip, you will manage

 Not too difficult but you may need some basic skills

 You will need to be fit, with lots of stamina and may need specialist qualifications

 You need to be fit and determined—not for the faint-hearted*

 This is for the serious adventurer— physically and mentally challenging!*

Sometimes only part of the trip is very hard and there may be an easier option

 Comfort rating: Indicates the degree of hardship you can expect, where 3 is comfortable and 1 is uncomfortable. This category not only covers accommodation, but also
 factors such as climate and other conditions that may affect your journey.

Specialist equipment: Advice on any equipment needed for the journey, covering specialist items like diving gear, and also clothing and photographic gear.

◢ SECTION 3 · PAGES 257–320

"Blue Pages"—*Contacts* and *A–Z of Activities*—begin with selected contacts specific to the 25 main adventures. Here you'll find names referred to in the main stories, including tour operators, with addresses and contact numbers.

The A–Z lists a wide range of the best activities available in the region, with general information and full contact details of the outfits and organizations able to help you plan your journey. Finally, the book ends with a comprehensive index and gazetteer.

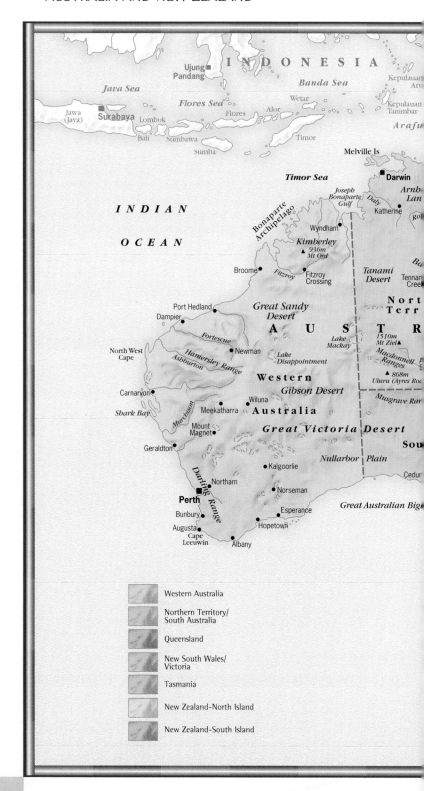

INDONESIA

Ujung Pandang

Java Sea

Banda Sea

Kepulauan Aru

Flores Sea

Wetar

Kepulauan Tanimbar

Jawa (Jaya)   Surabaya

Lombok   Flores   Alor

Arafu

Bali   Sumbawa   Timor

Sumba

Melville Is

Timor Sea

Darwin

INDIAN

Joseph Bonaparte Gulf

Daly

Arnh Lan

Katherine   Ro

Wyndham

Bonaparte Archipelago

Kimberley
936m
Mt Ord

OCEAN

Broome   Fitzroy   Fitzroy Crossing

Tanami Desert

Ba

Tennan Cree

Great Sandy Desert

Port Hedland

A   U   S   T   R

Dampier

North Terr

Fortescue

Lake Mackay

1510m
Mt Ziel▲

North West Cape

Hamersley Range   Newman

Ashburton

Lake Disappointment

Macdonnell Ranges

S

Western

Gibson Desert

▲ 868m
Uluru (Ayres Roc

Carnarvon

Wiluna

Meekatharra   Australia

Musgrave Ran

Shark Bay   Murchison

Mount Magnet

Great Victoria Desert

Geraldton

Sou

Nullarbor Plain

Kalgoorlie

Cedur

Northam

Darling Range

Norseman

Great Australian Big

Perth

Esperance

Bunbury

Augusta   Hopetown

Cape Leeuwin   Albany

Western Australia

Northern Territory/ South Australia

Queensland

New South Wales/ Victoria

Tasmania

New Zealand-North Island

New Zealand-South Island

Practical Matters

TRAVEL DOCUMENTS

Although a passport is the first thing to be packed by most travellers, it is worth checking to ensure that it is valid for much longer than your stay, and there are enough blank pages left for visa stamps. Many immigration officials are reluctant to stamp previously used pages, no matter how much space is left on them. It is also important to carry several copies of the passport, especially the front cover, personal details page and those pages containing any essential visas. These copies can speed up a new passport should it be lost or stolen. It is also worth leaving copies at home with friends or relatives, in case you lose everything.

Check at least a couple of months before you leave about the visa requirements for the countries you are visiting. Obtaining visas has become much easier in the last decade or so as governments have realized that tourism numbers increase with a reduction in red tape. Many countries now allow tourist visas to be issued on entry, especially if you arrive by air, although others still require you to obtain a visa before travelling. If possible, get a visa for the longest duration possible and certainly for longer than you intend to be there. This allows you to stay on if you like it too much to leave, and provides leeway for any problems with delays departing the country, such as cancelled flights or illness.

HEALTH MATTERS

Nothing can make such a difference to your enjoyment of an adventure as your health, so it is worth taking as many precautions as possible to maintain it. Necessary vaccinations vary with the country you are visiting and even which region of the country you go to, but ensuring your protection against tetanus is current is important wherever you go. Give yourself plenty of time, at least six weeks, to get all the necessary vaccinations, as some require more than one visit to the doctor. Also, if you think you already have a full complement of inoculations then it is still worth checking with a doctor before travelling as situations change regularly and there can be sudden outbreaks of diseases. Record your vaccinations on an International Health Certificate and carry it with you.

Don't ignore the dentist either in preparation for a trip. Get your teeth checked out at home as it can cost a surprisingly large amount of money to get dental work done in other countries; costs that may not be covered by your travel insurance. It's particularly important to have your teeth in good working order when visiting very cold places, as the temperature can cause problems with fillings.

INSURANCE

Unless you are fabulously wealthy or a big time gambler then comprehensive travel insurance is essential. It may seem to cost a lot for something you are unlikely to use, but if things do go wrong then it could not only save your holiday, but it

---

❛❜ LANGUAGE

English is the major language spoken throughout Australia and New Zealand. The Australian Aborigines and the New Zealand Maoris have their own languages, but all speak English too.

LOCAL CURRENCY

Australia's currency is the dollar (A$) and comes in notes of A$100, A$50, A$20, A$10 and A$5 with coin denominations of AU$2, AU$1, 50 cents, 20 cents, 10 cents and 5 cents. New Zealand's currency is also called the dollar (NZ$) with the same denomination notes and coins as in Australia.

In both countries there are A.T.M. cash machines that accept international credit and debit cards in most major towns and all cities. VISA and Mastercard are very widely accepted for payment and American Express to a lesser extent.

could save you going bankrupt too. If you aren't convinced then consider the cost of being airlifted from a mountain environment with a serious injury then transferred to a suitable hospital. Think in tens of thousands of U.S. dollars and suddenly the insurance fee seems a bargain. If you want to ensure the best care then take out a good policy, including cover for personal accident, medical and air ambulance, personal liability, legal expenses, cancellation, personal baggage and loss of passport. Make sure the policy covers "adventure" activities, which are usually excluded from ordinary policies. With the baggage cover, check the single item limits as expensive items, such as cameras, can fall outside this. If you're lucky enough to travel a few times a year, consider an annual policy. They can be cheaper than several individual policies.

Keep receipts for anything you buy to go away, or instead take a photograph of all your gear laid out. With more fraudulent claims taking place every year, insurance companies are even keener to prove ownership. Each insurance company has differing requirements for lodging a claim but the very least you will need to do for theft cases is obtain a signed local police report

detailing the incident and every item that was taken.

MONEY

There are several useful ways of getting access to money while travelling that reduce the risk of loss through theft. A very popular option is to take travellers' cheques, which can be converted into local currency at banks and larger hotels or even used to pay directly. The most widely accepted travellers' cheques are Thomas Cook, American Express and Visa in US$. Be aware though that on top of the commission fees most issuers charge to issue the cheques, you are often charged another commission fee to use them, which can result in significant loss of value (3 percent or more). But they are easy to replace, if you keep records.

With the spread of automatic bank teller machines (A.T.M.s) to even remote areas, an easy way to get money is via a credit or debit card. If you have a Personal Identification Number (P.I.N.) and a card that is linked to one of the international transaction systems, such as Link or Cirrus, you can withdraw local currency up to your daily limit. Many machines detect the nationality of your card and provide instructions in your

VACCINATIONS

There are no compulsory vaccinations needed for travel to either Australia or New Zealand, though it is wise to ensure your tetanus jab is up to date. There is no malaria either, though the far north of Australia is occasionally susceptible to very small outbreaks.

CUSTOMS/ENTRY REQUIREMENTS

All visitors to Australia who do not hold an Australian or New Zealand passport must obtain visas before arriving in the country. Three and six-month tourist visas are easily obtained from Australian consulates around the world. Twelve-month working holiday visas are available for 18–25-year-old single visitors from the U.K., Japan, Canada, Korea and Holland (the age restriction is sometimes open to interpretation).

New Zealand issues six-month tourist visas on arrival to nationals of the United Kingdom, and three-month tourist visas on arrival to nationals of many other countries, including the U.S. and most European countries. If you are aged 18–30 and from the U.K., Japan or Canada you can enter New Zealand on a 12-month working holiday visa, but this has to be obtained from a New Zealand consulate before entering the country. New Zealand has strict regulations on bringing in organic matter. This may mean they insist you clean your muddy boots or camping gear before they let you through customs!

own language, just to make things even easier. This is a very safe way of carrying money and can be very cost effective on debit cards. However, credit card companies treat foreign currency withdrawals as cash advances. Wherever you travel, carry some cash with you, but don't make it so much that losing it could spoil your trip. The more remote the area you are visiting the more important it is to carry smaller denominations, as sometimes change for large notes can be hard to come by if you are only buying a snack.

There is no completely safe method of carrying your money but a travel money belt or neck pouch are particularly popular as both are concealed under your clothing and are big enough to

carry a passport too. It is wise to carry a small wallet with a little money in that is easily accessible so that you do not have to rummage under your clothes to buy small things. It can also be a useful decoy if thieves accost you. Avoid revealing your main stash of cash in crowded places, such as markets. Do not leave money hanging around in hotel rooms, no matter how exclusive a place it is. We all bow to temptation some time, so avoid tempting room cleaners and hotel staff with wallets or expensive equipment. Use the safe deposit box, making sure you get a full receipt. Many insurance policies don't cover valuables stolen from a room if a box is available.

Right: Starting the Overland Track in Tasmania

 ## TIME DIFFERENCES

	London, noon G.M.T.	New York, noon E.S.T.	San Francisco, noon P.S.T.
Western Australia	+8	+13	+16
Northern Territory, South Australia	+9½	+14½	+17½
Queensland, Victoria, New South Wales	+10	+15	+15
Tasmania	+10	+15	+15
New Zealand	+12	+17	+20

No account has been taken of Daylight Saving Time, which operates during the summer and puts the clocks forward one hour.

Travelling Safely

WHAT TO TAKE

While the majority of things you take with you when you are travelling are specific to each country, there is a core of travel gear that can be considered important on all trips.

BAG IT UP

Although travellers can be seen using all sorts of luggage carriers, some are just suckers for suffering. Unless every single aspect of your trip is sorted beforehand and you are doing everything from a base then forget about taking a hard suitcase. They are unwieldy and generally not suited to more adventurous trips. Hold-all bags, available from outdoor stores, are large, robust, have good carrying handle options and some even have tuck-away backpack straps for short hikes to hotels or stations. However, if you plan on doing any lengthier walks with your luggage then it is worth buying a suitcase-style travel backpack. Most have excellent harnesses for carrying heavy loads over a reasonable distance. The straps all pack away to make the luggage look smarter in hotels and prevent straps snagging on conveyor belts. The main compartment opens up fully like a suitcase, so it is easier to keep clothes neat and they have numerous extra pockets and storage areas for organizing your luggage. Top loading backpacks, or expedition style packs, are only really necessary if you envisage doing long hikes where you need to carry a lot of equipment.

In addition to your main baggage a daypack is invaluable for use as hand luggage on aircraft and for carrying around towns or on day trips. If you can avoid taking more than two bags then you will find things a lot easier when taking public transport. Make sure you have some way of securing all bags, such as a lock or a strap.

CLOTHING

Clothing requirements will very much depend on what you intend doing and where you intend doing it. For flexibility in varying climate conditions, it is better to take a number of thin layers rather than one or two thick layers. Most trips require a lightweight waterproof jacket and a warm layer, such as a fleece jacket, to keep the chills at bay on cool evenings. Footwear is heavy and bulky. Seasoned travellers will take just one pair of shoes and maybe lightweight sandals or sand-shoes for relaxing times and visits to the beach. There is plenty of good travel footwear available these days, with shoes or boots that are okay for light hiking but still smart enough to wear out to a bar.

ACCESSORIZE

Useful accessories include a universal sink plug (you'll be amazed how many hotels do not have sink plugs!), a lightweight travel towel, a pocket knife, and some duct tape, which can be used for backpack repairs. A basic first aid kit is essential too.

FILM

For photographers it is wise to take as much film as you think you'll need for the entire trip (over-estimate rather than run out of film when things get exciting). Film is generally available in major cities around the world but it is hard to ensure quality of storage conditions in some places, so play safe and take it with you. Keep the film in your hand luggage for all air travel and, except in airports in developed countries with "film safe" X-ray machines, insist on having it hand searched at X-ray machines. This is usually agreed to with little fuss. X-ray effects build up on film with each pass through a machine, so avoid taking left-over film from previous trips.

What to Avoid

A few simple precautions can make your trip a lot safer.

Drugs and Other Traps

It may seem obvious, but using or carrying illegal drugs of any kind whilst travelling is asking for trouble. If you're caught then it may not just be a fine or the drugs that you lose, but your freedom too, possibly for years. In countries that still operate the death penalty, drug smuggling is often one of the qualifying crimes.

Perhaps the easiest trap to fall into is purchasing souvenirs made from parts of endangered animals. Check your own country's customs regulations before travelling to ensure that you do not unwittingly contravene the laws. Penalties for smuggling endangered animals, dead or alive, can be as severe as those for drug smuggling in some countries. Never carry anything for anyone else through customs, no matter how friendly they may seem or how much they offer to pay.

Personal Safety

Whilst staying safe is very important on your travels, there is little point in becoming so obsessed with it that it spoils your holiday. Using the common sense that comes naturally to most people when visiting any big cities is really all you need on adventures in remote regions too. A healthy level of scepticism will help prevent you falling foul of the various tricks and scams that travellers encounter.

Travellers Tips

• Treat any stranger that approaches you with caution. The more eager the person, the more caution is necessary.

• Learn to say no with some conviction.

• Stay as calm and clear-headed as possible, though this can be hard in stressful, crowded situations.

• Take a second or two before answering any question from a stranger.

At Night

Talk to friendly locals that you have met, such as hotel owners and tour guides, and ask about safe and unsafe areas to visit. It is very much in their interest that you remain safe for the sake of the tourism business. If possible, when you arrive somewhere, take time to get to know the place before heading out for a big night of partying and don't drink too much. Avoiding getting very drunk is a major factor in staying safe.

Avoid wearing any signs of wealth. Even if your watch and jewellery are not that expensive in your own country, they are relatively valuable in many other countries where incomes are much lower. The majority of impromptu attacks are money related so keeping your valuables out of sight is a good idea. Use a money belt or pouch that fits under your clothing and avoid accessing it in public areas. When going out around town, leave any large sums of money in your hotel safety deposit box.

Dress Sense

Dress conservatively. Flashy or revealing clothes all attract the wrong sort of attention. For women, it is sensible not to expose too much of your body no matter how strongly you feel that your personal rights should allow you to wear whatever you want. This is particularly important in countries where it is culturally insensitive to wear such clothing.

Be Honest

On active adventures there is often an inherent but usually small risk of personal injury or worse involved. Be very honest with tour operators about your own abilities. There are often easier options available. Halfway down a big, wild rapid in a raft is not the time to divulge that you cannot swim. Take responsibility for your own actions, think on your feet rather than being led like a sheep and voice concerns over any safety issues that you are not happy or comfortable with. Any good operator won't take offence at such questions.

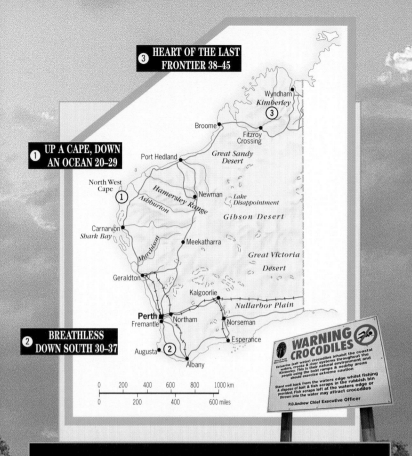

③ HEART OF THE LAST
FRONTIER 38–45

① UP A CAPE, DOWN
AN OCEAN 20–29

② BREATHLESS
DOWN SOUTH 30–37

WARNING CROCODILES

Estuarine (salt water) crocodiles inhabit the coastal
waters, creeks & river systems throughout the
Kimberley. This is their natural environment and
people using the boat ramps & nearby areas
should exercise extreme caution

Stand well back from the waters edge whilst fishing
& dispose of bait & fish scraps in the rubbish bin
provided. Fish scraps left at the waters edge or
thrown into the water may attract crocodiles

P.D.Andrew Chief Executive Officer

WESTERN AUSTRALIA

Western Australia is big, very big. Covering just over
2.5 million sq. km (965,250sq. miles), the state is ten times
larger than the United Kingdom and over one-quarter the
size of the entire United States of America, yet it has only 1.8 million
inhabitants (the vast majority of whom live in Perth). There is no need
to squabble over elbow space here. It is also the state with the widest
variety of natural environments in Australia. There are vast inland
deserts, forests of giant trees in the southwest, the remote wilderness
of the northern, Kimberley region, and a sensational, 12,500km
(7,767mile)-long coastline overlooking pristine coral reefs. With such
diversity, such space, and so few people, the opportunities for the
adventure traveller are almost limitless. Throw in a climate that means
it is always warm and sunny somewhere in the state, and it is easy to
understand why increasing numbers of travellers are heading west.

*The airstrip at Mount Hart Station; the nearest shops are 250km (155 miles)
away*

1 Up a Cape, Down an Ocean

by Steve Watkins

Jutting out from Western Australia's coastline into the Indian Ocean like a rhino's horn is the Cape Range Peninsula. Bordered by the internationally renowned Ningaloo Marine Park and dissected by the primordial hills of the Cape Range, I sought out a variety of enthralling ways to explore them both.

The town of Exmouth, located 1,272km (790 miles) north of Perth, is the only settlement on the entire Cape Range Peninsula printed in large typeface on an atlas. It boasts only around 3,100 inhabitants, not exactly a large-typeface kind of place. However, what the town lacks in history and size, its surroundings more than make up for with ancient Aboriginal sites and major natural attractions.

One of the most exciting aspects of Exmouth's coastal location, at the meeting place of both temperate and tropical waters, is that no matter what time of year you visit, there is always some ocean creature in the area guaranteed to elicit "ooohs" and "aaahs." The most renowned of these creatures is the enormous, but thankfully human-friendly, whale shark. These speckled giants, which can grow to over 12m (39ft) long and weigh up to 1,100kg (11 tons), are the biggest fish species and largest cold-blooded animals in the world. They pass through the Ningaloo Marine Park between mid-March and June each year. When the whale sharks are not in town, the role of principal local attraction switches to the humpback whales, which migrate north from Antarctica to breed in the warm waters off Exmouth between August and November. I headed down to Exmouth Marina to join Jeff Bubb on his 12m (40ft)-long vessel, Ocean Quest, for an afternoon of whale-watching out in the protected waters of Exmouth Gulf on the eastern side of the cape. The small marina was full of prawn trawlers. Jeff explained that they were all in port for four days because the brightness of the full moon causes prawns to hide, making trawling futile.

A THREATENED HISTORY

Unsurprisingly, it is a very recent trend for people to take pleasure from simply observing whales. As early as the 1830s, American whaling ships worked off the northwest coast of Australia. Despite seemingly low catch rates of just three or four whales a day, the whale population soon became depleted and whaling finally ceased altogether in the area in 1963. Humpback whale numbers have since recovered slightly, although they are still endangered. These behemoths of the ocean can grow to 15m (49ft) long. Fortunately for whale-watchers, the

---

3 Exmouth and the activities in the surroundings area are suitable for people of all fitness levels and ages, including families. A reasonable degree of fitness and swimming ability is needed for the diving trips.

★ For a small town, Exmouth has a wide range of accommodation to suit all requirements, from campsites and backpackers' hostels to motels and well-appointed hotels.

⚒ All specialist diving and snorkelling equipment is available from the dive centres, although you can take your own to save on costs. No specialist equipment is necessary for the other tours. Dive courses are available in Exmouth.

humpbacks take full advantage of their slack travelling pace to frolic, and it wasn't long before the first cries of "Whale!" went up from passengers on the boat. Out to starboard, some distance from us, two large adult whales were joyfully engaged in a bout of flipper-slapping. The bright white underside of their exceptionally long side-flippers stood out sharply against their black bodies as they lay on their sides and slapped the water with all the playfulness of children in a swimming pool. Jeff headed slowly towards them, taking great care not to encroach into the 100m (110yd)-no-go zone that has voluntarily been adopted by the whale-watch boats in the area. Of course, that does not stop the whales deciding to come closer themselves. "Humpbacks are very inquisitive and will often circle the boat to check it out," said Matt, Jeff's assistant. Our presence raised no interest from the two slappers, but a real treat was awaiting us moments later.

To cries of wonder a mother appeared with what seemed to be an albino calf; this was the first time that even Jeff had seen one. He cut the engine, and slowly the two whales edged closer to the boat, circling anticlockwise, occasionally surfacing to send spouts of water shooting into the air from their twin blowholes. The mother proudly nudged the unique youngster nearer until it was almost within touching distance. It was a precious moment as the calf rolled on its side, revealing its characteristic knobbly head and one of its deep black eyes, and looked intently at me. On the way back to the marina we saw several other humpbacks spectacularly launching themselves from the depths in a manoeuvre known as breaching. All too soon they came crashing down with such force that the waves rocked our boat.

DEEP KNIFE CUT

Such is the beauty of the beaches and ocean around Exmouth that it would be easy to forget to explore the inland hills that give the peninsula its name. To delve deeper into the 50,000 ha (124,000 acres) of the Cape Range National Park and Aboriginal history, I joined five others on a one-day four-wheel-drive tour operated by Exmouth Bay Village Resort. Although the national park covers the western portion of the peninsula, the most direct routes into the range go via the eastern gulf road. Following a trail cut in the 1950s, the road climbs up into what used to be coral reef formations over 10 million years ago. Today, the limestone gorges are impressive indeed, and the area is riddled with caves where remnants of Aboriginal settlements have been discovered dating back over 30,000 years. As we neared the top of the climb, dramatic views opened up to our right. The ragged and often vertical walls of the Charles Knife Canyon are almost 300m (985ft) high in places.

As we rounded the dry, scrubby lands of the North West Cape at Vlamingh Head Lighthouse and began heading south down the Indian Ocean side of the peninsula, it seemed to take forever to lose sight of the huge transmitters for the US naval base at Exmouth. The Indian Ocean side has a unique ecosystem that consists of three distinct environments, ranging from the stony hills of the high country to the coastal plains and mangrove swamps nearer the water. Yet the most striking feature as we drove along the coast was the increasingly turquoise-coloured ocean that butted seamlessly on to pure white sandy beaches, the sort of pristine strands that act as backdrops to bronzed bodies in magazine ads for sunscreen.

Near Osprey Bay, we were enthralled to see a family of emus trot past us through the scrub, mother leading the way with six youngsters trailing in her wake. These large (only the African ostrich is larger), long-necked, flightless birds have a tumble of black and grey feathers on their backs that shimmer and shake like a cheerleader's pompom. Just 10km (6 miles) south of the bay, at Yardie Creek, the coastal road ends for all but the most experienced off-road drivers as

it crosses the river via a notoriously difficult sandbar. We had no intention of traversing the creek though, instead joining Neil and Rhondda McGregor, of the multi-award-winning Yardie Creek Tours, for a boat cruise up the river.

GROOVY WALLABIES

Snappily dressed in his impeccably pressed captain's whites, Neil welcomed us all aboard his 40-seat, flat-bottomed cruise boat and slowly set off upriver through the pretty red-rocked gorge. The tour lasted just an hour, but Neil's

Left: *Black-footed rock wallabies at Yardie Creek*
Below: *Vlamingh Head lighthouse rises above a lonely landscape of grassy slopes, white sandy beaches and blue ocean*

entertaining, rapid-fire commentary contained enough information about the gorge to make the journey feel like a day-long roller-coaster ride through an ancient history museum, a botanical

Below: *Fish painting in the door of the Exmouth Dive Club Centre*
Right: *Crest on Exmouth's council offices*

WESTERN AUSTRALIA

garden, and a zoo all rolled into one. High on the rock face, Neil spotted one of the gorge's most renowned inhabitants, a black-footed rock wallaby, its brown ears and black-striped head barely peeking from behind a rock. These agile, miniature kangaroos have inhabited western Australia for over 30,000 years but are becoming increasingly rare; Yardie Creek is one of the few places travellers are guaranteed to see them. The wallabies move around steep rock faces, at times with quite breathtaking speed and daring, in search of grass, leaves, or fruits to eat. This particular one remained perfectly still in the hope of avoiding detection as we passed, but Neil promised that there would be plenty more to see along the creek.

The rust walls of the gorge were pocked with caves that once provided shelter for early Aboriginal inhabitants. Refuse heaps containing piles of leftover shells have been found throughout the Cape Range area, indicating that Aborigines were eating shellfish here at least 32,000 years ago. Nowadays, the rocks, caves, and crevices play host to a range of birds. White-feathered little corellas, medium-sized members of the parrot family, occupied some of the smaller holes in the gorge and emitted alarming screeches. High up on the front ledge of a scalloped cave, two large, lumpy nests of grey sticks lay abandoned, having recently been used by white-bellied sea eagles. However, it was hard for anything to steal the show from the rock wallabies, and as we made our way back to the river mouth, we stopped several times to watch more of these endearing creatures leaping around the cracks and ledges.

SHARK ENCOUNTER

We headed back up the coast to visit exquisite Turquoise Bay for a first look under the water. With everybody geared up in snorkel, mask, and fins, we swam the short distance to the reef. In the shallow, glassy water, a blue-spotted fantail

ray glided over the sandy floor, uncovering shellfish for eating by blowing water jets out of its mouth. The biggest thrill came when we passed over a large bommie, or isolated coral outcrop, and spotted two menacing-looking whitetip reef sharks hiding out in a rock hole. Although I knew they lacked the desire to devour humans, I still couldn't bring myself to get too close.

Having whetted my appetite for the undersea world, I was looking forward to spending the next couple of days scuba diving at two of the region's best dive sites: the Muiron Islands, 12km (7½ miles) off the peninsula's northern tip and the renowned naval base pier at Point Murat. The low-profile limestone Muiron Islands are rather dull and devoid of any features, so the contrast between the above- and below-water scenes is even more startling. Our first dive site, dubbed The Spit, was on the north island. Mick, our divemaster, explained that the dive followed an 18m (60ft)-deep wall, with a large bommie at one end and a couple of swim-throughs (accessible, cave-like holes that go through the reef system) at the other end. We would have plenty of time to stop and look around during the 40-minute dive. I was partnering Elko, who was training to be a divemaster. After double-checking our equipment, we donned our masks, slipped breathing regulators into our mouths, and took a giant step off the back of the boat.

FINGER-NIPPING FISH

As I looked down the anchor line, which faded into the blue below, two potato cod slowly emerged. These giant fish, which have brown-flecked bodies as big as labrador dogs and thick-lipped mouths, are completely protected in western Australian waters. Mick had forewarned us that their inquisitive nature, linked with poor eyesight, leads them to inspect divers from very close quarters. He also suggested that we kept our hands tucked tightly into our bodies in case the rock cod mistook our fingers for edible fish. As one of the cod turned and started towards me, I was torn between wanting to swim away at pace or to stay put to see just how up-close and personal these fish get. Keeping my nerves at bay, I chose the latter, and stared wide-eyed as the cod edged ever nearer until it stopped so close that I could have licked its lips. Disappointed that I was too large to eat, it swam off in search of smaller prey.

The wall loomed large above us on the right-hand side, and was elaborately decorated with corals in the shape of fans, whorls, plates, and brains. Near the mouth of a small cave, a green turtle glided gracefully by, its flippers pulling through the water with power and ease. It is the most common species found in the marine park, and its name stems from the colour of its fat, which was once used in soups, rather than the colour of its shell, which is speckled dark brown.

UNDERWATER SINGING

Just moments later we had a real treat, but this time it was audible rather than visible. At first, the medium- to high-pitched tones sounded like one of the other divers sighing and gasping at another underwater delight. It soon became clear, however, that this was the haunting, beautiful sound of humpback whales singing. The tones faded in and out of the endless blue depths ahead of me, and each time one melted away I hankered for another. Humpbacks are often referred to as the singing whale because they produce more vocalizations than any other whale species, with the males crooning for up to half an hour at a time during the mating season.

Moving further along the wall, I saw a tiny, unidentified species of nudibranch, a bizarre-looking and flamboyantly decorated sea slug, crawling over a piece of coral. Near the end of the wall, Elko checked my gauge to ensure I had sufficient air to enter the swim through. The entrance was wide enough for a couple of divers, but I was shocked and confused to see Jason, our dive-boat driver, swimming casually up alongside me with just his swimming trunks, snorkel, and mask on. I checked my depth gauge, which read 12m (39ft), and double-checked that indeed I did have scuba gear on. While I looked on in astonishment, Jason swam through the cave and off up to the surface. Later, back on the boat, I learnt that he is an experienced free diver and can hold his breath for long enough to swim around happily at such depths!

As I carefully negotiated narrow passages, I passed below natural roof holes where sunshine arrowed in, spotlighting fish. A little further in, a sizeable blacktip reef shark was lurking in a small side cave. Although these sharks are not considered dangerous, they certainly look the part—even more so than the whitetips. Five minutes after entering the swim-through, I emerged in a stream of bubbles at the top of the reef. The upper reef was around 7m (23ft) deep, so we spent the final, safety part of the dive exploring there.

LOGGERHEADS

Lunch was spent at aptly named Turtle Beach. Scores of loggerhead turtles were swimming in the bay, waiting for the right mate to come along to breed. It was a remarkable sight, and we swam to the

---

CYCLONE VANCE

On March 22, 1999, Cyclone *Vance*, the most powerful cyclone ever to hit Australia, drove its way across the North West Cape, hammering the town of Exmouth in the process. At Learmonth Airport, 35km (22 miles) south of the town, wind gusts of 276kph (172mph) were recorded and there was widespread structural damage. Incredibly, despite this terrible natural onslaught, no lives were lost and the town has recovered remarkably quickly.

Above: *Preparing for a glass-bottomed boat tour*
Left: *Heading off into the deep blue*
Inset: *The shallow draft of the boat allows it to pass right over the coral reef giving a wonderful view of marine life*
Right: *Gleaming silver in the sunshine, shoals of fish circulate endlessly around the reefs off Muiron Island*

shore with our snorkel gear to enjoy a close-up view of these magnificent, but sadly endangered creatures. In the afternoon we were taken to dive over a reef system off the south island and although we saw plenty of fish and even a white-eyed moray, the spring tides and a growing sea breeze had churned the water up and reduced visibility. However, I still had the following afternoon's dive on the renowned navy pier to look forward to.

WESTERN AUSTRALIA

BEAUTIFUL SLUGS

Nudibranchs ("naked gill") are some of the most enchanting underwater creatures to look at, but they are really just slugs. There are over 3,000 species of nudibranchs, with probably many more undiscovered. Despite their colourful, flamboyant appearance, they are still easy to miss, because they are small (some grow no bigger than a beer-bottle top) and move painfully slowly over coral that is often just as colourful as they are. Nudibranchs have an outer layer of potent chemical and biological defences that make them the slugs that fish love to hate. They themselves eat anything, including anemones and sponges, and some species live for only a few weeks. When they breed, they do it in style, producing colourful fans of jelly that contain up to a million eggs.

When the United States' base was established in Exmouth, the navy built the substantial Point Murat Pier, 11km (7 miles) north of town. The underwater inhabitants of the region also found the pier useful as a home, and it is now considered to be one of the top ten dive sites in Australia. To explore there, I joined up with the well-run Village Dive operation at the Exmouth Cape Tourist Village, one of only two operators permitted to dive on the pier. During the dive briefing, Dave Stewart, our divemaster and a marine biologist, explained that the 70m (230ft)-long, T-shaped pier is only safe to dive at slack water, the lull between tidal flows. Otherwise the current is too strong to negotiate the many beams and pillars that hold the pier up. "This dive is all about fish. There are over 150 species living under the pier," Dave said, before adding a warning: "There are stonefish, lionfish, and fire coral under there too, so if I show you the 'don't touch' hand signal, please don't be tempted to do otherwise," he said with a knowing smile.

Manoeuvring carefully past beams and around rusting pillars, we slowly began descending to the base of the pier. Almost immediately, exotic fish that I had never seen before swam by. Lurking near a broken-off sheet of metal was a wonderfully elaborate common lionfish. It was showing off its white and brown fanned fins, which resemble the headdress of a Native American chief. Shafts of light shone down eerily through the structure as we moved up the central section, where Dave spotted a striped anglerfish poking its head out of a pipe. A little further on, where we had to ease our way between two metal beams, I almost lay on a well-camouflaged tasselled wobbegong shark. These flat-headed and flat-bodied sharks are fairly harmless unless provoked, and are distinctive for the rows of fleshy tassels they have around their lips. I had to suck in my breath sharply and hold it to stop myself from sinking down on top of the shark. We encountered a common reef octopus hiding in a rock hole, a poisonous striped catfish and four grey-coloured slate sweetlips. I have dived in many places in the world but never before have I seen so many exciting species of fish in one small area, and could only agree that the pier rated as one of Australia's top dives.

My final angle on the underwater world was from a glass-bottomed boat, owned by Richard from Ningaloo Ecology Cruises. The shallow draft of the vessel allows it to pass right over the coral reef without damaging it, and permits non-divers and hydrophobes a wonderful look at the marine life. Richard is committed to maintaining this pristine environment for future generations. He religiously documents the species he sees on each trip to monitor changes in populations and behaviour. We spotted many species of fish during the absorbing two-hour trip, including a huge manta ray happily resting beneath a bommie. Exmouth might not be a large typeface kind of place, but the fortunate travellers who make it here will remember it with awe.

GOING IT ALONE

INTERNAL TRAVEL

Exmouth's location on the Cape Range Peninsula means that you have to make a positive decision to go there, as you will never just pass through, but it is certainly worth the effort. Skywest Airlines, part of the Ansett group, have daily flights to Learmonth Airport from Perth, while Greyhound Pioneer Buses run three direct services a week, also from Perth. By road, Exmouth is 1,272km (790 miles) from Perth and 3,366km (2,091 miles) from Darwin, so whichever route you take it is a long journey, but it is also a fascinating one if you have the time and inclination.

Once you are in Exmouth, if you choose not to join an organized tour you will need to rent your own vehicle as none of the attractions is within walking distance. Major car-rental firms, including Budget Rent-A-Car, have offices in Exmouth, but book early as availability can be a problem. Alternatively, the Ningaloo Reef Bus operates a daily return service along the western side of the peninsula to beaches and other attractions, including Yardie Creek, Turquoise Bay, and the Ningaloo Ecology Cruises departure point at Tantabiddi.

WHEN TO GO

Exmouth is truly a year-round destination, with consistently warm temperatures and rare days of extreme heat. It is a favourite place for Western Australians to retire to because of the agreeable climate. There are also very few days when the sun doesn't shine. Whale sharks appear off the coast from mid-March to mid-June, while humpback whales are seen from August to November.

PLANNING

All the tours and diving featured can be booked at relatively short notice, although if you travel at peak times more notice will be needed. If you don't dive, there are plenty of good snorkelling locations just off the numerous beaches. Check with the very helpful Exmouth Tourist Bureau for information (see Contacts).

TRAVELLERS' TIP

❏ Taking pictures under water is an artform in itself, but you can get some reasonable pictures here even with a cheap single-use camera as the visibility is so good and there is plenty of light when snorkelling. If you have an underwater compact camera, then use ISO/ASA400-speed film for the best results as the fish move very quickly and the wave motion rocks you about, thereby making it difficult to keep the camera steady.

WHAT TO TAKE

❏ You can take your own scuba-diving gear to save on costs, although the centres all hire out reasonable equipment (the standards at Village Dive are particularly good).
❏ Sunscreen is an absolute must, along with a wide-brimmed hat and sunglasses. Remember that the sun reflects strongly off the white sand and the water, so you need sunscreen on all exposed skin. There is little natural shade at the beaches, so consider taking or buying a beach umbrella if you have your own vehicle.
❏ Exmouth's nightlife is rather quiet (aside from the Potshot's Saturday night disco), so a good book may prove useful.

HEALTH

Any health worries in Exmouth are likely to be related to the sun, so use plenty of sunscreen and avoid spending the whole day out in the sun. If you go scuba diving then ensure that you do not have any difficulty equalizing the pressure in your ears (this can become a temporary problem if you have a head cold). The boat trip out to the Muiron Islands can be a little rough at times, so either take up the offer of seasickness tablets from the dive company or take your own. There are mosquitoes in the region, so use a repellent and keep your body covered at dusk.

FURTHER READING

The Marine Life of Ningaloo Marine Park and Coral Bay by Ann Storrie and Sue Morrison (CALM, 1998)
This lavishly illustrated general guide to the various life-forms in the ocean waters around Exmouth covers everything, from the beautiful corals and sponges to the breathtaking sea horses and whales.

2 Breathless Down South

by Steve Watkins

Western Australia's South West and Great Southern regions are best known for their wineries, yet they are also glorious adventure playgrounds. I spent a week catching thrills on a self-drive activity extravaganza that included biking, caving, hiking, surfing, and scuba diving.

Many travellers "do" Australia by looping from Sydney up through Alice Springs and back round via Queensland's Gold Coast. Of those who choose to head west, many confine themselves to Perth, Kalbarri and Broome, without giving a thought to visiting the southwest (which includes both the South West and Great Southern regions). However, if you don't want to miss out on one of the best adventure spots in Australia, then break from the crowds, stock up on adrenalin and head south from Perth. I hired a Toyota Landcruiser and a mountain bike and set off for a maximum-adventure, multi-activity week that promised to leave me breathless.

With the sun beating down from a cloudless sky, the wind rushing in through the open windows, and music drumming out of the stereo, I hit the open road with a feeling of elation. I was taking the scenic route—Coastal Highway 1—to Dunsborough, 260km (160 miles) south of Perth on the Cape Naturaliste

Peninsula. Between Bunbury and Dunsborough the highway follows the gentle arc of Geographe Bay, where the Indian Ocean is consistently as placid as a well-fed baby. The small, peaceful town of Dunsborough, set at the base of the cape, is a popular weekend-break destination for Perth-dwellers. I checked into a spacious villa at the Dunsborough Bay Village Resort, signed up for a wreckdiving trip the following morning, then unloaded the bike for a short, late-afternoon jaunt up to the lighthouse at the tip of the cape.

OUT OF THE VOID

In December 1997, Kim Hancock, with the aid of a Canadian team of explosives experts, sank the Australian Navy destroyer HMAS *Swan* just 1.3km (¾ mile) off Meelup Beach. The ship was sunk with much media-friendly pomp and ceremony to create one of Australia's most accessible and exciting wreck dives. The sinking location was painstakingly chosen to ensure that all divers, no matter how qualified or experienced, could dive the wreck.

After Greg, manager of Cape Dive, gave a full dive briefing, I buddied up with his wife, Gaby, and with our tanks and masks on we jumped off the boat's rear platform. With a mutual thumbs-down sign, we initially descended to the ship's crow's nest, which sits in about 7m (23ft) of water, before continuing to deck level

A moderate to good level of fitness is needed to undertake most of the activities featured, although there are always options to suit other levels of ability.

There is a complete range of accommodation options throughout the region, from basic camping facilities to luxury hotels and lodges.

If you have your own bike, scuba-diving gear, or rock-climbing equipment then consider taking them to save on costs, although all are available for hire or are included in the organized tours.

Right: Abseiling down the sea cliffs at Wilyabrup
Inset: *For sheer drama and beauty there are few rock climbing areas in Australia to match that to the north of Margaret River*

at a depth of about 18m (59ft). The dark hulk of the wreck was an awesome sight, although it is so big, at 113m (371ft) long, that it was impossible to see both ends at once. The *Swan* was cleaned out meticulously before she was sunk, so if you hold a wreck-diving qualification it is possible to enter the holds. I haven't undergone any wreck training, so I had to be satisfied with peering into the void from outside. Back at the central tower, Gaby pointed to the bridge and indicated that this was a section I could enter. A special exit hole has been cut in the bridge roof so that divers without wreck qualifications can still go inside. After carefully adjusting my buoyancy via my breathing, I eased through the bridge door and chuckled out a burst of bubbles at the sight I encountered. The captain's swivel seat was still in situ, but a shoal of common bullseye fish now surrounded it. They peered intently out through the windows, as if they were part of the ship's watch. I couldn't resist parting the shoal momentarily to sit in the seat myself and play captain. Easing my way out through the roof, I then swam along one of the outside galleys. Towards the bow of the boat, we finned around the turret that used to hold the two guns, before ascending back to the crow's nest for our safety stop prior to surfacing. It had been an outstanding dive, and I found myself wishing that I had a wreck diver's certificate.

That day was to be a particularly challenging one on the activity front, for no sooner had I changed out of my dive gear than I was on the road heading south to Margaret River. Caves Road is a wonderfully scenic route that twists and turns through eucalypt and karri forests, and passes a bewildering array of wineries. There was no time for wine-tasting though, as I had an appointment with Helen Lee, owner of Cave and Canoe Bushtucker Tours. Helen's canoe trips depart from the stunning Prevelly Beach at the mouth of Margaret River, 8km (5 miles) from the town itself. Kitted out with buoyancy aids and paddles, a group

WALKING THE WAUGAL WAY

Western Australia has only one long-distance walking trail, but it is world class. The 963km (598-mile) Bibbulmun Track runs from Kalamunda, east of Perth, all the way to Albany on the southern coast. Named after an Aboriginal tribe, the trail is waymarked by distinctive yellow and black triangles bearing the Waugal, or rainbow serpent, central to Aboriginal mythology. The track passes through remote wilderness forest, including the Darling Range and Valley of the Giants, and pristine coastal areas, such as Nuyts Wilderness. Track amenities include cosy, wooden sleeping shelters and tent sites, but the trail is also suitable for day walkers.

of around 20 of us set off upriver. The waterway snaked through a series of S-bends below Walcliffe's limestone cliffs and onto the Ellensbrook Homestead.

CRUNCHY GRUB EYES

The homestead was our high point on the river, and we turned around here to enjoy an even easier paddle with the current back to a small, enchanting stand of paperbark trees. We pulled the canoes to shore, and wandered into the eerily quiet wood. Local Aboriginal people believe the spot to be full of bad spirits because nothing grows here except the trees and not even mosquitoes inhabit the area. However, the scientific explanation is that the trees cause the void rather than bad spirits. Paperbark trees give off a eucalypt-oil aroma, which saturates the air and drives mosquitoes away. The oil is also given off through the trees' roots and prevents other plants from growing in the vicinity. Satisfied that there were no evil spirits, we sat around the knowledgeable and enthusiastic Helen to learn about and, sometimes reluctantly, to sample bushtucker food. After dabbling in nature's larder—including bardi-grub paste, complete with crunchy eyes, and bush raisins—we utilized our newfound knowledge to create a custom sandwich, wrapped in damper, delicious bush bread cooked in the sand. I chose a couple of slices of roasted emu and kangaroo meat, topped off with a coating of bardi paste and bush lettuce. It was a taste sensation and nutritious, too.

Any thoughts of a gentle paddle back to Prevelly Beach were dashed when Helen announced the traditional "no rules" race home. On the count of one, everyone whirled into action, trying every trick in the book—apart from capsizing opponents—to gain an advantage.

ROCKY DILEMMA

Rest is only for the lazy or the dead, so after grabbing a quick lunch, I met up with Trevor McGowan from Adventure In for an afternoon of rock climbing on awe-inspiring sea cliffs at Wilyabrup, to the north of Margaret River. For drama and beauty, there can be few climbing areas in Australia to match these rust-red lime-stone cliffs. I soaked up the endless view up the rocky coastline, while far below me huge waves rolled in off the Indian Ocean before erupting against fallen boulders.

With the climbing rope set up on a medium-grade climb on a face known as One for the Road, I abseiled down to the bottom, pulled on the tight-fitting and sticky rubber-soled climbing shoes, tied into my harness, and set off up an obvious crack line. Initially, the route was easygo-ing, but once I reached the halfway point I suffered a case of climber's block. No mat-ter how hard I tried to psych myself up to stretch for a small rock flake that would only accommodate two fingertips, my body wouldn't react. I rehearsed the move mentally and dipped my hands into my chalk bag a dozen times, hoping for inspiration. Trevor shouted up some help-ful hints, and eventually, and with a deep breath and a mouthed "Come on!", I com-mitted to the flake and held it. A satisfying flush of achievement washed

over me. Higher up the route, with arms pumped full of pure pain, I took a brief rest on the rope to study the options. A little shimmy with my feet gave me better balance, and I stretched up to grab the last hold. As I sat safely on top of the cliff, I looked out to the ocean and pondered whether life could get any better. By the time we had completed a second climb, the sun was finally setting on my action-packed day.

DOWN UNDER

With so much limestone around, it is no surprise that the whole area is riddled with outstanding caves. The following morning, I travelled north via Yallingup to Ngilgi Cave to join the only adventure-caving tour on offer in the region. The whole cave system is 730m (800yd) long and spreads out in a series of arms from the main chambers. Mark, the adventure-tour guide, and I headed off together to explore just a few of them.

We entered via the impressive and superbly lit show cave, descended steps between First Chamber and the Amphitheatre, then turned on our head-torches and clambered down a rocky incline to the start of Riverbed Crawl. As its name suggests, there isn't room to stand up here; in fact, at times there is barely enough room to lie down. With our helmet lights piercing the darkness, we got on our hands and knees and shuffled into the gap, following a line of white marker stones. We emerged on the other side to find ourselves in a small chamber with several wonderful examples of helectites, hollow straw-like formations that grow in all directions, including upwards.

Soon after we returned to the main artery, we encountered a rather chilling reminder of the consequences of being trapped in a cave: the skeletons of three possums lying on the sandy floor where hunger overcame them. It was hot and humid in the cave, and the high levels of carbon dioxide made us feel slightly short of breath, but the fun of exploring

WESTERN AUSTRALIA

Above: *The intriguing rock formations reward you for adventurous crawling, but not if you suffer from back problems or claustrophobia*

underground was more than sufficient distraction. One of the more technical parts of the tour is the aptly named Pinch Gut, a short climb and squeeze through a very narrow gap between a boulder and the cave roof. Mark went through first to show how it was done, before I contorted my body, like a double-jointed circus performer, to follow him. On the other side was a marvellous rotund stalagmite covered in ribs and a gigantic boulder precariously balanced on a ledge.

Throughout the system there are countless examples of magical formations. In a big chamber known as Pot Belly, a stalagmite shaped like a pot-belly stove sits on a platform. Below it spreads a large area of flowstone: pools of smooth white calcium carbonate that look as if somebody has poured a carton of milk over the floor. To get out of the cave, we squeezed our way up through the narrowest part of the system. It was so tight that, once I was in the gap, I found it almost impossible to move my legs, and I had to inch my way up by wriggling like a caterpillar. Adventure caving may not be for everyone, but if you can handle the tight bits then the rewards are infinitely richer than a mere wander around the show cave.

FIRST WAVE

My afternoon mission that day was to attempt to become a real Aussie by learning to surf. There can be few more apt places for a first taste of surfing than Margaret River, the spiritual home of surfing in Western Australia and host to a round of the World Surfing Championships. I figured a lesson with state champion Josh Palmateer would be a good step. After Josh demonstrated the basic techniques for catching a wave and standing on the board, surprisingly I managed to get up on my first attempt. Unfortunately, that was a dry run on the beach, and things seemed to get more challenging once we were in the water.

Most of the group had been having lessons for a while, and were soon getting straightforward, wildly applauded, rides into the beach. Then it was my turn. I lay on the board, Josh gave the wave warning, and I paddled with my arms as strongly as possible. The back of the board lifted and I ignored the temptation to stand, just as Josh had suggested. After another couple of strokes I was on the wave. With one firm push from my arms, I was up and standing, harnessing nature's power with all the grace of a drunken nightclub dancer. "Beauty!" I screamed, and promptly fell off into the turbulent white water. I emerged to hear the dying round of applause, so I swam out again to prove that the first attempt was not beginner's luck. Josh's love and enthusiasm for his work was infectious—by the end of the session I was catching rides regularly, and felt like rushing off to buy a corked hat, a pair of thongs, and a tinny!

That evening I began my journey to the south coast, stopping off overnight in the enchanting Karri Valley Resort near Pemberton. The resort is set in a beautiful karri forest at the side of Lake Beedelup, and offers a range of activities. At sunrise the next morning, a fine layer of mist rose off the calm lake while the sun lit the trees along the far shore. Donning my hiking boots, I followed the Beedelup Falls loop trail, which circles the lake and visits the waterfall I could hear from my room. On the far side of the lake it briefly joins the Bibbulman Track, the longest marked trail in Western Australia, which runs from near Perth all the way to Albany, my evening destination—although I would be

Above: *Surf lesson in Margaret River, the spiritual home of surfing in Western Australia*
Below: *Forest of karri trees*

travelling by car.

Albany and its surroundings are well worth exploring, so I spent the morning at the pristine, little-visited Two People's Bay Reserve to the east of the town. My main goal, however, was to hike in the dramatic Porongorup and Stirling Range national parks to the north of Albany, and

WESTERN AUSTRALIA

FORESTS OF GIANTS

The southwest region of Western Australia is home to the world's only forests of the giant karri and jarrah trees. While jarrah trees can grow up to 30m tall (98ft), karri trees are the true giants, soaring up a whopping 85m (279ft). The wood from both trees is popular with home and furniture builders, but supplying this demand has led to a significant decrease in original forest growth in the southwest, a topic high on the environmental agenda. For visitors, there are a couple of locations that offer unique perspectives on these wooden giants. The Gloucester Tree, near Pemberton, is a 61m (200ft)-high karri tree that brave travellers with a head for heights can climb via a spiral ladder. Another place to get a bird's-eye view of huge trees, this time in a red tingle forest, is in the Valley of the Giants, between Walpole and Denmark, where an incredible treetop walkway gradually leads you up into the canopy.

so I joined John Healy from Escape Tours for a one-day visit that took in both.

The 2,511-ha (6,205-acre) Porongorup National Park is just 40km (25 miles) from Albany. There are plenty of easy to moderate walking trails to the main peaks; we chose to hike the gentle and varied 1.5km (1-mile) track to Castle Rock at the eastern end of the park. Initially, the trail twisted through dense acacia bush and then entered more open land dotted with moss-covered granite outcrops and isolated karri trees. Amongst the karri grew vivid splashes of wildflowers. Nearer the summit, we threaded through narrow gaps between boulders as big as elephants, including the much-photographed Balancing Rock. This huge boulder is perched precariously atop a granite outcrop and seems to need only a small nudge to send it rolling off to the plains below. Beyond it, a short

scramble took us to the bottom of an iron ladder that leads to the summit lookout point on the granite dome of Castle Rock.

HIKE OF AGES

Despite the overcast sky, the view south over the plain was still impressive. The Porgongorup Range was pushed up during the powerful collision between the Antarctic and continental Australian land masses that created the supercontinent Gondwanaland. Looking north, the jagged silhouette of the Stirling Range, our afternoon destination, broke the skyline. These mountains rose up during the disintegration of Gondwanaland, so in just one day John and I were going to hike on peaks that were formed millions of years apart. As we drove towards the Stirling Mountains, it was hard not to be awed by their commanding appearance above the otherwise flat landscape. The range's highest peak, Bluff Knoll, rises to 1,073m (3,520ft), and has become increasingly popular as a long and testing day hike. With only half a day to spare, we chose instead to tackle the slightly lower but none-the-less challenging peak of Talyberlup.

After 40 minutes of unrelenting steep ascent, I reached the rock band and skirted around to the left to reach an enormous vertical fissure. I climbed up through a small hole in the roof, to emerge near the small, stone windbreak shelter that marks the summit. The vista was both stunning and vast. To the west, the peaks of Mount Magog and the more distant Hume Peak and Donnelly Peak stretched with simple majesty towards the descending sun. To the east lay Toolbrunup and Bluff Knoll. Far below, the bushland wilderness rose and fell in smooth sweeps into the haze. Although time demanded my descent shortly, I sat awhile and enjoyed the rewards of the short but challenging climb. After all, following such an exhilarating, action-packed week in the magnificent southwest, I could hardly begrudge myself a little rest.

GOING IT ALONE

INTERNAL TRAVEL

If you intend to travel around the southwest region of Western Australia it is preferable to hire a car as public transport is very limited. The only options for the latter are based around Westrail's daily train service to Bunbury and the infrequent bus service the company operates from there to the other big towns of the region, including Margaret River and Albany.

All the major car-hire firms—including Budget Rent A Car, Avis, and Hertz—have offices in Perth. While four-wheel-drive vehicles are necessary if you want to explore the myriad forest and coastal tracks of the southwest, all the main roads are paved and in excellent condition.

Although the region is well suited to cycle touring, there are no long-term bike-hire outlets, so it is best to rent one from a Perth-based company such as About Bike Hire.

WHEN TO GO

As most of the southwest's rain falls between May and September, when the temperatures can be quite chilly (it has been known to snow on the Stirling Range), most people choose to visit outside of these months. However, this is a good time to see the country at its most lush, and the cooler weather makes for more pleasant hiking than in the height of summer. In the summer months (January–March) the country dries up significantly and the temperature can become too hot for biking and hiking. If you are particularly keen to see the abundant wildflowers, then early to mid-spring (October and November) is the best time to travel.

PLANNING

This trip was very much a bespoke one that was put together by contacting the operators independently. If you want to book it all—or most of it at least—through a single operator, try the Traveller's Club Tour and Information Centre in Perth (see Contacts for details), an independent operator with excellent contacts for adventure sports activities throughout the state.

WHAT TO TAKE

❑ If you wish to take advantage of the sporting action on offer and you have your own equipment, such as bike helmet or rock-climbing shoes and a wetsuit or other dive gear, then consider taking them. However, all this specialist gear is supplied as part of the tours, so it is not essential to have your own.

❑ For caving at Ngilgi, take some old, sturdy clothes such as jeans and a long-sleeve sweatshirt as you will get dirty.

❑ A warm jacket or sweater will keep the evening chill at bay.

❑ Take plenty of waterproof, high-factor sunscreen and a decent sun hat.

TRAVELLERS' TIPS

❑ Driving the long distances around the southwest can be tiring, so don't push things too hard. Stop regularly at the roadhouses even if it is just to stretch your legs.

❑ Beware of driving at dawn and dusk. The kangaroos have a tendency to bound out of the bushes suddenly and across the roads. They barely allow you you any time to react.

❑ Along the coast near Margaret River, the ocean currents can be very strong. There are frequent rip tides that will whisk you out to sea before you realize it. Take notice of the swimming safety signs and always seek local advice before you enter the water.

❑ It is quite a bit cheaper to run your hire car's fuel supply down on the return journey and then fill up in Perth than to use pumps at the roadhouses.

❑ Don't be tempted to drink and drive or break the speed limit, simply because you are out in the country on open roads. Australian police regularly patrol all the major highways and can be particularly tough on drink-drivers .

HEALTH

There are no major health risks associated with travel in the southwest. However, you should be reasonably fit to undertake the activities included in this feature, particularly rock climbing, surfing, and scuba diving (for which official certification is needed—courses are available locally).

As with any sporting endeavours, it is important to drink plenty of fluids (though you should avoid alcohol as it merely increases your levels of dehydration). Sunscreen can be washed away by sweat or water relatively quickly, so reapply it regularly to avoid sunburn.

WESTERN AUSTRALIA

3 Heart of the Last Frontier

by Steve Watkins

The Kimberley is one of the world's most remote wilderness regions. It boasts magnificent scenery, Aboriginal art, and wildlife, and is home to some extraordinary people. I hired a four-wheel-drive vehicle and set out to meet a few of the characters who live a little further off the increasingly popular Gibb River Road.

Take a moment to consider where two to three hours' driving can take you in your own country. It may include several cities, crossing state or county borders, or even entering a different country. In the remote Kimberley region of northwestern Australia, tagged the "Last Frontier," such a drive will most likely get you only as far as your neighbour's house. The region covers 423,000sq. km (163,320sq. miles), over three times the size of England or New York state, and is one of the least populated areas on Earth. Yet it is surprisingly accessible and, given a modicum of common sense, quite safe to travel around independently. I hired a Landcruiser in Broome, and set off with Simon, a friend from Perth with previous Kimberley experience, for a week-long journey to Kununurra, via the Gibb River Road. This 647km (402-mile) unsealed highway begins near Derby, north of Broome, and traverses the heart of the Kimberley.

This tour is not physically demanding, but there is a lot of exciting driving and you need to be generally active to undertake the hikes and canoeing. Temperatures can get quite high (20–34°C, or 68–93°F).

★★ The levels of accommodation off the Gibb River Road vary from basic, self-sufficient camping and luxury tent cabins to comfortable homesteads and motels. Only El Questro offers a luxury lodge. You will have to be flexible as it is difficult to plan your trip around one style of accommodation.

Operators provide all the necessary specialist equipment for the activities. A four-wheel-drive vehicle is essential for this trip.

Broome is an idyllic place, with stunning beaches and a seriously laid-back atmosphere, so it was hard to convince ourselves that a week "going bush" was preferable to sipping cocktails on nearby Cable Beach. However, we managed to drag ourselves away and headed up the Great Northern Highway to Derby. If you drive anywhere in outback Australia it will soon become obvious that roadbuilders in these parts have a penchant for horizon-reaching, dead-straight stretches, and the road to Derby is no exception. I felt a real sense of journey and freedom each time we crested a ridge and saw the bitumen arrow across the vast plains ahead and peter out in a distant haze.

Some 2¼ hours after our departure, we rolled into Derby, where we met up with two further companions for the trip to Windjana Gorge, our first overnight stop. Richard, completing his medical studies at Derby's hospital, was another friend from Perth and Sam Lovell, a renowned Aboriginal character of the Kimberley. After quitting cattle mustering in 1981, Sam established Kimberley Safaris, the first Aboriginal-owned tour company in Western Australia.

ASSIMILATED SADNESS

We topped up the fuel tanks at the BP roadhouse on the edge of town (it is wise to fill up whenever possible in the Kimberley) and I joined Sam in his vehicle for the drive to Windjana. The Gibb River Road starts just 4km (2½ miles) back down the Derby Highway and is

Above: *Top up your fuel wherever possible in the Kimberley region*
Right: *Sam Lovell, a famous face in the Kimberley*

sealed for the first 63km (39 miles), until it reaches the vast, open flats of Napier Downs. Along the way, Sam told me a little of his incredible life story. Born to a white father and an Aboriginal mother, he was taken from his parents at the age of three under an assimilation programme that put thousands of Aboriginal children into institutions to raise them in a European lifestyle. Sam never saw his parents again. "They promised a better education, a better life. We got neither." Yet he has no time for recriminations. "Nothing they [the government] can do can give us back what was taken from us, but we have to look forward. We have to find a way to work together."

Sam worked as a cattle drover, and became one of the most respected drovers in the Kimberley. As we crossed Napier Downs, Sam pointed out routes he used to follow. "I have driven cattle all over this area. We used to drive up to 500 cattle for weeks at a time with only five stockmen, all on horseback," he said proudly. As we arrived at Windjana, an old stock-camp location, he showed me the pens, now rusted and decrepit, where they used to hold the herds. By then it was almost dusk, so we took a quick hike a short distance into the impressive gorge. The sun's rays lit up the 90m (295ft)-high red-rock walls, making them glow warmly like coals on a dying fire. Cut by the waters of the Lennard River, the gorge is part of what was a prehistoric reef system and fossils of extinct animals have been found in some of the caves high up in the cliff faces. Further upstream, small freshwater crocodiles hung motionless in the water, their noses and eyes barely protruding above the surface, while black and white archerfish swam around them.

As darkness crept into the gorge and blackened its walls, we hiked back to the campsite and set up our mosquito nets and swags, canvas-covered sleeping mattresses originally used by stockmen. After bidding Sam a fond farewell for his return to Derby, we cooked up a pasta feast on the fire and settled into our swags for a wonderful night's sleep under a star-swept sky.

WESTERN AUSTRALIA

SNAKING TRAIL

One of the advantages of sleeping outside is that it seems natural to get up at dawn, so I headed off into the gorge as the sun crept over the range on one side and the three-quarter moon sunk below it on the other. The track through the gorge is easygoing and only 3.5km (2 miles) long, but it is worth allowing a couple of hours to explore. A large flock of little corellas, white-feathered members of the parrot family, was raucously making its way through the riverside trees. Windjana's riverbanks are thick with river cadjeput trees, whose whitish-brown bark peels off in rough strips, like a chameleon shedding its skin. With the sun higher in the sky, the temperature in the gorge rose rapidly, and I was glad to have brought fresh drinking water along. On reaching a sandy flood plain, I headed back to camp.

After breakfast, Richard also returned to Derby while Simon and I continued eastwards through the King Leopold Range National Park. Occasionally, other four-wheel drives passed us or we would pull over to allow road trains, massive three-trailer trucks unique to Australia, to thunder past. An hour after leaving Windjana, we arrived at the turn-off for Mount Hart Station. The 50km (31-mile) long picturesque "driveway" was in good condition, but as it was narrower and twistier than the Gibb River Road the going was slower.

Mount Hart homestead is set amongst a large stand of trees, ferns, and large-leaf plants, and the tranquillity of its surroundings was palpable. Mount Hart's brochure convinced us of both its remoteness and of its owner's, Taffy Abbott's, tongue-in-cheek nature: "The driveway is only fifty kilometres long so that you are not annoyed by the garbage truck first thing in the morning. The shops are only two hundred and fifty kilometres away, just in case you have forgotten something!" Only strong characters choose to live in such remote locations, and down-to-earth Taffy, with his long bushy beard and weathered face, easily qualifies.

Mount Hart is no longer a working cattle station and the emphasis while staying there is on relaxation, although there are wonderful bushwalking and birdwatching opportunities. Simon and I swam in the beautiful, tree-lined, and crocodile-free waterhole behind the homestead. Later, we enjoyed a scrumptious feed, including Taffy's own freshly-baked bread and fresh fruits plucked from nearby trees.

In the afternoon, we met Taffy's dingoes—three semi-wild ones—named Stock, Casserole, and Ratbag, the last a three-month-old puppy. Taffy found Casserole, the mother, abandoned as a pup and helped rear her.

HOT FUEL

The following morning we loaded up the Landcruiser and headed back down the driveway on our way to Old Mornington Stock Camp, some 200km (125 miles) away to the south of Gibb River Road. The track began to wind its way up into the King Leopold Range, threading through impressive red-rock outcrops. There was no fuel at Mount Hart, so we stopped to fill up at Imintji Aboriginal community. Even at ten o'clock in the morning the

IT'S A DINGO'S LIFE

Introduced to the Australian mainland by Asian sea merchants around 4,000 years ago, the dingo was readily adopted by Aboriginal people and used for hunting kangaroos and possums. European settlers quickly branded them as livestock killers. This led to the use of wide-ranging poisoning to eradicate them from farming areas. Although they often hunt alone, dingoes have a social structure similar to wolves. They are rarely seen as they wander constantly through the bush, but one evening we chanced upon three near Drysdale River. They actually came nearer to us when we got out of the car, possibly hoping for food, but they were too nervous to come very close.

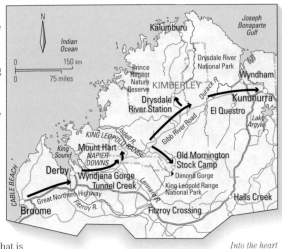

Into the heart of the Kimberley

heat blasted at us as we stepped out of the air-conditioned Toyota. Aboriginal children were playing around the gas station's store, while their parents sensibly sat in the cool shade of the veranda. Once back on the road, we soon reached the junction for Old Mornington. This is the start of the Tablelands Track, a route to Halls Creek that is beginning to attract more adventurous drivers who dislike the continuing improvements to the Gibb River Road.

Initially, the Tablelands Track was in excellent condition and crossed a sweeping grassy plain. With dust rising up behind us, as if a steam train was passing through, we made good progress until the track narrowed and deteriorated for the last 14km (9 miles). Old Mornington Stock Camp is set in a grassy clearing some 92km (57 miles) south of the Gibb River Road. Owned and managed by Michael Kerr, the camp offers upmarket tented accommodation next to the lovely Anna Creek. Before dinner, we joined Michael at the Bull Bar for a few beers and learnt a little about his past. He grew up in outback Queensland and spent much of his childhood hanging around with Aboriginal children, learning to appreciate the landscape and wildlife in the same way that they do. He moved to the Kimberley over 20 years ago on a short-term project, bought Mornington Station and never left. Cattle are still worked on the 404,700ha (1 million-acre) property, although tourism is becoming more important. The principal attraction for visitors is Dimond Gorge on the nearby Fitzroy River, where we planned to canoe the following morning.

We were up at dawn for the hour-long journey to the canoe put-in point. Along the way, we spotted a pair of bush turkeys, while nearer the gorge a herd of wild donkeys momentarily held up our progress by defiantly blocking the track. The final, short section down to the Fitzroy River was incredibly steep and covered in deep sand, requiring faith in the vehicle's ability to conquer seemingly impossible terrain. After applying a thick layer of sunscreen, we hiked over a rocky outcrop and were silenced by the view of the immaculate Dimond Gorge, which cuts through the King Leopold Range. With the limestone cliffs and blue sky perfectly reflected in the glass-like water surface, it seemed a pity to put in a canoe and disturb the serenity.

BOILING BILLY

Michael and Christina, the camp's cook, teamed up in one canoe and Simon and I in another. The paddling was easy, and the scenery became more spectacular the further into the gorge we headed. The only sounds we could hear were from the paddles as they dipped gently in and out of the water, and birds singing from the riverside trees. On top of the cliffs, Michael spotted a euro, a medium-sized member of the wallaby family, bounding its way across the skyline. The dark river water is up to 25m (80ft) deep in places,

is crystal clear, and is completely safe for
swimming—an irresistible combination in
such heat. Deeper into the gorge, at the
end of the navigable section, we disembarked and took a hot but rewarding
short walk across a huge boulder field to a
peculiar hill of loose black rocks. They
were piled high enough that the summit
offered dramatic views of the entire
gorge. Back at the river, Michael quickly
got the billy boiling on a small fire, and we
tucked into delicious sandwiches and
fruitcake to build our energy reserves for
the paddle home.

The next day
promised to be a special
one. An Aboriginal rock-
art site had recently been
found on the property,
and although it had
yet to be opened to
the public (the pro-

Above: *The only sounds we could hear came from
the dipping of paddles in the Dimond Gorge*
Below: *Friendly dingo—these animals follow a
social structure similar to wolves*
Right: *Ancient cave paintings in Old Mornington*

ject should be completed by the time of
publication), Michael agreed to take us
there. He warned us that it would be a
very rough ride, as he hadn't graded a
track there yet. Tortoise pace was the
maximum speed we achieved over an
endless series of potholes and past severe
drop-offs. On reaching
the gorge, it was
safe to say that
very few people
in human his-
tory had ever
been there. We
clambered up
some low rocks
into the long,

body. Wandjina is a generic term used to describe a group of Aboriginal ancestor beings that came from the sky and sea to help maintain balance in nature. Other images included a large crocodile figure, kangaroos, and fish. It seemed that the longer we stayed, the more we saw. Next to the paintings were silhouetted handprints, created by placing a hand on the rock and blowing paint all around it. Caves were important social gathering places for the Aborigines, and this one was a temporary shelter for hunters rather than a permanent living, hence the predominance of animal paintings. With such overwhelming ancient history and spirituality around us, it wasn't hard to imagine tribal members sitting around a fire swapping tales of the day's hunt while comets streaked overhead.

AN OUTBACK WEB

The next morning we were back on the road for the lengthy drive to Drysdale River Station, 314km (195 miles) to the north on the way to Kalumburu. The road condition worsened slightly, with deeper corrugations and patches of surface water, as it headed through a dense gumtree forest interspersed with the bright yellow flowers of kapok bushes.

sloping cave. As our eyes adjusted to the low light levels, images emerged from the coloured rocks. First, I saw a dull orange ball with speed lines trailing off the back of it, a depiction of a comet or perhaps a shooting star. Below it, a similar image had been painted over with a curved, white arrow as if to suggest motion or direction. The night sky, shooting stars, and comets still bewitch us today even though we know more about their origins, so their magical nature must have been quite staggering thousands of years ago. Michael is unsure of the age of the paintings. Some looked relatively recent, but tribes traditionally "maintained" original images by repainting them.

Close to the comet was a small Wandjina figure with short, spiky white hair (which represents clouds or lightning), a characteristic large, white head, round black eyes, no mouth, and a rotund

WESTERN AUSTRALIA

THE DEVONIAN REEF

Over 350 million years ago, a vast sea covered much of Australia's northwestern region and the Kimberley was encircled by a coral reef that measured over 1,000km (660 miles) long. These reefs now form the region's exposed ranges, including Napier and King Leopold, which are up to 100m (330ft) high in places. They are some of the oldest exposed rocks in the world, and scientists are regularly making new discoveries here and finding fossils of extinct sea animals.

John and Ann Koeyers have owned Drysdale River Station for over 14 years and it is still a working station. After settling into our comfortable rooms, we joined them for a delicious buffet dinner. Over a glass of red wine, Ann revealed few days pass without herself, Michael Kerr, and Taffy Abbots chatting over the phone. Having driven the vast distances between the stations, it was strange to perceive them suddenly as a community with as much gossiping and mutual support as takes place in a tiny village.

We were awake before dawn to watch a contract cattle team move bulls around the pens. There were four catching buggies, made from cut-down, short-wheelbase Landcruisers. Captured animals were loaded into a couple of six-wheel-drive trucks, which shuttled back and forth to a road train that would ship the cattle off to market. A dedicated road grader drove tracks into new areas of the property, and the team usually enlisted the help of a helicopter to flush cattle out of dense bush. The only vehicle that doesn't "go bush" on a daily basis is the mobile kitchen! It is tough and dangerous work, and this team had been on the road for five months. As the vehicles revved up and set off in a blaze of sunlit red dust, it looked like a scene from a *Mad Max* movie. There's an Aboriginal rock-art site and a particularly good lagoon for birdwatching near Drysdale, but we were short of time and needed to head off for our penultimate day's drive.

EL QUESTRO

Our last overnight stop was to be at El Questro Wilderness Park, a well-established resort that has pioneered modern tourism in the Kimberley region. It is nearly 280km (174 miles) from Drysdale, and the scenery *en route* is perhaps the most awesome along the entire Gibb River Road. The majestic, multilayered hills of the Cockburn Range dominated much of the journey, along with sightings of the mighty Durack and Pentecost rivers. Soon after we crossed the latter river via a long causeway, we arrived at the El Questro junction.

Opened in 1991, the wilderness park was the dream creation of an English millionaire. Set in 405,000ha (1 million acres) of prime Kimberley scenery, the park offers accommodation for everyone, from campers to wealthy travellers. After taking a quick look at the resort's most expensive suite, we checked into the more affordable tented cabin accommodation at Emma Gorge, a quieter spot within El Questro. In the early afternoon, we took a relaxing boat trip up idyllic Chamberlain Gorge to an Aboriginal rock-art site to see Bradshaw figures, possibly the oldest art form on Earth. Modern-day Aborigines dismiss these unusual, lanky figures, with their tall head-dresses, because they say they were painted by the people who inhabited the Kimberley before the Aborigines. To finish off the day, we hiked for 40 minutes up an easy trail through Emma Gorge to a swimming hole surrounded by 50m (164ft) cliffs draped with waterfalls.

Our journey was nearing an end. Rejoining the bitumen near Kununurra, we looked back at the distance markers for the Gibb River Road. It certainly was a long journey for a short cut, but the memories of untamed wilderness and the remarkable people who call it home were going to linger much longer.

GOING IT ALONE

INTERNAL TRAVEL

It is possible to travel the Gibb River Road from either direction, although most people start in Kununurra. Both Ansett and Qantas have daily flights to Broome and Kununurra, and Ansett now also operates an international flight to Broome from Bali. If you are flying in from other countries the nearest international airport for access to Kununurra is Darwin.

All the major vehicle-hire companies, including Budget Rent-A-Car and Avis, have offices in Broome and Kununurra, and offer one-way hire deals.

WHEN TO GO

April to mid-October is the only time when you can drive along the off-road tracks as they regularly become impassable or very treacherous in the wet season. Although there is more potential for inclement weather, the cusp months do offer a different and possibly more rewarding view of the Kimberley. At this time there are also fewer vehicles on the road.

PLANNING

There are numerous tour companies based in the major northern and Kimberley towns, and also in Darwin and Perth, which run trips that include the Gibb River Road. Few, if any, include all the stations visited in this feature, and some operators tend to have very tight schedules. That said, such a tour will most likely be cheaper than renting a four-wheel-drive vehicle yourself.

TRAVELLERS' TIPS

❑ The biggest and best tip is to fill up on petrol whenever you can, even if you don't need much. Things in the Kimberley have a habit of doing the unexpected, and fuel is your ticket out of there. This advice hit home to me one Sunday, when we met a guy at Mount Barnett road-house who didn't have enough petrol to get to Derby. That day was the first Sunday of the wet season, so Mount Barnett was closed and the Inmintji community only sells diesel. As a result, he had to wait three hours until another motorist came by who had some spare petrol to sell him.

WHAT TO TAKE

❑ Treat the Gibb River Road journey with an expedition approach. Take plenty of food, including snacks for the long driving sessions, and always carry plenty of drinking water—think in tens of litres rather than litres.

❑ You will need to have all your own cooking equipment and sleeping gear. Swags and mosquito nets are ideal, especially if you have a roof rack on which you can sleep. Tents are adequate, but they can get very warm on hot and humid nights.

❑ A cool box is essential for carrying any fresh or dairy produce, and should be kept well protected from the sun when in the vehicle—swags or sleeping bags can be very good for this.

❑ Ensure that your vehicle has the necessary tools for changing tyres, and ask the hire company to include two spare wheels. There is usually no extra charge for this and you don't want to be stuck without a spare.

❑ A blanket or sheet is useful for covering all the gear in the vehicle to prevent it becoming coated in road dust.

❑ A pair of binoculars is essential for wildlife-spotting.

HEALTH

There are no special health requirements for travelling in the Kimberley, although the heat is the most likely thing to affect you. Drink plenty of water throughout the day, especially if you are active. Use mosquito repellent at dusk and keep yourself covered up.

FURTHER READING

❑ *The Kimberley—An Adventurer's Guide*
Ron Moon and Viv Moon (Kakirra Adventure Publications, third edition 1997)
This is a comprehensive four-wheel-driving guide to the Kimberley, with detailed route maps and descriptions, and brief notes on the places along the way. It covers all the major tracks, including Gibb River Road, Tablelands Track, and Kalumburu Road.

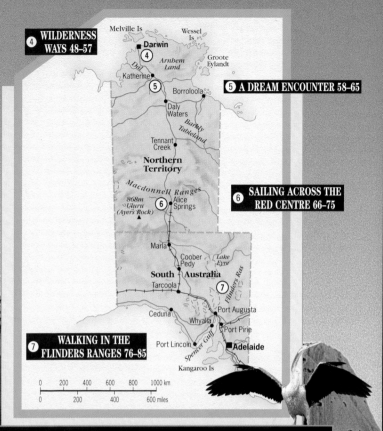

Melville Is

Wessel Is

■ **Darwin** ④

Arnhem Land

Groote Eylandt

Katherine ●

⑤

Borroloola ●

Daly Waters ●

Barkly Tableland

Tennant Creek ●

Northern Territory

Macdonnell Ranges

868m *Uluru (Ayers Rock)* ▲

⑥ Alice Springs

Marla ●

Coober Pedy ●

Lake Eyre

South Australia

Flinders Ras

Tarcoola ●

⑦

Ceduna ●

Whyalla ●

Port Augusta ●

Port Pirie ●

Port Lincoln ●

Spencer Gulf

■ **Adelaide**

Kangaroo Is

| 0 | 200 | 400 | 600 | 800 | 1000 km |

| 0 | 200 | 400 | 600 miles |

NORTHERN TERRITORY·
SOUTH AUSTRALIA

The Northern Territory contains Australia's most famous landmark, Uluru (or Ayers Rock), in the central desert, and the landscape backdrop to the country's most famous film, *Crocodile Dundee*. Yet, the region still does not have full state status and only became a self-governing territory as late as 1978. Lack of political independence has held back development and ensured that the Northern Territory remains the most adventurous part of Australia for travellers. Tourism infrastructure in some areas, such as Kakadu National Park, has improved in recent years, but there are still large areas—mostly Aboriginal-owned requiring special access permits—where few travellers have ever ventured. South Australia, meanwhile, is the driest state in the country. Beyond the Flinders Ranges, the isolation of the desert can be disconcerting yet immensely rewarding. Include both of these regions in a trip, and you will get a taste of Australia to match many of its classical images.

The visual power of Uluru, better known as Ayers Rock

4 Wilderness Ways

by Steve Watkins

Dubbed "God's own country," northern Australia boasts world-class wilderness areas. I got close to wildlife, wet in waterfalls, and was wowed by Aboriginal rock art in the national parks at Litchfield and Kakadu, both highly rated public showcases for this natural beauty.

No matter where I travelled in northern Australia, whenever I mentioned my imminent trips to the national parks at Litchfield and Kakadu, opinions were passionately polarized. Some people loved "unspoilt" Litchfield and disliked the "commercialization" of Kakadu, while others found the smaller Litchfield "uninspiring" after the "grandeur" of Kakadu, Australia's largest national park. To have the best chance of finding some special spots in both parks, I joined two separate tours, both led by enthusiastic tour leader Annette Cook.

Litchfield National Park covers 146,000ha (360,850 acres) and is located on the western side of the Stuart Highway, just 100km (62 miles) south of Darwin. It's an easy destination for a day trip, and at weekends or during school holidays the more accessible waterfalls and plunge pools are busy. To get to the more pristine and less visited areas it is better to stay at least one night.

Generally, the trip is fairly easygoing, with plenty of options for people of varying degrees of fitness. Some of the hikes can be rather hot and humid if you are travelling during the pre-monsoon season.

There is a motel within Kakadu National Park, at Cooinda, although most people (including those on the tour I joined) use the excellent camping facilities. Camping is the only option within Litchfield.

No specialist personal equipment is needed for this tour. A four-wheel-drive vehicle is essential to get off the beaten track in Kakadu.

The northern half of the park is centred on the impressive Tabletop Range, a sandstone outcrop from which numerous waterfalls tumble throughout the year. The major falls maintain their flow during the dry season because the rain-permeable top layer of the range soaks up water during the wet and releases it slowly during the dry season. The southern part of the park consists of more open land that is bordered to the west by Reynolds River. To kick off the tour, we travelled down a rough track that took us past fields full of the marvellous, grey, magnetic termite mounds, which resemble gravestones. These tiny creatures build large, slim mounds that all align almost exactly in a north–south direction. A couple of bush turkeys scuttled off as we approached our destination, and a flock of sulphur-crested cockatoos squawked and played in a cocky apple tree. Surprise Creek is a lovely twin-tier cascade with deep swimming holes on both levels. A couple of invigorating leaps from the surrounding rocks prepared me for the return hike along the track and the journey north to Odyssey Safari's exclusive Minjungari Camp.

HOPPING DRUMMERS

The camp, with luxury raised platform tents, is located on a billabong (a permanent waterhole) down a secluded track at the very western edge of the park. We set off straight away to explore along the billabong, where blue waterlilies stood tall above the dense cover of green leafy pads. It was a wonderfully tranquil spot,

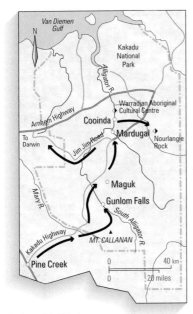

On the trail in Kakadu

and as I rested on a tree trunk a group of antilopine wallaroos emerged from the bush cover and hopped towards the water. I hardly dared breathe for fear of scaring them off, and I watched unnoticed as one stopped, stood up high, and scratched its stomach, its small front paws rubbing up and down with the rhythm of a marching drummer. Later, after savouring Annette's pasta treat, we heard scraping noises outside the eating hut. With torches in hand, we followed the sounds until we discovered two small northern brown bandicoots foraging for insects in the leaf litter. Almost unaware of our presence, they came within an arm's length of our feet at times, before I accidentally made a noise and they scurried off into the dark.

Early the next morning, we set off for Tjaynera Falls, also known as Sandy Creek Falls. The falls are approached through beautiful paperbark woodland, where the ground layer was covered with various species of ancient cycad plants. Tjaynera, which drains into the Reynolds River, is widely regarded as Litchfield's best waterfall and it was easy to see why.

The dark cliffs of the Tabletop Range arc around a large plunge pool at the base of a tall, narrow cataract. It is just how a tropical jungle paradise pool should look and Annette nearly had to drag us away.

Before heading back towards Darwin, we stopped off at the relatively busy Tolmer and Florence falls. As attractive as they both are, we had been spoilt by tranquil Tjaynera and Surprise Creek, so we took only short swims to freshen up before the two-hour journey back to Darwin.

BIG BROTHER

Litchfield's big brother, Kakadu National Park, lies a couple of hundred kilometres to the southeast of Darwin, on the eastern side of the Stuart Highway. It covers almost 20,000 sq. km (7,725 sq. miles), roughly the size of Switzerland, making it Australia's biggest national park. A World Heritage site, it encompasses the entire catchment area of the South Alligator River system and it boasts over 1,600 plant species, almost 300 bird species, and more than 5,000 Aboriginal rock-art sites. New species and sites are regularly being found. Annette was the perfect guide for a journey through a region so rich in wildlife. She had an unerring ability to identify birds, lizards, and noises in the night, even if they were the length of a football pitch away.

FRILLY LIZARDS

The group was two days into a seven-day tour, when I joined at Manyallaluk, near Katherine. We entered the park along the surfaced Kakadu Highway from Pine Creek. One of the great attractions of Kakadu is that it is possible to reach the very heart of the park without a four-wheel-drive vehicle. The infrastructure is superb, including well-appointed campsites, while strict management controls ensure that the impact of rising visitor numbers (over 240,000 people in 1998) is minimal. However, the real gems are to be found on challenging off-road tracks beyond the range of ordinary cars. From the Kakadu Highway, we joined a dirt road that took us past Mount Callanan and stopped briefly to collect deadwood for the evening fire. Just ahead of the car, Annette spotted a frilled lizard sitting warming itself on the gravel. These spectacular creatures have a huge, fan-shaped flap of skin around their necks that they lift to scare off predators or to attract female suitors.

Our first night was spent at Gunlom Falls, a camp near a beautiful plunge pool below a high escarpment. The falls form part of the headwater area of the South Alligator River. Odyssey Safaris has luxury tents permanently set up here, so we just moved in, lit the fire, and cracked open a beer to watch the sunset. The local Jawoyn Aboriginal people called the area "sickness country," due to mysterious illnesses suffered by resident tribal members, almost certainly caused by the deposits of uranium, mercury, lead, and arsenic that are found underground in the area. Luckily, none of these deposits lie near the camp! In the morning, I hiked up

a steep, rocky path to the top of the escarpment, where serene pools were contained by strangely sculpted salmon-pink, black, and grey rock formations. Although the pools are beautiful, the principal reason for climbing so high is to enjoy the spectacular vista over the distant rolling hills and vast flatlands of the South Alligator Valley. Seeing our tiny camp far below, as small as a town looks from a cruising aircraft, reinforced the sense of endless wilderness—a feeling that can be both overwhelming and enlivening if you have spent most of your life in built-up areas.

CROC WARNING

Back at camp, I load the trailer for the journey to Maguk, also known as Barramundie Gorge. A pleasant feature of the setup at Kakadu is that there are few swimming holes and gorges that you can drive right up to. Many of them require short, enjoyable walks through varying bushland from the car parks. Large signs

Below: Gigantic cathedral termite mounds dominate the landscape in Litchfield National Park
Right: Frilled lizard basking on hot tarmac
Far Right: Tjaynera Falls —a real paradise we didn't want to leave

warning of crocodiles dominate the start of the Maguk trail, and Annette ensured that we all took the time to read them. The 2km (1-mile) hike initially crossed shallow, sandy pools before winding through a narrow stand of monsoon woodlands. Annette stopped to show us a delicate purple flower and a little later we spotted archerfish swimming in a deeper section of Barramundie Creek. When the trail opened out into a rocky section, two

KAKADU'S ABORIGINAL SEASONS

The local Bininj and Mungguy Aboriginal people recognize six distinct seasons beyond the accepted wet and dry:

❑ *Gudjewg* (January to March) The "true" wet season, with heavy rain, thunderstorms, high temperatures and humidity. A good time to collect edible eggs.

❑ *Banggerreng* (April) Clear skies return and floodwaters recede. Violent winds ("knock 'em-down" storms) early in this season can flatten fields of spear grass.

❑ *Yegge* (May to mid-June) Temperatures and humidity levels drop. When the Darwin woollybutt flowers, it is time to burn the woodlands to "clean the country."

❑ *Wurreng* (mid-June to mid-August) The "cold" and dry time of year, when temperatures drop to 30°C (86°F) in daytime and 17°C (63°F) at night. Creeks stop running and floodplains dry out.

❑ *Gurrung* (mid-August to mid-October) A hot, dry season. A good time for hunting file snakes and long-necked turtles.

❑ *Gunumeleng* (mid-October to late December) Pre-monsoon time; hot and humid. Afternoon thunderstorms produce some rain and the land starts to turn green again. Aboriginal people moved to the high stone country to avoid the coming floods.

of us chose to head to the top of the gorge while the others continued along the creek to the swimming hole. The waterfall at the end of the gorge emerges from a deep, narrow cleft in the sandstone cliffs. Another small tour group was frolicking in the upper pools, while we waved down to our companions swimming towards the fall. The intense midday heat soon had us backtracking to the river to join them.

In the afternoon we went to Mardugal, where we joined a boat trip onto Yellow Waters (Ngurrungurrudjba in the local Aboriginal language), a pristine wetland area that forms part of the South Alligator River's floodplain. Large, flat-bottomed boats each seat around 50 passengers— not a particularly personal way to interact with the abundant wildlife, but it controls the impact of so many visitors. Just make sure that you get a seat on an outside edge of the boat if you want to see well. Our guide explained that this, the end of the dry season, is the best time of year to see wildlife as the water—and thus the birds and animals—is concentrated in small areas. Within a minute or so of leaving dock, the menacing, dark, scaly figure of a saltwater crocodile broke the surface near the boat. Everybody jostled to get the best view, cameras clicking paparazzi-style. These remnants of the dinosaur era always look capable of causing damage no matter how big a boat you are in and, as excited as I was to see the saltie, it was a relief to watch it submerge once more.

HONKING MAGPIES

For birdwatchers, Yellow Waters is a veritable paradise. The tree- and mangrove-lined banks, grassy floodplains, and numerous mudflats make ideal habitats for a large number of species. Lines of plumed whistling ducks hugged the riverbank, while a couple of huge jabirus stalked through the mangroves on their long, reddish-pink legs. High up in trees, two majestic white-bellied sea eagles sat guarding their large, clumpy nests. As we eased quietly downriver, dense flocks of black-necked, white-bodied magpie geese were massed, like regiments, on the vast grassy plain. Their noisy, deep, resonant honking sounded similar to hundreds of vintage car horns. In amongst them, small herds of wild horses grazed. We continued to spot more saltwater crocodiles all along the banks, including one that was close to 7m (23ft) long. Where the river widened, the edges were dominated by swamps of paperbark trees, their exposed roots entangled with river debris. Overhead, against a darkening sky, squawking squadrons of red-tailed black cockatoos flew home from their daytime feeding, whilst colourful kingfishers continued their search for food from low-lying tree branches. Within weeks, the coming rains would raise water levels and, once again, the birds and animals would disperse.

OUR SECRET DESTINATION

An early start the next morning saw us on the very rough track to Graveside Gorge at the best time of day for seeing some of Australia's most famous creatures, namely kangaroos and emus. Graveside Gorge is not marked on any maps of Kakadu, and nor mentioned in any guides—until now—so I have no intention of revealing all here either. I would like to think that keeping the location quiet might allow others to find it as we did. Odyssey Safaris have been coming here for several years now, but few others venture this way, part of the reason it remains so special. The track twisted persistently through gorgeous open woodland, subtly lit by the warm rays of the morning sun. As we rounded a corner, a flurry of movement on the passenger side of the car turned out to be a startled emu. Strangely, it paraded back and forth in front of us, edging closer without ever making much real progress. This remarkable, almost comic encounter lasted for ten minutes, before the bird suddenly took fright and sprinted off into thicker bush.

At times the track was pocked with deep holes and washouts that required snail's pace driving from Annette and fine judgement on where to place the wheels. Up in the trees, Annette's sharp eyes picked out a blue-winged kookaburra. The kookaburra is known throughout Australia for its prolonged staccato call, which sounds like a laughing chimpanzee, but it is only in the northern woodlands that the psychedelic blue-winged version is found. At one long sandy section of track, we had to get out of the vehicle to ensure it didn't get bogged down and then rejoin Annette further on. The track crossed more open grassland, where the landscape was dominated by the gigantic mounds of cathedral termites. We occasionally saw brightly coloured rainbow bee-eater birds, their green bodies contrasting with their blue and yellow wings as they flew in search of insects.

Two hours after leaving camp we reached the start of the one-hour walking trail that leads to Graveside Gorge. A bushfire had recently gone through the area, wiping out the old trail in places, but Annette was confident (well, at least she looked confident!) that it would be easy enough to find our way. Starting out over a bed of fragmented pink rocks and sand, the hike was fairly easygoing, but the sun's intensity was already starting to increase, making it essential that we carried water and wore wide-brimmed hats.

LIVING FOSSILS

Cycads have been around since the dinosaur era and continue to thrive today. There are numerous species spread all around the world, but all have dense, sturdy, palm-like leaves with a small fruit growing at the core. Some plants can live for over 2,500 years, and the genus has survived two periods of mass species extinction on Earth. A secret of their success is the bowl shape that develops around the base of the trunk, which traps water and nutrient-rich litter to ensure the plant's survival through even the most extreme dry spells. They can grow in sand and rock.

NORTHERN TERRITORY & SOUTH AUSTRALIA

Above: *The leaves of a cycad with its fruit at the core*
Below: *Nourlangie Rock, infused with Dreamtime stories*

From the rocks, we crossed the burnt-out section of woodland, where small, green shoots pushing through the blackened soil indicated that the plant life was already making a comeback. We crossed a creek bed via large boulders and emerged through trees into the beautiful, deserted gorge. To have it as our own private playground for a few hours was a real treat. Surrounded by craggy, rust-red hills, the two-level pool here had a small waterfall at its far end and a rock platform down its left-hand side. We swam, relaxed in the sun, ate a plentiful lunch, swam again…you get the picture. It was a hard

place to leave, but we had to get back along the track before dark.

After another night at the Mardugal Campsite, we again left quite early to get to the famous Aboriginal rock-art site of Nourlangie Rock. Kakadu has one of the greatest concentrations of rock art anywhere in the world. To date, over 5,000 such sites have been recorded, and it is thought that perhaps double that number remain to be seen by non-Aboriginals. The art was created over a period that extends from possibly 35,000 years ago right up until the 1970s, making it the longest continuous art form known to

Above: *Nourlandie's rock art details an encyclopaedic history of Aboriginal life in this region*

man, one that details an encyclopaedic history of Aboriginal life in the region. Access to the site is easy in any vehicle, and recently, a raised wooden boardwalk, parts of which are suitable for wheelchair users, has been constructed.

ROCK OF CREATION

Nourlangie Rock is a sandstone outlier of the Arnhem Land escarpment, and dominates the landscape for miles around. We chose to walk the 1.5km (1-mile) trail in reverse direction to get an overview of the site first from the Gunwardewarde Lookout. Nourlangie slopes downward at one end where a large boulder sits, precariously balanced. As with all parts of the landscape it is infused with Aboriginal Dreamtime stories. For some of the clans in the area, Namondjok (pronounced "nar-mon-jock") was a Creation Ancestor who travelled through the Nourlangie area and broke the kinship laws, designed to control relationships within a clan, with his sister. Namondjok's sister took a feather—the boulder—from his head-dress and placed it at the end of the rock after they had broken the laws.

Next we came to the art site known as the Main, or Angbangbang, Gallery. The principal figure on the wall, protected from the elements by a large, overhanging section, is none other than Namondjok. Some regional clans have a different, less damning, view of him, seeing him as a Creation Ancestor of the sky, who can be seen only at night, appearing as a black void amongst the dense stars of the Milky Way. Beside him is a weird, white, skeletal figure, a common image throughout Nourlangie's art. This is Namarrgon, the Lightning Man, who during Creation charged out of the sky with an arc of lightning and stone axes on his elbows, knees, and feet, which he used to bang and split the storm clouds to make thunder. Below him is his wife, Barrginj, also white and skeletal, along with a procession of elaborately dressed tall people.

The stories these paintings depict are as old as human history, but the

Angbangbang paintings were the last great works created at Nourlangie. Aboriginal art was a way of telling stories, and paintings were regularly repainted, as a means of staying in touch with the Creation Era. Only clansmen who were initiated to a high level could repaint.

EVIL DANCERS

Further along the trail, a group of stick-like human figures with gangly arms and legs are described on the sign as dancers. Annette, however, informed us that the images were actually evil Narmarndis spirits that Aboriginal people are unwilling to talk about to outsiders. Another gallery had old paintings of kangaroos and other hunted animals, dating back around 20,000 years. Even having seen the art and heard the stories, it was still hard to comprehend the period of history on show at Nourlangie Rock. However, the spirituality was more obvious, and we left with a much deeper respect for the meaning of the Dreamtime and what it continues to signify for the Aborigines today.

CREATION OF A DREAM NATION

The religious life of Aboriginal people is based upon the Dreamtime. Creation Ancestors, such as Rainbow Serpents, the Wagilag Sisters, Lightning Men and Wandjina, travelled across the shapeless world, leaving Dreaming tracks as they went, and created everything in it. The stories of the Creation Ancestors have been passed from generation to generation through word of mouth, ceremonial dancing, and art. The Dreamtime provided a framework for people to live in harmony with their surroundings. The breakdown of traditional Aboriginal clan and family structures may soon reduce the Dreamtime to a distant memory recorded on a painting in an overseas art gallery.

GOING IT ALONE

INTERNAL TRAVEL

Darwin is the obvious base for visiting the national parks, and is well served by all the major forms of transport. Qantas and Ansett both offer domestic and international flights to Darwin, and other international carriers, including Singapore Airlines and Malaysian Airlines, also offer flights there. If you are flying domestically, you can get significant fare reductions (certainly helpful given the price of flying to Darwin) by purchasing tickets seven or more days in advance.

There are good highways leading to Darwin from all the major cities in the country, even if they are rather long! Greyhound Pioneer buses run daily to Darwin from around the country. If you have your own transport, then both Litchfield and Kakadu national parks are easily accessible, although you will need a four-wheel drive to see the best parts. All the major car-hire firms, including Budget Rent A Car and Avis, have offices in Darwin city centre and at the airport.

WHEN TO GO

Although it would be something special to see the parks in the height of the wet season, when the waterfalls are pumping and the land is lush, it really isn't feasible unless you want to stick to the main highways. Therefore, almost all visitors go there between April and October, with the middle months the most popular. Personally, I think that a tour during the cusp months—March/April or October/November—is a good idea as you get to see the transition between seasons, although be warned that access on the four-wheel-drive tracks at these times can be tricky or impossible.

PLANNING

There are plenty of tour operators in Darwin that offer one-day or multi-day trips into both parks. Accommodation is usually on a camping basis, although it is also possible to book hotel-based tours.

OFF-ROAD DRIVING TIPS

Ever wondered why off-road vehicles cost so much to hire? It's because they get damaged so frequently. Most hirers have little or no previous experience of driving on the dirt and accidents are all too frequent. First of all, slow down. It is very easy to lose the vehicle's back end on loose gravel, especially if you are moving at high speed. Braking distances are also greatly increased as the vehicle struggles to gain grip. On narrow, bumpy tracks, it is important to anticipate and choose your route carefully through the holes and over the bumps if you want to keep the vehicle on four wheels.

WHAT TO TAKE

- ❏ Good-quality, comfortable hiking boots.
- ❏ Sunscreen and a wide-brimmed hat.
- ❏ Portable water bottle.
- ❏ Torch for use in camp.
- ❏ Mosquito repellent. Mosquito headnets are useful if you find the persistent and numerous flies a nuisance.
- ❏ Swimming costume and towel.
- ❏ Small daypack for use on hikes.

HEALTH

There are no major health concerns when travelling in the national parks. Drink plenty of water when bushwalking as dehydration can strike quickly, and wear a brimmed hat to combat the intense sun. You are very unlikely to encounter snakes on the trail (they normally feel your approach and move away), but if someone in your party is bitten, it is very important to keep the patient calm as panic causes the poison to be pumped more quickly around the body. Wrap the bite area tightly, as you would for a twisted ankle, and then seek help. It is enormously useful to medical staff if you identify the snake, but don't try anything rash to achieve this. Avoiding snakes is the best protection, so wear high walking boots, thick socks, and long trousers when bushwalking.

FURTHER READING

- ❏ *Kakadu—Looking After the Country—The Gagudju Way* (J.B. Books, 1998) by Stanley Breeden and Belinda Wright. Lavishly illustrated with beautiful photos, documenting an 18-month stay with the Aboriginal people of Kakadu.
- ❏ *Kakadu—Natural History Guide* (Steve Parrish Publishing, 1996) by Ian Morris. A unique, very readable guide to Kakadu's flora and fauna, based on the Aboriginal seasons.

5 A Dream Encounter

by Steve Watkins

For at least 40,000 years Aborigines have lived in Australia. Nowadays, their rich and vibrant culture remains strongest in the Northern Territory. I joined two distinctive, award-winning tours, at Manyallaluk and Bathurst Island, to learn something of Aboriginal ways.

 The tours are very easygoing and are suitable for people of all ages and fitness levels. The walks are short and pass over easy ground.

★★ At Manyallaluk, Odyssey Safaris provides large canvas tents with comfortable swag mattresses. The Tiwi Islands tour is just a day trip, so you stay overnight in Darwin, where there is a complete range of accommodation options.

 No specialist equipment is needed for these tours.

In an attempt to get as broad a view of Aboriginal life as possible during my limited stay, I joined two very different tours in the Northern Territory, both of which have won national indigenous tourism awards. The first of these was to the community of Manyallaluk (pronounced "man-yalla-look"), southeast of

Katherine, 314km (195 miles) south of Darwin, which offers guided bushtucker walks, and craftmaking and spear-throwing lessons. To get there, I joined an Odyssey Safaris tour, which included an overnight camping stay at the community. My second tour was a day trip with Tiwi Tours to Bathurst, in the Tiwi Islands, 80km (50 miles) north of Darwin in the Timor Sea.

Manyallaluk is home to around 150 Aboriginal people from the Mayali, Rembarrnga, Ngalkbon, and Jawoyn language groups. The community land covers 3,000sq. km (1,150 sq. miles) and its enviable location borders Nitmiluk National Park to the west, Kakadu National Park to the north, and Arnhem Land to the east.

GOING BUSH

The first seeds of tourism were sown here in 1990, when a tourism initiative was developed that would allow the Manyallaluk community to work towards being self-supporting. By 1999, tours were booming, there were more than 20 regular Aboriginal guides, and the whole community spirit had improved immensely. After being warmly welcomed by Quinton, our enthusiastic guide, we hiked off into the bush with him to learn how Aboriginal people use the natural resources around them. Quinton's knowledge was staggering, and it seemed that every few steps he would point out an edible plant, a root that could be used to paint with, or a tree out of which weapons were made.

Near a small creek, Quinton peeled a strip of loose bark off a stringybark tree and swiftly fashioned a water-carrier by making a simple boat shape and wrapping the ends round. The soft bark is waterproof, and we took turns drinking refreshing creek water from it. The impermeable bark is also ideal for building shelters, called humpys, which hunters used. When set on fire, the bark also smoulders endlessly, making it an excellent means of carrying fire from one camp to another. Quinton explained that the leaves were used to add flavour when cooking kangaroo meat. As we moved below an open, rocky slope, two antilopine wallaroos—large kangaroos with fine fur similar to that of an antelope—bounded across in front of us, followed moments later by two excited dogs from the village. Quinton smiled and said, "Roos always win... them got big step!"

On the way back to the village, we learnt of a plant, called *yering yering* in Jawoyn, with leaves so rough that they serve as sandpaper for smoothing

Left: *Practising the skill involved in weaving baskets and mats from pandanus leaves*
Above: *Face painting is part of the preparation for the welcome dance*
Below: *Carved and painted ironwood figure*

didgeridoos. Quinton also explained how the Cooktown ironwood tree was used in the past to make clubs for women to settle their differences (men used spears). Nowadays, he revealed, with a big grin on his face, the women pull hair and the men box. To wrap up the walk with startling effect, he picked up a handful of green ants, briefly let us smell their pungent acidic odour, and then ate them! Apparently, these ants help stave off stomach illnesses. Strangely, no one in our group was feeling unwell enough to try them. Messing with green ants is not recommended, however, as they can squirt acid up to 8cm (3in), far enough to give peering intruders a very sore eye. Back under the shelter of a large tree in the village, Manyallaluk's head chef served up a buffet feast of native food, including roasted emu and kangaroo meat, grilled squashes, and barramundi fish. This was all washed down with a cup of billy tea served off the fire.

A LEAFY FAILURE

Having seen the versatility of plants found in the bush, we enjoyed an afternoon sitting on the grass with Diane, a cheery middle-aged Aboriginal woman,

TEN USES FOR THE PANDANUS PLANT

The pandanus is impossible to avoid on any visit to Aboriginal communities in northern Australia. It is used:

❑ For basket-weaving.

❑ As a paint brush and as a green-grey dye.

❑ As an antiseptic—the soft white heart, or cabbage, at the apex of the stems is chopped out and crushed into a coarse paste to make an antiseptic that is applied directly to infected sores, scratches, and boils.

❑ For headaches—young pandanus leaves are pulled out and stripped of their thorns, and then tied tightly around the forehead to ease headaches.

❑ A a bandage—the antiseptic paste is held over the wound by what else but a pandanus leaf!

❑ As food—the cabbage is rich in carbohydrate, and is eaten raw or boiled. The seeds, bright red fruits, and the fruit stalks are all eaten.

❑ Musical instruments—the stems of the plant become light and hollow after they fall to the ground, and can be turned into didgeridoos.

❑ As boats—tied together to make ocean-going rafts.

❑ As fire carriers—dead branches make excellent fire-carriers as, once lit, they rarely go out.

❑ As toys—the root is fashioned into childrens' dolls.

learning about how one of those plants, the spiral pandanus, was used to make colourful baskets and mats. If any of us had underestimated the skill involved in working with plants, we soon changed our minds. Diane took hold of the sharp end of a pandanus leaf, and, using her thumb, effortlessly split the thin front layer of long fibrous leaf from the back layer, peeling it away as if she was tearing off strips of wallpaper. "Now, it's your turn, who wanna go?" Confidently, we all picked out a leaf, bent it over backward near the tip and thumbed at the resulting crack. Minutes later, we were still thumbing. Persistence turned to frustration and we thumbed more erratically as the leaves simply refused to part. Unwilling to admit defeat, several of us continued to thumb haplessly at the leaf throughout the rest of Diane's weaving demonstration. The split leaves were wetted to make them supple, then using a sewing needle (they used to be made from kangaroo bones) and blanket stitch Diane gradually transformed the leaf into a swirling mat. The leaves can also be coloured by boiling them with brilliant red or blue dyes produced from local plant roots.

Later, Quinton and another guide showed us how to make slate paintings using ochre colours and—you guessed it—a pandanus leaf as a fine paintbrush. The mesh-like art style, known as X-ray art, is commonly used to depict animals such as kangaroos and crocodiles. However, we were all keen to try our hand at spear throwing, and we joined several of the community's best throwers to learn the necessary techniques. To gain extra leverage, the long spears are launched using another stick called a woomera, which has a small hook lashed to its end that fits into a depression in the tail of the spear. Our teachers showed how to hold the two together, and then launched flat-arm throws that saw the spear whizzing low through the air, often hitting the small cardboard-box target some 25m (82ft) away. When Aborigines really hunt, the incredibly sharp, ironwood spear tips are coated with a paralyzing poison made from a mixture of native plants. I balanced mine carefully on the woomera as I had been shown, then unleashed my schoolboy javelin technique. The spear spiralled skywards, like a poorly made paper aeroplane, and I also managed to let go of the woomera, which, much to the amusement of our instructors, landed nearer the target than the spear!

After dinner, Little John, a rather large fellow like his Robin Hood namesake, came to our camp to tell us a couple of lengthy and enchanting creation stories from the Dreamtime. It would have been an ideal time to sip a glass of red wine as we sat by the fire, but Manyallaluk is a strictly alcohol-free community and there are hefty penalties for one who breaks this law. We headed to bed, rolling up our tent windows to enjoy the cooling breeze and a view of the stars. That decision proved foolish, however, as at around three o'clock in the morning a sudden rain and lightning storm hit and we all had to rush out to seal the tents. We left next morning a whole lot wiser and more appreciative of Aboriginal knowledge and skills than when we arrived.

REAL PEOPLE

Physical isolation can have a unique effect on the development of cultures, and there can be few more striking examples of this in Aboriginal Australia than Bathurst and Melville islands, collectively known as the Tiwi Islands. Although the Tiwi people share many common traits with mainland Aboriginal groups, there are also several remarkable differences. Tiwi means "real," or "only," people, as the islanders thought they were the chosen ones, the only people worthy of living on the islands. No one else was considered real or human enough, and even mainland Australia was known as Tibambinum, meaning place of the dead. Any attempts to visit the islands before 1900 usually met with outright violence,

further adding to their isolation. These days, thankfully, welcome is much warmer. I joined a one-day trip offered by the islanders' own company, Tiwi Tours, to take a look at their distinct culture.

Flight time from Darwin to Nguiu, the main town on Bathurst Island (the smaller of the two islands) is just over 1¼ hours and is spent mainly over the open ocean. As we came in to land, I saw that much of the island was densely forested, undulating rather than hilly, and dotted with sandy bays guarded by small cliffs. Our enthusiastic guides, Lloyd Tipiloura and Berna Timaepatua, met us at the airport's tiny office, which is painted with Aboriginal-style kangaroo figures. Even the public lavatories just outside the airport have the full Aboriginal art treatment.

NEVER SINGLE

We travelled on the Tiwi Tours bus through the wide, downtown streets, remarkably tidy and litter-free compared to many mainland communities. There was hardly

WHAT'S YOUR SKIN?

Aboriginal social structure is governed by a couple of core concepts: the clan and the kinship system, both handed down by the Creation Ancestors during the Dreamtime. Clans normally include a few family groups that share overlapping land areas. The kinship system defines how everybody within an extended family, which includes uncles, aunts, cousins, and so on, can relate to one another. Family groups are allocated "skin" names and then the kinship system dictates how people from different skins can behave. The most obvious way it is applied is to control who can marry whom, resulting in girls and boys from prohibited skin combinations even refusing to acknowledge one another as they pass in the street. Penalties for breaching the kinship system are substantial and very painful, even today.

anyone out on the streets though, so I asked Berna why this was. "There's a wedding today, everybody going. Lloyd and me, we'll go after to the party." Before the Catholic mission was set up on Bathurst in 1911 and islanders were converted to Christian ways, marriage was driven by a rule—possibly unique in world society—whereby every female had to be married, regardless of her age or wishes. Females were nominally married at birth and there is no word in the Tiwi language for single females. This rule stemmed from the generally held Aboriginal belief that spirits, and not men, make women pregnant. As spirits were uncontrollable, women could theoretically become pregnant at any time, so this enforced marriage situation guaranteed that all newborn Tiwi children had fathers. Even an elderly woman would have to remarry immediately should her husband die, which meant that such marriage ceremonies took place at the departed husband's graveside. Even today, not all Tiwi women have been won over by the Christian faith. One woman I met told me, "Weddings are a Catholic thing. I'm not getting wed. We have our own religion."

Our first stop was the museum, set in a tin-sheet building that used to be the mission teahouse. The exhibits gave an excellent insight into the lifestyle, culture, and history of the islanders. There is also a fascinating collection of black and white photographs from the early mission days, alongside more modern memorabilia, such as children's paintings of Japanese bombers flying over the island on their way to attack Darwin during World War II. Other displays include elaborately carved and painted hunting

Left and below: *The clapboard Nguiu church contains a wonderful mixture of indigenous art and Christian imagery*

spears, an art form the Tiwi took to a far higher level than any mainland Aboriginal group. Missing were two items that you would ordinarily expect to see in any Aboriginal community: the woomera and curved boomerang. To the amazement of anthropologists, neither of these implements was ever used on the Tiwi Islands, reinforcing just how isolated they had remained.

Within walking distance of the museum, past an old aircraft propeller that serves as a memorial to those who fought in World War II, is the colonial mission church. Built in 1934, the white clapboard church is set on a raised platform. Inside, shafts of sunlight shone through numerous shuttered windows and reflected off the pale yellow walls to create a warm, homely feel. There were enough rickety benches neatly aligned to sit up to a couple of hundred worshippers. The domed altar area is a wonderful mixture of indigenous art and Christian imagery, summed up best by a small brass figure of Christ on a cross that is painted with a traditional Aboriginal dot design.

A MODEL WIFE

Paintings and items created by the islands' artists have become much sought after around the world, and exports now total more than A$1.5 million per year. Tiwi Designs' bold and vibrant screen-printed products, including T-shirts, cushion covers, and rolled fabric, have brought the Tiwi name to the high streets of cities throughout Australia and

Above: Tiwi Ladies burst into ceremonial dance, stamping and flinging their arms in the air
Below: Traditional crafts are eagerly learnt by the younger generation

Europe. The company's store and workshop are open to the public, and it all proved too tempting as I came out with a painting and, of course, a couple of ceremonial headbands made from woven pandanus. Another art workshop, called Ngaruwanajirri, employs islanders with learning difficulties. I was particularly taken with a quirky looking, lopsided head carved from ironwood and decorated with ceremonial face painting. The artists told me that Thomas Munkanome, the man who was getting married that day, had carved it. After I bought it, one joked that Thomas had modelled it on his wife, sending the other artists into fits of giggles.

For morning tea, we drove to a clearing on the outskirts of town and joined the Tiwi Ladies, a group of four women who were to show us their craft skills and a series of ceremonial dances. First, we tucked into the delicious fresh damper

NORTHERN TERRITORY & SOUTH AUSTRALIA

(traditional bread that is baked in the sand under hot coals) and billy tea they had made for us. Three of the women—Doreen Tipiloura, Mary Orsto, and Ruth Kerinaui—were quite old, with shocks of white hair, while the fourth, Mary Rose Tipungwuti, was only in her twenties and just beginning to learn the skills and dances. It was refreshing to see a young person eager to acquire the knowledge of community elders; a number of mainland communities are in fact suffering because the traditional skills, few of which are written down, are dying out with the older generation.

The women sat in an arc on the floor and patiently decorated their faces with ochre paints in readiness for the dancing. Then, lined up before us, and with Lloyd joining in too, the Tiwi Ladies lit bunches of pandanus leaves and burst into ceremonial dance action. Stamping the ground and flinging their arms in the air, they moved in mesmerizing circles and swirls before scuttling up to us and waving the smoking leaves all around our bodies in order to attract good spirits. This was the welcome dance. Each lady then took it in turn to perform an animal dance while the others sang and chanted. The dances they showed us were public ones; only people initiated to the right level can see the numerous other ceremonial dances.

AN OLD TABOO

The last part of the tour took us to a remote traditional burial site in thick bushland overlooking a beautiful bay. Perhaps the most striking of the unique Tiwi developments are the large, carved and painted totems, known as *pukimani* poles, that are placed around their graves. *Pukimani* is a generic word used for anything sacred, untouchable, or forbidden, and covers everything from mourners at a funeral to women who have just given birth. The burial site had eight 2m (6.5ft)-high poles, elaborately carved with human and animal faces, and arranged in a circle around the

stone-covered grave. Each pole had a woven bag over its top to indicate that the site was no longer considered *pukimani* and could thus be visited. The names of dead people are *pukimani*, too, and Berna insisted strongly that I shouldn't write about the person buried at the site. The list of *pukimani* acts and places is almost endless, reflecting just how strong a hold taboo has on the islanders. Before flying back to Darwin, we all took a relaxing swim in Tantipi waterhole and reflected on the confident enthusiasm of the Tiwi people.

The process of enmeshing Aboriginal and European culture in Australia still has a long and hard road to follow, but a more independent and proud Aboriginal population is one of the key steps to success. Travellers should not miss out on seeing the country through Aboriginal eyes, and there is, at last, a convincing glimmer of hope that the incredible Aboriginal story has yet to reach its final chapter.

ABORIGINAL LANDS?

When Europeans first settled Australia, the country was deemed *terra nullius*, or empty land, despite the presence of some 300,000 Aborigines. The dispossession that followed colonization was catastrophic for the Aborigines, whose culture and lifestyle were so closely linked to the land. The 1976 Land Rights Act, allowed some Aboriginal people, now deemed "traditional owners," to reclaim land, but only in the Northern Territory. Over half the state became Aboriginal owned over the following 20 years. Further laws extended the land claims and, by 1998, around 13 percent of Australia was legally owned or controlled by traditional Aboriginal owners. Is that too great a compensation for the previous destruction of their culture? Some people still think so.

GOING IT ALONE

INTERNAL TRAVEL

Darwin is a natural base for exploring the northern part of the Northern Territory, and getting there is easy by both plane and road. Ansett and Qantas have regular domestic flights to Darwin from all the main cities in Australia, and a number of carriers now offer international flight access direct to Darwin.

If you are not joining an organized tour you really need to have your own vehicle as bus services are either nonexistent or infrequent. All the major car-rental firms, including Budget and Avis, have offices in Darwin.

WHEN TO GO

The most popular time to visit the Northern Territory is during the dry season (April–September), but it can be advantageous to visit outside of these months as there are fewer tourists and the scenery starts to "green up." I visited in late October, and although some of the days were hot and humid, it was certainly bearable. The Aboriginal communities' tourism programmes tend to quieten off from November onwards, so do try to visit before then.

PLANNING

Access to Aboriginal land is strictly controlled, and anyone not from that community requires a permit to enter, except when passing through on designated highways. If you join an organized tour the permits will automatically be arranged for you. If you wish to travel independently, contact the relevant land councils in advance. Permits are usually granted, but the traditional owners do have the right to refuse entry (for more information, see Contacts). The only way to visit the Tiwi Islands is with Tiwi Tours; permits are not granted for casual independent visits.

TRAVELLERS' TIPS

❑ Aboriginal people are inherently shy, so don't expect gregarious welcomes or conversations. As with all people, they respond best when you show a genuine and intelligent interest in them and in their life. Those involved with tourism are usually open to having their photograph taken—so long as you ask first—but avoid snapping away at strangers. Children are always keen to have their picture taken and to borrow your camera so that they can take photos of all their friends, and this is a good way to break the ice—as long as you have enough film!

❑ Even after you have learnt about bushfoods at the communities, avoid the temptation to indulge in eating plants you don't know very well indeed: there are several species that can leave you feeling unwell or much worse.

WHAT TO TAKE

❑ Clothing requirements are minimal whatever time of year you visit as it is always warm or hot, and only occasionally cool at night.

❑ High factor sunscreen is vital to protect you from the damaging effects of the sun.

❑ A wide-brimmed hat, and sunglasses are essential.

❑ A water bottle is a good idea, even for general travelling. Dehydration creeps up slowly but can hit hard.

❑ A torch is useful as most of the Aboriginal community settlements are rarely lit at night.

HEALTH

There are no major health worries concerned with travelling in the Northern Territory. The intense heat and strong sunlight can cause such problems as dehydration and sunburn or heatstroke, so take it easy when you first arrive and allow yourself time to acclimatize. Following the arrival of refugees from East Timor in 1999, several cases of malaria were reported in Darwin. Although this is not a serious threat, it is wise to use insect repellents as mosquitoes also carry other diseases, including Ross River virus, which leaves you feeling exhausted after the easiest of tasks.

FURTHER READING

❑ *The Tiwi of North Australia* (Dryden Press, latest edition 1988) by C.W.M. Hart, A.R Pilling, and J.C. Goodale. A readable and comprehensive anthropological study of the Tiwi people and their culture. The anthropologist authors visited the island over an extended period from the 1950s.

NORTHERN TERRITORY & SOUTH AUSTRALIA

6 Sailing Across the Red Centre

by Simon Richmond

There are many adventurous ways to explore the desert heart of Australia: from a helicopter or a hot-air balloon, in a four-wheel drive, or on a horse or mountain bike. But best of all is to experience it from the back of a camel.

 Riding a camel is practically child's play, and the creatures are nowhere near as aggressive as they are sometimes made out to be. That said, you should be prepared for sore leg muscles and perhaps even blisters. You'll need some previous experience and good general fitness to tackle the off-road mountain-bike tracks around Alice Springs. There are hikes to suit everyone at Uluru, Alice Springs, and Kings Canyon, although you'll need to be in tip-top shape for any extended trips, such as the Larapinta Trail.

★★ Camping facilities are a cut above the basic level, with hot-water showers and a choice of accommodation in a hut or tent (although sleeping under the stars is best). In Alice Springs and the resort complex that caters for Uluru, every level of comfort is available, from camping grounds to five-star hotels. Come prepared for hot, dry days and, from June to September, for cold nights.

You'll need a wide-brimmed hat, sunscreen, sturdy shoes, long trousers, and a torch at all times of the year for the camel ride. Warm clothing is also essential for the cold winter nights, including a woolly hat if you're planning on sleeping outside. A basic first-aid kit should be carried on any treks across remote country.

You'd think there would be better places to find yourself, at 6.30 in the morning, than in the midst of the central Australian desert, shivering in the half-light on a roadside with a couple of hundred other camera-toting spectators. But there we were, ready to witness and record the rising sun's rays gradually warm and set afire a monolithic 348m (1,260ft)-high sandstone rock. This ancient, sacred totem is now known as Uluru, the name it was given, several millennia ago, by the local Aborigines. You might know it better as Ayers Rock.

I had come to the Red Centre—as the rusty outback heart of the Australian continent is nicknamed—to ride a camel across the desert. My camel journey would begin some 400km (250 miles) northeast, on the road to Alice Springs,

Above: *Deflating a hot-air balloon at Alice Springs*
Right: *The Valley of Winds, viewed from a thrilling helicopter ride over the multicoloured desert floor*

NORTHERN TERRITORY & SOUTH AUSTRALIA

central Australia's largest town. But despite the three-ring circus that gathers for Uluru's sunrise and sunset photofests, I knew it would be sacrilege to tour the Red Centre without first paying my respects at the Rock. The visual power of this Australian icon makes it easy to see why it's such an important site for the local Anangu Aboriginal communities.

BEYOND THE ROCK

Visitors can walk around the base of Uluru. The full 9km (5½-mile) circuit takes around four hours, but there are several shorter trails. Some of these can be done in the company of expert Aboriginal guides, who will explain the Dreamtime significance of Uluru. You can climb Uluru, but the Anangu have requested that visitors do not do so, as they hold it sacred. The climb is strenuous and monotonous (especially the initial chained section), and at least one person dies each year through slipping off the rock. If you're at all unfit or nervous of heights, don't do it. The 3.2km (2-mile) round trip takes around two hours. It's best undertaken early in the day while the temperature is still relatively low (the climb is closed 10am–4pm, when the temperature peaks at over 38°C, or 100°F).

The name Uluru refers to a waterhole near the summit of the Rock; this was always an important source of water for the Anangu, and up close you can see black streaks down the Rock left by waterfalls that run after the rare rainstorms. The scaly texture of the monolith, which is naturally grey under its oxidized surface, is also striking, as are the wavelike caves that are scattered around its base.

To take a different look at Uluru and nearby Kata Tjuta (the Olgas), an equally impressive and in some ways more mysterious rock outcrop some 50km (30 miles) east of the Ayers Rock Resort, I boarded a snazzy yellow and purple chopper for a thrilling 30-minute flight over the desert. First, we headed to Kata Tjuta (meaning many heads), a conglomerate rock mono-

lith that once would have dwarfed Uluru, but which has been worn down over millions of years into 36 separate domes. Much of Kata Tjuta is off limits; of the two walks you can undertake here, the best is the 7km (4½-mile) Valley of the Winds loop trail. The helicopter swung smoothly around and headed towards Uluru, which looked like a giant, burnt, bread bun bursting from the sand. From this height I could also see how the desert's multi-coloured surface—the clusters of pale green and yellow spinifex grass, the red and ochre rocks, the dark brown dots of mulga trees—has inspired Aboriginal art.

QUEEN OF THE DESERT

It was another pre-dawn start for the trip to Alice Springs, which would take me via Kings Canyon, my nomination for the Red Centre's most jaw-dropping geological feature. This 1.2km (¾ mile)-long gorge, with sheer walls that shoot up 270m (890ft), lies in the Watarrka National Park and gained international fame in the movie *The Adventures of Priscilla, Queen of the Desert*. The short burst of effort needed to tackle the initial incline to the top of the canyon is amply rewarded by the views and by the strange weathered sandstone landscape (nicknamed the Lost City) found there. The 6km (4-mile) trail takes around three hours, although you'll want to stay longer. If it's warm enough, go for a dip in the waterhole at the end of the aptly named Garden of Eden, a lush gum tree- and cycad palm-filled valley that meets the canyon's apex at right angles. If you don't feel up to the rim walk, there is a much easier track along the bed of Kings Creek.

A TOWN CALLED ALICE

Alice Springs nestles at the foot of the MacDonnell Ranges. The Alice, as it's affectionately known, still has a touch of the outback cowboy atmosphere about it, what with its Camel Cup races in July and surreal Henley-on-Todd Regatta—a bottomless boat race down the dry riverbed—in October. But since it now thrives predominantly on tourism, Alice is also surprisingly sophisticated, with good restaurants, art galleries, and excellent facilities for somewhere that lies slap-bang in the middle of the desert.

There are many ways to experience this magnificent desert terrain. Alice has carved out a niche for itself as an outback hot-air ballooning mecca, with three companies offering daily dawn trips over the McDonnell ranges. Another enjoyable, though energetic, way to see the area is on Steve Albury's mountain-bike tours. Steve has the full-suspension bikes necessary if you plan to tackle the off-road tracks to the west and east of town. So rugged are these tracks that at times it's as much a ramble as a bike ride, as I found myself having to wheel the bike up the rocky inclines. A recent shower had coaxed yellow, pink, and purple desert flowers out of the ground, adding splashes of unexpected colour along the route. Steve advised me to keep the wheels straight to tackle the sandier parts of the track, and to stand off the saddle and bring the pedals level when going down bumpy hills. "I call this the downhill extreme challenge," he said, before plunging over a savagely steep slope. I opted for the gentler route down. If you keep your eyes peeled you might see kangaroos—you'll definitely see their tracks and droppings.

SHIPS OF THE DESERT

Camels were found to be ideally suited to transporting men and supplies across the continent's vast arid regions, and before the railway and sealed roads arrived camel trains provided a lifeline of goods for outback settlements. There are now estimated to be over 250,000 camels roaming the outback, and 57 farms across Australia breed the animals for export, meat, racing, and the tourist trade. Noel Fullerton's Camel Farm, 80km (50 miles) south of Alice on the Stuart Highway, is one of the longest running and is the only operation that organizes camel safaris where you actually get to ride your camel.

CAMEL-RIDING TIPS

- ☐ Mount from the left side, throwing your right leg over the saddle. Adjust the stirrups so that your legs are in a comfortable position.
- ☐ To get the camel to stand, pull back gently on the reins and say "Hup." To steer, pull the head around to the required direction. To stop, pull the reins out and say "Hold." To dismount, do the same and say "Hush."
- ☐ Camels are intelligent but wilful; in this case, a firm tug on the reins is required.
- ☐ For the most comfortable ride, try to keep a relaxed posture in the saddle, going with the motion of the camel's gait. If you're heading downhill, lean back in the saddle to keep your balance.

Noel's camels are not roped in a train; you set the pace and can decide on the direction yourself.

Our three-day trip was led single-handedly by Crispin Gargan, a young ex-policeman who now runs the farm with his wife Michelle, Fullerton's daughter. We began with the introductions. My fellow cameleers were Cathy and Mark from Canberra, who had done a five-day safari the year before and enjoyed it so much they were back again, this time with Cathy's brother Dan, his wife and their teenage kids, all from New York. Our group of nine was completed by Australians Barry and Angela, a couple of "greying nomads" who had sold up and were touring the country.

Next came the introductions to the camels. I would be riding Taboo, a 16-year-old lady, who, hardly batting her lengthy eyelashes, took a toilet break as I strapped my day bag to her saddle. After a few brief instructions on how to ride, we were off, crossing the Stuart Highway and heading into the outback, not a cloud marring the vividly blue skies. The safari had begun.

GETTING INTO THE OUTBACK

It was an eight-hour ride on the first day to reach the base camp, just outside Rainbow Valley Conservation Reserve, some 30km (19 miles) from the farm. To get there we crossed part of a cattle station the size of Switzerland. There are some 2,500 head of cattle here, which have become a little less docile since helicopters were introduced to help with the mustering. Thus, when we approached cows, Gargan steered our group away,

just as he did when we passed groups of wild camels. "A bull camel will steal away the females," explained Gargan. And to show us how, Gargan's bull male Sharka cheekily blew out its dulaa, the bubblegum-like throat lining used to attract the girls.

Right: *Rainbow Valley—faded handprints, stencils and other unfathomable scratches on the rock*
Below: *Camels are ideally suited to transporting people and supplies across the continent's vast arid plains. They're also environmentally friendly*

NORTHERN TERRITORY & SOUTH AUSTRALIA

The camel is one of the most environmentally sensitive ways of travelling across the desert. Their soft-padded feet make minimal impression on the ground, and since we were not always riding in a line we could spread out so as not to leave tracks. What the camels do to the passing foliage—a movable feast, if ever I saw one—is another matter entirely! By the time we stopped for lunch, we were beginning to get the measure of our four-footed partners—as bright as an eight-year-old child, and about twice as smart as a horse.

ABORIGINAL REMAINS

Manny's Waterhole, where we had our lunch, is dry now, but once the site was home to an Aboriginal community. Gargan led us on a walkabout of the area, past grinding stones, scattered flints and sharp stones used as knives, and a midden containing a pile of rocks on which kangaroos were cooked. It was as if the Aborigines had just upped and left days ago. The reality, however, is that massacres and Spanish flu wiped them all out by the early decades of the 20th century.

On the long afternoon ride we spotted turquoise-green Port Lincoln ring-necked parrots flying among the spindly mulga and river red gum trees. From a hillside, a couple of euros, a kangaroo-like marsupial, eyed the camels curiously before bounding off to higher ground. By 5pm we had reached base camp, which consisted of a few tents, a shower room, and camel barracks, all set around the aptly named Stagger Inn, otherwise known as the kitchen. A campfire was started and the swags—sleeping bag, pillow, and foam base inside a protective cover— were distributed. There were rusty iron bedsteads to keep the swags off the ground; together they made a much more comfortable bed than would first appear.

ACROSS RAINBOW VALLEY

As amazing as it is to drift off to sleep under the overarching Milky Way, watching shooting stars fall to Earth, the early morning desert chill bites to the bones in the midwinter here. I snuggled down into my swag, cursing myself for not having brought thermal pyjamas and a woolly hat like my well-prepared American companions. Gargan was up before us all, preparing breakfast and saddling up the camels for the day's trek into Rainbow Valley. The name comes from the colours of the rock layers here, which span the spectrum from mauve and orange to yellow and cream. As I rode through the narrow gap in Mushroom Rock, past the towering sandstone bluffs and cliffs that are part of the James Ranges, I felt like Chips Rafferty, Australia's answer to John Wayne. We dismounted the camels and clambered up the slope to a lookout that gives a panoramic view of the reserve, including a large, smooth claypan and two lonely outcrops, Coroboree Rock and the oddly named Cricket Ball Rock. Before we set off again, Gargan sketched animal tracks in the sand for us to look out for. Then, while we sipped our morning tea, he trotted away on Sharka, only to appear moments later, galloping and yahooing over a nearby dune in a flurry of sand like a one-man Charge of the Light Brigade. The bolder members of the group were given the chance to repeat this rowdy performance. Taboo very reluctantly brought up the rear, and at the brink of the dune decided she'd rather amble down, yelping or no yelping. At least I reached the bottom in one piece; Dan slipped off his camel and fell into a bush.

ANCIENT CARVINGS

An overhang provided a cool lunch spot out of the blistering midday heat, and a gallery of 10,000-year-old Aboriginal art. The surface of the rock was covered with faded handprints and stencils. Over the top were the ochre paintings of desert oaks, the crescent-shaped symbols for women, similar figures crossed by a line for men, spirals signifying waterholes, and wavy lines for lightning. More mysterious still were some of the carvings we saw after lunch, when we were led on foot along a creek to a virtually dried-up waterhole, past indelible emu tracks, to see long-limbed warriors, sunbursts, and other unfathomable ancient scratches. A little further along was a shaded hollow where male initiation ceremonies once took place; the dark patches on the walls here are human bloodstains.

CAMPFIRE POETRY

Considering he is a one-man band, Gargan's catering efforts were admirable, but would perhaps be best termed "authentic" rather than "gourmet" Aussie tucker. For example, breakfast included tinned spaghetti on toast, while the second night's dinner was a slap-up barbecue of sangers (that's sausages) and steaks. His most impressive culinary achievement was a perfectly turned-out damper, a dense flour-and-water loaf baked in a ground oven formed from the embers of the campfire. It was ready for us to tuck into, drizzled with syrup, after a torchlit ramble in search of more Aboriginal rock carvings in the gullies around the camp.

If you can't go without your creature comforts, take advantage of the fact that your luggage is transferred out to the base camp. Mark and Cathy learnt this lesson on their first safari, and second time round kindly brought enough wine for us all to enjoy with our meals. Perhaps it was wine—although I prefer to think it was the grandeur of the landscape—that inspired several in the party to poetry. The winning campfire oration went to Mark, whose *Ode to Angela* was highly pertinent: "If you ever ride on a camel, A most peculiar mammal, To take care of your bum, Here's my tip old chum, Have it sprayed with a high-gloss enamel."

THE RIDE HOME

Angela, with her sore behind, opted to ride back by four-wheel drive with the luggage on the last morning, so we waved goodbye to her as our camels plodded out on the final leg of the safari. The 8am start, Gargan told us, indicated to the camels that we were headed back to the farm. To prove his point, Sharka took the correct fork in the route without any steering, following a creek of the Hugh River, part of an old shortcut on the Alice–Adelaide trail. Magnificent ghost gums, their bark a spectral white against the paprika sands, lined the creek. In the branches of one was the nest of a wedge-tailed eagle, perhaps the one that had flown over Rainbow Valley the day before.

The journey back was another hot day's ride, and not for the first time was I glad of the water canisters that hung from my saddle. As we came over a hill I could see the corrugated-iron buildings of the farm once again and hear vehicles speeding along the Stuart Highway. We were back at the brink of the modern world and, symbolically, the big blue sky was filling with clouds. "It'll rain within the next three days," said Gargan. I dropped the reins, took in the scene, and let Taboo find her own way home.

THE LARAPINTA TRAIL

Starting at the Alice Springs Telegraph Station, and ending 220km (137 miles) later at Mount Sonder in the West MacDonnell National Park, is the Larapinta Trail. When completed, the trail will be the longest desert walking track in the world. The beginning and end stages are already open; the 23km (14 miles) from the Telegraph Station to Simpsons Gap, for example, is an overnight trek, and you could continue from here to the dramatic Standley Chasm. Before you start, register your plan with the National Parks and Wildlife Service in Darwin. Take plenty of water: a minimum of 4 litres (7 pints) per day is needed in warm weather. It's also recommended that you hike in a group of at least three people. Return transport from the end of your trek can be arranged in Alice Springs.

GOING IT ALONE

INTERNAL TRAVEL

There are daily flights from Sydney, Melbourne, Perth, Adelaide, and Darwin to Alice Springs, and from Alice Springs, Cairns, Perth, and Sydney to Uluru. The most romantic route to the Red Centre is by the train know as the Ghan. A new 1,555km (966-mile) route was built in 1980. The traditional start of the overnight journey is Adelaide, where the train departs every Monday and Thursday, returning from Alice on Tuesday and Friday. There are three classes on board, first class including comfortable sleeping cabins with their own bathrooms, and gourmet meals in elegantly furnished dining cars. Longer direct Ghan services now also run from Melbourne and Sydney.

If you don't have your own transport, getting around the Red Centre takes some planning. There are a few scheduled bus services linking Alice Springs with Uluru, but if you also want to visit Kings Canyon, your best option is to take an organized tour such as that offered by AAT Kings (see Contacts). Also note that the Ayers Rock Resort is 20km (12 miles) from Uluru and 53km (33 miles) from Kata Tjuta. If you're not taking a tour to visit these places, transport to suit your own schedule can be arranged through Uluru Express, which runs shuttlebuses throughout the day from the resort to the national park.

WHEN TO GO

The Red Centre is prone to extremes of temperature. In July and August, the days can be very pleasant, but the night temperatures plummet dramatically, sometimes to below freezing. In December and January, midday temperatures can exceed 50°C (122°F) in the shade, with night temperatures stuck in the 30s°C (90s°F). The best times to visit are from April to June and from September to early November. When it rains, the downpours tend to be short and very heavy.

PLANNING

Accommodation is usually in high demand during the cooler winter months (June–September), particularly at Uluru, so make sure you have accommodation booked in advance of your trip. Accommodation options are more plentiful, but not unlimited, at Kings Canyon and around Alice Springs. The same advance preparation applies to hiring a car.

Entry to the Uluru-Kata Tjuta National Park costs A$15 (children under 16 are free); the ticket lasts five days and should be carried it at all times during travel in the park.

CAR-HIRE TIPS

❑ When hiring a car in the Red Centre, all deals include no more than 100km (60 miles) of free mileage, which won't get you very far. Before other charges, you'll be looking at least A$50 a day for the cheapest economy sedan and around A$90 for a small four-wheel drive.

❑ You do not need a four-wheel drive on all unsealed roads, but make detailed enquiries about road conditions before you decide on what type of car to hire.

❑ Paying extra for car insurance cover will only lower, not eliminate, the costs if you have an accident.

❑ Because it is common for wild animals to run across the roads suddenly at night, it is not recommended that you drive in the dark.

❑ Be wary of becoming fatigued while driving along the long, straight roads; take frequent stops.

WHAT TO TAKE

❑ Aside from a hat and sunscreen, wear a good pair of sunglasses to protect against eye damage.

❑ Stout walking shoes are essential for tackling the rocky, thorny desert floor.

❑ For extended outback trips, binoculars and a pocket knife are useful, as are a torch and a small mirror—the best way to signal to a passing plane should you need help.

HEALTH

The major health hazard in the outback is overexposure to the sun. Make sure you wear a wide-brimmed hat, apply plenty of sunscreen, and always carry plenty of water. Attacks by snakes, dingoes, or other wildlife are very rare; you are much more likely to be pestered by harmless flies. If you are spiked by any splinters or thorns, make sure they are removed immediately as wounds can quickly go septic.

Left: *Looking along the sheer rock wall of Kings Canyon*
Inset: *Perched on a cannon-like promontory above the magnificent Valley of Eden*

7 Walking in the Flinders Ranges

by Matt Cawood

The Flinders Ranges begin in lush farming country 200km (125 miles) north of Adelaide, and spear 420km (260 miles) into the dry outback. The highest mountains, and some of their most spectacular gorges, are found in the central region; it was through this area that I took a hiking tour over a period of four days.

The Flinders Ranges lie well off the beaten track for most international visitors to Australia, but they offer a diversity of experience that few other regions can rival. The long, broken spine of the mountains, along with the geological detours and asides that put the plural "s" in "Ranges," spans latitudes that extend into lush farming country in the south and arid outback in the north. This, and their rain-attracting height above the fringing plains, has created the wide variations in climate and habitat that enable the hills to support a remarkably rich collection of flora and fauna.

Walking a variety of foot tracks, most well marked and documented—anything from an hour to a day—is the best way to see the Flinders Ranges. Keen backpackers can plan a variety of multi-day walks, particularly along the 320km (200 miles) of the 1,500km (930-mile) Heysen Trail, which winds through the Flinders.

Accommodation in the Flinders is limited only by your wallet. Camping is popular and inexpensive. Many stations rent out converted shearers' quarters, with basic amenities, at budget rates. Some also offer excellent cottage accommodation with every comfort, in secluded locations. Pubs and motels are also located throughout the Flinders, with varying standards of sophistication.

If you are on an extended walk you will also need a compass and relevant 1:50,000 maps. For users of 35mm SLR cameras, a polarizing filter helps tame the outback glare. A soft-drinks cooler can prevent camera film from overheating in hot weather.

Nearly half of South Australia's 3,100 recorded plant species grow in the ranges, providing home and sustenance for 283 species of birds from desert, forest, and sea habitats, and 86 species of rock-loving reptiles. Four species of kangaroo are readily seen here, and the porcupine-like short-beaked echidna, an ancient form of spiny marsupial that lays eggs and suckles its young, is sometimes spotted bumbling along in search of termites. The ranges nourished Aboriginal people for thousands of years, both physically and spiritually, until European colonization in the mid-1800s. The newcomers brought with them domestic stock, feral animals such as the rabbit, and a scant regard for Aboriginal life—a lethal combination for an environment and culture that had been delicately tuned over millennia. As a result, nearly half of the ranges' mammals have since become extinct and traditional Aboriginal culture is receding into history. Meanwhile, the scattered ruins of stone cottages and old graveyards show that the colonizers' ignorance was destructive to themselves as well as to the landscape and its inhabitants.

HITTING THE TRAIL

The most frequently visited features of the ranges are found in the 947sq. km (366 sq. mile) Flinders Ranges National Park (F.R.N.P.), which embraces some of the mountains' best scenery and natural and human history. The park's most

NORTHERN TERRITORY & SOUTH AUSTRALIA

popular attraction is Wilpena Pound, a spectacular ring of ranges offering activities for people of all abilities. I planned to walk to Wilpena from Parachilna Gorge, along a section of the Heysen Trail that traverses some of the most scenic country in the Flinders. Although the distance from Parachilna to Wilpena is about 50km (31 miles) as the crow flies, my route would meander over about 80km (50 miles). I planned on taking four days over my journey, walking at a leisurely pace for six to eight hours a day. It could be done in less, but not if I wanted to take a look around *en route*.

The walkers' book at the Parachilna trailhead has an entry from someone who walked the entire 1,500km (930 miles) of the Heysen Trail, finishing there in the gorge—"Made it!" My four-day excursion seems like a garden stroll in comparison, but nevertheless I feel apprehensive as I step alone over the stile at the

THE HEYSEN AND THE MAWSON TRAILS

One of the world's great walking tracks, the Heysen Trail, meanders about 1,500km (930 miles) from Cape Jervis, 80km (50 miles) south of Adelaide, to Parachilna Gorge in the central Flinders Ranges. The trail crisscrosses the spines of the Mount Lofty and Flinders ranges, passing through national parks and conservation reserves.

The Mawson Trail, a cyclists' companion to the Heysen Trail, follows a network of road reserves and fire tracks over an 800km (497-mile) route between Adelaide and Blinman, 63km (40 miles) north of Wilpena. Like the Heysen Trail, cyclists can get on and off the Mawson at will.

Walkers and cyclists can access both trails at dozens of points along their well-marked length, for one-hour taster trips or full-blown multi-week treks.

northernmost point of the trail. Friends who were to accompany me have dropped out, and along this dry route the cautious approach is to walk in groups of four—hence my worries. The European history of the Flinders is littered with the tales of people who have underestimated how quickly lack of water can kill. Still, I have plenty of walking experience, local knowledge, and 7 litres (15 pints) of water sloshing gently in my pack, which I can refill at Aroona, 20km (12 miles) away. I also have ample food, a tent, the relevant Heysen Trail map, and a desire to see the ranges at walking pace. I lean forward and set off.

PAINTERS AND SERPENTS

From Parachilna Gorge to Aroona, the Heysen Trail wends its way along the narrow valley between the Heysen and ABC ranges, sometimes in a creek bed, sometimes over stony slopes that carry groves of northern cypress pines. The less striking ABC Range is so named because it supposedly has as many peaks as there are letters in the alphabet—a neat if somewhat dubious coincidence. Throughout the trail's considerable length, energetic volunteers have marked its route with steel pegs set at 1km (½-mile) intervals, or within sight of each other over difficult ground.

Aboriginal myth and science offer vastly different explanations about the creation of these two ranges, but each has its own fascination. In Aboriginal legend, the sinuous ridges mark the track of two giant water snakes, or *akurra*, which slithered down from the north to ambush an Aboriginal ceremony being held at Wilpena. Geologists believe that these mountains are formed of compressed and folded sediments forced up out of a deep trough in the Earth's crust about 500 million years ago. It's speculated that, until erosion took its toll, the Flinders may once have been a range of Himalayan proportions. The Heysen and ABC ranges are merely the weathered stubs of that prehistoric range, yet they retain a presence out of all proportion to their relatively modest height.

STEPPING OUT ON THE OCHRE TRAIL

I slog out my first afternoon in the mounting heat that comes before a storm, reviving briefly when I see the iron fan of the Pigeon House Bore windpump turning above the trees. My hopes of a drink of freshly pumped water are dashed, however, when I see that the bore hole, once a watering point for sheep, has long since fallen into disuse. Disappointed, I rest in the shade of the rusting tank and reflect on a far older piece of history adjacent to the bore. There lies Pukardu, an ancient ochre mine guarded by its inaccessibility and

Below: *Creek-side camping at the foot of the Heysen Range in the Flinders Ranges National Park*
Inset: *One of the 86 species of rock-loving reptiles in South Australia*
Right: *Kangaroo-like euros are a familiar sight on the Heysen Trail*

status as a protected site. Ochre, a fine red rock powder, was used throughout Aboriginal Australia to paint ceremonial dancers, rock galleries, and implements. Pukardu ochre contains flecks of mica, which glittered on the dancers as they stamped in the firelight—a quality that gave it widespread fame. Men from distant groups would walk hundreds of miles to mine Pukardu. Even as recently as the the 1860s, ochre from Pukardu was traded by Aboriginal groups as far away as the shores of the Cape York Peninsula, some 2,900km (1,800 miles) distant.

NORTHERN TERRITORY & SOUTH AUSTRALIA

AROONA VALLEY

My arrival at Aroona, my first camp, is signalled by a Flinders Ranges National Park sign. Until this point I have been walking on Alpana Station land, one of the big sheep ranches that often cover hundreds of square kilometres. Visitors can traverse the stations providing commonsense rules are observed: do not interfere with stock, and leave all gates as you find them. I leave Alpana and walk out of the pines and into the head of the Aroona Valley. Light from a stormy dusk picks out the steep walls of the flanking ranges in a magnificent display that makes me appreciate afresh why the Flinders Range National Park is the most popular of the ranges' reserves. At the head of the valley, I drop my rucksack gratefully at a restored pine stockman's hut. I replenish my water containers from the hut's rainwater tank, then walk the hundred metres or so into the popular Aroona campground, where I soon find the merits of its toilets and barbecues outweighed by my desire for solitude. I retreat, and carefully pitch my tent between five dark columns of ants that crisscross bare ground beside a dry creek, above which the Heysen Range rears up 865m (2,837ft). A freeze-dried dinner is soon developing on my spirit stove. No wood can be collected for fires within the national park. As I complete my welcome meal, the surrounding gum trees bend before a suddenly chill wind, and raindrops patter on the fly as I zip up the tent. Whenever I awake that night, it's to the sound of rain drumming a few centimetres above my head.

TRAILSIDE VISIONS

The Aroona Valley looks freshly rinsed when I rise with the first dawn light. Small, fresh clouds drift around the peaks of the Heysen Range. I'm cold beneath my pullover. There's a sense of revival in the air, even if the ant columns have broken ranks and a busy army is foraging over my cooking gear.

The Bulls Gap Track, the beginning of my next leg, follows a climbing, disused vehicle track into pine-covered hills and through creeks dense with gums. Emus, a smaller version of the ostrich, are by far the most common sight on the trail, as are their splattered droppings, although this is too dainty a word for the emu's cowpat-sized productions. Western grey kangaroos and the similar-looking euros appear frequently, while goats, a pest in the park, remain a distant sight, their bleats drifting back on the breeze.

I stop at Red Hill Lookout to brew a mug of tea and admire the view across to my destination, the distant peaks of Wilpena Pound. Today, they are almost obscured in the cool blue haze and are topped with a froth of cumulus cloud. The walk from Red Hill is largely downhill, the vehicle track meandering through bushland that is highlighted by the yellow pompom blooms of wattle, yellow-flowered sennas, and red-flowered hop bushes. I reach the broad, stony bed of Brachina Creek in the early afternoon. Here, instead of following the trail straight on, I deviate right, bound for Brachina Gorge. This is a 5km (3-mile) detour from the trail, but I know I'll find fresh pools of water and a magnificent campsite. My aching feet protest, but my mind successfully argues that it's worth the extra effort.

BRACHINA GORGE

Brachina is one of the most beautiful gorges in the ranges, the long, slanting rock striations of its cliffs set off by gum-fringed, limpid pools. I set my tent away from the tempting water: camping close to pools is discouraged because of the importance of water to wildlife, in particular the yellow-footed rock wallaby, known to Aboriginal people as *andu*. This rare little kangaroo is at home among Brachina's cliffs, and they are often seen around the scree face at a sharp bend midway through the gorge. As I approach the scree, I unseeingly walk so close to an andu that it takes fright and bounds away up the rocks. The wallaby's spectacular

CAMPING TIPS

❑ The sight of flood debris caught 2m (6ft) up trees that are rooted in creek beds is a clear message to those tempted to camp here—don't! A distant storm can unexpectedly send a wall of water that is capable of tumbling a car end on end down these mostly dry creek beds, and yet within hours the creek will have stopped flowing again.

❑ Do not be tempted to camp beneath the inviting spread of a river red gum. Like many Australian trees, these eucalypts regularly shed their massive limbs without warning.

markings, striking when seen in isolation, provide perfect camouflage in its habitat.

My schedule doesn't allow the explorations Brachina Gorge deserves. The gorge is the focus of the 11km (7 mile)-long Brachina Geological Trail, which showcases a great tilted sandwich of rock 9km (5½ miles) thick, its sediments ranging from 640 to 520 million years old. Excellent interpretive signs along the way take you through the development of the Flinders. The most visible fossils are at the Wilkawillina Limestone site, three-quarters of the way through the gorge.

SHEPHERDS AND BEAUTIFUL BUNYEROO

I resume the Heysen Trail with gusto, helped by a lightening pack and acclimatizing legs. I soon pass the disused Elatina stockmen's huts. The men who occupied these shepherds' huts lived lonely lives, watching their flocks and keeping an eye out for any Aborigines who were intent on snaring an easy meal of mutton. Of the 12 Europeans known to have died in Flinders frontier clashes, most were shepherds. Past Old Elatina, the trail follows a disused vehicle track that loops across rolling hills, through low woodlands of yellow-bloomed wattle, towards the ramparts of Wilpena Pound. I take lunch in a creek bed, my back to an

immense red gum with a trunk that is 3m (10ft) thick. As I munch on a health bar, a bird dropping makes an unexpected and unwelcome appearance on my boot. Thankful that emus don't fly, I crane my neck to spy a little corella on a branch high above, and, near by, its nesting mate snapping at flies from within a branch hollow. Only big old gums have had the time necessary to develop the hollow limbs in which these large white cockatoos like to nest.

The descent on sliding shale from a series of rocky little hills into magnificent Bunyeroo Creek is steep and sometimes treacherous. The creek is broad for the Flinders, its dry bed of rocks and sand flanked by cool avenues of mottle-barked red gums. The track sometimes had me rock-hopping, sometimes crunching over sand, and sometimes out of the creek altogether in the flanking woodlands of pine and wattle. I find a camp near the junction of two creeks, within sight of a little spring that comes from nowhere, trickles through a series of clear little pools, then disappears again into the sand. Tent pitched, I explore my surroundings before returning to camp to observe quietly the passing of a perfect evening. I watch the thin crescent moon sink behind the dark outline of the rocks and the stars as they begin to pierce the indigo sky, then gratefully turn in for the night.

THE FINAL LEG

I awake on my last day of pack-toting to the sound of a pair of aptly named clamorous reed warblers duelling in noisy song, their ruckus overpowering the less vigorous contests of other birds high in the trees. The track soon takes me to the top of a 490m (1,607ft) hill, where walls of Wilpena Pound, once impossibly distant, loom directly ahead. Above soars a wedge-tailed eagle, Australia's largest raptor. I descend, and find myself near the base of those walls in no time at all, heading south on my final leg.

St. Mary Peak, the most imposing

Above: *Venerated by Aboriginal people for at least 15,000 years, the vast natural amphitheatre of Wilpena Pound once hosted great ceremonies. Today it's a major attraction for visitors to the Flinders Ranges*
Inset: *A sleepy lizard and purple flowered Salvation Jane*
Left: *One of the many scattered pioneer ruins near Hawker*
Right: *Some of the excellent climbing to be found at Moonarie Gap, Wilpena Pound*

upthrust of the Pound, and at 1,171m (3,510ft) the highest peak in the Flinders, moves past imperceptibly to the crunch of my tread. The track meanders over the gullied ground, through scrubby tracts of pine and gum, until the landscape opens out into a spacious forest of big pines near the outflow of Wilpena Creek. In the shade of these trees, western grey kangaroos scramble up from their nap to observe my passage. Half an hour later, I walk into the vast Wilpena campground, seemingly full of people drinking beer. It seems a good idea: I keep on through the site towards an appointment with a shower, a razor, and a cold ale.

ABORIGINAL WILPENA

Before the invasive onslaught of European colonization, groups of Aboriginal people from the length of the ranges and the surrounding plains met at this immense natural amphitheatre of Wilpena Pound, 35km (22 miles) in circumference, to perform religious ceremonies. They left the symbols of their beliefs in ochre and charcoal paintings at Arkaroo Rock, a natural gallery at the foot of the Pound's southeast wall, and in petroglyphs at Sacred Canyon, a few kilometres from Arkaroo Rock. The pamphlet *Interpreting Rock Art of the Flinders Ranges*, available at Wilpena Information Centre makes sense of the galleries' cryptic circles and lines, the vestiges of an all-but-vanished religion. Dating of cooking-fire ashes near Arkaroo Rock suggests that Aboriginal people may have been painting in the gallery 15,000 years ago, long before the world's great civilizations were born. Unfortunately, there are no walking trails direct from Wilpena to the sites. If you're without a vehicle, make arrangements through the Wilpena Pound Resort reception desk for a special trip. For other insights into traditional life, an Aboriginal guide leads walking tours inside the Pound that look at plant foods and parts of the landscape that are incorporated into Aboriginal mythology.

INTO THE POUND

There are just two ways to see the Pound. You can slog it out on foot (though admittedly some of the trails are very short and relatively easy). Or you can fly over it and see it laid out from the air. A network of well-marked walk trails offers walks ranging from 800m (880yd) to 16km (10 miles). A leisurely half-hour amble from the resort gets you to a pioneer homestead inside the Pound, but you need greater commitment to reach the heights of St. Mary Peak or Mount Ohlssen Bagge, or the lip of the 18m (60ft)-drop over Malloga Falls in Edeowie Gorge. Inside the Pound, the going is level and easy through woodlands of red gum and wattle, or, higher up, heath that in spring is rich with subtle blooms.

The clamber up the outside of the Pound to St. Mary Peak is strenuous, but having made it, the views are stupendous. I trace the sinuous path of the mythological *akurra* down the Heysen and ABC ranges to the Pound, where the story relates how they encircled an Aboriginal initiation ceremony and became the walls of the Pound. The female's raised head is symbolized by Beatrice Hill, on the western wall, while the male's head became St. Mary Peak. The features of this story, and of the whole Dreaming landscape hereabouts, are even more evident from the air. Scenic flights can be booked at the resort. Flying within a few hours after dawn or before sunset is preferable, because the low-light shadows lend a scale to the ranges that disappears in the flat light of midday.

AND BEYOND...

I do some dreaming of my own on the bus back to Adelaide, and find I'm already plotting further walks in the Flinders Ranges. My walk had covered a fraction of the ranges' 420km (260-mile) length. There are a lot more trails to explore, and hundreds of square kilometres of trackless and little-known country. And all of it is within a day's drive of a cappuccino in Adelaide.

GOING IT ALONE

INTERNAL TRAVEL

Premier Stateliner runs a seven hour bus service between central Adelaide and Wilpena, via Port Pirie and Port Augusta, available in both directions on Wednesdays, Fridays, and Sundays. Airlines of South Australia visit Hawker *en route* between Adelaide and Leigh Creek on Tuesdays and Thursdays. Bookings can be made through any travel agent. Hire cars are available out of Adelaide and Port Augusta and, soon, out of Hawker; check when you make your arrangements. Most of the ranges' roads and tracks can be accessed in a conventional vehicle, although some unsealed routes north of Wilpena soon become inaccessible in wet weather. A sturdy four-wheel drive is necessary for those who want to penetrate the wilder reaches of the northern Flinders Ranges.

WHEN TO GO

You can visit the Flinders at any time. Between November and March, day-time heat, which often rises above 40°C (104°F) in the northern regions, seems to add depth to the warm hues of the rocks. However sections of the Heysen Trail outside the national parks are closed from December 1 to April 30 due to fire bans. In autumn (March–May) the mountains can be explored in near-perfect weather. During the cool, occasionally wet winter (May–August), when average temperatures range from 20°C (68°F) down to around 3–4°C (37–39°F), the Flinders are often clad in green, unlike their summer austerity. And in spring (August–November), when most people visit the ranges, waterholes are usually full and the subtle displays of wildflowers are at their peak.

PLANNING

Getting to and from Parachilna Gorge, the northern trailhead for the Heysen Trail, needs planning. There are no facilities in the gorge; the nearest accommodation is at Angorichina, or "Ango," several kilometres' walk away. This is basic but comfortable, and food must be supplied and cooked by residents—it is easier to start walking at Parachilna and to end at Wilpena. John Henery of Alpana Station provides transport from Wilpena to Angorichina and Parachilna Gorge. Alpana, about 20 minutes' drive from the trailhead, also offers its own accommodation and tours into remoter areas. The Prairie Hotel at Parachilna railway siding, about 20km (12 miles) west of the gorge trailhead, will pick up walkers at Hawker and drop them off at Parachilna Gorge, providing they spend a night in the hotel or in its backpacker accommodation. Pricing for the Prairie's drop-off service depends on the size of the party and the options chosen.

TRAVELLERS' TIPS

❏ Purchase good maps. A wide range of material is available from Flinders Ranges and Outback SA Tourism (see Contacts).
❏ Mobile-phone coverage in the region is limited.
❏ If you are venturing off well-used routes, let people know where you are going. If you become stranded while driving, stay close to your vehicle under all circumstances.
❏ Avoid camping near, or swimming in, waterholes. These are a vital source of water for many animals, particularly in times of drought. Swimming in the pools stirs up brackish water in their lower levels, which may cause animals some distress.
❏ Open fires are not permitted from November 1 to April 15 in the southern and central Flinders, and to March 31 in the northern areas. Collecting of wood for fires in national parks is not permitted.

WHAT TO TAKE

❏ Sun hat and strong sunscreen.
❏ Durable footwear.
❏ Water (minimum 1 litre, or 2 pints, per person per hour when walking in hot weather).
❏ Warm clothes for the cool evenings.
❏ Maps and compass.

HEALTH

Take insect repellent and a basic first-aid kit. Always carry ample water, whether driving or walking. In cool weather, 3 litres (6 pints) will be enough to sustain a day's hike. In heat, walkers may need 1 litre (2 pints) during each hour of walking. It's best to set off with too much—you can always pour some away. Don't drink from waterholes frequented by campers; you expose yourself to the risk of an illness. Never go to the toilet in or near a waterhole. In areas without toilet facilities, bury faeces and paper at least 15cm (6 in) deep and 100m (330ft) or more from waterways and campsites.

Map labels:

Torres Strait
Cape York
Weipa
Cape York Peninsula
Great Barrier Reef
Cooktown
Gulf of Carpentaria
Mitchell
Cairns **8** **10**
Normanton
Townsville
Charters Towers **9**
Mount Isa
Cloncurry
Hughenden
Mackay
Winton
Georgina
Diamantina
Great Dividing Range
Barcaldine
Rockhampton
Emerald
Gladstone
Yaraka
Windorah
Maryborough
Charleville
Miles
Brisbane
Ipswich
Cunnamulla
Toowoomba
Gold Coast

0   200   400   600   800   1000 km
0   200   400   600 miles

QUEENSLAND

Queensland, Australia's second-largest state, sits in the northeastern corner of the continent, its sandy coastline lapped by the waters of the Coral Sea and the South Pacific Ocean. Running virtually parallel with the mainland is the world's largest living organism, the Great Barrier Reef, a World Heritage Site and a scuba diver's paradise. Fun-in-the-sun resorts slither up this coastline as far as a dense band of protected tropical rain forest that continues towards the vast wilderness of Cape York Peninsula, Australia's northernmost tip. Inland, the forests make way for an arid outback of cattle stations and old gold-mining towns; this is crocodile country. The "sunshine state" presents a microcosm of the continent, and is totally geared to tourism. It has off-the-beaten track adventure, and culture to rival any destination, including Aboriginal sites and expeditions in the footsteps of great explorers, as well as a unique diversity of wildlife. In fact, everything you ever wanted from Australia.

Sea coral on the Great Barrier Reef—a colour-rich fantasia

QUEENSLAND

8 Exploring Queensland's Outback

by Lee Karen Stow

*West of the Great Dividing Range in northern Queensland, under a burning sun, I
explored the solidified aftermath of volcanic eruptions, walked the property of
Aborigines, and then slept beneath the stars in Australia's endless interior.*

Two to three hours' driving time
from Cairns places you in the hot,
dusty grip of the outback to the
west of Queensland's Sunshine Coast.
Here, where rain forest thins into sclero-
phyll woodlands of gum trees and
paperbarks, is a sparsely settled land of
saltpans, cattle stations, and pockets of
wilderness. Aborigines are trying to preserve whatever is left of their culture, in a
world that is far removed from the cheap
backpackers' breakfasts and scuba divers
of the coast.

The Gulf Savannah is a fairly flat mon-
soonal region, roughly crescent shaped,
covering some 186,000sq. km (71,800 sq.
miles) and slotting into the top left-hand
corner of Queensland. It brushes the
southern coastline of the Gulf of
Carpentaria and stretches from the Great
Dividing Range in the east to the
Northern Territory to the west. In the dry
season this is a parched land, with empty
creeks and riverbeds, while in the wet it is
grassy green, replenished, and sometimes
flooded. Our quest—mine and Danny
McMahon's—was to drive through the
fertile Atherton Tablelands and colourful
landscapes of the north Queensland
outback to the Gulf Savannah, in a
four-wheel drive loaded with swags, a
kettle, and enough drinking water to fill
Sydney Harbour.

OUT TO THE OUTBACK

I discovered Danny, my guide, after touring Queensland's rain forest with a few
others, and persuaded him to accompany
me further into the outback. Before arriving in Queensland, Danny had lived on an
island teaching Aboriginal children, and
had been adopted into an Aboriginal family there. This Sydneysider of Irish
descent had a passion for the outdoors
and the knack of navigating by the stars,
and didn't need reminding that the way to
entice Australia under your skin is to
stray off the beaten track to the bush. It
was early December, not the best time to
visit the Gulf as this is the wet season,
with stifling temperatures, intense
humidity, and the threat of flash floods.
But my time in Australia was running out,
and I had more wildlife to unearth and
silence to appreciate. So onwards we
went, with a few stops along the way.

Heading southwest from Cairns, we
crossed the Atherton Tablelands to the
foot of the Great Dividing Range, where

 Provided you and your vehicle are equipped
for the outback with enough supplies should
problems occur (including breakdowns and
dehydration), driving in the region is not difficult. For bushwalking, you need a good
level of fitness, although there are no high
peaks to scale and the boulder-hopping is
optional.

 Temperatures can rise to 35°C (95°F) in the
outback, so an air-conditioned vehicle is a
must for maximum comfort. Accommodation
mostly involves camping out at designated
camping facilities that have clean toilets,
shower blocks, and other amenities.
Otherwise, there are charming hostels and
hotels at the old mining towns.

 A swag with a zip-up insect net is essential
for real outback camping, along with a few
pans for cooking. If you book an organized
tour, everything is provided, even the food.

thick rain forest recedes into a sparsely wooded land littered with conical termite mounds and piles of red boulders shaped like giant toasted bread-crumbs. By high noon, the bitumen had taken on a watery shimmer in the heat, and pausing to take pho-tographs was like stepping into a blast furnace.

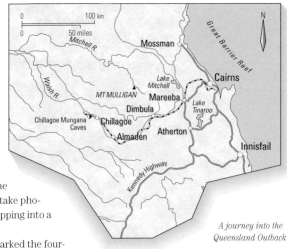

A journey into the Queensland Outback

Undeterred, we parked the four-wheel drive in a clearing of gums in what little shade we could find, layered on the sunscreen, and filled our water bottles to begin a two-hour bushwalk to a viewpoint on a granite ridge, where the wattle tree flowers blaze the same yellow as that in the Australian national flag. Somewhere up a cliff, we found a ledge decorated with Aboriginal art, a long baton striped with ochre that I later learned was a form of calendar. Our first swimming hole, slot-ted into more slate-grey granite, was a pool of milky jade water whose surface was skimmed by dragonflies. We plunged in to cool off, but by the time we had climbed out our hair was being frazzled by the sun again. The way back wound down a dry riverbed and along a solidified lava flow stacked with boulders.

UPSIDE-DOWN STARRY NIGHT

Back on the road, the bitumen gave way to rusty tracks that raged fire-red like hot coals on a barbecue. The panorama was breathtaking, the red road backed by green-topped white ghost gums that punched upwards into an incredibly blue sky. As the sun lowered, this richness intensified, and I sat back in the passen-ger seat, Australian rock music on the stereo, absorbing it all. An eastern grey kangaroo powered by its mighty thigh muscles, raced us until a herd of wild horses emerged from the eucalypts.

There's a billabong where the horses go to drink and swim. As it happens, there's a camping spot on its shore where we spent the night, the sand engraved by arches of hoofprints. Bleached trees forked out of the water, darkening to eerie silhouettes as the sun fell behind them. In Queensland, the sunset is rapid; spend too long filling the can for your billy tea and you will miss it. We rolled out our swags, and put the damper on the fire to cook, shovelling hot coals on top of the iron pot and underneath it. But the heat from the coals escaped into the sand below and dinner was ready too late to savour. Instead, I lay on my back, folded in the canvas of the swag, and traced the Southern Cross in the night sky. As I lay there waiting for a satellite to pass, I sank into a bush sleep from which I failed to wake even when the horses came to the billabong.

PLAYING THE DIDGE WITH TOM

The next day, we crossed near the Great Dividing Range, driving on dirt roads until we reached sleepy Irvinebank, site of the deepest and richest tin mine in the coun-try. The town, where we stopped for a cold beer, is a living museum, but not as

enthralling as having tea with Danny's friend Tom Congoo. We found Tom's place, 43km (28 miles) from the town of Dimbulah, by following an etched plaque on a gum tree that advertised "Didgeridoos for sale." Tom is an Aboriginal elder of the Barbarrum people, and lives with his family in several corrugated-tin shacks in the dry bush. He was born in 1928, and his eyes were as clear as the sky on the day we visited. He has lived here for 20 years, not far from an Aboriginal burial site. He likes the bush because, "If there's no other noise, you can hear yourself think."

The day had crept to a blazing noon. Tom sat in the shadow of a corrugated-tin awning, the back wall painted with a rainbow snake and an iguana. A row of didgeridoos, ranging from thin to fat and crafted from brown gum wood,

Above: Tom's place
Right: Danny gives us a tune on a beautifully polished and painted didgeridoo
Below: Aborigines are trying to preserve what is left of their culture, and ask the tourists who visit these areas to respect this

yellowjack, and polished blood wood, displayed the proud paintings of animals of the land—other people's totems. Tom's grandson, Juan, explained how a dead branch on a tree, its innards eaten away by termites, is first chopped down and stripped of its bark using a flint, before being polished and painted to make a didgeridoo. He said that the early white settlers named the instrument the didge because when they heard it being played they thought the sound called out "didge, didge."

The Aborigines call their instrument a *yikki*, and say it imitates the sound of animals in the bush. Putting the hollow end to his mouth, Tom moulded the wax rim with his thumb to fit his lips, and began to blow, controlling the sounds with his tongue and throat. He played the "doing, doing, doing" sound of a kangaroo springing through the grass, while Juan hoisted a brown gum didge, its bottom blown out like a bell, to imitate the amusing sound of road trains passing a

OUTBACK DRIVING TIPS

- ❑ Don't park your vehicle in a dry riverbed or creek and never camp in one. A flash flood could rush down it, growing to 3m (10ft) in minutes.
- ❑ Unsealed roads can change quickly when wet, becoming slippery and boggy.
- ❑ Carry a few days' supply of food and more than enough drinking water.
- ❑ Many outback roads are unfenced, so wild animals stray on to the road.
- ❑ Check weather and road conditions before you set off.
- ❑ If exploring more isolated areas, notify the authorities of your destination and expected time of arrival.
- ❑ Rest often—the heat and monotony of the landscape can cause fatigue.
- ❑ Carry basic spare parts for your vehicle, including an extra spare tyre.
- ❑ In case of breakdown, stay with your vehicle. You can die of dehydration if you wander off in search of help. Make a shade with blankets, or lie under the vehicle.

hitchhiker on the road. I hoisted a didge etched with a red-back spider, painted by Tom's nephew Harold Go-Sam, and spluttered the gargling call of a strangled crocodile.

ON SACRED LAND

Tom made us tea, and although shy at first, he rambled on with stories until late afternoon. When he was sixteen, he told us, an Aboriginal man appeared from the bush and said: "One day you will be a leader. You must be obedient, because obedience is better than sacrifice." Tom remembered: "He went away as quietly as he came. Then, one day, some government people visited me to talk about land. I had no education, and I had to talk to these people."

The meeting resulted in Tom putting in a land claim for 1.5 million ha (3.7 million acres) for his people, the latest of many such claims that has seen Aborigines win back land that was taken from them by European settlers. Tom looks after more than 612 people in the Barbarrum community, some of them scattered around Australia, including the cities of Melbourne and Sydney. Some are too old to come back. "It's not a job, it's a responsibility," Tom acknowledges. "If you go into some other tribal traditional lands, they do not want you there, because what's happened to them is like a bitter taste in their mouth that's been handed down. But we all got to start anew." As a parting gift, he placed in my palm a sprinkling of dry spiral leaves gathered from the bush. "Shampoo," he insisted. That afternoon, to cool down, we stopped at a creek with a rope hanging from a branch, where I washed my hair.

OUTBACK ON HORSEBACK

It's not all four-wheel driving in the outback. There are times when you can saddle up and ride horseback through creeks and along meadows. This type of trail riding is available at Springmount Station, a 24,300ha (60,000-acre) cattle ranch. Here, you camp out, learn to throw a boomerang, and join in the cattle muster to round up the livestock, before dozing in the shade of the ranch veranda.

We rode for an hour, which was enough for me as I wore the wrong shoes. My arms roasted in the afternoon sun, and try as I might I couldn't budge my horse into a pace faster than a gay trot. It was just one of those days. Perhaps I'd become too accustomed to the four-wheel drive, I thought, as we later bumped along off road. Our aim that evening was to slap down our swags opposite the sheer cliffs of Mount Mulligan, once devastated by a huge coalmining explosion, so that the next morning we could photograph the glow cast on the rock by the rising orange sun. To those with an overactive imagination,

Mount Mulligan presents itself as a haunting place, with the kind of twilight remoteness captured by film-makers of gory horror movies. As if I wasn't scared enough, once the sun had disappeared we took a nightwalk around the Mount Mulligan graveyard. All that's left by the mountain is the former hospital, now a homestead where you can stay overnight and take bushwalks. Piles of rusted baked-bean cans, and fragments of tea cups are evidence of men once busy at work. At the Richard's Creek swimming hole, the miners would emerge from the pits filthy and sweaty to swim, carving their names and the dates (we saw a 1922 and 1930) into the granite boulders.

INTO THE VOLCANOES

We entered the deep, red-brick soils of the Forty Mile Scrub National Park, and saw evidence of its tumultuous volcanic past. This is the lip of the McBride Volcanic Province, a mantle of basalt laid down by 164 volcanoes in a series of eruptions that raged for more than 2.5 million years. When the Undara Crater erupted, boiling lava smothered the land, blackening and twisting the once green forest. As the lava streamed down riverbeds, its surface cooled rapidly. Below, it drained to form the hollow tunnels of what is considered to be the longest lava-tube system from a single volcano, stretching more than 160km (100 miles). It is understandable then why it is called Undara, the Aboriginal meaning for a long way.

You can visit Undara for the day, taking a guided torchlit tour of the tubes, or you can stay overnight in restored 19th-century Queensland Rail carriages. Lined up along an old cart track, these burgundy carriages—the oldest dating back to 1888—were mainly used on the Brisbane–Cairns run, and together with platform signals form an unexpected sight out here in the bush. There's even a plush dining car with napkins on the tables, where grilled kangaroo steaks are washed down with chilled wine.

Before dinner we took a Sunset Tour, a safari interrupted by a summit walk up Bluff Hill to see the sun fade as a purple globe behind the volcanic peaks and to hear the buzz of the cicadas. As we sat with a glass of champagne in hand and a platter of pineapple and cheese, we didn't feel the least bit guilty about not roughing it for a while.

The beauty of the Gulf Savannah plains is reminiscent of that of the wide grasslands of East Africa, yet this is a dry bush that doesn't have to be observed from a distance for fear of lions and tigers. Here, I could touch it and sleep in it. Wildlife is, in fact, prolific. On the safari drive around the park, we sighted the rounded ears of wallaroos and the pointed ears of some nine species of kangaroo. They played in the pink glow of red nuttal grass scattered with daisies and lilies, and under the brown pod fruit of the native kapok tree rosella birds flitted from branch to branch, as did ravens, laughing kookaburras, parrots, and lorikeets. Thomas, our guide, stopped to pluck a frilled lizard from its hold on some bark and spread its membraneous ruff to convince us that it should play a starring role in the dinosaur movie *Jurassic Park*. It made Danny's day.

As dusk fell, we perched at the entrance to one of the lava tubes to see, sense, and feel the flutter of 100,000 eastern horseshoe bats using sonar navigation to fly off for their nightly feed. Apparently, sometimes as many as seven snakes dangle from nearby tree branches to snatch at the passing bats. The best was to come: the sighting of a black-headed python curling out of a hole in a tree branch above our heads, its shiny body wrapped around the waist of a kookaburra, which it was squeezing to death.

But the python had trouble deciding whether to consume the kookaburra body or beak first. Then, without warning, it let go. The bird fell from the sky and landed on the grass, where it twitched spasmodically, still alive. Thomas put it out of its misery, admitting that even he had never witnessed such a sight.

Danny and I decided to ignore the comforts of the rail carriages, and instead rolled out our swags amidst the eucalypts. The next morning I awoke to the cawing of ravens and a party of kangaroos grazing mere strides from my head.

Back on the track, trundling along in the rosy dirt, I wondered aloud how we could better what we had just experienced. To prevent tiredness, we stopped regularly, sometimes putting the kettle on the stove or wandering into the bush. Controlled burning had scorched one patch of land charcoal-black, where stubs of brittle grass were still smouldering, ready to start sprouting anew. Low flames

crept like an orange wave across the ground, sending quivering heat lines that drunkenly blurred the horizon.

CORALS IN THE CAVES

The former cattle station of Chillagoe remembers its days as a copper-, gold-, and lead-mining town in its stiflingly hot museum through displays of black and white photographs. Smelters in Chillagoe formed one of the largest metallurgical developments in Queensland prior to World War I, the town boomed to a peak population of 10,000, and supported ten hotels, a far cry from its ghostly mood today. Once we had looked at the rusting

Left: Chillagoe-Mungana Caves—caverns of ancient coral that 400 million years ago were coral reefs, deep below the ocean
Above: The colours of the outback are a striking melange of parched red earth, dark green vegetation and brooding blue-grey skies
Inset top: Crimson rosellas flit from branch to branch
Inset bottom: Wild horses grazing in a leafy glade
Right: Weather Rock, Chillagoe—outback humour from the town's mining heyday

QUEENSLAND

smelting works and quiet chimneys, crumbled brick buildings and a spoil heap as wide as a hill plateau, we went to play down at the Chillagoe-Mungana Caves.

These limestone formations were discovered as early as 1883 by prospectors exploring the Walsh River, and boast crystal stalagmites and stalactites sparkling in the shafts of light. Spiders had spun their gossamer webs across gaps, the intricate lacework emphasizing the centre, behind which the spider awaits its prey. It's a photographer's dream. I rubbed my eyes in disbelief at the caverns of ancient coral that 400 million years ago lay hidden below the ocean. Only weeks before I had been diving above the vibrant colours of the Great Barrier Reef, and here I stood under a similar, fossilized formation the colour of campfire ash.

We drove to a camp near Dimbulah, by a river where owls hooted. Too tired and sunburnt to cook supper, we crept into our swags for some welcome sleep. In the early hours I was spooked by the sound of grunting and of horses whinnying frightfully. "Pig bush, I mean bush pig!" I screamed, walloping Danny with the torch. It couldn't have been anything worth moving camp for, however, because the next thing I recall was the dawn sun stirring my slumber and the smell of fish frying gently in butter. Danny

had also put the kettle on. You know that feeling, when you never want to leave?

THE TIN TWINS

The prospect of returning to the artificial lights of Cairns loomed, so to delay the inevitable we called in on two exceptional bush characters, Bill and George Fewtrell, otherwise known as the Tin Twins. The brothers are in their mid-seventies and live in the middle of nowhere at an abandoned tin mine, their home a jumble of a corrugated-tin shack secured by low walls that are strengthened with hundreds of empty brown beer bottles, or stubbies. Originally from Birmingham, England, they arrived in Australia in 1948, filtering up to the Queensland outback to prospect for tin and gems, and so find their fortune. To date, they've clocked up 30 years of living in the bush.

Bill poured us weak tea and cut wedges of fruitcake, pointing out a snoozing bat in a crack in the roof above me. The twins sat on separate spring beds under fastened mosquito nets, behaving like a long-married couple as they reminisced over the days of tin mining. The brothers spend their days swatting flies and cutting bottle glass, topaz, and aquamarine found around their home into copycat jewels. They read library books or tune in to the BBC World Service on a short-wave radio. "We're waiting for the price of tin to rise, so we can get digging again," they told us.

Dusty, scorched, parched, and agog with star-gazing, python-watching, and wallowing in billabongs, we headed back to Cairns. The day was clear, and Mount Bartle Frere had lost its eyebrows of cloud and stood bare. Behind it lay the Coral Sea, and beyond that the Great Barrier Reef. After stopping at Peet's Falls, a cascade of white water dropping into a black pool, to wash away the dust of the outback, we were ready again for backpacker meals, boat trips, and an electric kettle. But it was with a sinking feeling in my stomach that I remembered I would be sleeping under a ceiling again.

OTHER ACTIVITIES

There are a number of other options for those wishing to explore north Queensland's outback: four-wheel-drive safaris to Cape York Peninsula, one of Australia's last frontiers, through endless eucalyptus woodlands and some rain forest; fishing for the highly prized barramundi on the rivers and creeks that flow south from the Gulf of Carpentaria; fossicking for agates, topaz, garnets, and aquamarines; panning for gold; stays on working cattle stations; horse riding; and crocodile spotting. (See Contacts for details of operators.)

GOING IT ALONE

INTERNAL TRAVEL

You can reach the Gulf Savannah from Cairns in the east, by following the pioneer trail through central Queensland along the Matilda Highway, or by heading across the Great Top Road from Darwin in the Northern Territory. Roads are both sealed and unsealed. A four-wheel drive is the best choice for those not experienced in outback driving. Unsealed roads are generally fine for conventional cars, a four-wheel drive, on the other hand, can access off-road routes and, more often than not, can also overcome the difficulties of driving on unsealed roads in wet weather.

Alternatively ride on the Savannahlander Outback Train along the original 90-year-old railway line that serviced the pioneer mining towns of Forsayth, Einasleigh, and Mount Surprise. The train runs twice weekly and slows and halts regularly so you can admire geological features, wildlife, and flora, and take photographs. Likewise, the Gulflander train runs from the station at Normanton weekly through to Croydon. You can also fly to Undara, site of the volcanic lava tubes.

WHEN TO GO

December to March is the monsoon season, when heavy rainfall causes the landscape to change dramatically. The roads may be closed due to flooding, and there are high temperatures and high humidity. April to October is the dry season, the best time to travel through the Gulf Savannah, especially as the warm days are combined with cooler nights. November to early December, just before the arrival of the monsoon, is the time to see the landscape turn green and the numbers of birds increase. Throughout the year, average daily temperatures stand at 30–35°C (86–95°F). Remember that Australia's summer is the Northern Hemisphere's winter.

PLANNING

You can easily spend a week, a fortnight, or longer exploring the outback, even venturing right out to the west. A good base to start from is Cairns, because here you can decide whether to hire your own four-wheel drive from one of the many operators in town or book an organized tour instead. You can combine a trip to the outback with the Wet Tropics rain forest area or with an exploration of the Great Barrier Reef; this way you will be assured a complete change of scenery.

TRAVELLERS' TIP

❑ It is worth getting up early to drive through the outback at sunrise: the heat is less intense at this time and the colours of the landscape are incredible.

WHAT TO TAKE

❑ More drinking water than you think you might need (allow at least 4 litres, or 8½ pints, per person per day).
❑ Maps.
❑ Telephone numbers of places to stay and of local authorities.
❑ Sunscreen and sunhat.
❑ Insect repellent.
❑ Swags or sleeping bags and a tent.
❑ A simple lightweight cooking stove.
❑ A few days' supply of food should you become stranded, particularly in the wet season.
❑ A camera with UV and polarizing filters.

HEALTH

The main hazard of outback travel is dehydration, so drink plenty of water. Sunstroke is also a danger, so wear a hat, stick to the shade whenever possible, and apply sunscreen liberally and at regular intervals. Although the outback is inhabited by venomous snakes, it is rare for them to attack unless you stand on one unintentionally. To lessen your chances of being bitten, wear walking boots and long trousers or socks when walking through the bush. Some species of spider can also cause a nasty bite, so the advice is not to touch. Estuarine crocodiles inhabit some rivers and waterholes. Be choosy about where you swim, wash, and gather water for boiling. Unless you know otherwise from a reliable, local source, always assume there are crocodiles present.

FURTHER READING

❑ *Australia's Wet Tropics and North-eastern Outback—the Driving Guide* (Little Hill Press Explorer Guides, 1997) by Ian Read. It details routes right across the outback and advises on what equipment and supplies you should carry.

QUEENSLAND

9 Diving the Great Barrier Reef

by Lee Karen Stow

Said to be the largest structure on Earth built by living creatures, the Great Barrier Reef is a busy, breathing, natural phenomenon. Like the legendary explorer, Captain James Cook, I was struck by this colour-rich fantasia, where I sailed, snorkelled and dived.

Seen from space as a quivering white ribbon in the green-blue South Pacific Ocean, the Great Barrier Reef is not, as I initially imagined, one long, continuous fence. Instead, it's a chain of 2,900 reefs and sand cays that stretch 2,300km (1,429 miles) from the Gulf of Papua in New Guinea at the northern end to Australia's Lady Elliot Island in the south. And, as English explorer Matthew Flinders, who surveyed these waters in the *Investigator* in the early 1800s, also wrongly believed, it is not impenetrable.

 Snorkelling is suitable for all abilities—you don't even need to be a good swimmer. But before you begin a diving course, you may need to undertake a medical and you must prove that you can swim and tread water for ten minutes.

 The ocean is warm all year round. Facilities and accommodation on cruising and sailing boats are good.

 Tour companies provide all equipment and instruction, as well collecting you from your accommodation, feeding you, and at the end of the activity, returning you to your base.

JETLAG IN THE CAPITAL

Rather than flying directly to Cairns, the tourist trap for trips out to the Great Barrier Reef, I preferred to be fed Queensland in bite-sized chunks. So after a spending a night in Sydney, I caught the Greyhound Pioneer coach for a 3,049km (1,895-mile) run up the Sunseeker Route that edges the coastline. With an Aussie Pass in my pocket (it promises flexible travel on a budget), air-conditioning blowing, a video rolling on the screen, and chilled water on tap, I sank back in an effort to shake off the jet lag. A sore throat, aches and glaring eyeballs convinced me never again to attempt a straight 26-hour flight from London.

The first leg of my journey was a daze: coffee and toilet stops at service stations, where women fried chips and called me "darl," and black roads illuminated by steel road trains. By the time I reached my 11th-floor hotel room in Brisbane, I was sneezing wildly and convinced I'd left half my brain back in England. I looked out through the window to see Christmas fairylights draped around a town that

signed up for a three-day, two-night safari to Fraser Island, with eight others, driving our own four-wheel drive. We stocked up with food for the trip, packed the lot into Eskies (iceboxes), and then piled in the tents, sleeping bags, and a cooking stove supplied by the travel company. After a military-style briefing on how not to overturn the four-wheel drive in the sand and how to treat a bite from a black funnel-web spider, we set off to catch the ferry to the island.

We had a map and a list of places to see, beginning with a vine-wrapped rain forest of brush box, satinay, strangler figs, and creepers, all alive with the flapping of king parrots. We swam backwards down a flowing creek, made footprints on the miles of flat beach, and plunged into Champagne Pools, natural rock pools washed by the surf. We didn't swim in the actual ocean for fear of tiger sharks, but climbed the rocky outcrop known as Indian Heads to watch them and the turtles show their fins and heads in the blue bay below. While the kettle hissed on the campfire I took a sunset dip in the orange-stained waters of Lake Boomanjin, where the tea-tree grows. Toasted marshmallows brought out members of the 160-odd dingo population to sniff and try to steal, their alert ears just visible above thin, wolfish faces.

Our trip was going too well, so it was no surprise when we became bogged in an uphill sand road on our way back to the ferry. There was only one alternative: reverse back down the hill, head for the beach, and speed along it before the tide rolled in. It worked, and we arrived back in Hervey Bay just before my next leg on the Greyhound. Hoisting my backpack onto its usual snug position, I screamed in agony at the raw sunburn on my shoulders. Great, first jet lag and now lobster looks. And Cairns would be even hotter.

Away from the roadside are fields of fawn-skinned beef cattle, which seems normal enough until a kangaroo bounds in between them as though on an obstacle course. We drove through Proserpine,

with its sugar industry and guided tours of the mills during crushing periods, and rested for pies, nicotine, and caffeine. I noticed that the uniforms of the drivers shrank the further north we travelled: shirt sleeves became cropped, navy shorts replaced trousers.

SIDETRACKED BY THE WHITSUNDAYS

As the resort town of Airlie Beach approached, I hankered after another stopover. By the time the Greyhound pulled in, however, the promised sun-drenched paradise disappeared under seamless clouds and I scuttled for cover from the downpour. "The rainy season is early this year," remarked the rep from the backpackers' hostel. "Could be set in until March."

I was faced with the choice of sitting out the rain along Airlie's main street of Internet cafés, with their jumbo prawn and avocado salads, overdosing on blueberry muffins, or of doing something nautical. I chose the latter and turned up at the marina the next morning to board *Anaconda II* for a sail around the Whitsunday Islands. Not for the faint-hearted, this 25m (82ft) fibreglass maxi-yacht, said to be the largest in the world, has won some major sailing races and has circumnavigated the globe twice. But it wasn't the boat that amazed me, rather the 30-odd revellers who were boarding her. There were girls with hand-kerchief-sized bikinis (one even wore stilettos) and gap-year kids with animal teeth around their necks and big watches strapped to their wrists, all carrying bags of bronzing sun lotion, endless changes of sarongs, cigarettes, lighters, and raunchy paperback novels. Standing on the gangplank, clutching my bottles of mineral water and cola while everyone balanced beer and boxes of South Australian Chardonnay, I had an inkling that somewhere along the line I'd gone off course.

Later, when we were offshore and heading for the islands, I stood on deck in a yellow sou'wester with needles of rain

QUEENSLAND

stabbing my bare legs, and wondered whether someone would notice if a box of their wine went missing. But when in Queensland, the Whitsundays are a must, whatever the weather and company. So I zipped up my hood, faced the spray, and enjoyed it.

The Whitsundays are actually the summits of volcanoes that were ferociously active over millions of years. Evidence suggests that Aborigines fished and hunted around the Whitsundays for at least 8,500 years. Now, most of the islands are national parks; tourist resorts have sprung up on several (including exclusive Hayman Island, with US$1,200-a-night rooms that attract film stars and politicians), while the rest are left alone. We made an impromptu stop out of the rain at South Molle Island. Holidaymakers on the island ignored the weather and canoed, jet-skied, or sprawled on sands fronting rows of screw pines, a tree resembling a palm but with a spiral trunk.

By the time we anchored in a fjord off Hook Island, which rises to a jade summit of 451m (1,479ft)—the highest point in the Whitsundays—and is pocketed with caves decorated with Aboriginal rock paintings, the sun showed its face dazzlingly. As I toyed with the idea of swimming, my decision was made for me in a dramatic way. A crew member, ignoring the fact that I was fully clothed, picked me up and hurled me over the side. The party was just beginning.

BEER, BULLETS, AND TOGAS

The next day the weather proved better. White-mackerel clouds hung in wisps across the sky, making ideal conditions for diving off the boat to swim, eating

Left: *Diving instruction*
Below Left: *The range of fish to be seen around the Reef is immense: it would be easier to list the species I didn't see*

sliced fresh pineapple, and lazing on deck to the blare of techno and reggae. It could have been Ibiza. Trade winds—locally nicknamed bullets—blew in sharp bursts to relieve the sunburn. We took advantage of the breezes in the afternoon, and hitched a ride by sail to a snorkelling bay where scissor-tailed sergeant fish and yellow and blue damselfish pecked at my face mask. Snorkelling is easy, for you simply float above the coral in shallow water, watching the sun's rays penetrate the surface to colour a different world.

By sundown *Anaconda II* had been transformed into a floating nightclub. Jo, the cook, who had initially appeared to be a quiet girl, was the first to ditch her swimsuit in favour of a bedsheet, wrapping it round her as a toga. As the last

Left: *Lazing on the deck of Anaconda II*
Below: *Boom netting—all part of the frolics during our sail around the Whitsunday Islands on a maxi-yacht*

Q U E E N S L A N D

QUEENSLAND

drops were drained from the wine boxes, others tied on the togas and it was party-time in the Pacific. The next morning we had a fantastic sail back to Airlie Beach, with *Anaconda II* on her side cutting through the waves, chasing the swooping white-bellied sea eagles. Hangovers worsened. As a farewell that night, we danced on the tables at the resort's Moroccos music bar in front of a wall-sized video screen that flashed hits from the 1980s.

CAIRNS AT LAST

And so to the final stretch of my Greyhound journey, through sleepy towns of more Queenslanders and Red Rooster Drive-thru's serving hot chicken. Saltpans shimmered in the sun, the water in them evaporating to leave salt that is then scraped up, packed, and used for tanning cattle hides. The shopfronts here are like pop-up birthday cards. Sugarcane fields sprouted tall blades that arched like green fountains, and at banana plantations polythene bags covered the already ripened claws.

A number of passengers alighted at Townsville, with its Great Barrier Reef Wonderland attraction, including an aquarium with living coral, sharks, and rays. From here, you can take a catamaran ferry to Magnetic Island. I stayed firmly aboard for my next big stop, the finale of my trip—Cairns.

THE DIVE OF A LIFETIME

Something certainly draws people to Cairns in their thousands, although the resort has no beach, only mudflats washed by the ocean and trodden on by pelicans. Joggers pace the Esplanade, but I didn't want to jog. I wanted to see the Great Barrier Reef. Long before Cook and Flinders, the Aborigines made the first explorations of the reef in outrigger canoes to harvest fish and shellfish. It is Captain Cook, however, whose name stands out, his orders being to try to locate the legendary great southern continent that geographers believed existed. After circumnavigating New Zealand, he

> # WHALE-WATCHING
>
> Humpback whales were almost totally wiped out in Australian waters during the 1950s and 1960s, but since 1963 the whales have been protected and their population should recover to an estimated 10,000 by the year 2020. The humpbacks, which measure up to 12m (40ft) in length, migrate from their feeding grounds in Antarctic waters to their breeding grounds in the warm tropical waters of the Great Barrier Reef. They are renowned for the "breach," in which they leap into the air in a magnificent display.

was driven north and sighted the eastern coast of Australia on April 19, 1770. Unknowingly, he sailed within the Great Barrier Reef, noting in his log a "wall of Coral Rock rising all most (sic) perpendicular out of the unfathomable ocean."

To dive or snorkel the Great Barrier Reef is to be faced with an overwhelming number of options. Fast catamarans can transport you straight to its more spectacular outer edge for a day's diving and snorkelling, while others cruise gently, combining sightseeing with a little diving. Trips on dive boats last from one day to five nights. Some dive operators offer intensive PADI dive courses for beginners and advanced divers, including such specialities as wreck diving (more than 1,000 19th-century shipwrecks have been recorded here) and underwater photography (cameras provided).

I booked with a mainstream diving company that offers cheap day dives and snorkelling at the reef, by way of a double-deck boat that was as crowded as a passenger ferry. Our destination was Hastings Reef, home to Wally, a 45kg (100-pound) maori wrasse that nudges his humped head softly against the diver's shoulders, followed by an afternoon dive to locate turtles feeding around the Breaking Patches corals off Michaelmas Cay. The boat took more than two hours to reach the reef, by which time many passengers had dozed off or were clutching paper bags, heads bent as if praying their seasickness would disappear. The crew ran out of wetsuits; I had to squeeze into a child's, and the fins I was handed pinched my feet. We were given no commentary about the reef, and I saw as many rubber fins as I saw fish.

Back at my hostel, someone mentioned *Jungle Diver*, a 16m (51ft) Randell boat that speeds at 18 knots from Cape Tribulation and in about 40 minutes is anchored off Mackay Reef at the outer edge. "Mackay is our little hidey-hole," confided Cod, the skipper when I joined the trip. "It's beautiful with soft and hard corals, and is a turtle nesting site. It's also protected from the winds and swell, so is easy for snorkellers and for introducing divers to the reef."

We moored near a sand cay crowded with common noddy terns and brown boobies, as white ripples broke on the reef. Kitted up, I strode off the back of *Jungle Diver*, and immediately the coral appeared to come to greet me. The formations appear as weeds: bushy, with branches, or with needles that poke you. The coral is dime-shaped, spongy, hairy, lacy, a transparent tapestry, a web of intestines. I saw staghorn coral with blue tips, and coral as complex as a human brain. Algae in reds, browns, greens, and yellows play their role in the balance of ecology on the reef. Small fish eat plankton, bigger fish eat worms and molluscs, and even bigger fish eat the other fish. And so it continues.

SEND IN THE CLOWNS

It's like a city down there. By day it's hustle and bustle, with pickers, scavengers, and fish living in harmony. By night the lights turn up bright: neon pinks, greens, and purples. Feeding intensifies, hunts begin. Lurking in alleys are the big guys, waiting for a victim. My shadow spooked the 70-year-old giant clams, their pea-green optic nerves sensing danger so that they slammed their purple lips shut.

Mauve Christmas tree worms popped back into holes as though sucked in by a vacuum cleaner. And as for fish, it would be easier to list the species I didn't see.

After lunch, we plunged back in for a drift dive. Cod dropped us off and moved the boat to the end of a thick, crusty, vertical wall of coral, perforated and stacked with ledges. Then Cod dived in to escort me on an exclusive visit to the Clown Fish Hilton, a fragile mass of coral animated by clown fish. Blue sea stars formed a regular pattern on the bare bones of dead coral. Shoals of silvery fish, each individual no bigger than my fingernail, joined the theatrics, while sea cucumbers conserved energy, lying motionless on the sand like sausages.

After a dive, there is usually a post-mortem discussion of sightings over a can of beer. I really did believe those who had seen a tiger shark and a hammerhead shark. And I was overcome with jealousy when I heard a beginner say he had spotted a manta ray with a fin span measuring more than 4m (13ft). Fish, fish, and more fish littered my memories as I left Cairns, this time flying back briskly to Sydney. What a send-off. As the plane rose over the reef, I saw a tie-dye fabric of diaphanous jade-green swirls on blue. Now I can say that I've seen Australia's magnificent barrier from every angle, although there's always that view from space.

CORAL ORGY

Each year, following November's full moon, a spectacular "coral orgy" occurs beneath the waves. On the same night all along the Great Barrier Reef, corals, which are not plants but animals, spawn simultaneously, and thousands of pink eggs and sperm float upwards. Fish gorge on this cocktail, and what they don't eat is fertilized, ensuring the ongoing survival of the coral reef. A peculiar side-effect of the event is that the ocean stinks for days afterwards.

GOING IT ALONE

INTERNAL TRAVEL

Currently, Qantas (Sunstate) and Ansett are the major regional airlines, with flights from Sydney and Brisbane to Cairns. Popular coach networks are Greyhound Pioneer, McCafferty's, and the colourful Oz Experience.

A Greyhound Pioneer Aussie Explorer Pass offers 12 pre-set routes, while an Aussie Kilometre Pass enables you to buy 2,000–20,000km (1,243–12,428 miles) before you travel anywhere on the network, and then top them up if necessary. An Aussie Explorer Pass links all the resorts from Sydney, through Brisbane, and on up to Cape Tribulation. There's also a service heading inland to Mount Isa, which links up with Alice Springs in the Northern Territory. You can combine your coach travel with a VIP Backpacker membership card, which offers discounts to the 44 backpacker hostels in Queensland and gives further reductions on tours and adventures.

WHEN TO GO

Water temperatures range from 22°C (72°F) to 28°C (82°F), which makes for comfortable diving and snorkelling all year round, although the main tourist season runs from April (autumn) to November (spring). From April to September, the Queensland coast is wafted by southeast trade winds. Cyclones can occur at any time during

Left: It's amazing how close it's possible to get to some of the reef's inhabitants
Inset: Getting a close-up view of an intricate tree-like coral

the summer rainy season (November–May), although they are most likely in February or March.

Maximum summer temperatures in Brisbane reach 29°C (84°F); in Cairns, they soar to a very humid 31°C (88°F), with most rain falling in January. Even when it rains, it's warm enough to dive, although visibility underwater may be reduced. In winter, the sun continues to shine, nights are cooler, and fewer mosquitoes and irritating marsh flies make this a pleasant time to visit.

PLANNING

All visitors to Australia need a visa which you can apply for well in advance by phoning your nearest Australian consulate or embassy. The visa is processed electronically, payment is taken by debit or credit card, and when you arrive in Australia your details are already logged.

If you have time to explore (two weeks or longer), take your time travelling up or down the eastern coast, calling in at the resorts and taking trips out to Fraser Island, the Whitsundays, and Magnetic Island at the very least. If you just want to visit the Great Barrier Reef, you can try to get a direct flight to Cairns' international airport.

If you plan to dive, choose a boat you like the look of and find out how many passengers it takes (some carry more than 400, which means that you see little other than your fellow divers). Look for a boat that takes 40 people or less and speeds out to the reef. If you have never dived before, book an inexpensive

introductory dive first before splashing out on a whole course.

TRAVELLERS' TIP

If you want to hire a guide for visits to Fraser Island and other destinations, try the tour operator offices that line the streets of popular tourist areas. Alternatively, backpacker hostels and hotels can arrange any excursions or activities.

WHAT TO TAKE

❑ Lightweight clothing, including beachwear, sandals, and deck shoes.
❑ Sunscreen, sunglasses, and sun hat.
❑ Camera and films (an underwater camera is a good idea, although these can be hired on the diving courses).
❑ Your own snorkel and mask, although again these are supplied by operators.
❑ Tents and sleeping bags for camping on Fraser Island (these are provided or can be hired).

HEALTH

Some dive courses request that you undergo a (locally-arranged) medical before you can take part. Australia is exceptionally clean, with few health hazards, and standards of hygiene are high. Sun protection is strongly advised, even in overcast weather and especially out on the ocean. Wear a broad-brimmed hat, a shirt with collar and sleeves, and high-factor water-resistant sunscreen. Snorkellers should wear a "shortie" wetsuit or T-shirt to protect their back against sunburn. From October to April, it's unsafe to swim in shallow waters near the coast: box jellyfish inflict stings that can be fatal, especially to children.

QUEENSLAND

10 On Safari through the Wet Tropics

by Lee Karen Stow

Some of the oldest tropical rainforest on Earth is found in northeastern Queensland, creeping down mountain slopes to greet the fringing corals of the Great Barrier Reef. Cutting through this dense canopy of giant ferns and poisonous leaves are rushing rollercoaster rivers.

Sandwiched between the dry outback and the sweeping beaches are the densely forested coastal mountain ranges of Queensland, the wettest in Australia. This is a humid, magical place, with the highest diversity of animal and plant life found anywhere on the continent. The plants here were once used as food and tools by 16 different Aboriginal tribes and fossilized pollen has proved that some areas pre-date the breakup of Gondwanaland (the ancient southern supercontinent that encompassed Africa, India, South America, Antarctica and Australasia) 50 million years ago.

 Whitewater rafting is challenging and can result in serious injury, although the major rafting companies make safety a priority. You don't need to be able to swim to take part. Bushwalking through the rain forest is easily manageable, but the going can be slippery at times. There are short paths or full-day walks to choose from. Horse riding is available for all abilities, and tuition can be provided.

 Accommodation can be in roadside hotels or within the rain forest at lodges. Here you will find either dormitories or single and double rooms with verandas overlooking the forest. Beds and facilities are all of a high standard.

 No specialist equipment is needed for the whitewater rafting as everything, is provided. You will need stout walking shoes for the treks and, ideally, footwear with a heel for the horse riding. Don't forget to pack waterproofs, especially in the wet season. Good maps and a compass are essential if you plan to walk through the rain forest without a guide.

Australia's rainforest grows predominantly along the continent's eastern coast, from Cape York to Tasmania, and is either tropical, subtropical, or temperate. It is only in northeastern Queensland, however, that the tropical rainforest flourishes, yet sadly only a fraction of its original grandeur remains. With the arrival of Europeans, trees were cleared for cattle and horse grazing, for sugarcane farming and logging, causing massive destruction to virgin rainforest. A sizeable portion of what's left is now protected as national parkland, a World Heritage Site covering at least 7,500sq. km (2,900 sq. miles) between Cooktown and Townsville and including the Daintree area and the Atherton Tablelands.

IT'S WET IN THE TROPICS

"Soggy Start to Wet," read the front-page headline of the Cairns Post newspaper, dated December 2, 1999. The lead story went on to report that Cairns had been soaked with more than twice its usual November rainfall (apparently, it had rained for 29 of the 30 days).

I realized how lucky I was to have packed my own waterproofs when, on a half-day's horse ride into the rainforest behind the resort of Airlie Beach, I refused the stablehand's cape which, when shaken, disgorged an army of cockroaches. The hens in the yard went frantic, chasing after the insects and pecking away at this impromptu banquet

MANGROVES

Australia has more than 30 species of mangrove. They grow along the shoreline in tropical Australia, and make a valuable contribution to the local environment and food chain. Mangroves trap sediment and nutrients, providing a shady home and feeding ground for crabs, molluscs, worms, spiders, lizards, crocodiles, prawns, snakes, and wetland birds. Because the bases of the trees are engulfed by the tide every 12 hours, and because the mud in which they grow is starved of oxygen, the mangroves have adapted a root system that grows upward to take in oxygen directly from the air.

until they had swallowed the lot. A spider the width of an apple dropped from the cape's hood and it, too, was dismembered. The actual horse ride was a joy. Rain droplets bounced off the leaves of mango trees and water sank into the soil, transforming it into terracotta-coloured soup. Hoofs splashed through pools that were a deep salmon colour as my horse plodded past the purple trumpets of the violet morning glory bush. The rainy season here is kind of pretty, with steam rising from the valley bottoms to settle as mist on the treetops.

It was still pouring when I sat warm and cosy in a four-wheel drive a few days later on a jungle safari into the rainforest with a group of eight others.

An hour earlier, all had been clear as we drove from Cairns along the Bruce Highway. Walsh's Pyramid rose greenly behind a sign saying "Turn left for the Crocodile Farm." This free-standing 922m (3,025ft) mountain slopes upwards at a 45-degree angle in a constant climb that takes the average fit person three hours to conquer. Every August, a fun run is held, when competitors race from Cairns to the mountain's summit. At the time of writing, the record of 1 hour 20

minutes had just been smashed by a New Zealander knocking a few minutes off the total. The Aborigines believe the mountain was created in the Dreamtime by the Australian bush turkey. Mounds of leaves and earth, about 1m (3ft) tall, are built by the bird with its large feet, and are then used as incubator nests for the eggs. We saw plenty of these miniature pyramids on our walks through the forests.

UNDER THE CANOPY

We turned off the Bruce Highway and headed up through the sugarcane fields of the Mulgrove Valley. As we crossed the river we noticed cyclone debris of uprooted trees and withered barks by the roadside. A lace monitor skirted across our path before the lush rainforest heralded our first venture into its labyrinth.

To reach a thunderous waterfall, we trod on a sodden carpet of red, brown, and golden leaves like those of an autumnal woodland back home. Droplets from the overhanging canopy fell large, and more came, washing away the numerous bugs. It was midday, yet the forest giants of silkwoods and bumpy ash, mahoganies and rosewoods, and the floppy ferns darkened to a medley of greens and browns, damp and mysterious.

In the distant past the whole of the continent appeared like this. When Australia broke free from the supercontinent of Gondwanaland it floated northwards towards its present position, taking its flora and fauna with it. It then became more arid, changing its face to dry desert, and the rainforest contracted to the wetter areas along the eastern coast. Today, 13 of the world's 19 primitive flowering plants occur in the Wet Tropics. Scores of species are endemic to this particular area. The chameleon gecko, for instance, is one of 18 species of reptile found only here. Geckos are funny creatures that, when they are disturbed they shed their tail, which then continues to twitch independently.

Aside from its wildlife, the Australian rainforest is one of the most complex

ecosystems in the world, boasting around 800 species of trees and 1,200 species of flowering plants, plus native gingers, mosses, ferns, and fungi. Crowns of tall trees—some, like the northern silky oak, rising to 30m (100ft)—form a canopy that intercepts sun and rain, causing the understory and the forest floor to thrive in a different microclimate. Strangler figs make amazing subjects for photographs, their knobbly caramel-coloured fingers draping down to the forest floor, twisting and creeping. Their life cycle is a fascinating one. A bird eats a fig seed, then passes the seed through its digestive system. The seed germinates on a branch and grows into a new plant, which sends its roots down to the ground; these strangle the host tree as they expand. The host eventually dies, leaving the fig tree standing majestically. The so-called "Curtain

Left: *The rainforest canopy displays some of the many species that flourish in this area*
Above: *The densely forested mountains of Queensland support some of the oldest tropical rainforests on Earth*
Right: *The roots of a strangler fig drape down to the forest floor, engulfing the host tree*

Fig," a well-known example of this species that we saw on our walk, is 500 years old and has the texture of a chocolate flake, with aerial roots that are spattered with snow-white, button-headed fungi. The reason for this particular tree's gothic formation is that when its host fell, due to the crushing weight of the fig, it was supported halfway down by another tree. The fig then continued to grow, draping over the pair like a curtain.

Among this wet wonderland, we watched insects suck the nectar out of crimson petals, and briefly saw the brilliant red plumage of the male king parrot. We gave a wide berth to the stinging tree, or gympie-gympie, whose heart-shaped flowers are coated in silica hairs that are full of toxins; if you brush against them they inflict a severe pain that can last for months.

Hair on the crown of my head became caught up in the barbed vine of the lawyer cane, or wait-a-while. Once it buries its spikes in your skin, T-shirt, or boot laces, it never lets go. Many hands made light work of the wait-a-while until I was free, but as we emerged from the rainforest a friend glanced at me and screamed, pointing to my eye. A tiger leech, tapered like a black liquorice strip and with a sucker at each end of its body, had anchored its backside to my eyebrow. The leech could have ingested up to ten times its body weight, had the guide not flicked it off briskly. Then, he plucked a green ant from a twig and sucked its rear end, assuring me that the liquid inside was pure vitamin C and acts as a remedy for nose and throat infections. Aborigines would crush hundreds of these ants' abdomens in order to make a nutritional cordial that mothers apparently smeared on their nipples before breastfeeding their babies.

WEAVING UP TO THE TABLELANDS

More than 260 hairpin bends wind 760m (2,493ft) up the steep Gillies Highway to the top of the Atherton Tablelands, another World Heritage Site. This fertile oasis, standing at altitudes of 400–1,100m (1,300–3,609ft), stretches between Cairns and the sugarcane town of Innisfail, and is set off by striking soil formed from a base rock of basalt lava

that is as red as the rust on the farmhouses' tin roofs. Grazing the pastures are Fresian cows, reared for milk and butter, while avocados, mangoes, tea, coffee, teatrees, and macadamia nuts all share the territory. Even sugarcane is edging its way in.

Until a century ago, the Atherton Tablelands were covered in rainforest. Then white settlers discovered gold and tin, and subsequently further deforested the region through logging and agriculture. From Gillies Lookout the view is beautiful, stretching to Queensland's highest peaks, Mount Bartle Frere, at 1,657m (5,437ft), and Mount Bellenden Ker, at 1,591m (5,220ft). Breaking the expanse of greenness is Lake Eacham, a clear circle of water in a volcanic crater, forming an idyllic swimming spot with a picnic place that steals hours from your afternoon. We chased the bush turkeys from our sandwiches, and scouted around for the musky rat kangaroo that lives behind the toilet block. This is the smallest macropod, and although it is related to the kangaroo, it resembles a rat and springs around on all fours, not just its hind legs.

Sites as peaceful as Lake Eacham are located on tourist trails and maps, and are easy to find. However, there are secret places that only a few tour guides are privileged to. Luckily, we were blessed with such a guy, who led us over a path of lime-green clover to a bat forest. I was ecstatic. Never before have my ears experienced the deafening squawks of flocks of sulphur-crested cockatoos battling for perches at the top of the forest canopy. Trying to sleep through this racket were spectacled flying foxes, hanging like clusters of brown seedpods. Adding to the cacophony was a laughing kookaburra, the largest of the kingfishers, which cackled hysterically from its treebranch perch.

CANOEING BY DARK

Sleepy dairy towns and former timber settlements populate the Tablelands. The town of Atherton itself is a sizeable agricultural centre, full of stores and services, while at the smaller old tin-mining town of Herberton you can buy fuel and bread, and read on a wall the story of the settlement's history. We stayed at Yungaburra. This used to be an overnight resting place for miners from the coast heading for the tin and gold mines to the west, and is a village noted for its listed architecture. In the afternoon, we drank beer in the white hotel, where dairy farmers in check shirts, sat glued to the seemingly ubiquitous Sky Sports on the television screen.

Nightfall in Yungaburra is prime time for spotting wildlife, especially from a canoe paddled in the dark on the restful surface of Lake Tinaroo. The two-man, red plastic canoes come with single or double oars, and all you need to take is a life jacket and a torch. By night, the insect hums and bird calls are magnified in the stillness, and the trees on the lake margins are silent, shadowy thickets. However, the moment your spotlight shines on a pair of red eyes peering out through the leaves, you know it's a good safari. We were more than lucky, sighting three Lumholtz's tree kangaroos, including a mother and baby, a red-legged pademelon, and a musky rat kangaroo. It's peculiar to think of kangaroos climbing trees, but that's how a Lumholtz's tree kangaroo gets around, using its stout, heavily clawed forelegs for gripping, and its long, thick tail for balancing. We watched the kangaroos for ages, but the red-legged pademelon leapt briskly away on its powerful hind legs as soon as the spotlight caught it grazing on the fallen leaves.

CROCS AND BUGS AT DAINTREE

From the famous scenic veil of the Millaa Millaa Falls, we headed to the Daintree-Cape Tribulation region, with its pure virgin rainforest, once the home of the Kuku Yalanji Aborigines. We stayed overnight at Crocodylus Jungle Village, a

gathering of green-canvas dormitories and lodges, where a long-nosed bandicoot scurried along the top of the dining tables as we ate. Overnight, rain pounded on the fabric roofs as we slept. Frogs chimed a continuous beat and insects hissed louder than a kettle on the boil. In the early hours a melomys, or native bush rat, crept stealthily into our dorm. It nibbled through a rucksack, half-attacking an apple and, sacrilegiously, took a bite out of a paperback novel.

One morning I took a three-hour horse ride through the rainforest and, surprisingly, it didn't rain once. I rode Chucky, a half brumby (wild horse), on slopes churned to mush by the November wet. As I steered through the rocky creeks I watched shrewdly for hanging wait-a-whiles and bloodthirsty leeches, but nothing lassoed or bit me during what I found to be the best horse ride in Queensland. Even though the roadside is punctuated by "Cassowary Crossing" signs, it's only a few fortunate (or unfortunate) travellers who actually come across one. For this huge, flightless, blue-black-feathered bird, with a red and blue

ESTUARINE CROCODILES

The saltwater ("saltie"), or estuarine, crocodile is the largest of all 23 species of crocodile. The saltie is not restricted to salt water, but can be found over 100km (60 miles) inland, lurking in rivers, billabongs, and pools. Estuarine crocodiles can grow up to 6m (20ft) long and weigh 720kg (1,600 pounds), and can stay submerged for over an hour. Signs warning you that "Estuarine crocodiles inhabit creeks and rivers," are common in the rain forest. You might spot them on a Daintree River cruise, but to be sure of a sighting and a photograph book a cruise through the mangrove wetlands to the Cairns Crocodile Farm which houses over 10,000 individuals.

Above: *The Atherton Tablelands are a fertile oasis stretching between Cairns and Innisfail*
Left: *The saltwater crocodile can stay submerged for over an hour*

neck and a vicious-looking horn atop its skull, can, if provoked, head-butt anything that should have the misfortune to get in its path.

One beast you don't approach, is the estuarine crocodile, which can be seen floating in many rivers and creeks in the rainforest. If you wish to see these creatures, along with snakes and birds, the best idea is to join a safari cruise along the Daintree River in a steel sightseeing boat—although there's no guarantee of a

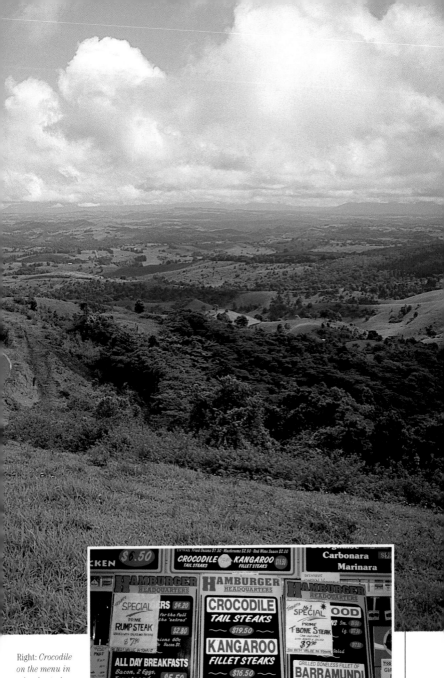

Right: *Crocodile on the menu in a local eaterie*

sighting. Unfortunately, the wet season is the time when the female crocodiles nest, laying about 30–80 eggs that the males then hide around in the undergrowth with them. All we saw were a few spiders in webs wrapped around the mangroves and the electric-blue flash of the Ulysses butterfly, the symbol of tourism throughout Queensland. I was, however, told that crocodiles also inhabit the lower reaches of the Tully River. Did someone mention the Tully?

FOAMING ON THE RAPIDS

With an almighty thud, one instructor smashed his helmet-protected head on a boulder at Full Stop Drop. Then someone bounced over the side of a dinghy like a rubber ball and plunged into the rushing Tully River. "Man overboard!" His team mates reached into the foaming rage of water with the handle of a paddle, pulling him in, but the dinghy was speeding rapidly. He couldn't make it back on board. He lost his grip and was eaten by the torrent, only to be spewed back up again. We were in the dinghy behind, watching helplessly. The instructor grasped the man's life jacket and held him to the dinghy, so that he was pulled along like a villain being dragged behind a cowboy's horse. Within seconds, they hauled him back in, and the rapids gave way to a slower, smoother stretch. Drenched from head to trainers, the rescued fellow lifted his oar in the air and hollowed the customary, "Yee-haaaaaaagh!" Now that's what you call whitewater rafting.

The Tully River cuts through the Tully State Forest, a dense green corridor of basalt rocks and volcanic lava flows, until it drains into the ocean at Tully Heads, south of the town of Tully. "Do you like my office?" joked Mike Ward, the outdoor education instructor of Raging Thunder, one of the two major rafting companies that are allowed down the Tully. He perched at the back of our raft, steering and guiding us through 44 rapids, ranging from Class III to Class IV, on a 14km (9-mile) stretch of river.

JOINING THE QUEUE FOR THE TULLY RIVER

I had joined a coachful of rafters, many of them complete beginners, for the two-hour trip from Cairns to the Tully River. Once there, we donned life jackets and helmets, and each took up a paddle. Because I am light, I had been placed in the back of the dinghy, an adventurous seat, but it caused me to be thrown around like a ragdoll on caffeine. Mike sat alongside, issuing orders. Tully rafting is a very popular activity, so there can be more than a dozen dinghies stacked up in the queues waiting to raft down one rapid.

We rafted 4km (2½ miles) downstream over a couple of hours, tackling most of the major rapids. Double Waterfall is a big hydraulic, sucking you into its force and spitting you out only when it wants to. Then there's the Staircase, with 175m (574ft) of consistent water, and the Theatre, where a lot of the drama comes from the build-up of rapids—before the culmination at that headache-inducing Full Stop Drop. Wet, laughing, and trembling with adrenalin, we pulled the dinghies up to an awning in the rain forest where lunchtime barbecued burgers sizzled. Then we jumped back into the dinghies to meet the Double D rapid, so named when a German girl flipped out of her raft and swirled around in a current so strong that it somehow managed to dislodge her bra.

At Guide's Revenge we dropped our paddles and gathered in a rugby scrum at the head of the boat, hanging onto each other's life jackets for a rollercoaster dip that threw us, minus our dinghy, up in the air and back down into the river with a crash. No one was spared the ducking, except of course the guides, who waved their paddles in victory and repeated the distinctive and slightly smug "Yee-haaaaaaagh!" war cry.

THE RELAXING DRIFT DOWNSTREAM

The day ended with a relaxed drift downstream. Cormorants perched on boulders waiting for us to pass so they could dive for fish, blue dragonflies skittered around our legs, and irritable marsh flies stabbed their probosces into our skin to draw blood. Aside from the bites, I suffered from a sprained hand and broken fingernails, so was let off lightly by what can be a dangerous sport. And yes, I'd do it again, and yes, I might be brave enough to be at the front of the dinghy next time. Oh, and yes, I do like the rainforest rain.

GOING IT ALONE

INTERNAL TRAVEL

Many international airlines fly direct to Cairns, which is a good base for touring the rainforest. Should you fly to Sydney first, there are daily coach services up the coastline. Numerous Australian-based operators offer tours to the rainforest and to the Atherton Tablelands, from one day to around a week.

In the dry season, you can reach the places in this feature by self-drive car; these can be hired at main resorts. In the wet season, it is important to drive slowly and take it easy. The Kennedy, Gillies, and Palmerston highways all lead to Atherton, and the sites are well signposted. This is also true of the rainforest sites to the north of Cairns along the Captain Cook Highway towards Cape Tribulation.

WHEN TO GO

The main tourist season in Queensland runs from April to November. Summer (December–March) is the wet season, when it can be uncomfortably humid with plenty of insects and frequent downpours. That said, the rainforest looks exceptionally beautiful. The best time to visit the Wet Tropics and tropical northeast is around April to October (the dry season), when the days are warm and nights cooler. Some rain is to be expected and there may be frost at night in the Atherton Tablelands, where the temperature can drop to below 10°C (50°F). Summer temperatures on the coast average 30°C (86°F) in the wet season and about 20°C (68°F) in the dry.

PLANNING

You can happily spend up to a fortnight exploring the Atherton Tablelands and rainforest area, with a half-day or day's rafting included, or even longer if you take the rafting package on the North Johnstone River. Cairns is the most obvious base for tours and trekking into the rainforest. However, the Tully River is a good two hours' drive from the resort, so if you wish to go rafting there it's probably best to base yourself at Mission Beach. Another popular option is to hire a car and caravan or a campervan so that you can go as you please. Alternatively, there are hostels and hotels, ranging from the basic to the luxurious, which can be booked in advance.

TRAVELLERS' TIP

❑ Guides are available for hire at all the main tourist resorts. Park rangers, based at national park offices in the towns and at ranger stations, are invaluable sources of information.

WHAT TO TAKE

❑ Waterproofs, even in the dry season.
❑ Stout walking boots.
❑ Walking trousers or shorts with long socks.
❑ High-factor sunscreen and insect repellent.
❑ Camera with a fast film for photography under the rainforest canopy.
❑ Old shorts and T-shirt or swimsuit for rafting.
❑ Warm sweater.
❑ Plenty of drinking water.

HEALTH

The best advice when walking through the rainforest is to hire the services of a guide. If you do intend to walk alone, read thoroughly about the species of plant that can cause you harm and make sure you know what they look like. Crocodiles inhabit many creeks and rivers in the rainforest, so be choosy about where you swim, wash, and gather water for boiling. Unless you know otherwise from a reliable, local source, always assume that crocodiles are present. To deter leeches, wear long trousers or socks, and apply insect repellent to your ankles or rub some eucalyptus oil on your lower legs.

WHITEWATER ALTERNATIVES

Those wishing to try something less challenging than the Tully could try the Barron River, which is a smaller river with Class II to Class III rapids, and can be tackled in half a day on an organized trip. The North Johnstone River, between Townsville and Cairns, is a major whitewater rafting stretch but has Class V rapids in parts and drops that even some instructors squirm at. This river is accessed by helicopter, which means you fly in and raft out. Expeditions to the North Johnstone River include rainforest walks to spectacular waterfalls and overnight camping deep within a remote part of this World Heritage Area.

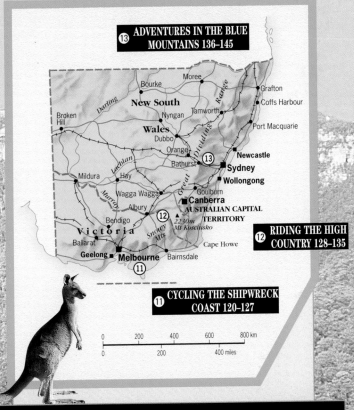

Moree
Bourke
Grafton
Coffs Harbour
New South
Broken Hill
Darling
Nyngan
Tamworth
Port Macquarie
Wales
Dubbo
Orange
Newcastle
Lachlan
Bathurst
⑬
Sydney
Mildura
Hay
Wollongong
Murray
Wagga Wagga
Goulburn
Albury
Canberra
⑫
AUSTRALIAN CAPITAL
Bendigo
2230m
TERRITORY
Victoria
Snowy Mts
Mt Kosciusko
Ballarat
Cape Howe
Geelong
Melbourne
Bairnsdale
⑪

0   200   400   600   800 km
0   200   400 miles

NEW SOUTH WALES•
VICTORIA

The southeastern corner of Australia is home to the states of New South Wales and Victoria and the Australian Capital Territory, surrounding Canberra. Here, the South Pacific's waves break on innumerable beaches, there are magnificent national parks and major rivers flow down from the Great Dividing Range as it splits the coastal strip from the sunbaked outback. Perhaps because Australians are the most urbanized people in the world, the majority living in the cities of Sydney and Melbourne, they like nothing more than "going bush." Sydneysiders head for the Blue Mountains, offering everything from gentle rambles to heart-pumping canyon action. Near Canberra, the Snowy Mountains are an ideal escape in winter or summer, while at any time of year the scenery of Victoria's Great Ocean Road is hard to beat. And hinterland towns such as Lightning Ridge and Broken Hill provide a taste of real outback adventure.

Climbing in the breathtaking Blue Mountains

NEW SOUTH WALES & VICTORIA

11 Cycling the Shipwreck Coast

by Simon Richmond

The Great Ocean Road is undoubtedly one of the world's most scenic drives. However, if you want to experience the full drama of this route, which hugs the rugged, wind-whipped coast of Victoria, make the trip by bike.

For the most part, the Great Ocean Road, which hugs the jagged contours of Victoria's southwest coast, is less romantically known as the B100. Officially, it runs for 285km (177 miles) from the beachside community of Barwon Heads, some 20km (12 miles) south of the Phillip Bay port of Geelong, Victoria's second city, to Warrnambool, the state's premier whale-watching location. The route was created as a memorial to those who died fighting in World War I, and at the same time also happened to be a handy works project that employed over 3,000 returning soldiers. In places tracks had to be carved out by hand with pick and shovel along plummeting cliffs with workmen dangling precariously by ropes from trees to hack the initial footholds in the rock. But then danger has never been a stranger along these shores, as the frequent memorials to shipwrecks testify.

VICTORIAN STYLE

Cycling solo or in a small group along the most scenic sections of the Great Ocean Road can be accomplished in around five days, depending how frequently you care to stop. The easiest way is to join a bus-supported tour, which provides the options of skipping the more gruelling sections or having a rest when you've done enough biking for the day. In addition, all your accommodation and meals are taken care of, and you don't have to carry your luggage in panniers. My six-day trip with Boomerang Bicycle Tours began in Queenscliff, a 19th-century resort town at the southern tip of the Bellarine Peninsula, 103km (64 miles) from Melbourne. Many of the charming cottages and grand mansions of the early days remain, including the Ozone Hotel, my group's elegant home for the night.

I had been picked up at Melbourne Airport by tour leader Konrad, the 30-year-old owner of the company. Attached to the back of the minibus was the trailer that would transport our luggage and the company's hybrid bikes between the various sections of the ride. I was beginning to feel that my lack of experience might hold people back, until Ann, a 60-year-old from the U.S., announced, in her Lauren Bacall accent, "I don't like hills. I'm very particular." And then she limbered up for the first evening's ride around Queenscliff

Seasoned cyclists will find the undulating road well within their capabilities. There are some steep and sustained hills and the going is often affected by strong head winds. More casual cyclists will find it a challenge and could use a support vehicle. Be prepared for rain and cold weather, even at the height of summer.

Seaside resort towns are dotted all along the Great Ocean Road, and you'll find accommodation ranging from backpacker hostels and B&Bs to historic hotels.

You'll need a hybrid or mountain bike if you wish to stray from the asphalted main road; otherwise, a racing bike is fine. You are required by law to wear a helmet (which the operator will supply along with puncture-repair kit, water bottle, and pump). Cycling clothes, shoes, and gloves are all recommended. Take thermal or polypropylene underwear and all-weather gear for the cold, rainy days, and high-factor sunscreen and a sun hat for the fair-weather days.

with a shot of whisky and a cigarette. I was in good company.

QUEENSCLIFF TO TORQUAY

We set off on our first full day on the road—45km (28 miles) to the surf Mecca of Torquay, followed by just over 20km (12 miles) after lunch to the kangaroo-occupied golf course at Anglesea. Konrad cycles with us for the initial few kilometres and then returns to pick up the bus, following on behind to scoop up any weary stragglers.

Blue skies promise perfect weather as we ride past the terminus of the Bellarine Peninsula Railway and along a cycle path for 5km (3 miles) towards Point Lonsdale, dominated by a handsome white lighthouse that guards the infamous Rip. This is the name for the 1,200m (1,300yd)-wide entrance to Port Phillip Bay, one of the most hazardous stretches of water in the world. The tides flow through the 15m (40ft)-deep channel at up to 8 knots, and have dragged scores of ships to their doom.

From the lighthouse we turn inland and pedal up the first of the day's hills, a steady rise to the outskirts of Ocean Grove, the next beachside community, where we pause for morning tea at Raafs Beach. The ride from Barwon Heads past the lengthy Thirteenth Beach ends at a towering wind generator, giving an indication of the gusts that hit this exposed

stretch of asphalt. I pause at the tiny Torquay Airport to take a thrilling scenic flight in a Tiger Moth, swathed in jumpsuit, leather jacket, flying hat, and goggles, before rejoining the others for a picnic lunch on Torquay's grassy esplanade.

WHAT'S A WINKI POP?

The first real test of our cycling stamina comes on the road out of Torquay where the B100 climbs for 3.5km (2 miles) towards the turn-off to Jan Juc, a classic surfing location. We continue up and down the rollercoaster-like Bells Boulevard towards the coast. The final hill, however, defeats me and I

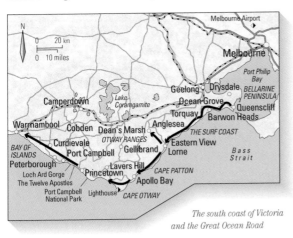

The south coast of Victoria and the Great Ocean Road

have to push my bike to the crest, which provides a panoramic view across fields towards one of the world's top surf beaches. Named after local 19th-century landowners, Bells Beach is a real beauty, secluded and totally uncommercialized. Wooden steps lead down to the gritty sand and the breaking waves, which are not too powerful today but at their best rise to heights of up to 4m (11ft). There's a sign proclaiming this is a "Winki Pop Conservation Area." We look at the pink flowers blooming on the cliffs and wonder if these might be the elusive winki pops, but Konrad isn't too sure. Later, a savvy local informs us it's a surfers' slang name for a surf break.

It's past 4pm, and for most of the group the day's ride ends here, with Konrad loading the bikes onto the trailer. Only Doug and Kathryn cycle the remaining 10km (6 miles), past the unsightly Alcoa Power Station and its huge open-cast coal mine, to the long downhill sweep into the sleepy settlement of Anglesea. We meet them by the sand-dunes and finish the day at Anglesea's golf course, where the resident mob of kangaroos nibble contentedly on the fairways.

LOST IN THE RANGES

Our overnight base is the luxurious self-catering King Parrot Holiday Cabins in the foothills of the Otway Ranges. The surrounding bush is home to a multitude of wildlife, including bush wallabies, bandicoots, glow-worms, and platypuses. After a barbecue dinner that we all help to prepare, Konrad leads those who are keen on a torchlit ramble.

The first 5km (3 miles) of the next day's ride is along Dunce Track, a fire trail that is largely an uphill slog with several muddy sections to negotiate. The difficulty of the terrain has caused the group to spread out. Doug waits at the crossing and points me to the left, which I happily whiz down. Several kilometres later I realize that I should have turned right instead. By the time I make it back up to the crossing, the group has moved on and rain is beginning to fall. I pedal furiously to catch up, but in my haste I misread the cycle notes and head in the wrong direction again. Just when I'm at the point of giving up and carrying on to Lorne, our coastal destination for the day, by another route, Konrad turns up with the minibus.

Left: *The Ozone Hotel in Queenscliff is a grand mansion dating from the early days of European colonization*
Right: *It was reassuring to know that Konrad and the trailer were never far behind*
Below: *The ride was panoramic from day one, though seldom flat*

The rain is falling heavily now, so it's not surprising to find only Doug sheltering at the lookout over Erskine Falls, a 30m (80ft)-high cascade; the other members of the group have pedalled on to the lunch meeting place. Doug hops in the bus, too, and we drive to the Erskine Falls Café.

I have now learnt two lessons. The first is not to trust fellow cyclists on directions; always check the route on the map yourself. The second is to pay more careful attention to the cycle notes, which give precise and almost infallible instructions.

INTERLUDE IN LORNE

There's little chance of getting lost on the afternoon cycle to Lorne, a largely downhill route with a short uphill detour to Teddy's Lookout. This provides what Konrad has taken to calling "an amply

NEW SOUTH WALES & VICTORIA

SURFERS' PARADISE

Between Anglesea and Lorne, the Great Ocean Road runs along what is called the Surf Coast, where you'll find some of the best surf breaks in Australia. Torquay has the world's largest surfing museum and next door, in Surf Coast Plaza, you can buy or rent all the gear you might need to sample the waves at classic surf beaches such as Jan Juc. The main surfing destination is Bells Beach, venue for many world championships. It's packed in summer, even though the surf is reputedly best in winter, when you'll certainly need a wetsuit to brave the icy waters.

rewarding view" for our efforts, and as I gaze out at the Great Ocean Road below, snaking its picturesque way around the estuary of the St. George River and the surrounding cliffs, it's impossible not to agree. We are based in Lorne—one of the state's oldest and most fashionable seaside towns—for a couple of days.

The wettest day of the trip falls on Day 3, our rest day from biking. We spend the morning exploring another part of the Angahook-Lorne State Park on foot with Ian, an enthusiastic and entertaining guide who is beside himself at a rare daytime sighting of a koala munching on leaves up a blue gum tree. We continue along the densely wooded track, on the lookout for wallaby tracks and the sleepers of the old logging railway that once covered the same route. At a soaring gum tree with teethmarks up its bark, Ian introduces us to his favourite of the forest inhabitants, the gliding possum.

LORNE TO CAPE OTWAY

There's more, much more, of the same beguiling sea and cliff views on Day 4 of the ride, which initially takes us 44km (27 miles) along the most serpentine stretch of the Great Ocean Road, between Lorne and Apollo Bay. A sign at the start warns that this is a "High Accident Zone," no

doubt because drivers lose control as they zip recklessly around the hairpin bends or become too engrossed in the scenery to notice danger on the road. The highest point is the lookout at Cape Patton, beneath which ships once floundered on the perilous voyage up the Bass Strait. It's mainly downhill from here towards Apollo Bay, where stout cypress trees line the beachside approach to a town that is less studiously trendy than Lorne. Weird wooden sculptures of fish, lizards, seals, and distorted faces decorate the lawns outside the excellent visitors' centre.

After lunch, we tackle a heart-bursting series of hills into the Otway National Park. The park's lush rain forest couldn't be more of a contrast; at Maits Rest, we dismount to stroll through a shady gully bursting with giant ferns and centuries-old myrtle beech trees smothered in moss.

The toughest section of the trip over, we pedal along a more gentle road for 12km (7 miles) towards the 21m (58ft)-high historic Cape Otway lighthouse, arriving just before it closes for the day at 5pm. It is possible to stay overnight in this remote, beautiful, and windblasted spot in one of the whitewashed sandstone cottages that once housed the keepers. But we return to Apollo Bay, to rest up before what will prove to be the best day yet along the Great Ocean Road.

TOWARDS THE LIMESTONE COAST

The 47km (29 miles) from Apollo Bay to the top of Lavers Hill, the highest point on the Great Ocean Road, is the toughest section for the cyclist. We are spared this considerable effort, however, by being driven up the hill for breakfast on Day 5 before starting our ride. The 18km (11-miles) route across the top of the range—with magnificent prospects out to sea—and then down a helter-skelter of a road to the Gellibrand River is the most thrilling bit of cycling yet. Again, we're blessed with the almost perfect conditions of blue skies and almost no wind. On crossing the small bridge over the river, we turn left onto Old Ocean Road, an unsealed track that winds through shaded woods and along the grassy river flats past dairy farms and wetlands teeming with birds. This makes for a much more pleasant, traffic-free route to Princetown, our meeting spot for lunch, than the B100, which bumps along the inland hills.

Between the hamlet of Princetown and Peterborough, 32km (20 miles) up the coast, stretches part of Port Campbell National Park, the jewel in the Great Ocean Road's already dazzling crown. We have the entire afternoon to cover the 15km (9 miles) to Port Campbell, allowing us time to explore fully the scenic wonders of the ravaged limestone headland that remain hidden from the road by a broad swathe of heath. First up are the Gibson Steps, a stairway which leads down to the kelp-strewn Gibson Beach for a stunning view of sheer 70m (190ft)-high cliffs and a pair of limestone stacks, staunch sentinels against the ever-pounding waves.

STACKS AND SHIPWRECKS

Once known as the Sow and Piglets, the now more heroically named Twelve Apostles justifiably hog the tourist limelight. Don't bother to count these towering sea-stranded pillars as some are hidden behind the headlands or other stacks.

Further along is the Loch Ard Gorge, named after one of the coast's most celebrated wrecks. This is a beautiful spot to explore. And if you have a bicycle it is all the more easy to get around the sinuous paths of the gorge's extensive area. This stretches from Razorback (a jagged slither of rock) past Mutton Bird Island (one of the largest sea stacks, and a nesting place for several hundreds of thousands of birds) towards Thunder Cave and the Blowhole, through which the sea gushes inland on the stormiest days.

The main base for the national park is Port Campbell itself, a relaxed, one-street town from where it's possible to take boat rides out towards the Twelve Apostles, or even to arrange a scuba dive to check out the remains of the wrecks. This is where we spend the final night of our tour.

THE FALLEN BRIDGE

After five continuous days of cycling I feel I've got into the rhythm, but the last day's unrelenting head winds slow us all down. We climb out of Port Campbell onto the exposed plateau to view one of the final sights of the national park, London Bridge. At least it was a bridge until January 15, 1990, when the landward arch collapsed without warning. A couple stranded on the now isolated rock had to be rescued by helicopter.

There's a pretty rock grotto to be visited further along, but we're really battling with the gusts as we come into Peterborough, cross the shallow estuary of the Curdies River, and slog on towards the Bay of Martyrs. The Bay of Islands, which is like a smaller version of the Twelve Apostles, is where Konrad calls a halt to the day's cycling so we can make the Boggy Creek Hotel pub in Curdievale in time for lunch and be back in Melbourne by evening. Here, winter gales, blasting unimpeded from Antarctica, can reach up to 90kmh (55mph) and waves as high as 30m (100ft) have been recorded. Even on this blustery yet relatively mild day it's not a place to linger.

Officially, the Great Ocean Road finishes some 50km (30 miles) further west at Warrnambool where, between June and October, southern right whales and their calves can be spotted surfacing off Logans Beach. From here, it's possible to catch a train back to Melbourne, but before leaving you could do a lot worse than pedal a further 17km (11 miles) to the architecturally appealing town of Port Fairy, where there are several National Trust listed buildings, and a bustling harbour full of yachts and fishing boats.

GOING IT ALONE

INTERNAL TRAVEL

Apart from cycling, the best way to experience the Great Ocean Road is in a car. One-way car rentals are available from all the major companies in Melbourne, or you can check out the noticeboards in hostels to see if people with cars are looking for driving partners.

The V/Line Coastlink bus runs daily services from Geelong Railway Station to Apollo Bay, stopping at Torquay, Anglesea, and Lorne *en route*. There's also a Friday service (and Mondays during December and January) from Apollo Bay to Warrnambool.

Regular trains link both Geelong and Warrnambool to Melbourne's Spencer Street Station. From Warrnambool there are three daily West Coast Railway services back to Melbourne. If you're continuing up the coast towards Adelaide, there are also onward bus services from Warrnambool, Port Fairy, and Portland.

WHEN TO GO

Unpredictable is the best way to describe the weather in Victoria. There is a better chance of sunny, clear weather from November to March than at other times of the year, but always be prepared for strong winds and driving rain.

The Great Ocean Road experiences its heaviest traffic at weekends and over the holiday periods. Also, since many organized day tours start in Melbourne, it's best to get on the road early before the tourist buses arrive. This part of the Victorian coast is a very popular holiday destination from December to February; if you plan to travel during these times, book your accommodation well in advance.

PLANNING

The prevailing winds change constantly, so the Great Ocean Road is just as easily cycled in either direction. Driving between Geelong and Warrnambool takes around 5½ hours. To cycle takes between three and six days depending on how fit you are. Factor bad weather into your itinerary, as well as time spent on the beach or exploring the national parks. Don't underestimate the effort needed for the hilly sections of the route, especially the push up Lavers Hill.

If you're short on time, there are plenty of companies that offer one-day bus trips from Melbourne. Among the better options are the backpacker bus trips run by Oz Experience and Wayward Bus.

WHAT TO TAKE

☐ Cycling clothes, shoes, and gloves.
☐ Thermal or polypropylene underwear.
☐ Wet-weather gear.
☐ Sunscreen and sun hat.

HEALTH

Drink plenty of water to avoid dehydration, and cover up exposed skin with sunscreen.

Left: *Bells Beach*
Below: *The beach at Gibson Steps with its dramatic cliff stacks*

12 Riding the High Country

by Simon Richmond

Skiing and hiking are both fine ways to explore the Snowy Mountains, Australia's winter playground and summer highland escape. But to do the epic scenery full justice, saddle up for a horse trek across the alpine plains.

"And down by Kosciuszko, where the pine-clad ridges raise/Their torn and rugged battlements on high." Ken, a veteran birdwatcher, was reciting the final stanza of a poem that is as evocative to Australians as one of Shakespeare's sonnets is to the English. Ken continued, "Where the air is clear as crystal, and the white stars fairly blaze/At midnight in the cold and frosty sky." Yes, I already recognized that bit. That morning I'd poked my head out of my swag (the canvas and foam bedroll that true Aussie cowboys and campers sleep in) to discover a land

that had become encrusted overnight in a gossamer layer of ice. It might have been late spring, but the Snowy Mountains were living up to their chilly name. "It's what George Orwell called good bad poetry," noted Ken, before continuing on his way, on the lookout for singing honeyeaters, satin flycatchers, currawongs, and swallows, and leaving me resting on the grassy banks behind the Tantangara Dam wall. Here, I was enjoying lunch on the first day of a three-day horseback trek through the very country that bush poet A.B. "Banjo" Patterson had enshrined in that classic Ken had recited by heart, namely *The Man from Snowy River*.

COWBOY COUNTRY

Stretching some 500km (300 miles) from the Brindabella Ranges near Canberra to the hills outside Melbourne are the Australian Alps. Although neither particularly high nor wide, the mountains are a spectacular aberration in a sunburnt continent where barely anywhere stands 300m (1,000ft) above sea-level. The peaks become cloaked in snow during the winter, causing a flood of ski-crazy urbanites to flock to resorts such as Thredbo and Perisher Blue. But it's only the section of the Alps within New South Wales, around the headwaters of the Snowy River, that is properly known as the Snowy Mountains.

These mountains fall within the 690,000ha (1.7 million-acre) Kosciuszko National Park, which includes Mount Kosciuszko (pronounced "kozyosko"), at 2,228m (7,310ft) mainland Australia's highest mountain. It would be at the

4 You'll need stamina and a tough backside and legs to weather the Snowies' rugged terrain for three to five days on a horse; take some riding lessons before you start. The hike to Mount Kosciuszko is straightforward, with a metal walkway making the going easy. There are other more difficult treks in the area. The downhill skiing is ideal for beginners and intermediates, while the cross-country skiing is more suited to those with experience.

★★ On the horse rides you'll either be camping outside or sheltering in very basic wooden huts, which don't always have toilets and never a bathroom. At the ski resorts of Thredbo and Perisher Blue there's an excellent range of accommodation, although only Thredbo is open all year round.

⛏ You'll be given the option of wearing a helmet, although a broad-brimmed hat is recommended as an alternative to shade your face from the strong sun. A pair of gloves, a pocket knife, and a torch will also come in handy. (Note that operators provide only helmets and possibly oilskins, which you may have to hire; you will need to take your own clothing and boots.) For winter sports, all gear can be hired at the resorts (prices are slightly cheaper in the nearby towns of Cooma or Jindabyne).

north end of this park that I would begin my horseback exploration of what is also called the High Country, the rolling plains on which the pioneer settlers of the mid-19th century carved a harsh life, grazing sheep and cattle and breeding horses. I would be riding with Cochran Family Tradition Horsetreks, a relatively new operation but one with an impressive pedigree. The owner, Peter Cochran, was born in the High Country and has been in the saddle since he was a small child. Stocky and resilient, Peter slept beside his horses each night, proving to be a credible candidate for a contemporary Man from Snowy River.

THE OLD HOMESTEAD

Peter's 19-year-old son, Richard, had already been guiding a couple of guests over the weekend when I joined their party late on Sunday evening. Together with my experienced co-riders, Kate and Mel from Sydney, I had been transported by four-wheel drive along a bumpy dirt road up to the century-old homestead of Currango some 30km (19 miles) from the Snowy Mountains Highway. Rides usually begin at the Cochrans' homestead of Yaouk (the Gaelic name of one of the old Scottish counties, pronounced "yayak") 20km (12 miles) north of the sheep-grazing and trout-fishing community of Adaminaby on the Upper Murrumbidgee River. But Currango, the largest and best-preserved example of a permanent settlement above the snowline in Australia, is something special, and Peter wanted me to see it before the ride began.

The lovingly maintained wooden homestead and some 25 outbuildings—including cottages, cattle sheds, and a corral for the horses—have an idyllic location close by the Tantangara Reservoir, one of the many lakes created by the mammoth Snowy Mountains Hydroelectric Scheme. It's a popular place with weekend fishermen and hikers, so we found ourselves camping out, huddled close around the fire to ward off the suddenly chilly air. After a dinner of

HORSE-RIDING TIPS

❏ The reins should be grasped firmly in both hands, brought up short when you need to control the horse but otherwise left loose.

❏ The tip of your boot should rest in the stirrup with your heel pointing down. You should have 60 per cent of your weight on the stirrups, with the remaining 40 per cent on the saddle.

❏ When you are riding downhill, lean back in the saddle for balance; conversely, lean forward when going uphill.

❏ Kick the horse's flanks gently with your heel if you need to speed up, and don't forget to rise to the trot if you want a smoother ride.

chicken and ginger, Thai-style beef stews, and rice pilaf, followed by homemade cakes, all prepared by the resourceful cook, Jo, Rick strummed a guitar while his dad span yarns about local characters.

SADDLING UP

The following morning, the bright spring sun soon burnt away the frost. It didn't take long to learn that a horse trek is not for anyone who is in a hurry. Before you set off, there's the saddling up, plus the loading of the packhorses with supplies and swags, a procedure that can easily take over an hour, even with several hands to help. Peter also took this opportunity to replace a lost shoe on Ringo, the good-natured chestnut I would be riding.

The morning route headed towards the foothills of Mount Morgan, and then on to Patton's Creek, where Kate took a tumble while crossing the water. Honour had been regained and embarrassment forgotten by the time we stopped for lunch near the Tantangara Dam, where we bumped into Ken, the poetry-reciting birdwatcher. Richard returned from here to base with the other guests, leaving

Peter, Kate, Mel, and me to retrace our tracks across the open plains of the Gulf and then to ford a narrow stretch of the Murrumbidgee River. Hairy clumps of tussock grass and orange speckles of heather dotted this prairie, while ahead, nestling on a hillside at the edge of the gum forest, was our home for the night—Townsend's Hut, a bare-board, two-room shelter with a corrugated-iron roof and a veranda.

THE INEVITABLE FALL

Everyone pitches in on these treks. So while Peter strung up an electric fence to corral the horses, Mel and Kate gathered wood for the campfire, and I filled the billy cans with water from the nearby stream. Inside the hut, a visitors' book proved amusing reading as dinner was prepared. In the summer one writer complained of plagues of March flies ("The humans are losing"), while we'd obviously not suffered the worst of what the winter could bring: "Froze my brass knockers off," noted one past visitor.

I must have slept well, because I didn't notice the possum that sneaked in and rummaged through our food supplies during the night. Grey, threatening clouds now hung over the mountains, and the frigid air made us throw on all our clothing and long oilskin coats for good measure. The ride up the hill soon warmed me up, especially since I was having a hard time keeping the slow-paced Ringo up to speed with the rest of the group as they threaded their way between the flaking, twisting eucalyptus trees. Then, the inevitable happened. On a short but steep slope

down to a small creek, Ringo slipped and I slithered out of the saddle and into the mud. At least it was a soft landing, which is more than can be said for the pummelling my backside received every time Ringo picked up speed. Something had to be done. At lunch, back at Currango, Mel kindly demonstrated the fine art of posting, or rising to the trot, whereby the rider's rises from the saddle coincide with the fall of the horse's feet. It was something I concentrated hard on perfecting that afternoon, for the sake of my rear end.

Above: To do the epic scenery justice, saddle up for a horse trek
Inset: Currango homestead
Right: Breakfast at Currango camp

WILD HORSE TRAIL

As we rode across the Currango Plain, we soon came across enormous piles of dung. This is how wild horses, known locally as brumbies, mark out their territory. In the distance, several dots materialized as a pack of seven galloping horses, including one jet-black stallion and a foal. Not wanting our horses to end up like Patterson's

NEW SOUTH WALES & VICTORIA

CYCLING IN THE SNOWIES

Between the end of November and beginning of May mountain-biking is a sure-fire winner. The Crackenback and Snowgums chairlifts at Thredbo can both be used to transport bikes up the slopes. Bikes can be hired, along with all the necessary safety gear. An initial guided tour is a must as this will show you how to get on and off the chairlift with your bike, and which tracks you can follow. Lessons and packages, from a half-day of unlimited rides on the lifts to two- and five-day dirt camps, which teach you how to perfect your mountain-biking techniques, are available. If you fancy working up a sweat go for the Kosciuszko Summit Assault, a 16km (10-mile) ride from the Skitube terminal at Blue Cow Mountain to the peak.

"colt from Old Regret," a thoroughbred whisked away by the brumbies, Peter kept us at a safe distance where we could still view the spectacle.

The brumbies would make a couple more far-off appearances through the afternoon, and with the whiff of wild horse in his nostrils, Ringo picked up his pace. We continued across small creeks, through woods, and over more open prairie along the Seventeen Flat Route to the Blue Waterholes. The blue colour of the water running through a dramatic limestone gorge here is caused by the high content of dissolved minerals. Kangaroos, used to frequent visitors, nonchalantly hopped around close to where we rested, reviving our weary bodies with chocolate and jaw-breaking mint sweets. In warmer weather the gorge would have been an ideal place to bathe, and despite my now sore shins the visit was still well worth the extra 2½-hour return ride from our shelter for the night. Pocket's Hut, in comparison to our previous abode, was palatial, with three bedrooms attached to

a living room that boasted a working fireplace, plus a veranda and a storeroom with a ready supply of firewood.

BACK TO YAOUK

There's little chance of sleeping in on these treks. Peter was up before us all at 6am to cook a pioneer's breakfast of sausages, beans, and corn fritters, all part of the carefully researched frontier experience. Thick mist from the defrosting grasslands obscured the views through the window, but by the time we hit the trail a few hours later, a panorama of rolling plains stretched ahead of us. To our left, Peter pointed out the Goodradigbee landing ground, where an airstrip had been constructed during the building of the Snowy River hydroelectric scheme. This was one of the most important engineering projects undertaken in Australia's history, encompassing seven power stations, 16 major dams and 140km (87 miles) of tunnels. Overgrown now, the airstrip has become a stamping ground for kangaroos, which showed a polite interest in us as we passed.

We were now on the Murray Gap Trail, climbing up over a wooded hill and down into a beautiful clearing, the site of Oldfield's Hut, one of the most picturesque within the park. This weathered structure, with a chimney at one end, a wooden bar to tie up the horses, and a long veranda overlooking a garden of alpine violets, sometimes serves as an overnight base for the horse treks. On we moved, tracing the route along which stockmen once herded cattle in the spring and autumn to and from the High Country. Between the peeling snow gums, tiny purple wildflowers speckled the grass.

The 500m (1,400ft) drop from the high plateau, down through a forest of soaring trees, was steep and hard going, but by now we were within 10km (6 miles) of home. The countryside opened up again into grassy pastures, and by mid-afternoon Yaouk was in sight. It had been a unique experience to tour the Snowies on horseback, which provided an elevated perspective of the grand landscape. But there was one last place I wanted to go, where no horse could follow.

STANDING ON THE ROOF OF AUSTRALIA

Hiking to the summit of Mount Kosciuszko is something of a national pilgrimage for Australians. From the pleasant resort village of Thredbo, a chairlift saves the effort of the initial climb up 600m (1,650ft). From the lift's Crackenback Terminal, Kosciuszko's peak is a 12km (7½-mile) return journey along a raised metal walkway, put in place to protect the delicate environment. At the height of the summer, it's not uncommon to share this path with 3,000 other walkers a day.

SKIING OPTIONS

Australia's ski season is short, with unpredictable snowfall, resulting in inflated prices for lift passes and accommodation. The two main resorts within Kosciuszko National Park are Thredbo and Perisher Blue. If you have your own transport it's relatively simple to visit both during one trip to the Snowies. A network of some 50 lifts connects the previously independent ski areas of Perisher Valley, Blue Cow, Guthega, and Smiggin Holes. This spread of terrain makes Perisher Blue an excellent option for cross-country skiers. It's a good idea to take the free guided ski tour to understand how the resorts link together and how to access them via the different lifts. In contrast, Thredbo is a single large resort. Although there are fewer lifts here, they are more modern and generally faster than those at Perisher. One drawback is that in order to reach the resort's highest point at 2,037m (5,589ft) you have to use a T-bar lift on an exposed plateau that can be lashed by high winds.

Thankfully, the route was nowhere near as busy when I came to make my trip. The picturesque alpine meadows were covered with spring flowers including yellow buttercups and marsh marigolds. Gilly, our guide pointed out small cream flowers nestling beneath the melting ledges of snow or bursting from clumps of moss at the edge of crystal-clear streams. We brushed our hands across an alpine mint bush to release its fresh aroma, and in a rock cleft discovered a mountain plum pine—possibly 800 years old—stunted like a bonsai through the hardships of surviving in this unforgiving environment. In the summer, the giant granite tors that protrude from the plateau like monoliths become the breeding ground for bogon moths, a nutritious food source savoured by the Aborigines.

AT THE SUMMIT

The closer you get to the summit of Mount Kosciuszko, the greater the sensation that you are walking through a wild and desolate place. The small glacial Lake Cootapatamba (Aboriginal for "the place where the eagle drank") cowers beneath the peak, not far from Rawson's Pass. Just beyond Rawson's Pass the more challenging main range walk begins, an overnight trek that can start or finish at Charlotte Pass, the site of Australia's coldest recorded temperature of -23°C (-9°F). Gilly spun a few cautionary tales of hikers and skiers who had come a cropper in sudden changes of weather, something we experienced on the return to Thredbo as sunshine gave way to freezing sleet.

From the lake, a track winds around the mountain to the top. Standing on the rocky, treeless pinnacle we could see lingering snowdrifts melting around us, feeding the essential streams and rivers. Beyond the ring of clouds, rays of light caught the circular panorama of the Alps' most prominent peaks, including the 2,061m (5,654-foot) Mount Jagungal, a brooding mass of black basalt 40km (25 miles) to the north. I had reached the roof of Australia.

GOING IT ALONE

INTERNAL TRAVEL

You can fly to the Snowies from Sydney to Cooma on Impulse Airlines; from here it's around an hour's drive to Thredbo, Perisher, or Adaminaby. During the winter there are also weekend flights from Melbourne.

Greyhound runs coaches year round to and from Thredbo, via Cooma and Jindabyne. During the ski season, Murrays also offers direct services from both Sydney and Canberra stopping at Jindabyne, Bullocks Flat (for the Skitube train to Perisher Blue), and Thredbo. The Wayward Bus backpacker touring service runs between Sydney, Canberra, and Melbourne via the Snowies.

If you are driving, take care. The Snowies are sparsely populated, with long distances between fuel and food stops; carry plenty of both in case of emergency. Police check that you have snowchains in your car between June and October and some routes will be closed. It is a long drive to the Snowies from either Sydney or Melbourne, so break the journey or consider stopping at Bullocks Flat on the Alpine Way. Then take the Skitube, an 8km (5-mile) train ride that calls in first at Perisher Valley, just a short stroll from the ski lift, before continuing to the Blue Cow Terminal. This is actually at the top of the mountain, so it's possible to step out and ski away immediately. Combined Skitube and lift passes are available.

WHEN TO GO

Snow and freezing temperatures across the High Country mean that horse treks are primarily a spring to autumn activity (October–May). The temperature rarely rises above 24°C (75°F) in summer, but you still need to guard against sunburn due to the rarefied atmosphere. Spring is an especially pretty time. The peak ski season runs from July to the first week of September; if you are planning a trip prices drop in September and there is still a reasonable chance of decent snow cover. The Christmas and New Year holidays are the peak summer period; book accommodation well in advance and be prepared for crowds.

PLANNING

Companies that offer horse treks can be found through local tourist offices or via the Internet. Before you sign up for the longer treks, consider your level of experience. Riding in the Snowies is no Sunday amble. The horses need to be young and spirited to tackle the terrain, and to a certain extent you need to be able to follow suit. If possible, get some practice in before you undertake such a tour. Check out exactly what is included in the cost of the trek; you may need to pay extra for sleeping bags and oilskin coats if you don't bring your own. Most operators are based around Adaminaby, a 40-minute drive from Cooma, the nearest town with regular bus connections.

Entry to Kosciuszko National Park by car costs A$12 per car per day or by motorbike A$3.50. If you're planning on staying for several days or want to visit other national parks, then consider investing in an annual pass for A$60. Park fees are generally included in bus fares.

TRAVELLERS' TIP

❏ Wearing the right clothes will make a huge difference to your enjoyment and safety while on the horse trek. Elastic-sided boots are safest, as they have no laces to catch on the stirrups. Jodhpurs or riding trousers will be most comfortable as they don't have an inside seam, which could rub your leg raw; thermal longjohns or tights worn under your trousers work just as well, and keep you warm at the same time.

WHAT TO TAKE

❏ You will need boots and suitable clothing, as only helmets and possibly oil-skins will be provided by the operator. Wrap up well in winter, but don't underestimate the possibility of cold snaps and storms at other times of the year.

❏ Insect repellent will come in useful during the summer months, as will a broad-brimmed hat.

HEALTH

Hypothermia can be a serious problem in the mountains if you're not suitably prepared for cold weather. By the same token, in the rarefied atmosphere the sun can easily burn unprotected skin, so cover up and apply sunscreen liberally on bright days.

Left: *The Snowy Mountains are a spectacular contrast to the classic image of a hot, dry continent* Inset:*In winter the Snowies become Australia's premier skiing location*

NEW SOUTH WALES & VICTORIA

NEW SOUTH WALES & VICTORIA

13 Adventures in the Blue Mountains

by Simon Richmond

The Blue Mountains' name comes from the azure haze that rises from the eucalyptus forests, but it's the plunging canyons, limestone caves, and sheer cliff faces that provide the setting for the area's top thrills.

There are more comfortable places to take in the beauty of the Australian bush than dangling off a ledge, high above the stony ground, trussed up like a devotee of some sado-masochistic cult. But for sheer thrills, the combination of abseiling (also known as rappelling)—the art of using friction to control your rate of descent down a rope—and the spectacular clifftop panoramas of the Blue Mountains on a sunny day are hard to beat.

The Blue Mountains lie just two hours by road or rail from Sydney. The highest point in the National Park, which covers 247,000ha (610,000 acres) of a deeply eroded sandstone plateau, stands at a mere 1,100m (3,609ft), but it's not to conquer lofty peaks that you come here. The park protects gaping valleys and vertigo-inducing ravines, where millions of years of exposure to the elements has carved sheer cliffs and deep canyons. So remote are many of these gullies that it was only in 1994 that Wollemi pine trees, thought to have died out over 60 million years ago, were rediscovered.

To explore these magical, mysterious canyons, home to an array of exotic plant and animal life, requires bushwalking, climbing, and swimming skills.

LEARNING THE ROPES

Katoomba is the largest of the Blue Mountains' townships and is home to the area's most famous landmark, the 910m (2,986ft) Three Sisters sandstone rock stack. It's also the place to head if you want to spend a day learning to climb or abseil. I join a group of 17 game abseiling beginners—including a mother and father with their ten- and seven-year-old daughters, and a party of four on a fun-packed hen weekend—in the Australian School of Mountaineering (ASM) office for the 9:30am start. From here we're driven in two minibuses out to the training site on Mount York, some 20km (12 miles) further north.

Before we get anywhere near a rope or cliff, the ground rules and safety procedures are made crystal clear. The helmets we must wear are to protect our heads

You must have a head for heights if you want to go abseiling, but otherwise anyone can take part. For adventure caving you need to be reasonably fit, agile, and not scared of confined spaces. Most hikes involve crossing hilly terrain. Canyoning is the most challenging and potentially dangerous activity on offer, although any good operator will make safety a priority; a high level of fitness is needed and you must be able to swim.

The Blue Mountains offer an extensive range of accommodation options, including many excellent hotels and guesthouses. Apart from the longer hikes, it's possible to complete most activities in a day and then return to Sydney. An overnight stay in the mountains is a better option, especially since the area has some great restaurants and cafés (the locals call their cuisine "food with altitude").

For hiking, you will need walking boots, binoculars, a compass, and maps. Operators provide all the equipment required for caving, canyoning, and climbing. If you plan to do any climbing independently, you will, of course, require all your own gear.

from falling rocks and other items. We're then shown how to put on the harness, to which is attached a metal clip known as a carabiner and an abseiling device called a figure of eight."No one is to go more than a body length towards a cliff edge without first being attached to a rope," instructs Chris, and with that we walk down into the gully where a range of routes have been roped up for us to practise on.

FOCUS THE FEAR

Abseiling essentially boils down to having the confidence that, when you step off the cliff into thin air, your rope and harness will hold you. We begin on a gentle incline that even my granny could have walked up. On the ground stands my partner (or belayer), who holds the rope in a tug-of-war position, but cutting enough slack to let me descend. When I'm ready to go, I shout out, wait for the reply "On belay" so that I know my partner is in position, and then simply step off.

As if standing on flat ground, I keep myself perpendicular to the cliff face to avoid head-butting the rock or tipping head over heels on the rope. "It's OK to be afraid," comforts Chris, who also advises "focusing the fear" to concentrate on the right technique. So that's exactly what I do as I approach the end of a ledge; I let the rope out so my bottom sinks lower than my feet, push off, and swing into the rock below. It begins to feel like child's play, and to prove the point, ten-year-old Alex follows me down the cliff.

After a hearty lunch of sandwiches, hot soup, muffins, and fruit, I join the "adrenalin-junkie" (as opposed to the "love-of-life") group for a couple of more extreme abseils. This time we're belayed from above. As I go over the edge I can feel the wind rustling around my helmet and my knees start to tremble. Around me the damp leaves of the eucalyptus trees sparkle in the sunlight, while climbers work their way up cliffs like human spiders. With such beguiling distractions, my fast-diminishing fear doesn't stand a chance.

THE RUSTLERS' HIDEAWAY

When I check into my guesthouse that evening, I find the place decked out with tinsel and streamers, and turkey and plum pudding on the menu. In the topsy-turvy world of the Blue Mountains, the austral winter season (late June–late August) is Yulefest time, an excuse to indulge in Christmas rituals that are out of place in steamy December. Sadly, I wake to find that Santa has bypassed the foot of my bed and rain clouds have enveloped Katoomba. Changeable and distinctly cooler weather is something that you need to prepare for, but fortunately there are adventure options on even the wettest days.

On a day like this, the best place to be is underground. The Jenolan Caves, on the western edge of the Kanangra Boyd National Park, 175km (109 miles) from Sydney, are an eye-popping network of limestone caverns. Before they started to be properly explored in 1838, cattle rustlers used to hide out here. You can understand the sense in this after negotiating the twisting hillside road that leads

THE ABSEILING ABC

Before stepping off that cliff, run through the following checklist for safety's sake:

A is for anchor—give the anchor rope a tug to check it's in place.

B is for buckles—touch each one to check that the straps are doubled back.

C is for carabiner—make sure that the gate clip is closed.

D is for descender—is the rope threaded correctly through the figure of eight?

E is for everything else—check your helmet, and make sure there are no loose straps or strands of hair that may get caught in the rope.

F is for friend—make vocal contact with your belay partner to let him or her know that you're ready to go, then wait for the reply before you jump off.

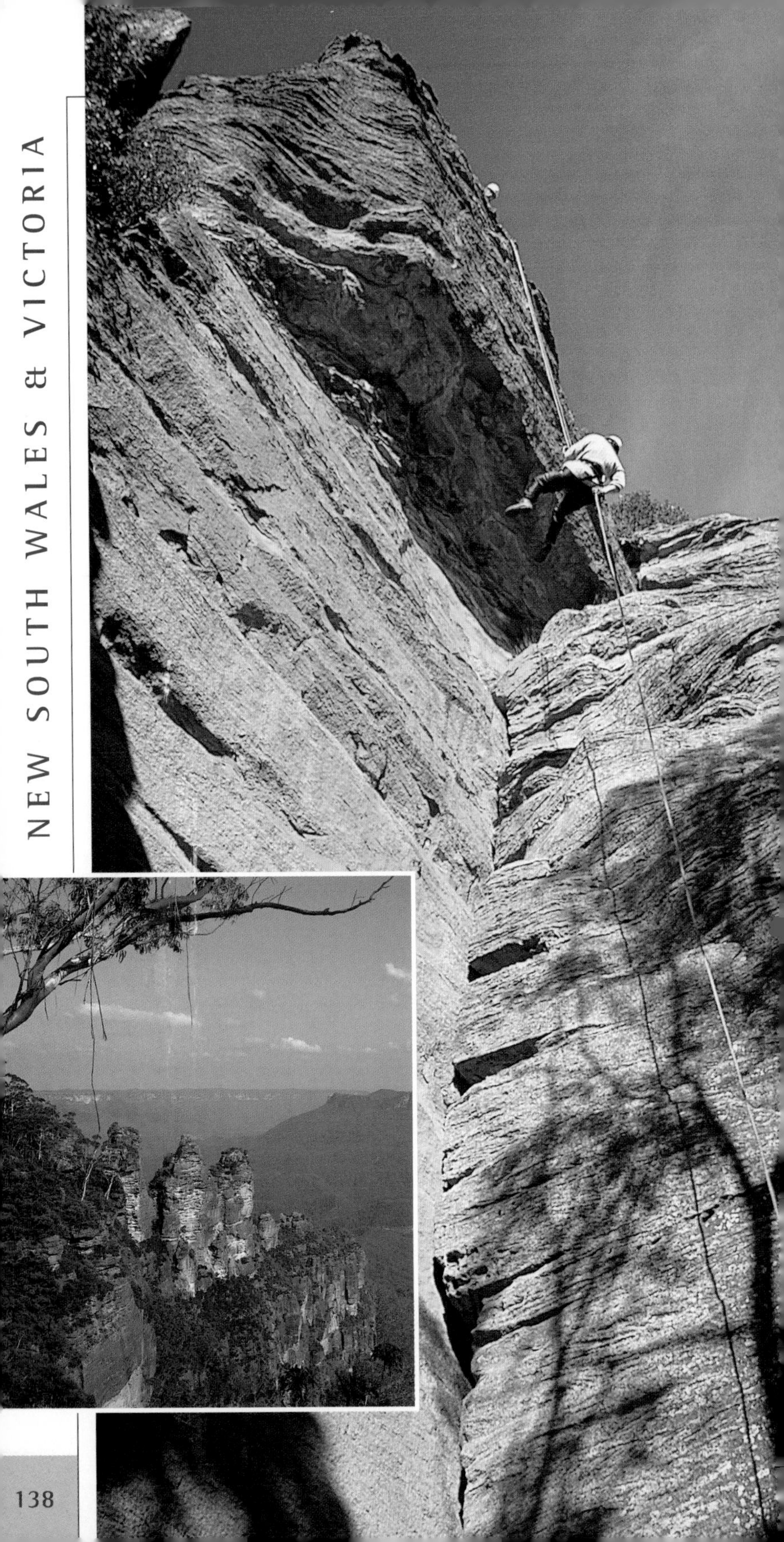

Left: *Adrenalin rush—abseiling down the sheer cliffs of the Blue Mountains*
Inset: *The Three Sisters sandstone rock stack*
Above: *All equipment is checked and double-checked before you go over the edge*

down to them, past the exotic Blue Lake, its aquamarine colour caused by dissolved limestone. Nine of the caves are open daily for guided tours that last from one to two hours. If you're short on time, rather than taking two separate tours, opt instead for the Jenolan Experience, a two-hour trip through highlights of the Temple of Baal, and River and Lucas caves.

AROUND THE S-BEND

Viewing the prettily lit Jenolan caverns, with their spectacular stalactite and stalagmite formations, from the concrete paths and steps will be exertion enough for many. But having plunged down the Plughole and slithered around the S-bend, I'd heartily agree that to have the most fun at Jenolan you need to get down on your hands and knees. The daily Plughole tour is a highly enjoyable introduction to the addictive sport of adventure caving, also known as potholing. When it's not raining, the tour begins with an abseil into the sinkhole, a gaping

NEW SOUTH WALES & VICTORIA

cavity in the hill above the Grand Arch. From here you enter Elder Cave, once a show cave for walk-in tourists. The route to the S-bend is a twisting, narrow passage that requires some body contortion, and takes in the Armchair, the Saddle, and the Wharf, all rock features that must be deftly negotiated. Thankfully, experienced guides are on hand to lead me, and fellow cavers, through the limestone maze. Boiler suits are provided to protect our clothes, and our miners' helmets have lamps with hefty battery packs that need to be swivelled round our waists as we manoeuvre our way through the gaps. No sooner am I up off my belly from the S-bend than I'm back down again to squeeze through one of the two Windows, a couple more narrow clefts in the limestone.

No daylight filters into these caves, as proved when we all turn off our lamps to experience the total blackness. Still, we find signs of life: a small puddle contains microscopic life-forms known as springtails; radiatta pine tree-roots dangle from above; and at the exit to the sinkhole, the guides point out the resident spiders stalking their lunch of cave crickets.

THE SIX FOOT TRACK

When tourism began in earnest to the Jenolan Caves in the late 19th century, the journey from Sydney took 24 hours. The caves were so popular that a faster route needed to be found, a feat achieved in 1884 when a government survey party crossed the Megalong Valley from Katoomba. The 42km (26-mile) bridle track—2m (6ft) in width, hence its name—slashed the journey time to less than eight hours.

The new route proved a hit with walkers and, despite periods of neglect down the decades, remains a local favourite, being the second most popular overnight bushwalk in Australia after Tasmania's Overland Track. Much of original route can still be followed today (it is clearly marked), and in so doing you'll gain a first-hand appreciation of the titanic

geological forces that have shaped the Blue Mountains' undulating topography. Only the supremely fit should aim to break the record time for covering the track, which stands at 3 hours 12 minutes and was set during the annual marathon run. Hardy backpackers could cover the distance in two days, camping overnight at Alum Creek, which is roughly the midpoint; to do this you'll need to hike with all your own gear and food, and arrange to be picked up from the end of the track.

The most pleasant way to cover the distance, however, is to take three days over it, and to go with a company that will arrange to transport your luggage between camps. This is not entirely the softy's option; even organized trips involve a fair amount of pitching in and roughing it. Nor should the actual walk itself be underestimated. The Six Foot Track mightn't be hardened bushwhacker's territory, but it still covers its fair share of steep gradients.

ACROSS THE TIGHTROPE

The first of the dramatic inclines, if you start at the Katoomba end, is near Explorer's Tree, and this is where I join a 16-strong group shepherded by Adam from Great Australian Walks, one of the most experienced trekking companies running trips along the track.

Before we start down the steep wooden steps, which drop 500m (1,350ft) or so into lush Nellie's Glen, Adam points out the nearby piles of stones that mark convicts' graves dating from the 1830s. Also visible along the route are remnants of settlers' cottages, but it's not the man-made features that make the Six Foot Track such a memorable way to reach Jenolan. Rather, it's the surrounding nature, from the towering mountain ash trees and the king ferns of Nellie's Glen, to the rolling pastures of the Megalong Valley and the rocky Cox's River with its inviting bathing pools.

It's particularly fine to walk the track in spring, as I'm now doing, some few months after my abseiling and caving experiences. Wildflowers add bursts of colour along the way, including bright yellow wattle and bushes of tiny, purple, native orchids, a swathe of which we pass after lunch. There are plenty of birds to spot, too, such as bright red crimson rosellas and black cockatoos. If you want to catch sight of wallabies and grey kangaroos, you'd be better off walking solo (and early in the morning), but even the largest group is guaranteed to see the odd cow munching away in the forest.

The biggest thrill of the first day comes when we cross Cox's River using Bowtell's Swing Bridge. This metal bridge, spanning 90m (300ft), is suspended 30m (100ft) above the river and is perfectly safe as long as you adhere to the written rule: "Strictly one person maximum." Edging slowly across the swinging construction is the closest I've come to walking a highwire. If you're not comfortable using the bridge, it's possible to cross at ground level further upstream as long as the river isn't in full flood.

CONQUERING THE BLACK RANGE

There's a good campsite just 500m (550yd) beyond the bridge, and this is also where Great Australian Walks has a comfortable bush lodge, with cosy bunk beds, hot showers, and log fires for its guests. Nibbles and wine are served on arrival, so that everyone is soon in the mood for the barbecue dinner.

The next morning, after a breakfast of cereals and toast, we're on the track at the civilized hour of 9am. This is a tough day, during which we'll be climbing from the valley, at 400m (1,300ft) to the top of the Black Range, at over 1,000m (3,300ft). It begins beguilingly easily, with a steady incline to the pastures of the old Kyangatha Homestead, where we pass six Shetland ponies frolicking in a field. There are two small streams to be crossed prior to lunch and one more after, before the sustained climb up the ridge of the Black Range. A fire is roaring on our arrival at the second night's camping

spot, this time in tents, and a supper of chicken stew, rice, green beans, and plum pudding and custard is on the go.

The third day's route starts along a wide fire trail shaded by gum trees that runs between the Jenolan State Forest and the Kanangra Boyd National Park. The paved road to Jenolan now follows part of the original track, so we take a deviation that runs parallel to it through the forest before rejoining the route at Binda Flats, a cleared area once cultivated as a vegetable garden for residents at the caves. The final downhill section is rocky and steep, and at one point narrows to just 30cm (1ft) rather than 2m (6ft). By the time we reach Carlotta's Arch, the end is literally in sight. Visible through this dramatically eroded limestone gap is the luminous Blue Lake, while just over the hill is the inviting form of Caves House, where celebratory beers and cappuccinos are enjoyed by all.

MORE CANYONING OPTIONS

Canyons are graded from 1, for beginners with no previous experience, to 4, the most difficult, strenuous, and challenging. The most popular Grade 1 choice in the Blue Mountains is Grand Canyon, where escorted groups are trained in abseiling techniques in the morning and then proceed by rope 15m (50ft) down to the canyon floor for a short exploration that involves some scrambling, wading, and swimming. Twister is a Grade 2, similar to Fortress Creek in that it's possible to explore if you've not been abseiling before and are not afraid of a water jump or two. Grade 3 adventures include Hole in the Wall, in the northwestern Newnes Plateau, and Claustral, reckoned to be the most adrenalin-pumping option of the regular canyoning trips. Its thrills include long abseils, water jumps, and an underwater swim through a tunnel.

THE ULTIMATE CHALLENGE

It's summer before I return to Katoomba once again, this time to go canyoning, the ultimate challenge in my programme of Blue Mountain adventures. Because the water flowing through the canyons can be freezing cold, it is best to explore them when the weather has warmed up. Even so, it's wise to be prepared for all conditions, so the suggested clothing list sent to me by the trip's organizers, ASM, includes rain jacket, fleece or warm sweater, beanie (woolly hat), thermal underwear, and spare shoes. "You will get very wet!" it warns.

None of this has deterred the group of seven other novice canyoners, all eager to explore Fortress Creek, a medium-grade canyon suitable for confident beginners.

Right: *Braving a jump in Fortress Creek: it's important to bend your knees to lessen the impact, especially as it's impossible to gauge the depth of the black water*
Inset: *Packing for the start of our canyoning trip*
Below: *The intense colour of Blue Lake is caused by minerals dissolved from limestone*

Reassuringly, our guides, Carl and Dave, are both highly conscious of ensuring the group's safety—a factor that is vital in the confined, potentially dangerous environment of the canyon.

Before we set off on the drive to the head of the trail that leads into the canyon, we're provided with our kit: wetsuit, helmet, harness for abseiling and a waterproof rubber backpack for carrying our gear. We also have a dry bag for storing things—most importantly, spare clothes and our packed lunch—safely away from the water. Brand-new, dazzlingly-white plimsolls are also available for us as a substitute for own footwear. I suspect they won't stay this white for too long.

TAKING THE PLUNGE

We have to hike for just under an hour across Fortress Ridge, spectacularly carpeted in white, yellow, purple, and red wildflowers, before heading steeply downhill to the point where the canyoning proper begins. Wetsuits are pulled on, and our other gear is carefully sealed in the dry bags. We then wade into the narrow, shallow stream, which gurgles around rocks and under lowslung ledges and branches.

It's less than five minutes before we meet the first challenge, a water jump of a couple of metres into a deep pool. Carl goes first, and after he does so tells us to keep our knees bent to break our impact as we hit the water. The icy water immediately refreshes me after the steamy hike into the canyon. With the protection of the wetsuit and thermal underwear there's little chance of chilling down too quickly, although the onset of hypothermia is something you need to watch for at all times. In addition to the lush ferns and soaring gum trees that stretch for sunlight from the canyon floor, there's plenty of wildlife to be found. Carl scoops up a plump tadpole the size of his little finger from water, and later shows us a yabbie, a freshwater crayfish with a red colour that makes it look as if it's already been cooked. Everywhere are spiders' webs, and on one sun-drenched rock sits a baby eastern water dragon, a lizard that can grow as long as a child's arm.

THE BEST VIEW

Earlier in the day, I had stood at Echo Point in Katoomba and looked out toward the Three Sisters and the Jamison Valley. It's a marvellous ridge-line panorama, but in it's own way, the view looking up from deep in the heart of a narrow canyon, such as Fortress Creek, where shafts of light catch the foliage, the water gurgles around you, and the rock walls billow out above, is just as breathtaking.

As we continue downstream, the canyon experience really begins to take hold, and I find it easy to imagine myself in some Indiana Jones epic, forging deep into an unknown land. And then the pipe dream in which I star as an adventure hero comes smack up against the reality of a water jump twice as high as the last. With heart pounding, I'm the last to take the leap, the only reassurance being my colleagues' whoops for joy at their own survival. After this, a 6m (20ft) abseil down slippery, overhanging rocks is a doddle. There's not much more of the canyon through which to swim and wade, before suddenly the water disappears underground and it's back to scrambling over huge boulders towards the light. As we emerge into the open air, the creek reappears, spreading out into a wider channel and forming whirlpools before plunging hundreds of metres over a broad cliff into the Grose Valley.

We dry off in the welcome sunshine, tucking into our sandwiches with grateful gusto, our canyon experience at an end and a strenuous uphill hike back to the minibus lying ahead. "With a view like this," says Dave, motioning to the yawning valley and sheer cliff faces spread out before us, "it doesn't matter what you bring for your lunch, it always tastes great." This is a tad unfair on the quite decent sandwich rolls, but we all know what he means.

GOING IT ALONE

INTERNAL TRAVEL

From Sydney's Central Station there are hourly trains to Mount Victoria, with stops at all the Blue Mountain villages. Combined rail and bus day-trip packages can be bought and there are also direct bus tours from Sydney, such as those offered by Mountain Escapes and Wayward Bus.

If you want to get off the beaten track, it's best to have your own transport. Car hire is widely available in Sydney, and the drive to the Blue Mountains along the Great Western Highway takes around two hours. There are also several car rental operations in Katoomba. There are a couple of bike rental outlets near the station and in Katoomba, and the Y.H.A. rents bikes out to its guests.

WHEN TO GO

It rains year round in the Blue Mountains, although the best weather occurs between September and May. Come in spring if you want to see the wildflowers, or in autumn for the changing foliage colours. Late June to late August sees the Blue Mountains come over all Christmassy for the Yulefest, when it will certainly be cold and wet. At any time of year you'll find the area much less crowded—and cheaper—during the week. Some guesthouses only take bookings for weekends as a two-day package, sometimes including meals.

PLANNING

To do the Blue Mountains full justice, taking in a few bushwalks and some adventure-tour options, you will need to give yourself five to seven days in the area. Katoomba is adrenalin-central as far as adventure-activity operators are concerned, but you could just as easily be based in Leura, Blackheath, or Jenolan. There's a lot of competition between the adventure-tour operators; check around and do not decide on price alone. Look into itineraries and what's included. If possible, meet your guides beforehand and talk to people who have taken a previous tour. Longer expeditions like The Six Foot Track require some planning, especially if you are going independently. Reckon on spending at least one night camping on the track.

TRAVELLERS' TIPS

❑ If there is a rock fall when you are abseiling, do not look up. Instead, look into the cliff face and the helmet you are wearing will protect your head.

❑ If you stay in the area rather than making a day trip from Sydney, you will not only be less tired but will also be able to enjoy some of the great local "food with altitude."

WHAT TO TAKE

Operators will provide all the equipment but if you are are going independently, abseilers and rock climbers will want to invest in a pair of climbing shoes, gloves, helmet, harness, slings, ropes, carabiners, and an abseiling device such as a figure of eight. Wetsuits, closed-in footwear (an old pair of trainers or plimsolls is best), and a helmet are essential for canyoning. Most canyons also require abseiling gear, and it's a good idea to have dry bags and thermal underwear. The usual camping equipment is required for any overnight treks. It can get very chilly at night, so bring more, rather than less clothing.

HEALTH

Wearing the correct clothing for both wet and cold conditions, particularly during the winter months, can help prevent hypothermia if you're caught in sustained rain. Play it safe by boiling or purifying all water taken from streams before drinking it.

FURTHER READING

For the fullest coverage of the state's national parks, turn to the *National Parks Association (N.P.A.)* guide in two volumes—covering the parks of northern and southern N.S.W. respectively.

Neil Paton's *Walks in the Blue Mountains* (Kangaroo Press) is a detailed guide to scores of walks in the area, mainly of a day in length, but several stretching over longer periods.

National Park Explorer, Around Sydney (Child & Associates) by Alan Fairley is a readable guide to the Ku-ring-gai Chase, Blue Mountains and Royal National Parks, including geological, flora and fauna details as well as suggested walks.

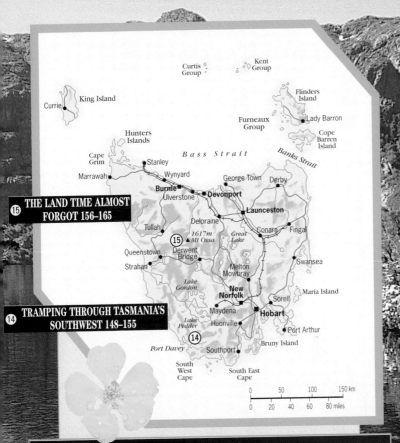

TASMANIA

T his lushly green, mountainous island at the foot of an otherwise dust-dry and flat continent is nirvana for the adventurous traveller. Over one-third of the state is protected, either by World Heritage Area, national park, or forest reserve, in regions that encompass mountains, rivers, lakes, and a rugged coastline that has been shaped by savage Antarctic winds. Tasmania is on a human scale (it is about the same size as Ireland or West Virginia), and its quiet roads are easily toured by car or bicycle. If you fly here, you'll arrive either in the capital, Hobart, or in the second city, Launceston, both pleasant and historically interesting places to base yourself. The Cradle Mountain Lake St. Clair National Park shouldn't be missed, but just as awe-inspiring is the Franklin Gordon Wild Rivers National Park on the west coast. But if you really want to get away from it all, fly down to the Tasmanian Wilderness World Heritage Area, in the state's windswept southwest corner.

Peaceful Crater Lake in Cradle Mountain Lake St. Clair National Park

14 Tramping through Tasmania's Southwest

by Matt Cawood

Tasmania's southwest is an isolated region of spectacular and sometimes severe beauty. Its forests, heaths, bays, and mountains have barely been touched by civilization, and its air is reputedly the cleanest in the world.

While Australia is generally best known for its dry and sunburnt open spaces, the far southwest region of Tasmania is decidedly different. Here, the landscape is reminiscent of Scotland: rocky mountains and damp, heath-covered moorlands, with a climate better known for its savage gales and rain instead of the sun of the mainland. The region possesses a wild beauty alchemized from seldom-scaled peaks, pristine beaches, the great blue-black sprawl of Port Davey and Bathurst Harbour—two faces of the same deep inlet—and isolation. For all Australia's vastness, few places have the remote quality of this region, part of the 1.38 million ha (3.41 million acre) Tasmanian Wilderness World Heritage Area. Although Aboriginal people lived here for millennia, the inhospitable climate has guarded against the encroachment of European civilization. The only way to reach the southwest corner is via a five- to ten-day walk with a pack, a long day on a boat, or a 45-minute plane flight. Once there, there are no shops, no phones, no conventional accommodation. You are left to explore the area, for hours or days depending on your whim, on its own terms.

FLYING IN

Few conventional tours operate in the southwest. I chose to visit the area with Hobart-based Par Avion. The family-owned company operates most of the flights that land in Melaleuca, site of the southwest's only airstrip and permanent habitation (a couple who operate a tin mine). With Chris, a friend who farms cattle, I turn up at the Par Avion base late one November afternoon to meet a scheduled flight, only to receive my first lesson in southwest travel: schedule in time for bad weather. Clouds over the Hartz Mountains have "socked in" the route. The first night of our long-anticipated adventure is ignominiously spent at a nearby caravan park, where we eat pizza.

Cloud still obscures the overland route the following morning, but nevertheless Chris and I, plus four others, jam into a little single-engined aircraft. The

---

3 In summer, it's possible to take a morning flight to Melaleuca, tramp down to Cox Bight or New Harbour, and return on an afternoon flight—a comfortable if energetic day, full of spectacular scenery. A multi-day walk is more demanding, especially in bad weather, but the rewards are commensurate with effort. Conversely, a trip aboard *Southern Explorer* may be completely relaxing.

★ Glorious one minute, lousy the next, the weather can reverse within hours. If you're a walker, this may cause some disagreeable moments. If you choose to use Par Avion's camp, you're assured of at least having a dry bed and good food. On board *Southern Explorer*, you have all the comforts of home, and almost certainly better views.

 Take clothes for wet, cold, and hot weather as all can occur on the same day. Sunscreen and a sun hat are necessary, and all-leather boots and calf-high waterproof gaiters make for the most comfortable walking. Among walkers' equipment should be warming foods and plenty of chocolate for energy.

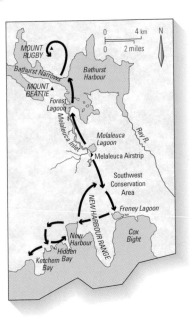

The Southwest Tasmanian Wilderness

tres along the South Coast Track to the coast, and then follow other tracks that lead into the southwest corner of Tasmania, a place with a cockleshell arrangement of ranges interspersed with lovely bays. Setting off past the scars of the tin-mining operations, we soon discover that wet and muddy feet are inescapable.

MOORLAND

Any qualms about the mud are soon overwhelmed by delight at the flowers. The peaty ground supports a tough heath made up of shrubs and grasses. We tread past an ever-changing display thick with the purple pompoms of melaleuca, yellow native primrose, golden pea and white waratah, to name a few of the moorland's 165 plant species. Skylarks sing from the heath around us, and we note the first of many wombat scats (droppings), their oblong shape hinting at a marvel of intestinal engineering. Despite odd tracts of mud, extensive stretches of boardwalk allow us to step out well along the valley to our first destination, a bay called Cox Bight. We pause only for lunch, during which we briefly exchange greetings with a couple heading for the Melaleuca strip after a seven-day walk from Cockle Creek. They prove to be the only people we see in three days of exploration.

spectacular vista that scrolls past our drizzle-streaked windows—a wild, wave-smashed coastline of jagged cliffs interspersed with virginal white beaches—looks untamed and uncomfortably bleak. Yet when the plane touches down onto the white gravel of the Melaleuca strip and the engine stills, we find ourselves emerging into a benign, if sullen, day. A single skylark sings into the great breezy silence. A sign saying "South Coast Track" points to the heath across the strip; we take its lead.

MAKING TRACKS

Walking the South Coast Track as it meanders for 85km (52 miles) is one of the world's great wilderness experiences: the route traverses mountain ranges, travels along pristine beaches, and plunges through tracts of rain forest. There are no concessions to civilization and each of the 2,000 walkers who use it each year must carry all their food and shelter. Depending on the weather and the fitness of those negotiating it, the journey can take between six and ten days. We have just four days of walking time and want to explore at a leisurely pace. Our choice is to walk a few kilome-

OCEAN AND RANGE

The blue-green Southern Ocean appears at Cox Bight after a gentle walk between two bare ranges and a short push through heavy scrub. This rocky beach is unlike anything on mainland Australia: heavy, limb-like strands of kelp lie stranded among the rocks and the whorls of unfamiliar shells dot the sand. A cold surf rolls in from a sea whose windswept aspect emphasizes that there is nothing between us and Antarctica. Having drunk our fill of the lonely sea, we backtrack, leave the main path, and make for New Harbour, a

large bay to the west where we intend to camp. On the map, our destination is just over 4km (2½ miles) away; in reality, the New Harbour Range intervenes. There's a track worn over the range, but the vulnerable ground has become so eroded by the passage of boots that it has been closed indefinitely for regeneration. These days, you either blaze your own path over, or you go round. Reluctant to backtrack, we start climbing, and soon discover that pioneering a path through heath up the steep side of a 556m (1,824ft) range is not an easy matter. Tough and unyielding knee-high bushes argue with every step, and a slippery jelly-like fungus that grows beneath scrub on damp ground makes for treacherous footing.

HARBOURSIDE CAMP

The emerging view of Cox Bight and the mountains beyond is spectacular. New Harbour gleams invitingly below, and when we set off downhill it looks a gentle saunter away. It isn't. We flounder through a scrub-choked gully, and tramp

Left: *Our path led us along rainforest tracks within earshot of surf*
Inset: *Access to the area is easiest by plane*
Below: *Climbing up the steep slopes of New Harbour Range on the way to Hidden Bay; the distinctive sweep of Cox Bight lies behind us*

down long slopes for about two hours, until we enter a gloomy rainforest within earshot of surf. When we emerge, it is approaching 9pm, but in the southern twilight we find a sublime campsite in trees fronted by a wide bed of moss bordering a dark stream. With tents pitched, we soon discover that it really was worth carrying steak, avocados, and a flask of red wine over the range.

The ringing calls of black currawongs and green rosellas feeding in the surrounding forest lend ambience to our first tentside breakfast. The stream that flows around our camp and out across the beach into the sea is, typically for the area, a deep inky black—a product of peat tannins. Although the water is deliciously drinkable, ever-present sea spray drifting over the heath has given it the same ionic composition as seawater.

After leaving our tents to steam off the night's dew in their idyllic setting, we wade knee-deep through the stream, boots in hand, and walk barefoot down the long beach in brilliant morning sun. We've scheduled a light walk of about 14km (9 miles) to Ketchum Bay and back. At the end of the beach trail climbs through luxuriant rainforest—a place of mossy fallen trunks and trickling streams—before it emerges onto heath.

The white ribbon of gravel winds down to Hidden Bay, another exquisite inlet, where we eat lunch and doze amid rocks beneath a cliff face on which flowers bloom. About 17km (10½ miles) off the Hidden Bay beach lies Maatsuyker Island, site of Australia's southernmost lighthouse.

VISTAS

The morning breeze has strengthened to a wind when we negotiate the last three ridges to Ketchum Bay. In places, the track has eroded to a chest-deep slit in the hillside, reinforcing the point that the area's soils are fragile. We linger at the top of each ridge, buffeted by gusts off the sea. In the days of sail, onshore gales sealed the fate of most of the 18 ships that sank along 120km (74 miles) of the coastline around Tasmania's southwestern tip. Today, the only visible vessel is a rock lobster boat setting traps.

Chilly wind blasts ensure that our stay is short. We make for home, reaching each ridge top in progressively more wondrous light. We reach the spine of the last ridge before New Harbour as the last rays of sun hit the sheltered waters of the bay. The rock-lobster vessel has moored below us, a small patch of white afloat in the harbour's deep turquoise expanse. Across mountains and valleys to the north, fanfares of sunlight break through the cloud and highlight patches of the immense uninhabited landscape. The drama has gone by the time we descend to the beach, but so has the wind: we emerge from rainforest into a calm seaside twilight. On our approach to our tents we startle a pair of red-necked wallabies, which leap off into the rainforest. A wombat foraging near our tents freezes. We stop and watch. After a moment the wombat quietly, unhurriedly, ambles away into the scrub.

BENEATH THE HEATH

The following morning is clear and fresh, and we make a leisurely departure when the sun is high, after eating,

---

VISITOR ETHICS

Tips for minimizing your impact on the World Heritage Area:

- ❏ Take a fuel stove. Wood fires are not allowed in the Southwest.
- ❏ Take a lightweight trowel to bury faeces and paper. Bury waste at least 100m (330ft) from waterways and campsites, and to a depth of at least 15cm (6 in).
- ❏ Everything taken in to the World Heritage Area must be carried out.
- ❏ Wash cooking equipment at least 50m (165ft) from waterways. Use sand and a scouring pad to clean pots, not detergent.
- ❏ Avoid widening tracks, even if it means ploughing through mud. Every step onto new ground increases erosion of the fragile soils.
- ❏ When walking in a trackless area, fan out. One person's passage is less damaging that that of a party walking in single file.

---

photographing, and packing, during which we marvel at the gear required to keep modern man alive for three days. When we leave New Harbour this time, it's to head north, across the heath back to Melaleuca, where we have an appointment with a boat. This is walking as we'd expected it. The track is squelchingly muddy, and where it dips through gullies it is crowded by rucksack-snagging scrub. It's unexpectedly hot, and except for a flock of yellow-tailed black cockatoos wailing from a stand of trees, there doesn't appear to be much animal life in the heath. This is an illusion, as the wombat scats attest and the vegetation is honeycombed with runs. Twice we scare another retiring creature of the heath, the brilliant green ground parrot. This bird has a reluctant relationship with the air. Those who fail to see the parrot may hear its bell-like call around dusk.

ORANGE-BELLIED PARROTS

Near the Melaleuca airstrip is a well-constructed viewing hide built overlooking a feeding platform that is frequented by the orange-bellied parrot, one of Australia's most endangered birds. There are only about 150 orange-bellied parrots left in the wild, so the opportunity to get a close-up look at one—a small, gorgeously coloured bird a little bigger than a budgerigar—is a privilege reserved almost exclusively for those who visit lonely Melaleuca. We were in the hide for perhaps just two minutes before a parrot turned up.

THE MAN FROM MELALEUCA

The most prominent human heritage in the southwest lies a short walk beyond the bird hide: the former home of "the Man from Melaleuca," Deny King, a tin miner who until his death in the early 1990s welcomed all visitors to his lonely, windswept retreat. He built the walkers' huts beyond his house, the only regular accommodation for visitors in the entire southwest.

Deny's house, now intermittently occupied by his daughters and their families, is hidden in a lush temperate garden. When it was built, it sat exposed on the heath, its Nissen hut-style semi-circular roof designed to resist the gales that sweep the moorland in winter. Deny's name has been given to another rare resident of the southwest, King's holly. Since Deny found the holly in 1937, botanists have determined that there are only 500 living specimens, all clumped together in one piece of bushland in the Cox Bight area. The species reproduces by cloning, so that every plant is exactly the same and fossilized pollen indicates that the same cloned plant has lived in the area for at least 43,600 years!

SOFT OPTIONS

Late in the afternoon a Par Avion flight drones into the airstrip. It disgorges its passengers in the form of guide Greg and three others, whom we join in a small boat to plough up Melaleuca Inlet. Champions of the wilderness have successfully fought all attempts to develop conventional tourism facilities in the southwest, but Par Avion maintains a small camp hidden in the trees in a corner of Forest Lagoon, an offshoot of Bathurst Harbour. With the boat tied up at some rocks, we walk on almost invisible trails to a small gathering of tents and an open-sided deck-cum-kitchen hemmed in by rainforest. Chris and I opt to pitch our tents down on the shores of Forest Lagoon, where we find even the superlative views across the mirror-still water to 771m (2,530ft) Mount Rugby improved with an avocado and a splash of whisky on the beach at sunset. However, we are happy to abandon our camp food for a meal of Atlantic salmon and wine up in the kitchen. As we are eating, a long, pink, whiskered snout snuffles through the cracks in the floorboards. The owner later reveals itself as the aptly named long-nosed potoroo, a football-sized marsupial. This one has developed a knack for scrounging. Those who want to lounge around the camp do so, while more energetic visitors are taken by dinghy to climb peaks and explore islands. The only other summertime accommodation in the southwest is aboard the Par Avion motorboat, the 18m (58ft), nine-berth *Southern Explorer*. We have an appointment with *Southern Explorer* the following afternoon.

BOATING, SOUTHWEST STYLE

Dark clouds begin to gather as we pick our way inland from Forest Lagoon on our last walk. We follow some ridges up to a promontory called Mount Beattie and lunch while the weather grows steadily bleaker over a wide and empty landscape. Beneath us the narrows divide Bathurst Harbour from Port Davey. On either side, water stretches away to jagged mountains in the east and an island-dotted sea in the west. Our descent from Mount Beattie's steep sides is ungraceful. I take a wrong turn, and Chris follows a wombat

TASMANIA

pad, or run, into scrub so thick that he finds himself hanging suspended over a gully. But by mid-afternoon we are stepping aboard the *Southern Explorer* at its mooring on an abandoned fisherman's jetty. We take a much-needed shower before joining shipboard society.

For the next three days, with six others we cruise over the sheltered waters of Bathurst Harbour and adjoining Port Davey. The southwest's bad weather is upon us, but we don't mind. We are snug in the saloon, eating the fabulous meals prepared by Bob, our cook and guide, or out exploring a corner of the harbour on foot, secure in the knowledge that hot showers and dry feet await us.

BATHURST HARBOUR

Skipper Don motors us up to the mouth of Port Davey and moors while we take the dinghy into Settlement Point, a spit jutting into the Davey River. Settled by a few families briefly in the 1880s, Port Davey, a magnificent harbour was hopefully surveyed in the mid 1800s, but no house was ever erected there. Even in late November, ostensibly during the southwest's

spring, the overgrown site of the long abandoned huts at Settlement Point presents a cold and damp prospect.

THE LAST GREAT VIEW

On our final morning in the southwest, Chris and I rose early. In a sombre dawn, Bob takes us in the dinghy to a tiny beach at the foot of Mount Rugby, a rocky peak that has dominated our horizons for the past seven days. It takes us two hours to get to the top, the last section a scramble in dense fog. Enveloped in damp grey, we only know we have reached our destination when we can climb no further. Luckily, as we are shouldering our packs to return, the fog begins to thin, until we are standing in clear sun with immense skeins of mist looping and eddying around us. Before us spreads our playground of the past seven days, a vast landscape of ranges and moorlands and the shining spread of Bathurst Harbour, with the *Southern Explorer* cruising slowly below. It was disconcerting to think that in a few hours we would be in Hobart, dealing with such distractions as telephones and money. But right now, we had everything we could wish for.

Left: *Orange-bellied parrot*
Below: *From the flanks of Mount Rugby, we viewed our playground of the past seven days*

GOING IT ALONE

INTERNAL TRAVEL

Flying is the quickest and most popular way to visit the southwest. Two small Hobart-based airlines, Par Avion and TasAir, take light aircraft into the area on demand. Walkers can fly into Melaleuca, explore the southwest on foot, and then fly out again. Memorable alternatives are to exit via the South Coast Track (six to ten days' walk) or Port Davey Track (four to five days' walk). Walking in and flying out is equally possible, but weather may halt incoming flights.

WHEN TO GO

The only certainty about weather in the southwest is that it will change. Despite a relatively mild climate on paper, visitors should go prepared for extremes. The brief southwest summer (December–February) coincides with the major holiday break in the Australian calendar. February's average temperature is 22°C (72°F), but it is also when the wilderness is at its least wild—up to 100 flights a month can set down at Melaleuca during this season.

Autumn (March–May) can be delightful, with calm, predictable weather. By May, the average temperature has dropped to about 16°C (61°F), with an average 22 rainy days for the month.

Gales, driving sleet, and snow-capped mountains characterize winter, although they can appear in the southwest at any time. However, many regard this season as the best time to experience the region—a clear, crisp winter day amid the mountains is a delight.

July averages 24 rainy days and a mean temperature of 14°C (57°F). Spring (September–November) can be wet. Unpredictable weather grounds flights regularly.

PLANNING

Fitness is perhaps the single most important thing to plan for if you intend to make an extended walk in the southwest. Try to train on hills and off pavements if possible, wearing the boots and rucksack (loaded) that you will take to the southwest. Tasmanian Expeditions hosts a nine-day trek along the South Coast Track. Participants have to carry a 20kg (44lb) pack, but transport, food, and equipment are provided.

Explorations of the Port Davey-Bathurst Harbour inlet can be made from the *Southern Explorer*, for those who want to see the southwest in comfort, or in sea kayaks. For regular summer kayaking tours of the inlet, participants must be reasonably fit, but kayaking experience isn't necessary.

TRAVELLERS' TIPS

❑ When planning your trip to the southwest, plot a schedule with plenty of room for aircraft groundings due to bad weather. Two expendable days either side of your visit will cover most eventualities.

❑ Be sure to track down the Parks and Wildlife Service pamphlet, *Essential Bushwalking Guide*, which details much of what you need to know about hiking in the area. You also need a Parks Pass.

WHAT TO TAKE

❑ Good-quality leather walking boots.
❑ Calf-high waterproof gaiters.
❑ Clothing for all weather conditions.
❑ Sunscreen and wide-brimmed sun hat.
❑ Compass and maps.
❑ Camping equipment, including a fuel stove as wood fires are not permitted.
❑ Toilet spade.
❑ All food and other requirements for the duration of your trip, plus additional supplies in the eventuality that you are delayed.

HEALTH

Attacks of "gastro" can occur even in the wilderness. If you're obliged to drink water near a spot that is heavily frequented by walkers, boil it for ten minutes before you do so. Water in areas with low traffic is usually safe to drink.

Clear air—the clearest in the world, according to science—and the southern hole in the ozone layer mean that the sun has bite here. Take plenty of sunscreen and always wear a shading hat.

Although they may appear contradictory, hypothermia (collapse due to internal chill) and heat exhaustion (illness due to overheating) are both possibilities. Prevention is simple: use modern climate-control clothing to ensure that you stay warm and dry during cold and wet conditions, take plenty of fluids and be careful not to overexert yourself in the heat.

Snakes are normally shy, and will vanish when they sense a walker's tread. Attempts to kill snakes are the primary cause of bites.

15 The Land Time Almost Forgot

by Simon Richmond

The jaw-dropping, glacier-sculpted vistas and unique flora and fauna of Tasmania's Cradle Mountain Lake St. Clair National Park are the location for one of Australia's greatest bushwalks—the Overland Track.

The Overland Track, which winds its way for 80km (50 miles) across the undulating, prehistoric terrain of Tasmania's Cradle Mountain Lake St. Clair National Park, is rightly considered to be Australia's greatest bushwalk.

You can go it alone, although the park authorities advise against this for safety reasons (the ideal group size is four). You must know what you're doing and be prepared to carry all your gear and food, which could easily weigh 25kg (55lb) or more. The second option is to form or join an organized group. By doing so you'll have a support network, not to mention other bodies to help carry the camping gear. You'll also have guides who can interpret the surrounding landscape, do

all the cooking, and help you set up camp. The third option is to go with Cradle Huts. You stay in wooden cabins along the route that are well stocked with provisions and offer such niceties as hot showers, heaters, and soft beds. This is long-distance hiking the easy way, however, it's still no pushover.

THE LURE OF THE WILD

For many, the fact that time has bypassed Tasmania is its very appeal. Colonial settlers created tidy towns and English-style fields separated by drystone walls and hedgerows. Yet across vast tracts it is practically as wild and untouched as it has been since creation.

The National Park and the Overland Track that runs through it is part of the 1.38 million ha (3.4 million acre) Tasmanian Wilderness World Heritage Area, one of the three remaining temperate wilderness areas of the Southern Hemisphere (the others are Fiordland in New Zealand and Los Glaciares in Argentina). Some 20,000 years ago, the whole area was covered by glaciers. When they melted 10,000 years later, they left behind an indented landscape of rugged mountains, alpine moorlands, and rain forests. Launceston, a genteel, compact town spread across hills at the confluence of the North Esk and South Esk rivers, is the starting point for organized treks into the park. My plan is to spend three nights camping with Tasmanian Expeditions (Tas Ex) on the company's eight-day walking tour, followed by a further three nights with the Cradle Huts operator on

4 You need stamina for the Overland Track. Climbing is comparatively minimal, except on side trips to Cradle Mountain and Mount Ossa. Try some advance training for carrying upwards of 10kg (22 pounds) across potentially boggy, wind-lashed terrain. If you don't feel up to the full five- to seven-day trek, there are plenty of one- to three-day shorter walks at either end of the park.

★★ For the full outdoors experience, camping is recommended, although be prepared to go without washing facilities (beyond ice-cold streams and lakes). Leeches come out in the wet, and a variety of bugs in the heat. If you can't quite abandon all the creature comforts, go for the Cradle Huts tours for a soft bed, a good meal, and, almost always, a hot shower at the end of each day.

⚒ Solo walkers or those in a self-organized group will also require a tent; a sleeping mat; a gas- or methylated spirits-fired camping stove; cooking pots, plates, and cutlery; food for at least seven days; and a map.

its six-day tour. Both tours involve at least 70km (45 miles) of walking, although you can opt for a ferry ride along the length of Lake St. Clair on the final day rather than completing the section of the track between Narcissus Hut and Cynthia Bay. To this, there's the option of adding on side trips up Cradle Mountain and Mount Ossa (Tasmania's highest peak), and to various waterfalls and other scenic spots.

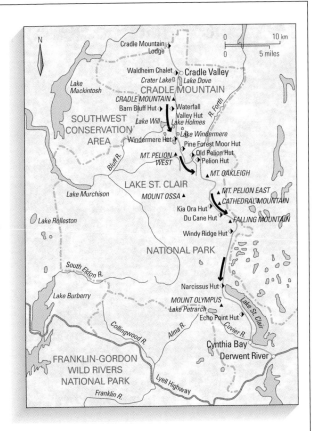

Trekking across the Cradle Mountain and Lake St Clair National Parks

All trips begin with a thorough pack inspection by the guides, who check that you take nothing unnecessary and that what you do carry is up to the job, underwear included. My wide-bodied travelpack fails the grade, and I gladly exchange it for a narrower rucksack that proves much more comfortable over the long haul. Simon, the lead guide outlines the importance of minimum-impact bushwalking. With upwards of 8,000 people walking the track each year, the park authorities are rightly concerned that the wilderness is suffering.

THE TRACK BEGINS

It's a two-hour drive towards Cradle Mountain, the northern head of the track, via Sheffield, the so-called "town of murals," which nestles beneath the brooding shadow of Mount Roland. We are to spend the first night of the trek in the comfortable public huts beside Waldheim. Waldheim is an easy 2.5km

(1½-mile) stroll from Lake Dove, the tract of glassy water in which the crenellations of Cradle Mountain are reflected in countless photographic images. Before we settle in for the night, we walk back from the lake across moorland covered with distinctive clumps of buttongrass, looking much more like giant spiky pom-poms than smooth-edged fasteners. A mother and infant wombat (which resemble overgrown hamsters) are spotted foraging around a creek, while closer to the huts, wallabies and their smaller cousins, pademelons, hop in and out of the trees.

Simon runs through some of the preparations necessary for the start of the trek. It's vital that we waterproof our packs with plastic bags and keep essential items, such as our sleeping bags and

spare clothes, in a further protective layer. Plastic plates, cups, and cutlery are dished out, as are Thermarests (self-inflating mattresses), bags of food, and tents.

The next day, we're on the track at 9am, climbing up through a shady forest of towering King Billy pines beside Crater Falls, down which cascades sparkling tannin-stained water. An hour

and a half after our start we reached the ridge of Wombat Peak, from where there are splendid views to Cradle Lake on one side and lakes Dove and Lilla on the other, all three shimmering in the dazzling light that shines down from a cloudless sky. A zigzag track, which is more of a scramble,

Far Left: *A currawong perched on the summit of Cradle Mountain*
Left: *The clover-like flowers of the lipstick-red Tasmanian waratah*
Below: *Lake Dove: a tract of glassy water reflecting the crenellations of Cradle Mountain*
Inset: *Kitchen Hut, an emergency shelter*

brings us panting to Marion's Lookout. Only a cinemascope lens could do justice to the sweeping panorama of Cradle Mountain lording it above Dove Lake, and of several hanging lakes nestling amid the rocky folds of the land, stretching away to the Walls of Jerusalem National Park in the east. The toughest uphill part of the track is now over.

CLIMBING CRADLE
From Marion's Lookout the next stage is an easy walk across an exposed plateau sprinkled liberally with the tiny white

TASMANIA

blooms of tea-tree bushes and the more fragrant lemon-scented boronia. This profusion of wildflowers is a bonus of walking the track in spring. Simon also points out the bright green, moss-like cushion plants, which despite their firm texture are actually very fragile; it can take 30 years for one plant to recover from a clumsily placed foot.

The unrelenting human assault that is being placed on this delicate environment becomes clear at our lunch spot, close to Kitchen Hut, an emergency shelter at the foot of Cradle Mountain. The 30-odd walkers who started with us in the morning are joined here by several day walkers, eager to reach Cradle's summit. At least we all have ideal conditions in which to make the climb; you'd hardly want to be tackling the slope's tricky boulder fields in anything less.

The only sure sign that you're on the right track up to Cradle are the less-than-secure metal poles (too wobbly to grab for support) and daubs of red paint on the rocks along the way. There are many huge boulders to clamber over and scuff boots on, and several false summits, each one providing excellent views across the plateau. However, putting in the extra effort to crack the 1,545m (5,069ft) peak is well worth it.

BEYOND FURY GORGE

From Kitchen Hut, where we left our packs, it takes us three hours at a leisurely pace to reach Cradle summit and make our return. It will be another couple of hours before we pitch camp for the evening at Waterfall Valley, 10km (6 miles) from Waldheim. The first section, towards Fury Gorge (where there's a striking prospect of the iconic Barn Bluff) is very rough underfoot, but soon after, the boardwalks that cover over 60km (40 miles) of the track begin, and we fly along Cradle Cirque.

Both of the public wooden huts at Waterfall Valley—an attractive spot in the shade of Barn Bluff—are full, but in such fine weather it's more pleasant to camp. Simon regales us with tales of how, in the worst weather, the huts resemble sardine cans stuffed to bursting with damp hikers and their gear. But on a calm summer evening, our alfresco meal of chilli and rice, followed by dried apple slices and custard, is delightful, and we're all so tired that it's an effort to stay awake until darkness falls. Before we retire for the night, we spot some of the Cradle Hut group trooping wearily towards their accommodation, 1km (½ mile) further along the track. Their trip had started that morning at 7am, making it a very long day for those who had gone for the Cradle summit challenge.

ALPINE WATERFALLS AND POOLS

Day two of the hike sees more endless blue skies. We're all beginning to think that the fuss about freezing, damp weather in Tasmania is a bluff. Today, there's only 8km (5 miles) to cover—a three-hour walk at most—to the next camp at Windermere.

Shortly after we start the walk, we down packs to explore Waterfall Valley's many cataracts. A muddy track leads to the foot of some delightful small falls, where carnivorous alpine sundew plants are breakfasting on bugs. Higher up, a 30m (100ft) cascade has relentlessly carved a shady overhang under which we shelter after taking a shower in the falling droplets. Rainbows bounce from the spray, and together with the palm-like pandanis plants it creates a surreal scene, out of which I wouldn't have been shocked to see lost dinosaurs amble.

We return to find that the black curra-wongs have got us. These rapacious birds, with white tips on their tail feathers, are clever enough to unzip backpack pockets. Ian's maps and books are scattered out of their protective plastic bag, and 20 muesli bars have been pilfered from Josh's pack—although we can't quite under-stand how the birds managed to zip his bag up again.

By the time we reach the small, shal-low Lake Holmes, another hour's walk across buttongrass-smothered moors, we're so hot that it takes little persuasion from Simon for us all to go for a swim. Skinny-dipping in a solar-heated alpine lake was not a pleasure I expected to experience on the Overland Track, and even Simon, with at least 50 traverses to his credit, had only bathed in this particu-lar lake once before, and then very briefly because the water was ice-cold.

HEADING FOR PELION CREEK

Just when I think the landscape can't pos-sibly get any more spectacular, it does just that at the viewpoint overlooking the islet-dotted Lake Windermere. Simon traces out the route we'll follow between the sturdy block of Pelion West to the right and the nipple-shaped Pelion East on the far left. Our campsite is a short dis-tance beyond the lake, and by the time we reach it, the combination of a weighty

rucksack and blazing sun has worn me down. This will be my last night in the tent, which given the obliging weather, the Thermarest, and my cosy sleeping bag has proved perfectly comfortable. If the rain and cold had struck, my feelings might have been quite different. The warmth has also brought out swarms of flies and mosquitoes, although the latter don't seem too inclined to bite.

The next morning I'm raring to tackle the hike to Pelion Creek, which Simon warns us will be a little more challenging than yesterday's walk. There's a possibil-ity that we'll encounter the Overland's famous mud bogs, so we strap on our gaiters for that authentic bushwhacker look. The first stage of the walk runs through a small forest of pencil pines and up onto the breeze-cooled plateau of Pine Forest Moor. A shallow, pebbly tarn reflects the rugged form of Pelion West, and a nearby ledge provides the perfect lookout across the hazy blue, densely wooded Forth Valley towards the jagged silhouette of Mount Oakleigh.

TAKING A MUD-BATH

For most of the rest of the day, we walk through forests of pine, leatherwood, and myrtle trees, the latter's tiny dried leaves scattered across the track like bronze confetti. Occasionally, a landslip opens up a narrow view in the foliage towards Mount Oakleigh, but otherwise the track remains shrouded, creating ideal condi-tions for mosses, lichens, and mud-pools between the tangle of tree roots. Close to the Pelion Creek campsite, I take the turn-off towards Old Pelion Hut, a side track that is notoriously boggy but which leads to an idyllic bathing spot at Douglas Creek. Here I join a guide from Cradle Huts, and one of his charges in a late-afternoon dip. Sloshing through the centre of mud patches is guaranteed to liberate the reckless child in all of us. One moment I'm snapping a photo of my com-panions as they stand up to their shins in the black stuff, the next I'm yanking out one of my own legs, having sunk up to my

phere continues after dinner with party games involving corks on pieces of string, candles, cards, and spoons.

What with all the fun and games, the guides forget to bake the fresh bread for breakfast and the lunch sandwiches the next day. So there's an early morning clatter in the kitchen as the loaves are thrown in the oven, followed by the pumping of water for the showers. If I was staying with Tas Ex I would be having a rest day at Pelion Creek, with the opportunity to climb Mount Oakleigh. Instead, I'm on schedule to scale Mount Ossa, at 1,617m (5,305ft) Tasmania's highest mountain.

CONQUERING OSSA

There's an average of just 32 days a year of fine weather in the park. Yet, despite some impertinent clouds, the rain holds off again as we climb steadily through mossy forests up to the open plains of Pelion Gap, at 1,126m (3,694ft), the crossroads on the track to either Pelion East or Mount Ossa. Some members of the group are not game to climb the mountain, and it is to the guides' credit that nobody is made to feel any the worse for that. Excess baggage is left at the crossroads, and we all clamber up the narrow, and in places steep and slippery, track to a grassy plateau beneath Mount Doris. This is our lunch spot, next to a stream with the freshest of water and with a panoramic view of Pinestone Valley, where the bleached arms of long-ago burnt gum trees claw out of the bush like witches' talons.

The climb to the peak from here, although steep—especially in its initial section—is less difficult than that up Cradle. A clear track winds its way past spiky scoparia bushes, tipped with scarlet

waist. It was a good job I could now clean up in one of Cradle Huts' famed hot-water showers. The showers work on a pump system, so my upper body gets a workout as I have to heave the pump lever back and forth for several minutes. At least there is sufficient rainwater in the storage tanks. Refreshed, I join the rest of the guests as they tuck into pre-dinner nibbles of Tasmanian Camembert, olives, and crackers, and contemplate whether they should go for the Chardonnay or the Pinot Noir with dinner.

AT THE PELION PIZZERIA

Typically, Cradle Hut clients are of an older age group, but on this trip the group ranges from a couple in their late twenties, to one in their early sixties. The guides are young and very enthusiastic. And everyone is getting on like they've known each other for years.

Several of the guests pitch in with the guides to prepare the evening meal—soup, homemade pizza, and apple crumble. The others relax in the cosy lounge-dining room, which is surrounded by four double bunk rooms and a gallery, where there are a couple more beds. When all is ready, the candles are lit, the wine is poured, and the guides make that extra effort to dress up in ties—drawn cartoon-style on paper. The zany atmos-

Above left: We enjoyed the luxury of fresh bread in one of the Cradle Huts
Right: Mount Ossa, the very summit of Tasmania, resembles a jumble of giant building bricks
Inset: Excess baggage was thankfully left as we clambered up the final ascent, stopping regularly to enjoy the view

flowers, over a boulder field, to a wind-blasted saddle between dolerite rock tors, and from here, it's a relatively easy hike to a small tarn. At its summit, Ossa resembles an unruly jumble of giant building bricks. It's a hop and a jump from the tarn to the tallest of these enormous fluted blocks, the very summit of Tasmania.

PADDY'S WINDSOR CASTLE

The route down to Kia Ora Hut is one of the loveliest sections of the track yet, a natural florist's shop lined with clusters of golden-orange prickly beauty, ground-hugging, buttercup-like guinea flowers, and the lipstick-red coronets of the Tasmanian waratah. At the hut—which is newer and of a different design to the others, with an outdoor deck overlooking the grand form of Cathedral Mountain—tiny brown-crested welcome swallows swoop in to greet us. Close by is the public hut, in an equally pleasant spot beside Kia Ora Creek. *Kia ora* is a Maori term meaning "happy, laughing, and playful." The next day we pass Du Cane Hut, the original King Billy-pine abode knocked up by Paddy Hartnett, a trapper and prospector who always walked in his trademark bowler hat. From the hut you can visit three waterfalls on the Mersey River. D'Alton Falls, where the river drops some 50m (165ft) over jutting copper and black blocks, is reached by a steep path leading away from the main track. Not far down are Ferguson Falls, where we sit within spray distance of the water enjoying lunch. At another turn-off are Hartnett Falls, which provide sweeping views back to Pelion East.

The route to Windy Ridge Hut takes us steadily up to Du Cane Gap, at 1,070m (3,510ft), where we rest at Campfire Creek in the lee of the appropriately named Falling Mountain, another precarious agglomeration of dolerite blocks. It's all downhill from here, through dark forests of pine and sassafras, and the prospect of more oven-warm scones at the hut spurs us on to complete the 10km (6 miles) from Kia Ora.

ACROSS THE SLEEPING WATER

The guides want us on the track for 9am on our last day so that we can all reach Narcissus Hut, on the north shore of Lake St. Clair, in time to have lunch before the 1pm ferry. The weather has finally turned and the rain is steady, shrouding the glacial cirque landscape beyond the stringybark trees. The change of conditions does, however, bring benefits. The earthy colours of the forest are refreshed, new smells hang in the air, and the lack of long-distance views focuses my ears on the sounds of birds calling and frogs croaking. It's also a relief to wear the rain jacket I've been lugging around for the last five days.

The 9km (5½-mile) walk takes around three hours to complete, and it is all pretty much downhill, through forests, and a buttongrass plain, to a swinging metal suspension bridge over Marion Creek. The widening Narcissus River, further along, flows into Lake St. Clair, where several damp walkers are waiting in the hut for the ferry. One points out the blood-gorged leech that is hitching a lift out of the park on my shin.

For the enthusiastic, the Overland Track continues for another 17.5km (11 miles) from Narcissus to Cynthia Bay (around five hours' walk). Views of the lake are limited since the track runs through the trees some 50m (55yd) from the water; a more scenic, but longer and more demanding route is the 23km (14-mile) Cuvier Valley Track, with campsites around Lake Petrarch.

I am satisfied to take the zippy ride in the small, twin-hulled ferry across the lake known to the Aborigines as Leeawuleena, which means "sleeping water." This is Australia's deepest lake, plunging to a depth of 167m (549 ft). Although I'm looking forward to peeling the boots off my blistered feet and shedding the heavy rucksack from my aching back, I suspect like everyone else on the boat that I'm already planning when I might again escape to this hauntingly beautiful wilderness.

GOING IT ALONE

INTERNAL TRAVEL

Both Ansett and Qantas offer direct scheduled flights from Sydney and Melbourne to Launceston or Hobart, while Kendell Airlines also flies to some of the smaller towns on the island.

Another option is the *Spirit of Tasmania* ferry from Port Melbourne to Devonport (14 hours), or the high-speed catamaran, the *Devil Cat*, which takes only six hours.

If you're driving or cycling to the park, Cradle Valley at its northern end, is 155km (96 miles) from Launceston and 85km (53 miles) from Devonport. Lake St. Clair, at the southern end of the park, is around 170km (106 miles) from Launceston and Hobart, Buses to both parks' access points and transfer services are offered year round by Tassielink and Maxwell Coaches.

WHEN TO GO

The hiking season runs from late October to early May. Throughout the year, the weather across Tasmania's central highlands is highly changeable. Avoid the peak holiday period (from around the end of December through January) if you don't relish walking the track with crowds. Don't trek in the winter unless you have plenty of experience.

PLANNING

The Overland Track can be completed in five days (if you opt to catch the ferry across Lake St. Clair). However, ideally allow yourself a week or more. The shortest organized tour lasts six days.

Accommodation is available on campsites or in cabins at both ends of the park, but you'll need to stock up on food supplies before you arrive. It's essential that you carry a tent. Take extra food and fuel for your camping stove in case you run into trouble or bad weather. For the Overland Track you'll need to buy a two-month pass, which covers all of Tasmania's national parks. Before you start, register at the information centres at Cradle Mountain and Lake St. Clair.

If you plan to take the ferry across Lake St. Clair, you must pre-book. You must also reconfirm your booking on arrival at Narcissus Hut using the radio telephone there. During the season, there are at least three trips a day, the last of which leaves at around 3:30pm.

TRAVELLERS' TIPS

❑ If you are tackling the Overland Track independently, go in a group of four, let the park authorities know when you set off, and inform them of your return.
❑ Waterproof your pack with a plastic bag, and wrap essential items such as sleeping bags and spare clothes in another protective layer.

WHAT TO TAKE

On an organized trip, you'll need the following:

❑ Sturdy lace-up walking boots, which are worn inside gaiters that protect boots and shins from mud and leeches.
❑ Sleeping bag which will keep you warm in temperatures down to -5°C (23°F).
❑ Waterproof jacket and overpants.
❑ Woolly hat and a broad-brimmed sun hat.
❑ Thermal underwear and gloves.
❑ Shorts for walking and lightweight trousers for the evenings.
❑ Fleece or woollen top.
❑ Water bottle.
❑ Torch.

HEALTH

It's safe to drink the water from streams along the way, but collect water upstream of where people swim or wash. Don't go to the toilet anywhere near a water supply, and alway bury any faecal waste and toilet paper. Drink plenty of water—even if the weather is cold and wet—to prevent dehydration.

RAFTING ON THE FRANKLIN

Most of this World Heritage Area rainforest, home to ancient Huon pines, is totally inaccessible, so rafting the Franklin River, a 8–14 day trip, is virtually the only way to experience it. The put-in point is the Collingwood River, 49km (30 miles) west of Derwent Bridge, from where it takes three days to reach the Upper Franklin. From here, it is white water, ravines, and dense forest all the way to the exit point on the Gordon River, south of Macquarie Harbour and Strahan. The rapids range from Class II to VI, and, coupled with the severe weather, should not be tackled by novices.

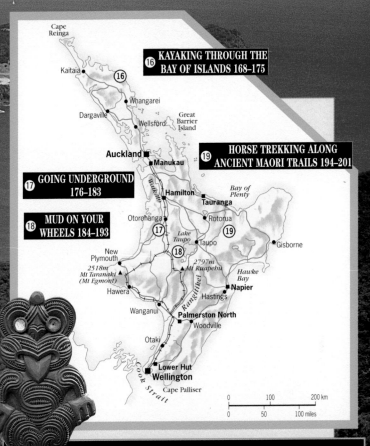

Cape Reinga
Kaitaia
Whangarei
Dargaville
Wellsford
Great Barrier Island
Auckland
Manukau
Hamilton
Bay of Plenty
Otorohanga
Tauranga
Rotorua
Lake Taupo
Taupo
Gisborne
New Plymouth
2518m Mt Taranaki (Mt Egmont)
2797m Mt Ruapehu
Hawke Bay
Napier
Hawera
Hastings
Wanganui
Rangitikei
Palmerston North
Woodville
Otaki
Cook Strait
Lower Hut
Wellington
Cape Palliser

| 0 | 100 | 200 km |
| 0 | 50 | 100 miles |

NEW ZEALAND•
NORTH ISLAND

Most of New Zealand's tiny population is to be found in North Island, and most North Islanders live in Auckland, New Zealand's largest city and a good jumping-off point for the multitude of adventures on offer. Beyond Auckland lie unspoilt and barely populated areas of fern-filled subtropical forests, gargantuan kauri trees, and virgin coastline. Here, there are opportunities for an extraordinary variety of adventure holidays, all carefully organized. On the northeastern coast are the beaches, inlets, and islands that make the Bay of Islands great for kayaking or for exploring by seaplane. The geological features of the central areas seem purpose-built for the adventurous—rafting through underground caverns and abseiling in the twilight world of the glow-worm. On the surface, you can bike in volcanic Tongariro, or take a horse trek through the jungle of Urewara, one of the last places where Maori traditions live on. In North Island, everything seems possible, everything accessible.

The luminous turquoise waters of the Bay of Islands

16 Kayaking through the Bay of Islands

by Christopher Knowles

The Bay of Islands is a scenic area fabled both for its beauty and as the birthplace of modern New Zealand history. Here I navigated mangroves in a kayak and took to the air in a flying boat.

No matter how you look at it, New Zealand is a long way from every-where. It comes as a physical shock to find that 27 hours of continuous travel are required to reach Auckland from Europe. I probably should have bro-ken the journey with an overnight stop, although I doubt that would have pre-vented my luggage from going missing. Thankfully it rejoined me next day at the hotel where I had collapsed in a fitful attempt to recuperate. Auckland is the largest city in the country, with one mil-lion residents—30 per cent of New Zealand's entire population. It is a city of wide, undulating streets flanked by mostly modern buildings that range over the islands and inlets of Stanley Bay. There is a lively, cosmopolitan mix of Asian, Polynesian, and European influences. It was Sunday, and although the New Zealanders' reputation for love of sport is well known, I was not prepared for the astonishing numbers of joggers pounding the streets. It was only after seeing a pair dressed as Batman and Robin that I realized that this was the annual marathon.

COLONIAL RELICS

The Great Sights bus picked me up, and over the course of the morning I was able to obtain a feel for the city. We passed by one of the largest marinas in the world (almost every New Zealander seems to own a boat) and the newly built Americas Cup Village. Then we went for a cruise around the harbour, starting from the old Ferry Building and finishing with a visit to the excellent Kelly Tarlton's Underwater World and Antarctic Encounter, where sharks and rays can be seen in their own habitat as you pass beneath them on a moving floor. Finally, we made an ascent of the 330m (1,082ft) Sky Tower. In the afternoon, I took a ferry across to Devonport, where there are several streets of delightful wooden residences and a number of fascinating period office buildings that have been converted into restaurants and shops. This is a charming part of the city that has developed a life and a character of its own.

TO THE BAY OF ISLANDS

The next day, by which time I was approaching some sort of bodily and men-tal equilibrium, I was picked up again by

---

1 For the kayaking, you need only be prepared to get wet (although the ability to paddle for a couple of hours is also useful), whilst for the seaplane flight, all you need do is sit back and photograph the stunning scenery below.

★★ Getting to and from the Bay of Islands area is easy and the climate is benign. However, the weather is changeable (except at the height of summer) and many of the activities depend upon clement conditions. Accommodation in the Bay of Islands area is plentiful at all levels, especially in the town of Paihia. You are advised to book in advance during busy times.

For the sea kayaking, a swimming costume, shorts, and footwear that is comfortable when wet are required, along with a water-proof bag for your camera and wallet.

Great Sights for the four-hour journey north to Paihia and the Bay of Islands. In many ways this is an excellent way to see the country, for the commentary from the driver/guide was informative, amusing, and clear. Apart from my introduction to the world of New Zealand cakes, an experience not to be overlooked, I learned of New Zealand's hybrid history. In my ignorance, I had thought only of Captain Cook, the Maori, and the early British settlers. But there were plenty of others, not least Dalmatians and Bohemians, for whom the countryside offered something that was familiar, and yet far sweeter and more yielding than in their home countries. We also caught glimpses of New Zealand's impenetrable native bush, allowed to flourish on hillsides that were too steep for settlers to cultivate. A short diversion was made off the main highway to see examples of the increasingly rare kauri tree. Native to New Zealand, it is said to be the largest in the world in terms of density (referring to the number of branches and leaves) and second only to the Californian sequoia in girth and height. The kauri was also a great source of amber, as so many trees were fossilized in bogland.

BOAT TOURS AND OTHER ACTIVITIES

Fuller's runs regular boat trips around the Bay of Islands that not only pass through the Hole in the Rock at Piercy Island, but also stop at Urupukapuka Island, where you can go swimming or snorkelling in the clear waters. If the weather is too cool for this, take a ride in the *Nautilus* instead, a sort of submarine from which you can obtain a glimpse of the bay's undersea life. Many of the numerous activities on offer in the Bay of Islands are highly weather sensitive. One option that is all the more fun during the rain, however, is a ride on an All Terrain Vehicle (A.T.V.) across the hills overlooking the bay.

FLYING DUCK

At Paihia, a small resort town strung along the bay, behind which rise forested hills, I was delivered to my hotel—located at one end of the town, a few metres from the water's edge. But there was not much time for relaxation. I was booked on the afternoon flying-boat flight, courtesy of the delightfully named Salt Air. In view of the days to follow, I was extremely lucky, for the weather was quite perfect: calm and sunny, the air burnished to a permanent autumn glow. The flying boat was moored at a ramp just behind the office, rocking to the lapping wavelets of perfectly clear seawater. The plane, a Grumman Super Widgeon, built in Long Island in 1946, is one of only 46 remaining in the world and is the only one operational in the Southern Hemisphere. Its design is reminiscent of a more leisurely era—it could have emerged from a poster for Imperial Airways—but the engines have been altered to increase the horsepower and cruising speed.

THE ISLANDS FROM THE AIR

We took our seats (everyone has a window seat) by entering the aircraft through the door at the back. The two Continental engines sprang into life, and we remained stationary for a couple of minutes as they warmed up, before taxiing gracefully into the water. Only a few seconds after we left the ramp, the wheels were retracted, the engines were opened up to full power, and we scudded across the water for just over half a kilometre before rising slowly into the air. I cannot say at what altitude we eventually levelled out, but it was low enough so that the details of the glittering seascape below were graphically laid out.

The Bay of Islands is indeed beautiful. The colour of the water is the most striking thing you notice from the plane—a luminous clear blue, yet so clear that it appears to merge with the sand—with mossy, rocky islets laid out as if on a tablet, like a children's cut-out. We passed close by some of them, and the pilot

Left: *A boat trip round the bay is relaxing way to get your bearings*
Above: *The Bay of Islands is dotted with forested rocky islets, only a few of which are inhabited*
Right: *In terms of density, the rare kauri tree is claimed to be the biggest in the world*

provided us with a commentary through our headsets. None of the islands was very much populated, although I did notice a flock of sheep being driven across one of them, the shepherd striding with measured pace behind whilst a pair of dogs ran to and fro in an attempt to keep their charges in some sort of order.

On a clear day it is apparently possible to see down through the water to a depth of about 12m (40ft). As I looked down, the water at one point appeared to be boiling but it was merely a shoal of fish feeding at the surface, seemingly oblivious to the attentions of a mako shark that was able to sate its appetite at leisure. As

we headed out to sea and cruised along the coast, a schooner in full sail struck out from behind an island, a quite glorious sight. Again, I felt part of an antique poster advertising the advantages of travel by air and by sea. The pilot pointed out some of the notable landmarks, such as the bird-covered Hole in the Rock (which I later saw by boat, also an experience worth trying), an islet that is pierced at one end, allowing boats to pass through when the conditions are right. From the plane the whole coastline is visible in all its glory, and we could see a complete picture of this subtropical haven.

HISTORICAL OVERVIEW

Below us, too, was the town of Russell, a short ferry ride across the bay from Paihia. Although most people are attracted to the Bay of Islands by its beauty or come to try various sporting activities, it is easy to forget that the area is the birthplace of New Zealand's modern history. Russell, now a sleepy harbour of some charm, with timber houses and plenty of trees, was the capital of early colonial New Zealand. Incredibly, or so it now seems, it acquired the soubriquet of the "Hellhole of the Pacific," from the early seaborne frontiersmen who came here for their wine, women, and song. The sheer beauty of the area leads one to forget that for the early settlers the Bay of Islands was not the picturesque resort it is today. To make a new life here over two centuries ago presented immense challenges, not least how to come to terms with the native people, the Maori. Beside my hotel is the Waitangi National Reserve, a place of enormous historical significance.

UP A CREEK WITH A PADDLE

By the following morning the weather had changed almost completely. But as I made my way at 8:30am across the Waitangi Bridge to the offices of Coastal Kayaking, it looked as if there would be enough sunshine to enable us to get underway. The office was a small beachside hut outside which a knot of people waited beside a row of kayaks.

Sam, our guide, indicated that we should sit in the boats in order to see if the pedals were correctly set up for our various heights. I had no idea that pedals were involved, and yet they are pretty vital to the successful manipulation of the vessel since they control the rudder. Next, we had to try on a life jacket and then a skirt. This looks pretty silly when you are wearing it out of the kayak but less so when you are ensconced in the cockpit, for you roll it over the cockpit rim to stop water pouring in. We were also given a paddle and a plastic bag, into

which we placed our valuables before pushing it into a watertight hold built into the kayak.

WATERBORNE

We carried the kayaks down to the water's edge, got them just about afloat and, with Sam's cheerful instructions about how to get in without capsizing ringing in our ears, managed to push off without incident. Sam told us to paddle around for a while in order to get used to the controls. This was not difficult as the water was flat calm, the wind low, and the kayak seemed to react pretty well to the pedals. That said, it was easy to forget which pedal took you in which direction and to establish the extent of your turning circle. Sam asked us to "Raft up," by which he meant that we should all gather together and cling onto each other's kayaks so that we formed a single floating unit, then he gave a rough outline of what we would be doing, before we all set off.

In a line we passed beneath the Waitangi Bridge and, beyond it, the Tui, an old schooner that is now a restaurant, to enter a fairly sheltered stretch of water. We followed Sam for about half an hour, heading for an expanse of low, thick vegetation. Your muscles do begin to ache by this time, and the slightly cramped conditions in the kayak mean that it is very important to get the pedal settings correct, for otherwise your knees can become jammed beneath the rim of the cockpit. All in all, I was glad when we rafted up again at what turned out to be the entrance to a vast mangrove forest. Sam allowed us to recover ourselves a little before paddling into the watery woodland.

INTO THE MANGROVE FOREST

Mangroves are remarkable plants, perhaps unique in their ability to grow in seawater, breathing by means of aerial roots (pneumatophores) that act like snorkel tubes. They also create an eerie, silent tangle of branches that require some care to negotiate; it was surprisingly easy to take the wrong route and find oneself having to duck overhanging limbs or extricate the kayak from the grasp of a tree.

Before long, we were once again out into the open air for another half-hour of gentle paddling along a wide, rippling stretch of water. A waterbird, rather similar to a grebe, bobbed alongside us. The banks on either side rose fairly high, covered in dense, green thicket, as we headed into the mouth of a creek. Then, round a bend in the creek, we found ourselves confronted by a waterfall that poured over a ledge above us. We rafted up and looked with a mixture of trepidation and excitement at the stream of water. "There are, in the world," Sam told us, "only two horseshoe-shaped waterfalls—Niagara and this one, Haruru." I could not make out whether he was serious or not. He didn't smile as he said it, so perhaps he is right. Well, Haruru is not Niagara by any means, but it still posed a fair test for a novice kayak pilot. First, however, we went to the shore to divest ourselves of any unnecessary items of clothing. And then, as we returned to the kayak, I succeeded in tipping myself into the water. This did not bode well for the journey behind the curtain of water. Sam had said that someone would surely topple in; well, he was right, although he was thinking of the waterfall when he said that. We set off back towards the cataract and rafted up. One at a time, we went in, feathering the rocky shore and heading for one end of the cascading water. The real aim was to pass behind the water and out the other side. Getting wet was unavoidable, but the question was, could a complete soaking be avoided?

Our first attempts were pretty lacklustre, but we were merely testing the waters, as it were. The next time, we were more determined. One girl who had tried kayaking before managed to get through and cling onto the rock behind the falls for at least a minute. Another of us toppled in. Then I, too, succeeded in piercing the stream, this time remaining

---

WAITANGI

The Waitangi Treaty, signed on February 6, 1840, established the direct sovereignty of the British government over New Zealand. Over 500 Maori Chiefs put their names to the document, many of whom, it seems, believed they were protecting their rights to land and trade, whilst acquiring the governorship of the British Crown. However, controversy has since surrounded the treaty. Many believe the Maori text and the English version were substantially different. The colonial authorities enforced the full sovereignty of the British parliament and the Maori communities have been attempting to re-dress the balance ever since. In 1975 the Waitangi Tribunal was established to resolve the problem, but it remains one of the most emotive issues in the country.

---

behind for some time as the water pounded onto the kayak before it was finally dragged back by the flow into open water. It was truly exhilarating, made all the more so as I had succeeded in remaining upright.

TEA BREAK

Then it was back to shore to dry off a little and to drink tea or coffee before climbing into the kayaks (we were all supremely confident by now) for the long journey home. The wind was up, the clouds were approaching, and my shoulder muscles ached; but we had passed through our waterfall and that was all that counted. We returned at our own pace, striking up a mechanical rhythm that eclipsed aches and pains, desultory conversations taking place between kayaks. It seemed a long way back, and the bridge was a welcome sight. We passed beneath it, beached our kayaks, and struggled up to the office with them. Sam removed his wraparound sunglasses and beamed at us genially.

GOING IT ALONE

INTERNAL TRAVEL

The best jumping-off point for the Bay of Islands is Auckland, which is served by air from all over the world and by many of the world's major airlines. From Auckland, there are two ways of reaching Paihia and the Bay of Islands: by road or by air.

The Bay of Islands airport is located about a 20-minute drive from Paihia. It is very small but Air New Zealand Link operates daily flights from Auckland (advance booking is recommended). By road, there are two possibilities: car hire or bus. Driving in New Zealand is, on the whole, a joy. There is very little traffic compared with Europe or North America, although the strict speed limit can therefore be an irritant. By bus, you can either take a standard service with one of several bus companies, or take a guided tour which includes stops *en route* and an informative commentary from the driver. Journey time is about three hours.

WHEN TO GO

The best time of year to visit the Bay of Islands is late spring or early summer (late November), when the weather is reliable and yet the area not too crowded. Avoid the Christmas period, especially the school summer holidays (mid-December–end of January).

PLANNING

The Bay of Islands is one of the best known of New Zealand's many scenic regions. It is located on the east coast of North Island, and is a very popular holiday destination, especially with Aucklanders. Accommodation should be booked well in advance, as should the seaplane flight.

The seaplane flight requires a minimum of two passengers before it will operate. It is also weather sensitive, so leave yourself plenty of time in case it is cancelled.

As for the kayaking, there is a choice of guided tours lasting from half a day to three days. You can also hire sea kayaks for your own use, for which a minimum of two people is required.

TRAVELLERS' TIP

❑ Make sure that you have a good waterproof bag or container for carrying valuables such as cameras when kayaking.

WHAT TO TAKE

❑ Swimming costume.
❑ Shorts.
❑ Footwear suitable for kayaking.
❑ Waterproof bag for valuables.

HEALTH

If you suffer from airsickness, take suitable medication before you go on the seaplane trip as it is prone to turbulence. When kayaking, apply sunscreen liberally as the reflection off the water increases the risk of sunburn.

Left: *A brilliant sunset was the perfect end to a strenuous but exhilarating day's kayaking*
Inset: *Kayaking near two killer whales*
Below: *We rested at the entrance of a vast mangrove forest before paddling in*

NORTH ISLAND

17 Going Underground

by Anna Carter

It isn't surprising that Waitomo is one of New Zealand's most sought-after adventure destinations. What is surprising, however, is that this beautiful little settlement has remained so quiet and unspoilt.

The tranquil Waitomo area boasts an unspoilt cave and karst landscape that is covered with a vast expanse of rich pastures and forest-cloaked rolling hills. The region is less than three hours' drive south of Auckland, the country's largest city, and three hours' drive west of Rotorua, the cultural heartland of New Zealand. Waitomo itself is home to a small population of 300 people and a minute number of shops and facilities. It could easily be perceived as a sleepy village, but more than 500,000 tourists visit the area annually to experience its natural beauty. Despite this, Waitomo retains its raw charm and can offer a host of "real Kiwi" activities ranging from gentle bush walks to extreme pursuits, with quality facilities that cater to every budget.

Underneath Waitomo stretch 50km (30 miles) of cave passages with a history

dating back 30 million years. These caves are part of a unique karst limestone landscape that has been sculpted by water into blind valleys, sinkholes, arches, and fluted outcrops. They are time vaults, natural stores of fossil deposits and magnificent crystalline formations from a time when Waitomo was below sea-level. You venture here on Nature's terms.

Although the majority of underground visitors prefer to view the glow-worm caves purely as spectators, a variety of trips are on offer to test not only a caver's physical agility but also his or her mettle. My own adrenalin rush was to be a double dip of black-water rafting and the Lost World abseiling trip, spread over two days and enjoyed in the company of Margaret, my reluctant companion.

AT THE WATERHOLE

Waitomo takes its name from two Maori words—*wai*, meaning water, and *tomo*, meaning hole. The torrential spring rains that had formed lakes of water in the fields left no doubt that this was an accurate description. After settling into the local hotel, we learned there had been a blow-out (flooding) and the caves had been closed for a day.

Luckily, the next morning shone bright, and a guide had been into the caves at 6am and deemed the conditions to be safe. As we took the five-minute drive to the Black Water Rafting Café and base, Margaret was still wondering how I had managed to talk her into this. After all, there were wetas (very leggy, albeit harmless, native spiders) down there, and eels too!

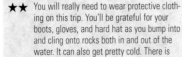

 Moderate fitness and surefootedness are recommended for this trip. While there are trained guides on hand to help, it is essential to listen carefully to instructions and to concentrate. At certain times of the year, when the water is high and fast, the difficulty rating is slightly higher.

★★ You will really need to wear protective clothing on this trip. You'll be grateful for your boots, gloves, and hard hat as you bump into and cling onto rocks both in and out of the water. It can also get pretty cold. There is plenty of choice of comfortable accommodation in the area.

 All specialist equipment necessary for the Black Water Rafting and Lost World tours is supplied by the operators. You need only take swimwear and a towel for the river tubing and loose clothing for the caving.

There are gentle cave trips at Waitomo, and then there are those designed only for thrill-seekers. Ours was the latter. Black-water rafting is, in fact, a misnomer because the trip is undertaken in a rubber tube. To do it you need average fitness, a keen sense of humour, a swimsuit, and a towel. It involves selecting an inner tube that fits over your backside, plunging into the Ruakuri Cave, and floating your way downstream and back into daylight. It sounded simple enough. New Zealand is the only country in the world where you can enjoy this particular form of lunacy under the care and guidance of a licensed operator. Since 1987, when Black Water Rafting first poked unsuspecting visitors into inner tubes and launched them into the glow-worm-studded blackness, more than 180,000 people of every conceivable shape and size have experienced it—and loved it, as the visitors' book attests.

Before we began, we had to complete medical declarations, and those who spoke English as a second language were asked to talk to the guides in order to ensure that communication difficulties wouldn't compromise safety. We were then issued with wetsuits, rubber socks, sturdy rubber boots, thick gloves, and caving helmets fitted with battery-operated lanterns. A brief training session showed us how to leap backwards and drop into the flowing water so that we arrived with our bottoms securely in our tubes. Although this isn't particularly difficult, it does involve a series of coordinated thoughts and movements roughly akin to learning to pedal a bicycle. We also learnt a fail-safe way of linking arms and legs to form a giant, black water snake; we'd be required to do just this at short notice later on.

WE PREPARE TO DESCEND

Our soggy sextet clambered into a minibus and set off for the 20-minute drive up into the hills through magnificent pastureland, while our three guides let us in on the extraordinary natural history of the area. We crossed through private farmland, before stopping in a field littered with ancient rock formations of stratified limestone. Looking like a cross between deep-sea divers and coalminers, we trudged to an opening in a hill and took our first look into what was to be our playground for the next few hours. The terrain was both fascinating and horrifying—a narrow, plummeting cavern shrouded in mist and looking for all the world like it had no end.

One by one, we lowered our heads and stepped into the cave. There was not a drop of water here, but then we had a lot of climbing down to do yet. These aren't small, tight caves, but gaping natural limestone caverns. You don't have be experienced in anything in particular to do this trip, but you do have to be careful. It is also advisable to own up to any phobias, as this is not the ideal place for a panic attack.

We stopped to adjust our eyes to the darkness before walking for about 20 minutes to the rushing river, which was gorged and turbulent with spring rains. Because of the speed and depth of the water, we were warned not to attempt to retrieve our tubes if they were swept away. The river flow was fast and, as I was about to find out, there were plenty of immovable objects down there that you wouldn't want to collide with at high speed. For some reason I volunteered to go first, over the precipice and backwards into the great swirling pool below. Then I was past the point of no return and paddling to stay facing the others as they hurtled towards me. I soon learned that the trick was to find something to hang onto, no matter how tenuous, and to kick off the cave wall to propel yourself into the current.

WILD, WET, AND WONDERFUL

Caving in this extraordinary environment can't be compared to anything else. Deeper and deeper into the dark we went, standing occasionally to negotiate sharp tight corners. What I hadn't considered was the noise that torrents of rushing water make, especially in such an exaggerated acoustic setting. It wasn't long before it was deafening—a sure sign that something big lay up ahead. At this point I also registered that, while our group was together in a sense, we were on completely separate journeys as we chose different routes across the rocky terrain and different tactics to negotiate our way. I followed the cave wall in knee-deep water, tentatively picking my way across rocks I couldn't see. All was black, and the lantern on my helmet produced only enough light to make out the shape of the cave. The water moving beneath me played tricks with my normal agility. I knew if I fell it was going to be hard, and I was also conscious of being one of six, so that if I stalled now I would be putting pressure on everyone else. A guide suddenly appeared at my side and, shouting over the roar of the water, told me to plant my feet down heavily. It worked. Suddenly I felt much more in command.

BLIND FAITH

The person in front of me stopped, and so I stopped. There was no room to move alongside him or even to crane to see what was happening beyond. All I could hear was deafeningly loud water, and I knew there was some hideous obstacle ahead, but I didn't know what. The man in front disappeared, and I inched around the corner. I was standing ankle deep now on top of a great rocky weir—a giant's step. The trick was to get over it without ripping my tube to bits; it was a timing thing. Ahead of me was a flattish area of rock and beyond it a roaring pool of black. I crouched carefully, steadying myself with one hand and trying to position my tube safely under me with the other. I was thankful for the protection of the gloves, and had to remember to hold onto the tube, at the same time hoping the speed of my launch would be sufficient to propel me into the flow and prevent me from pitching headfirst into the pounding water. I hurtled into the blackness, totally out of control.

A forceful thrust from my right spun me out and down to the relative safety of a blind wall, and I looked back to see that the shove had come from another strategically placed guide who had prevented me from being sucked into a treacherous rip. The rip was so forceful that it was difficult to stand, even when I hung onto rocks at the left of the cave. We grabbed each other's cuffs and waistbands, and reached out to hold the others as they hurtled towards us. We clung tentatively to the rocks until the last of the group was herded into the corner. From waist-deep water we then glued ourselves to the rock wall and shuffled around the corner. We were at the top of a thundering waterfall, and the noise was deafening as the water exploded into the cavern below. I planted my feet heavily so I didn't slip, quickly pulled my tube over my head and secured it tightly under my arms, and then jumped out as far as I could. Bang! Into the frothing mass. Even with the buoyancy of the tube I was under the water momentarily, before, breathless and slightly disorientated, I swirled towards the couple ahead of me. In black-water rafting everything happens very quickly, and while there's certainly no pressure to hurry there is a sense of urgency to know what lies in store around the next corner.

Left: Preparing for the descent: underneath Waitomo stretch 50km (30 miles) of caves dating back 30 million years
Right: Rafting underground is only for thrill-seeking adrenalin-junkies

MAORI LEGEND

Legend has it that an important Maori chief is buried with others in a recess on a ledge over the entrance to Ruakuri Cave. It is said that the ledge was reached with the help of trees that grew on the face of the precipice in olden times, but these have now disappeared and the spot can only be reached by means of a rope from the top. The locality of the recess and ledge is known by a quantity of *kokowai* (red ochre) which is still visible today.

HUMAN SNAKE

As we linked arms and legs to snake through the next hundred metres as a group rather than separating along a maze of ancillary routes, I realized I hadn't had time to think about whether I was cold, or to have a close look at this extraordinary environment. We were deep under the ground now. The water was very cold, and it was also suddenly very still and quiet. We floated apart and I lay back in my tube, switched my lantern off, and coasted. Above me, the brilliant lights of millions of glow-worms shone, the tiny larvae waiting to ensnare unsuspecting insects in the sticky threads they spin. This isn't just a river-tubing trip; it's a unique chance to be up close to natural history in the making, amongst magnificent, sculptural stalactites and stalagmites that have formed over thousands of years through the actions of water dripping from the roof of the cave.

As we floated towards daylight and clambered out of the hillside, I was astonished to hear that we'd been underground for nearly three hours. It was a short walk back to base before a hot shower, which stung against my skin, and a complimentary bowl of hot soup. Margaret and I bid farewell to our companions and headed back to the hotel for a congratulatory glass of wine, dinner, and an early night. Our Lost World abseiling trip was scheduled for the crack of the following dawn.

NEW DAY, NEW ADVENTURE

Having gone subterranean I was feeling quite confident about our next adventure, but subterranean on a rope was another thing altogether. As a little colour crept into the sky we climbed into the waiting van, and, on the road to the next pickup point, completed the requisite medical questionnaire. The sun rose higher in the sky, and I remarked that if this was to be our last morning on the planet it couldn't be a nicer one. Something told us our guides had heard such remarks before.

After crossing more private farmland and opening and closing numerous gates to prevent stock wandering, we arrived in a field housing a solitary shed that contained everything we would need on our four-hour trip into the cavernous underworld. We pulled on overalls, gumboots, harnesses, and hard hats. There is a magical waist loop, a rapid, a brake rack, and a thing called a cow's tail, which when looped a certain way becomes a lark's foot. We buckled ourselves into this paraphernalia and, still trying to remember the names of the knots, waddled awkwardly towards our next underworld experience—the Lost World.

This trip has a "Rambo rating" of 6/10 and is described as the ultimate abseil. But first there is a wonderful journey deep into the heart of this extraordinary world. This initial stage isn't a challenging passage, but you do need to be sure-footed. On the steep climbs I decided not to take any risks, and clipped myself to the rope bolted into the rock face. After descending hundreds of metres inside the caves, we climbed up into great rocky spires. I realized we were whispering, but this is a magical place and somehow it seemed inappropriate to break the spell of silence.

SUSPENDED BY SKY HOOKS

The Lost World trip isn't so much physical as mental. It is a challenge to work through your fears of the unknown. There was stunned silence when our eyes suddenly and collectively fell on the narrow metal platform in front of us. It appeared to be suspended by sky hooks, as did a series of ropes that hung perfectly still beside it, disappearing into a void. The Lost World is an enormous surreal hole in the ground, a heart-stopping descent down what is billed as one of the longest commercial abseils in the world.

I discovered that abseiling involves a close relationship with the rope. Rope is everywhere—in the traverse lines guiding you from point to point and, most of all, in the vital stretch between the top of this descent and the invisible bottom. Now we had to do something common sense told us not to: we had to reach out over this huge hole to grasp a piece of rope, swing around 180 degrees and lean our bodies back, and then sit on a metal bar above nothing and push off into space. This actual drop is just under 100m (300ft) but the bottom is an eternity away.

I was strapped to various safety devices, including one of the guides, but when the moment eventually came I had to remind myself to breathe. It was the guide's quiet prompting that eventually got me to begin gingerly to feed my rope. I made the mistake of looking down, and had to struggle to control a wave of panic. Margaret casually quizzed Brett about the rare ferns and mosses growing in the shaft while my mind focussed on the rope.

Climbing rope has built-in bounce for shock absorption. It is grafted onto you via your break bar, a simple but very effective device that clips to your waist and gives you control over your rate of descent. The break bar can even park you, mid-descent, like a fly in a spider's web. If you're brave you can release the friction and barrel down the rope at speed, although excessive speed and hard braking can generate enough heat to make the brake bar uncomfortably hot.

After a few minutes I had a good rhythm going, (the spring of the rope can leave you bouncing like a yo-yo), and found a leaning angle that didn't strain my back. Some 25kg (55 pounds) of rope

locked hard into the break bar by its own weight makes for tiring hand work, but as we crept closer to the rocky floor the rope lightened and the descent became a great deal smoother. At the midpoint I was even feeling relaxed enough to enjoy both the fabulous views and the thrill of the descent. The noise of the stream below us grew louder, and gradually the other adventurers came into focus beneath me. At the bottom there was a palpable sense of bonding, with much hugging, grinning, and gazing heavenward at the ropes that had now vanished into… thin air.

After a welcome orange drink and chocolate bar, we switched our lanterns on and paced and climbed through the star-studded labyrinth to our exit point, a narrow metal ladder that led 30m (100ft) straight up into the pitch-black cavern. This climb is possibly the most challenging part of the journey.

The Lost World adventure is a rare opportunity to observe nature at its most awesome, and an unforgettable chance to become part of a fantastic natural phenomenon that has developed over millions of years. I had put myself outside my usual comfort zone and had not only survived but thrived. As I glanced back one last time through the shafts of sunlight that streamed down around me, I sensed that I was leaving somewhere very special indeed.

MORE WAITOMO ADVENTURES

❑ *Black Water Rafting II* lasts five hours and combines abseiling, caving, cave tubing, and jumping over waterfalls. Includes a meal and a drink.

❑ *Haggas Honking Holes* gives four hours of abseiling, waterfall jumping, rock climbing, and crawling through spectacular caves.

❑ Several gentle trips to the glow-worm cave or nearby Ruakuri Caves are also available, as are horse trekking, self-drive jetboating and quadbiking.

GOING IT ALONE

INTERNAL TRAVEL

Waitomo is a three-hour drive south from Auckland, and boasts more than a dozen above- and below-ground activities that are unique to the area. Numerous tour buses and shuttles provide daily passenger services, including Newmans and Scenic Tours coaches, the Kiwi Experience and Magic Bus backpacker networks, and small shuttles such as the Waitomo Wanderer. Other options are Trans Rail, rental cars, motor homes or campervans, and off-track tours such as those offered by the Flying Kiwi. To reach Waitomo from Auckland, take Highway 1 to Hamilton, then Highway 3 before turning on to Highway 37.

WHEN TO GO

Because much of the activity in Waitomo takes place underground, it is a great place to visit year round. In the winter months of June, July, and August, you can still comfortably take walks and go horse trekking in just a warm jacket. After the spring and winter rains, the rafting becomes faster and more exciting than it is in summer.

PLANNING

Accommodation facilities in the area are ample and affordable, and range from campsites and backpackers' lodges to fully serviced hotel rooms. The Waitomo Caves Museum, at the heart of the village, takes bookings for every activity; it can also take care of ongoing travel arrangements, and along with the visitor information centre will arrange accommodation.

TRAVELLERS' TIPS

❑ Waitomo isn't on the way to anywhere, but there is so much to see and do it's well worth stopping here for at least two days.

❑ To understand fully the extraordinary natural history that makes the underground adventures possible, make time for a visit to the Waitomo Caves Museum.

WHAT TO TAKE

❑ Swimwear and a towel is all you need for the Black Water Rafting adventure.

❑ Comfortable clothes with plenty of flexibility to wear under the overalls provided on the abseiling trip.

HEALTH

Waitomo adventure operators are extremely safety conscious and won't allow you do take part if there is any risk of illness or injury. It is important to be honest about your medical history, phobias, and swimming ability. It is not possible to undertake the Black Water Rafting or Lost World trips alone or independently, and three highly experienced and trained guides accompany each group.

Left: Descending into the ancient landscape of the Lost World
Below: Taking a break in a dazzling shaft of sunlight

18 Mud on your Wheels

by Anna Carter

New Zealand's natural environment is incredibly diverse, ranging from alpine peaks and rainforests to grassy plains and golden beaches. But without a doubt, the wild and beautiful volcanic plateau of central North Island is the strangest.

The central North Island embodies the quintessential Kiwi outdoors. At its heart is the inland sea, Lake Taupo, home to leviathan trout that swim in its deep waters and up the world-famous whitewater Tongariro River. Skirting the shore of the lake and reaching into the mountainous hinterland is the magnificent Tongariro National Park. Not long after you turn off Highway 47 on the way to the apex of North Island's national park apex, a series of distinctive mounds begins to dot the roadside. This is volcano country. Steeped in history and Maori mythology, the peaks here reign supreme. They dominate not just visually, but in the reminders of their violent past—charred wood, pumice, and alternating beds of ash and scoria that tumbled out of the sky as scorching fingers of lava burned into the mountainsides.

The Ruapehu district lies almost midway between Auckland and Wellington; highways 1 and 4 provide equally good access and form the western and eastern boundaries. The connecting highways 47 and 49 provide the northern and southern boundaries respectively. The 80,000ha (198,000-acre) Tongariro National Park makes up most of this district, with its centrepiece of Mount Ruapehu rising dramatically 2,797m (4,176ft) from the surrounding countryside. Accompanying it are two smaller volcanic mountains, Mount Ngauruhoe and Mount Tongariro. Mount Ruapehu is the most active of the three, and every two or three years puts on a magnificent pyrotechnic display. It is also the site of the North Island's premier ski fields, at Whakapapa and Turoa.

A STRANGE AND ANCIENT LANDSCAPE

As I drove across vast plains of plateau tussock towards the oddly, but appropriately named village of National Park, the late-afternoon sky coloured the entire landscape deep blue, so that the only other colour was the bright white of the snowcap on magnificent Mount Ruapehu. The air was noticeably colder than it had been half an hour before, and I was feeling some trepidation about the following day's journey into this extraordinary terrain. The place is harsh yet beautiful, ancient and powerful, and its weird landscape presents a powerful reminder of the laws of nature. I was here to take on the 42 Traverse mountain-bike trail, one of the longest in New Zealand and, in some conditions, one of the most dangerous. Although National Park village would service my accommodation, dining, and entertainment needs very well, my journey would take me away from civilization and into the midst of hundreds of hectares of virgin forest and some of the

4 This is a long trip over rough terrain, so some recent mountain-biking experience is advisable, as is a good level of fitness.

★★ Preparation is the key to your comfort on the 42 Traverse, so ensure you take along all the recommended kit (see below).

 Good-quality cycle shorts will prevent chafing, gloves will reduce the risk of blisters, and more than one layer of clothing will guard against sunburn and provide warmth. A quality helmet is also a must, as are a well-stocked first-aid kit and bicycle-repair kit.

most spectacular landscapes in the North Island.

I turned off the main road into the tiny township to the warmth and comfort of Howard's Lodge, a favourite with backpackers. Peter and Sylvia, my hosts, had arranged the hire of a mountain bike for me, and after showing me to my room and giving me a quick tour of the facilities they introduced me to my means of transport for the following day. Peter provides a shuttle service to the start of the track for guests and independent riders alike, and is a seasoned mountain biker himself. He is also a long-time resident here, and as such is a mine of information; I was to be extremely grateful for his willingly imparted advice and tips.

Mountain biking on the bare slopes in the park is prohibited, so the 42 Traverse offers the best opportunity to get your adrenalin pumping up close to these mighty mountains. In New Zealand mountain-biking terms, the 42 Traverse is ranked 6/10 in the danger stakes and is also one of the most popular because the scenery is so spectacular. Many of the other rides in the North Island take you through vast corridors of fir plantations, but here you can experience the breathtaking grandeur of ancient virgin rainforest as well as admire the snow-capped Ruapehu, Ngaruahoe, and Tongariro mountains on clear days. The track is named for its Department of Conservation survey status, not its length—it is, in fact, 44km (27 miles) long, with an overall descent of 570m (1,870ft); experienced riders can reach speeds of 60–70kph (35–40mph) on the downhill stretches.

Over dinner at the corner café with a group of other pedal pushers, I began to wonder what I had let myself in for, as I was regaled with conquests I couldn't begin to compete with. It was with some relief that I met other relative rookies in the lodge car park the following morning. Here we helped Peter carefully load our bikes onto a trailer and climbed into the

Tongariro National Park

minibus for the 18km (11-mile) journey through barren desertscape to the mouth of the track.

MIXED FEELINGS

It was still chilly and the sky was threatening to release another deluge onto the already sodden ground. Dark clouds hung over the mountains, thinning only occasionally to reveal bright white snowcaps. It had rained heavily over previous days, and if it continued to do so today the trip would present serious challenges for inexperienced mountain bikers such as me. The camaraderie was, however, encouraging in our group of 16.

After we stepped off the bus at Kapoors Road, it was time for a final equipment check and a reminder from Peter that the route marker posts (which are placed 10m, or 30ft, before every major intersection) are picked off from time to time by hunters as target practice. He stressed we would be well advised to consult our maps if we had any uncertainties. This is a very isolated area and many bikers have become totally lost. This trip should not be attempted without a degree of caution. We then strapped on our helmets, pulled on our gloves and sunglasses, and methodically ticked off our checklists of maps, warm clothing,

Left: *Steeped in history and Maori mythology, the peaks here reign supreme*

Above: *Mount Ruapehu is an active volcano offering regular pyrotechnic displays as a backdrop to your cycling*

OUTSTANDING SITE

In 1990 Tongariro National Park, one of the most active andesitic volcanic regions on earth, was declared a World Heritage Area. This places it on an inventory of world sites which includes the Grand Canyon and Yosemite National Park in the U.S., and Tasmania's vast wildernesses. In 1993 Tongariro National Park also became one of the few world heritage areas recognized for possessing both natural and cultural values of "outstanding universal significance." Of the approximately 2,000 native plant species, nearly three-quarters are found nowhere else in the world. Dominating the Tongariro National Park forest are massive beech, rimu, totara, and kauri trees, as well as the manuka or tea-tree; the kowhai, the world's southernmost palm; the nikau, which grows wild here; and the strange, dead-straight cabbage tree. Also scattered throughout the area is the beautiful native climbing clematis, whose delicate white flower provides the only distraction among the myriad greens.

first-aid supplies, energy food and water, and comprehensive tool kits, including a spare tyre tube and chain breaker.

Compared to most mountain-bike trails in New Zealand, the 42 Traverse is raw and undeveloped. Paths have been forged through the vegetation, but the forest floor remains an uneven surface of rock and stone with occasional patches of shifting pumice and hard, smooth clay that can be slippery and treacherous when wet. I was keen to get on with it before my anxiety took a firm hold, and so I settled into the middle of the group. As we bounced across the first 7km (4½ miles) of loose stone, I was grateful for front and rear shock absorbers and for a windproof jacket that kept out the bitingly cold wind.

Six hours on a bicycle can be very uncomfortable if you're not used to it, especially over terrain like this, so some preparation is advisable. I had done plenty of road riding recently but was still concerned about holding up the rest of the group. With the exception of an English couple whose sole cycling experience was a gentle cross-country jaunt in France, I was amongst serious mountain bikers bent on reaching maximum speeds which they recorded on computerized speedometers.

PURE EXHILARATION

As I let the racers take an early lead, I glanced to my right to see the awesome sight of the now clearly visible Ruapehu, capped in snow. A right turn at the first marker took me on an undulating four-wheel-drive vehicle track and away from the stunted, windswept vegetation into deep forest. Suddenly, we were plummeting. This was the first downhill, which Peter had said would really wake me up, a fast and furious steep drop through a narrow, winding gully of uneven stone and dirt. The rush was fantastic, and as the greenery sped by I could hear whoops of delight from the riders ahead, who were already comparing maximum speeds at the base of the beautiful Waione River. With the huge mountains towering over us to our right, we slowly climbed 200m (650ft) before plunging down the valley again. By this time I was mud-spattered, beaming from ear to ear, and determined to set myself a pace somewhere between caution and intemperance.

The surface of the track changed from gravel to rain-ravaged, rutted soil and stones, and I put my weight well over the back wheel, fixed my eyes on the ground in front of me, and flew. Fantastic! So far, this trip was everything I'd been told it would be. On terrain as changeable as this, you can't afford to take your eyes off the strip of dirt directly in front of you. Concentration and anticipation is everything, but the rewarding thrill is superb. I could feel the strain in my forearms and realized I had the handlebars in a vice-like grip. I tried to relax my hands as I hurtled around the sharp bends, my entire being focused on making sure that the bike's front wheel went exactly where I wanted it to go, every muscle in my body reacting as an instant backup. It was pure exhilaration all the way.

We regrouped in a picturesque forest clearing with reports of descents of up to 55kmh (34mph). I lay my bike down, slipped off my day pack, and for the first time took in the majesty of the magnificent, lush rainforest. Vast stands of towering trees surrounded us, and the only sounds were the occasional bird call and the rattle of tyres on stones as the last riders approached. We had completed one-third of our journey without incident, and although this is a favourite place for deer hunters, today we seemed to have the forest entirely to ourselves.

DIRT, DANGER, AND ADRENALIN

As we pushed on, the mountains now at our backs and the spring sun trickling through the treetops, evidence of the recent rain suddenly materialized in the form of deep clay puddles. I was now literally plastered in mud from head to toe, and was completely in my element. This is escapism at its best: a bit of dirt, danger, and exertion topped off with a fantastic sense of triumph that you have successfully pitted yourself against the elements. I was feeling more confident and enjoying the manoeuvrability of my wide-tyred bike, but was also comforted by the fact that we were travelling only as fast as the slowest in the group.

As I pedalled on, ducking through a protruding grove of huge feathery toi toi pampas grass, I came upon a fellow traveller repairing what was to be the only puncture of the day and, as chance would have it, the only rider to fall, just a few metres further along. The fallen rider was expertly patched up with the help of one of our first-aid kits, and despite a heavily bandaged knee was back on his bike within minutes and sidling down the valley to our first ford and, that day, the only

---

EXPLOSIVE HISTORY

The Tongariro National Park lies at the southern end of the Taupo Volcanic Zone, and spreads out from Lake Taupo to Ohakune over a distance of 55km (34 miles). The oldest lava flows from Tongariro are about 260,000 years ago, although andesite pebbles from the region date activity back 1.7 million years. The park is also the site of one of the biggest volcanic eruptions to have occurred in the world in the last 5,000 years. Geologists estimate that about 1,800 years ago pumice was spewed to heights of 50km (30 miles). It levelled forests and buried everything within an 80km (50-mile) radius; the resulting crater eventually filled with water to form Lake Taupo.

---

non-rideable part of the trip. The knee-high water was fresh and freezing, and canopied by magnificent beech trees. One by one we lifted our bikes to the stony bank on the other side, while our injured friend was hoisted across in the interests of keeping his bandages dry. It was energy-food time, and a chance to register the fantastic isolation and beauty of the forest. For those who had been this way before, it was also time to laugh at the rest of us who bothered to remove our shoes and socks before wading through the water.

DINOSAUR TERRITORY

Resisting the temptation to stop for lunch, we eventually moved on. The toughest part was to come. In terms of distance we were halfway, but apart from a short stretch of undulating path and more water to wade through, the next 5km (3 miles) was a steady uphill grind which added almost an hour to the remainder of the trip. Determined to enjoy the scenery as well as the achievement of the traverse, I took Peter's advice

Above: *A welcome level stretch gives riders a chance to appreciate the fantastic view*
Left: *The vivid green slopes of Tongariro National Park, with Ruapehu brooding in the background*
Right: *A bust of Te Heuheu Tukino IV commemorates the Maori leader who gave Tongariro and Ruapehu to the people of New Zealand*

191

NORTH ISLAND

GENEROUS GIFT

In 1887, Te Heuheu Tukino IV, the paramount chief of the Ngati Tuwharetoa, gifted on behalf of his tribe, the summits of Tongariro and part of Ruapehu to the people of New Zealand. He wished to establish a three-way bond between the land, the Maori, and the Pakeha (New Zealanders of European descent). These sacred mountains are to be owned by no one and yet can be enjoyed by everyone. The Tuwharetoa people say the mountains of the south wind have spoken to them for centuries, and that they wish them to speak to all who come in peace and in respect of their *tapu* (sacred nature). For the mountains to remain sacred, every generation must honour the intentions behind the original Maori gift.

and made a short detour from the track to an expansive rock lookout. Stretched out below me was Echo Valley, containing a vast acreage of untouched native rainforest, and with sheer rock sides dropping hundreds of metres to the forest floor. As I stood well back from the edge in the now warm mid-morning sun, I wouldn't have blinked if a *Tyrannosaurus rex* had raised its head through the vegetation below. Echo Valley is mystical, spiritual, and untouched by time.

I soon caught up with the last of the group, a few of whom were now on foot. This trip is reported to be 99 per cent rideable, and having tried both, I found the smallest gear on the steep inclines a lot easier than pushing your bike. I also learned early on that keeping a steady leg rhythm by making full use of the gears is a lot less tiring than pedalling fast and then slowing down. Even so, I found it tough going up a series of steep, rocky cuts, and had to force my legs to keep pushing.

As I emerged panting over the top of our second near-perpendicular slope, I was met by a burst of applause from the pack leaders, who were by now devouring their lunch. Our friend with the heavily bandaged leg valiantly heaved himself off his bike, assured us that the pain wasn't too bad, and lowered himself onto a large, flat boulder. I wasn't sure I would have been so brave, but as he pointed out, there weren't too many choices—we were a long way from anywhere. One by one the remaining riders joined us, and as we chatted over our food I realized that I was the oldest here, at the wrong end of my forties. We were a disparate group of executives and professionals, plus a couple of teenagers who had been brought along for the ride by fathers keen to give them an experience of a lifetime. Three or four of the more experienced riders had handlebar extensions to give them, they said, more leverage on the uphills. I noted this for next time. Given that I had been concerned about spending up to six hours attached to a bike seat, I had taken the precaution of wearing good-quality padded cycle shorts, for which I was now profoundly thankful. I was aching a little already, and knew I couldn't have coped with chafing as well.

We had roughly another hour to go. Since we passed Echo Valley we had descended nearly 200m (660ft); the rest of the journey would take us on a gentle decline beneath a thundering waterfall and down to the magnificent Whakapapa River. Although this is definitely the easiest portion of the track, it isn't without its difficulties. Several of our group, a little weary and not prepared to chance injury, chose to walk the roughest stretches, and from the moment the first rider rolled quietly out of the forest to when the last emerged, more than half an hour had elapsed. As I lay on a warm boulder flanking the river I realized I'd done it, all 44km (27 miles) of it. The sense of achievement was fantastic. As we waited for Peter to pick us up I asked the young man sprawled next to me what he thought of the day. "Soul food with attitude," he grinned.

i

GOING IT ALONE

INTERNAL TRAVEL

The village of National Park can be accessed by shuttle-bus from Lake Taupo, which itself can be reached by train or coach from many main towns throughout the North Island. National Park lies southeast of Taupo via highways 1 and 47. To reach the start of the 42 Traverse, head northeast on Highway 47 from National Park township. After 18km (11 miles) you will reach Kapoors Road on your left and a parking area. Kapoors Road is too rough for most cars, but you should be able to negotiate it on your bike.

WHEN TO GO

While Mount Ruapehu protects the forest from bad weather blowing in from the southeast, it bears the full brunt of westerly storms. The coldest months are June, July, and August, and the warmest December, January, and February. In winter this track can be icy and dangerous, while in midsummer it can get very hot.

PLANNING

The 42 Traverse is recommended for intermediate mountain-bike riders. It is one of the longest such tracks in New Zealand and is also one of the most popular, but it shouldn't be attempted by anyone under 16 or without an average to good level of fitness. The terrain is rough and the trip will take you between three and six hours. Thrill wise, it rates at least 8/10. Remember this is a World Heritage Area and pristine rain forest, so you must take out everything you take in. Other

mountain-bike trails in the area are the John McDonald Loop, 40km (25 miles) over 4–7 hours; the Tongariro Forest Loop, 42km (26 miles) over 3–6 hours; the Owanga Loop, 33km (21 miles) over 2–4 hours; and the Fishers Track, 50km (31 miles) over 3–5 hours.

Independent mountain bikers can hire quality bikes from 42 Traverse & Bike Hire at National Park. Howard's Lodge accommodation, also in National Park, is excellent and well priced for individuals and groups alike, and also provides a cheap shuttle service to and from the trail. Booking is essential.

TRAVELLERS' TIPS

❏ Give your bike a quick once-over before you ride, checking for wobbly wheels, worn brakes, loose bearings and bolts, a dry chain, and frayed cables.

❏ Padded cycle shorts make this trip a lot more comfortable.

❏ A camelback water system from your day pack means you can sip without stopping.

WHAT TO TAKE

❏ Helmet.
❏ Gloves. Padded cycling gloves are best.
❏ Windproof jacket and warm lightweight clothes (fleece is ideal).
❏ Sunglasses and some device to keep them on your head.
❏ Tools to repair punctures and chains.
❏ Comprehensive first-aid kit.
❏ Map (available from local outlets at National Park).
❏ At least 1.5 litres (2½ pints) of water.
❏ Camera.

HEALTH

This is a very isolated area. Take extra clothes, food, and a first-aid kit, and make sure someone responsible knows what you're up to. A lightweight survival tent is also a good idea. Don't go alone, and consider taking a cellphone. If the Waione River is brown and swollen take extreme caution when crossing. Remember that hypothermia can kill. If someone shows signs of being cold, tired, and uncoordinated, prevent further cooling and arrange for his or her immediate evacuation.

FURTHER READING

Classic New Zealand Mountain Bike Rides (Kennett Bros, Wellington 1996) by Paul, Simon and Jonathan Kennett

A comprehensive and detailed look at mountain biking tracks throughout New Zealand, including good safety and equipment advice, maps, and degree of difficulty rankings. Available in New Zealand bookshops or via the internet on www.mountainbike.co.nz

Jonathan Kennett is also a co-author of *Classic New Zealand Adventures* (Compass Star Publications 1996)—a good starting point for any adventure traveller heading for New Zealand.

NORTH ISLAND

19 Horse Trekking along Ancient Maori Trails

by Veronika Meduna and Andy Reisinger

We enjoyed a timeless three-day journey on horseback through primeval forests to the Maori spiritual heartland of the Te Urewera ranges, learning about ancient traditions and legends of the Tuhoe tribe.

The rugged Te Urewera ranges in the east of the North Island form part of the 650km (400-mile) mountain backbone that stretches from Wellington to the East Cape. A striking feature of these mountains is the density of the vegetation, unbroken by pastures or plains. These magical, frequently mist-shrouded hills are the ancient home of the Tuhoe, a proud tribe of warriors who have lived in the area for more than 1,000 years. They led a spartan existence, resisting approaches by the colonial powers and missionaries for a long time. To this day, the Tuhoe maintain pride in their cultural heritage and traditions. They are the guardians of this forested land, where swirling rivers continue to carve the landscape on their way to the Pacific.

2 | The treks involve about four to five hours of riding each day, depending on the route you take and the condition of the tracks. Because the tracks are narrow, the horses walk most of the way, so even inexperienced riders will enjoy the trek.

★★ | The tents and inflatable mattresses provided are comfortable but basic. All meals are taken in the open air. At the camp, a shelter offers protection from rain, but it pays to bring an insect repellent to deter the tiny sandflies—their bites itch for several days and can be quite unpleasant.

 | The weather can change quickly, so both breathable waterproofs and sun protection are essential. Take warm, fast-drying outdoor clothing for the evenings, around the campfire and colder nights in the tent. Good walking boots are a prerequisite. A flash or fast (400 ISO/ASA) film are needed for photography in the dense forests.

PROTECTED FORESTS

A large part of the rainforest is now a national park administered by the Department of Conservation. The park area has a good network of walking tracks and huts, but apart from that, little tourism has entered the scarcely populated depths of this temperate jungle. During the three-day trip our small group met no other travellers.

The area surrounding Te Urewera, from Taupo to Rotorua and the East Cape, is rich in Maori history, and so it pays to start your journey slowly, taking in some of the Maori way of life. In Rotorua you can watch carvers at work, enjoy a Maori concert, and partake of a *hangi*—a traditional meal steam-cooked over hot boulders in an earth oven. Following these insights you can then head off the beaten track to share rather than observe Maori culture, on a journey deep into the Te Urewera forests. The region offers both an adventure and a voyage into a different world.

TAKING IT EASY

Our journey begins in Rotorua, the centre of New Zealand's geothermal area, with towering geysers, bubbling mud pools, and kaleidoscopic silica terraces. The odour of hydrogen sulphide pervades Rotorua day and night and

Above: *These magical, frequently mist-shrouded hills are the ancient home of the Tuhoe*
Right: *Ponga ferns on North island*
Below left: *Rotorua Maori wood carving*

has earned it the nickname Sulphur City. Heading south on Highway 5 to meet our fellow travellers, we pass a model Maori village that illustrates the way people used to live before the arrival of the first European explorers and settlers.

Beyond the Waimangu Volcanic Valley, with its fumaroles and steaming streams, Highway 38 turns east towards the coast to take us on a two-hour drive to Ruatahuna, a settlement of about 250 people and a traditional centre of the Tuhoe. Gradually, the straight and parallel trunks of pine trees, a Californian species that forms the backbone of New Zealand's timber industry, give way to dense bush and then to a wall of impenetrable native vegetation. Despite its designation as a state highway, the road is winding and unsealed for most of the journey.

LEARNING TUHOE CUSTOM

Even before we start our horse trek, we learn something about Tuhoe custom and hospitality. As we arrive at our guides'

NATIVE TREE FERNS

Several species of native tree fern grow in the rainforests of the Te Urewera. The tallest is the black fern or mamaku, which grows up to 20m (65ft) tall and has a crown of giant fronds topping a black trunk. The silver fern, or ponga, is New Zealand's national emblem and is easily identified by the silvery undersides of its leaves. It can grow up to 3m (10ft). Ferns form most of the undergrowth in the rainforest.

TE UREWERA NATIONAL PARK

The beauty of the Te Urewera ranges has been threatened several times during the last century. Large areas were set aside for settlement by servicemen returning from World War I, but the land proved too wild and rough. Later, during the Great Depression, the New Zealand government almost bowed to the pressure to mill the timber and clear the area for farmland. Finally, in 1954, more than 200,000ha (500,000 acres) of the forest-cloaked hills surrounding Lake Waikaremoana were put aside as the Te Urewera National Park. With the neighbouring Whirinaki Forest Park, this comprises the largest remaining pocket of native rainforest in the North Island. It is also one of the last places where the red-flowering kaka beak can be found in the wild.

home, we are asked to take our shoes off outside. The couple, Whare and Makere Biddle, also offer homestays at their home in Mataatua, about 4km (2½ miles) from Ruatahuna, so travellers often spend the night here before the ride. On our first evening, we share a generous meal with the other travellers, but our hosts don't join us at the table; it is Tuhoe custom to let the guests have their meal alone on the first night and for the hosts to eat what is left.

The Tuhoe are also very careful not to bring anything connected with the body, such as tissues and toiletries, near areas where food is prepared. Food has a special status that extends to the tables where it is eaten, the bench where it is prepared, and the fire where it is cooked. These rules also apply in the outdoors when food is prepared over a campfire.

EXPLORING THE RAINFOREST

Our small cavalcade is ready to leave late in the morning the following day. The

horses carry our gear, which is securely stored in kitbags, fastened at the front of the saddle across their shoulders. Although we have all been on horseback before, nobody in our group is particularly experienced or skilled as a rider. For the first half-hour we walk the horses along a rough farm road, which is enough to get used to the sensation before the track narrows and we are swallowed up by the forest.

The Whakatane River gurgles gently below us as the track gradually drops towards the valley along steep, narrow forest paths. We weave our way through dense clusters of tree ferns, past tall, ancient kahikatea trees, and down to the mossy banks of the river. The horses are very surefooted and know the area well, and even during the numerous river crossings we ride with trust and loose reins.

Altitude is the dominant factor in plant composition in the Te Urewera. As it increases certain trees appear, become abundant, and then disappear as more hardy plants take their place. The native trees growing in the lower reaches include rimu, northern rata, tawa, and the beech, the latter taking over completely above about 900m (3,000ft). Under the canopy grow rich stands of different types of tree ferns and broadleaf bushes, as well as many other plants unique to New Zealand. Virtually all landscape and botanical features that characterize inland North Island—grassy river flats, limestone bluffs, and podocarp and beech forests—are represented within the Te Urewera ranges.

CHILDREN OF THE MIST

Even on a sunny day, the early morning often envelopes the dense Te Urewera rainforest in mist, which rises through the canopy from the moist soil below. Maori mythology is based on the reverence of all living things, as well as shapes and features of the landscape. For many Tuhoe, the morning mists signify the presence of their ancestors, who still live in the

Horse trekking in Te Urewera National Park

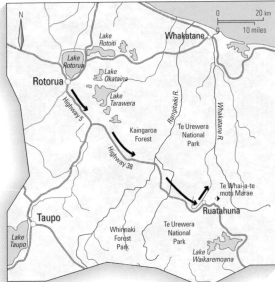

forests watching over them. For us, it adds spirituality and magic. Our guides tell us that, according to legend, the Tuhoe people are direct descendants of the marriage between Hine-pukohu-rangi, the celestial maiden of the mist, and Te Maunga, the mountain. In the Ruatahuna Valley a sacred flax bush used to mark the place of the gods' mythological union. Their firstborn, Potiki, is the main ancestor to whom the Tuhoe trace their beginnings in ancient times.

HIDDEN PA SITES

After about two hours the track starts climbing and, quite unexpectedly, the forest opens to reveal a clearing and the Ohaua Te Rangi Marae. This *pa*, as the Maori call fortified villages, dates back to the 1920s, and its handful of semi-permanent residents represent a fascinating link between the past and present.

All Maori meeting houses (*wharenui*) are built following the same architectural plan to represent a god-like guardian who watches over the people gathered within. The roof ridge is regarded as the backbone, while the triangle of front beams extending from the gable represents the arms, outstretched in a welcoming gesture. Inside, the meeting house is spacious. The single large room is framed by the side beams, interspersed with woven panels, which represent the guardian's ribs. In contrast to meeting houses built by other tribes, the Tuhoe design theirs with the entrance door off centre, towards the left. The larger space to the right is reserved for visitors, while the hosts make their beds on the left.

ON THE MENU

Although you will be camping and living in the outdoors, you can expect culinary delights and frequent cups of tea. Having a "cuppa" has become an integral part of New Zealand life, so a soot-darkened billy, plastic cups, and teabags are always in the saddlebags. The cuisine is traditional New Zealand, with Maori influences. A crisp roast of lamb comes with baked *kumara* (sweet potato) and pumpkin, followed by pavlova for dessert. New Zealanders and Australians still argue about who invented this sweet meringue filled with cream, and fruit. At breakfast you can choose between porridge or bacon and eggs. Double-decker sandwiches will sustain you during the day, and the evening meals are cooked over the open fire. A highlight of our trip was a lofty bread-and-butter pudding baked in the embers of the campfire.

Inside the meeting house, the beams are either painted or carved to represent the ancestry of the local people.

We are told that the Ohaua Te Rangi Marae meeting house is still used to welcome guests on to the *marae* (the open space in front of the meeting house) in the traditional way. In a ceremony outside, invitation chants, speeches, and songs are usually exchanged between the hosts and their guests, preceding the opening of the *wharenui*.

The *marae* is an unexpected island of human presence in the green wilderness around it, and it reminds us how tightly interwoven human existence and nature still are in this region. As we leave, the only sounds are the buzzing cicadas, the distant gurgle of the river, and the beat of the horses' hoofs.

A HOME AT CAMP TAWHIWHI

Just outside the national park boundaries at the riverbank, our guides have set up Camp Tawhiwhi, a small permanent shelter and outdoor kitchen built from tree-fern logs, timber, and pieces of

Left: *At Tawhiwhi our guides produced delicious hot food from this simple but effective outdoor kitchen*
Below: *Crossing the Whakatane River—like the forest, the river is linked with many myths and legends*

THE MAORI LANGUAGE

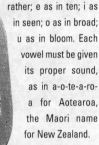

Te reo Maori, the Maori language, belongs to the Polynesian linguistic group, a fact that allowed Captain Cook's Tahitian interpreter, Tupaia, to translate for him during his voyage in 1769. Many Maori words have found their way into everyday New Zealand English, so it pays to learn a few terms. *Kia ora*, for example, meaning "may you be well,' has become a very common greeting among non-Maori speakers. In Maori, the vowels are pronounced as follows: a as in rather; e as in ten; i as in seen; o as in broad; u as in bloom. Each vowel must be given its proper sound, as in a-o-te-a-ro-a for Aotearoa, the Maori name for New Zealand.

aroha	love
awa	river
haka	war dance
hangi	earth oven
hongi	pressing noses in greeting
iwi	people; tribe
kai	food; eat
karakia	prayer
kaumatua	male elder
koha	gift
kuia	female elder
mana	spiritual power; authority
marae	area around meeting house
maunga	mountain
moana	lake; sea
pa	fortified village
pakeha	person of European descent
tapu	forbidden; sacred
waka	canoe
wharenui	meeting house

corrugated iron. As we arrive, water is put on to boil in a billy over the open fire, while we make our temporary homes in three tents equipped with comfortable airbeds. The shelter also doubles as a very handy storage room, which is regularly refilled so that there is no need to carry camping gear on the treks. The river here has carved itself a shallow bed with many smaller pools. During our overnight stay it provides us with an open-air bathroom and, most welcome of all, an opportunity for a refreshing evening dip in the cool water to soothe our sore muscles.

We all help with the dinner preparations as best we can, but Makere has developed outdoor cooking to an art form. Incredibly she conjures up a delicious bread and butter pudding, baked simply in the embers of a dying fire. By the glow of the campfire and the kerosene lamps we share the meal and listen to stories about the Tuhoe. We learn about their relationship to nature, and their religious beliefs. Nature and god are very closely linked for the Tuhoe, and Whare tells us that nothing is taken from the environment without a good reason.

Above: *Maori carving*
Right: *A woodcarver at work in Rotorua, a popular destination for visitors interested in Maori crafts*

MAORI MEDICINAL PLANTS

Tuhoe people prepare a number of natural remedies from native plants they harvest from the hills surrounding the Whakatane River valley. The gum of the native matai tree, or black pine, is collected and the gel-like extract used to treat burns. The manuka shrub, which is related to the Australian tea-tree, yields an essential oil with proven antimicrobial properties. The leaves of the karamuramu tree are used to prepare a kidney-cleansing potion, while extracts of the native clematis are boiled down to an ointment said to alleviate bruises.

THE BARKING SPIRITS OF THE RIVER

The next morning we wake to the sound of the river and a dawn chorus of native birds. The birds in these remote forests seem unusually tame, almost curious, and will often let people come very close. During our trek we come across several native wood pigeons, heavy birds that look elegant in the trees but are clumsy in flight. Smaller songbirds such as yellowhammers, fantails, tomtits, and grey warblers are our constant companions.

The second day takes us on a loop further along the river, following old paths and tracks maintained by the Department of Conservation. We plan to return to Camp Tawhiwhi for another night, so we travel light; this proves an advantage as the terrain gets more rugged and the tracks steeper. Sometimes the undergrowth is so dense that we find ourselves hugging the horses' necks to make sure we don't get pulled off by branches.

The track winds its way up and down the steep banks of the Whakatane river. We reach our turn-around point at the Dog *taniwha* (good or evil spirit). With a little imagination one can see the shape of a dog in a giant boulder in the middle of the river. Our guide tells us that the water-sculpted rock has long served as a

spiritual warning post for travellers. When the water rises and the Whakatane becomes too difficult to cross, the Dog starts barking as the river beats against the boulder's hollows.

Like the forest, the river is linked with many myths and legends. Its name, which means "to make a man," originates from the brave actions of Wairaka, the daughter of the captain of one of the original canoes that brought the Maori people to New Zealand. The Mataatua canoe landed in the Bay of Plenty during the 14th-century Polynesian migration. The men went ashore to explore the new land, but the boat started drifting out to sea. Women were not allowed to touch the sacred paddles, so they watched helplessly until the captain's daughter exclaimed that she would "act as a man." Others followed her example, and they brought the canoe safely back to shore. A modern statue of Wairaka stands on the rocks of Whakatane Heads.

SENSE OF TIMELESSNESS

From the Dog rock we retrace our steps to camp, and a day later travel back to our hosts' 20ha (50-acre) property in Mataatua, still following the river but taking different paths. The settlement is named after the canoe which brought the Tuhoe and other tribes to New Zealand. Once there, we are invited to visit the Te Whai-a-te-motu meeting house. It was built between 1870 and 1888 in honour of Te Kooti, a Maori rebel who founded the Ringatu religion widely followed among the Tuhoe. Te Whai-a-te-motu means "the chase of the island," referring to the rebel's imprisonment on the Chatham Islands and his later elusiveness. With its many traditional carvings, the meeting house is regarded as one of the most magnificent buildings of the Tuhoe. The carved centre poles depict the captain and the scout of the Mataatua canoe. The house is not open to casual visitors, so you have to ask permission, but a tour of this sacred place is a fitting finale to a journey into another world.

GOING IT ALONE

INTERNAL TRAVEL

The nearest domestic airport to Te Urewera National Park is Rotorua; Air New Zealand and Ansett provide daily links from all key cities in the country. The Geyserland Express travels daily between Auckland and Rotorua along a scenic train route inaccessible by car. There is also a train connection from Wellington. Several coach, bus, and scenic tour operators connect Rotorua with most North Island cities.

To get to Ruatahuna, your best bet is to hire a car or arrange to be picked up by your hosts or fellow travellers. Highway 38 is a good gravel road and the trip takes about 2½ hours.. From Ruatahuna, Highway 38 continues to Lake Waikaremoana, a good starting point for many walks within the national park, and then on to Wairoa in Hawkes Bay. Throughout summer, there may be a bus service between Rotorua and Frasertown near Lake Waikaremoana, depending on demand.

WHEN TO GO

The best time to go is in high summer (December and January), when the native rata and pohutukawa trees are in bloom and the weather is also reliably warm enough (25°C, or 78°F, during the day) for camping outdoors, although you may still experience rain. In spring (September and October), the weather can be very changeable. A few days of rain at this time can make the river crossings impossible. Autumn (March–May) tends to be more stable.

PLANNING

Summer is the busiest time and tours are often booked up in advance, but because of its remoteness, the Te Urewera is not yet on many international itineraries.

TRAVELLERS' TIPS

❏ Take your shoes off when entering people's homes. It is particularly important to respect this custom when entering a *wharenui*.

❏ Always ask permission before photographing the people in remote villages. Some Maori feel uneasy about having their photograph taken as for them it means giving some of their *mauri* (life force). The same applies to carvings, which are considered living parts of ancestors.

❏ Never sit on tables as places of food preparation are *tapu* (sacred).

❏ A *hongi* is the traditional Maori greeting, where two people press their noses together and hold hands or embrace. Leave it to your host to initiate a *hongi*.

❏ If you are invited to stay on a *marae* and expect to be welcomed officially, think of a song from your country to perform at the ceremony as such exchanges usually take place between the *tangata whenua* (people of the land) and the *manuhiri* (visitors).

WHAT TO TAKE

❏ All riding gear is provided, as are sleeping bags with an inner liner, and kitbags.

❏ Take good outdoor clothing for all temperatures, as the weather can bring four seasons in a day, particularly in the mountains.

❏ A pair of sturdy walking boots is good for the ride, but bring another pair of comfortable shoes as your boots might get wet during the river crossings.

❏ A sun hat, sunglasses, and sunscreen are essentials.

❏ Bring a pair of binoculars with you to watch the birdlife. The Department of Conservation shops at the entrances to the national parks have identification guides for native birds and plants.

HEALTH

There are no poisonous creatures in New Zealand, apart from a rare spider whose bite can be painful. However, the sandflies are a nuisance, particularly at dawn and dusk. The water from creeks and rivers in Te Urewera is drinkable without treatment.

FURTHER READING

Classic Walks of New Zealand, National Parks of New Zealand (Craig Potton Publishing, 1997 and 1998 respectively). Written and photographed by Craig Potton, each book devotes a chapter to the region, including a detailed description of the walk around Lake Waikaremoana, illustrated by images taken by one of New Zealand's best photographers.

WATCHING WHALES AND SWIMMING WITH DOLPHINS 204–211 ⑳

THRILLS AND SPILLS ON THE SHOTOVER RIVER 238–247 ㉔

ON THE ROUTEBURN TRACK 248–256 ㉕

HIGH COUNTRY ON HORSEBACK 212–219 ㉑

FLY FISHING VIA THE TRANZALPINE 220–227 ㉒

HIGH ON GLACIERS 228–237 ㉓

Cook Strait

Nelson · Picton
Westport · Wairau · Blenheim
Murchison
Greymouth · Maruia Springs · ⑳ · Kaikoura
㉒ · ㉑
375&m Mt Cook · Christchurch
Haast · ㉓ · Canterbury Plains
Tekapo
Timaru · Canterbury Bight
Wanaka · Waitaki
㉕ · Lake · ㉔ · Cromwell
Wakatipu · Queenstown
Te Anau · Alexandra
Manapouri
Gore
Invercargill · **Dunedin**
Foveaux Strait
Stewart Island
South West Cape

Southern Alps

0   100   200 km
0   50   100 miles

NEW ZEALAND•
SOUTH ISLAND

T he South Island is the home of extreme adventure. It is easy
to see why, for the landscape is an inspiration in itself. The
beauty of the Southern Alps, with Mount Cook as their highest
point, is a positive invitation to explore. As always, New Zealanders
have made the most of what nature has given them. To see the
mountains in comfort, take the TranzAlpine, one of the great railway
journeys of the world. To feel the snow and ice beneath your feet, take
a helicopter ride and clamber about the glaciers in Westland. In the
lowlands, there is some of the finest trout fishing in the world on the
west coast, whilst off the eastern seaboard at Kaikoura, there are
whales to spot and dolphins aplenty. Inland, not far from the picture-
postcard charms of Christchurch, you can take wonderful, rambling
horse treks . And then there is Queenstown, in the heart of Southland,
where bungee jumping was invented and where you can experience
the thrill of jetboating, or go tramping along the Routeburn Track.

Splendid coastal scenery stretches north and south from Kaikoura

20 Watching Whales, Dolphins and Seals

by Christopher Knowles

From Christchurch I went by road across the hills to Kaikoura, an old whaling port where the welfare of the whales, as well as of dolphins and seals, is now the main source of income.

Christchurch, on New Zealand's South Island, was built by settlers to resemble a cross between a garden city and an English university town. Although Christchurch is not quite as "English" as it is said to be, there are some very definite aspects of the city that are reminiscent of a certain type of Englishness. You can be punted on the River Avon through a very English park by helmsmen in straw boaters; statues of Victorian heroes and statesmen, in better condition than their equivalents in England, dot the city; and Cathedral Square is used for public speaking, much as Speaker's Corner is in London. It is from Christchurch that the famed TranzAlpine Express begins its journey across the Southern Alps to Greymouth, and near here where whales, seals, and dolphins frolic in the ocean.

1 Watching whales is not hard work as everything is done for you. The same is true of watching dolphins, although if you want to go in the sea with them you will need to be a confident swimmer.

★★ Accommodation of all kinds is available in Christchurch. It is also possible to overnight at Kaikoura, although the range of places to stay here is much more limited. You are advised to book trips in advance, especially the whale-watching.

All that is required is a swimming costume for the dolphin excursion (wetsuits and snorkelling equipment are provided), and some sort of protection against the wind on cooler days. Binoculars are useful, as is a good zoom lens for your camera.

THE WEATHER TURNS

On the day of my arrival in Christchurch, the grey, blustery conditions did not bode well for any seagoing adventure. Yet by the following morning, the weather had, in typical local style, changed entirely. It was warm, the sky was cloudless, and the country was suffused with a soft, burnished glow that is so characteristic of the light in New Zealand. It would, I was sure, be perfect for watching whales.

Ken Inglis of Royale Tours picked me up at around 8:30 in the morning. Apart from me, there were three others in the party: an American couple from Arizona and an Austrian who turned out to be a professional photographer specializing in wildlife photography. This became apparent only when he produced an impressive array of photographic equipment that would be beyond the means of all but the most enthusiastic and wealthiest amateur. We headed north to Kaikoura. The journey, which requires about three hours (including a short coffee break), took us across the neat farming country of the Canterbury Plain. However, it did not seem to me to resemble in anyway that part of England from which it takes its name, for instead of the rolling Kentish hills and narrow valleys it was fairly flat and open, with large farmsteads where enormous pine hedges had been planted as windbreaks. Huge and dense, the hedges had been pruned and trimmed with enormous care and attention, a perfect example of that tendency to do things properly, or not at all, that would seem to characterize the New Zealand outlook on life.

We left the Canterbury Plain and began to climb over the hills that separate it from the sea. The landscape here was smothered in brilliant yellow-flowering gorse and dense mossy green bushes, and watered by any number of gushing, crystal streams christened, with touching directness, Siberia, Chilly, and other equally appropriate names. There were creeks called Hewson or McDonald, natural memorials to the efforts of the earliest settlers, who thereby left their small mark on a new world. Scottish names in particular were widespread, and it seemed to me that although New Zealand is always said to be "more English than England," it is in fact more reminiscent of Scotland, particularly in terms of its colouring and in the contours of its landscape.

BESIDE THE SEASIDE

After an hour of traversing the hills, we glimpsed a sparkle of water and almost immediately found ourselves right beside it, for in this case the mountains really do come right down to the sea. We went straight to the Whale Watch terminal to check in and claim our tickets. A short film was screened to give us an idea of what lay in store, and the weather conditions were relayed to us. Even though the sea looked almost dead calm, it transpired that this can be illusory and that beyond the near horizon, where the whales lurk, conditions can be quite different. However, the chances of the boat being prevented from going out, were, so we were assured, "marginal." We were also told that the swell could be enough to turn the stomachs of the queasy, but Ken had very kindly acquired some acupressure bands, which when worn on the wrist are supposed to prevent seasickness. Whale Watch also rents them out—you pay a deposit which is reimbursed upon the safe return of the bands.

After the film, most people were invited to pose for photographs to

DEEP DIVERS

Sperm whales are present year-round in Kaikoura, and are attracted by the abundance of food. Their diet consists mostly of squid, and occasionally cod, grouper, and shark. Food is frequently swallowed whole, and sperm whales are even capable of gulping down a 3m (10ft) shark in this way. The whales are one of the deepest diving creatures on Earth. They have been recorded at depths of up to 2,000m (6,500ft), and can stay submerged for as long as two hours. They then need to surface for between 10 and 20 minutes to replenish their oxygen supplies. After surfacing, their first exhalation can be heard up to 1km (½ mile) away.

commemorate the occasion. Ken, however, whisked us away to the jetty so that we would be first in the queue and would therefore have the chance to claim places on the top deck of the boat, where there were only a dozen seats available for most of the trip. The view is supposed to be better from the top, and certainly it would be less crowded at the rails owing to the restrictions on the numbers allowed up there. The disadvantage is that, in a swell, the upper deck appears to sway far more than the lower deck. However, our group resolved to go for that upper deck, come what may.

WHEN OUR BOAT COMES IN

While we are hanging about at the water's edge, awaiting all the other passengers, a tractor, hitherto motionless, burst into life and backed a sort of trolley into the water. Then we noticed a boat, about the size of a large leisure cruiser, picking its way among the rocks and heading towards us. Soon it was very close to the shore, and we looked on fascinated as it headed for the submerged trailer, showing no sign of slowing its momentum. Nor did it slow its pace, until at the last second the engine was cut and the vessel slithered gracefully onto the trailer, whereupon the dripping hulk was immediately hauled out of the water and onto the quayside beside us. For some reason the whole operation delighted us all, and we exclaimed and gasped like children. Even if we weren't going to see any whales, at least we had seen the slickest beaching operation in history!

Of course, it is by no means guaranteed that you will see whales. Once we were on board, this is one of the things that was made clear to us, as the captain and his assistants introduced themselves to us over the tannoy. On the other hand, they said, the average sighting is at least one whale per trip, which clearly means that we would stand a pretty good chance. The boat, with us on it, was placed back into the water, the engines revved up, and we nosed gently out to deeper waters.

Behind us, as we headed out to sea, a classic New Zealand scene opened up, of

a shimmering jade sea lapping at the foot of snow-capped mountains that seemed to rise almost directly out of the water to reach up to the deep blue sky. Everything was white, blue, and green, and impossibly fresh and clean. The rain and grey of the day before were by now distant memories. It was, however, fairly cold as the sea breeze took hold, and when we reached deeper waters, the boat began to rock as we rose and fell with the swell. Still, the wristbands seemed to be working well so far.

Above: Sightings are of course not guaranteed, but most trips spot at least one whale
Inset: A tractor hauls the Kaikoura whale watching boat out of the water so we can get aboard
Right: The royal albatross—symbol of southern skies

LEVIATHAN

We were asked to remain seated until we were as close to a whale as is possible or permitted, whereupon the vessel would come to a halt and we would be given the chance to stand at the rails. We were also employed as lookouts, and were told not to look for a dark shape or a fin, but for a faint, translucent plume of smoke, which may well be the spout of a whale. The captain was in radio contact with other boats and with a helicopter, so if there was a sighting from one of those we would be able to race to the scene. Something had been spotted about 20 minutes away, and we set off; but too late, it had already submerged.

Then we were off again and this time we were in luck—it was a sperm whale. We approached slowly from behind and bobbed up and down on the swell. We were then allowed to get up from our seats and stand at the rail; a few others were allowed up from the deck below, but there was still plenty of room for all. We could see the outline of the creature, and hear a sort of wheezing noise as it breathed in air (a whale, it will be remembered, is a mammal, not a fish). It was just possible to distinguish the cliff-like front that distinguishes this species from other whales, the shape that seems always to characterize the whales of illustrations in old books and of cartoons. We could see the ridges on its blubbery, glistening skin, and then it disappeared briefly, as if taking one last, huge breath. "He is about to go under!" cried the captain. "Look out for the tail!" He did not mean, of course, that we were in any danger, only that we should have our cameras ready for the moment when the tail fluke flipped up like an umbrella, just immediately before the whale disappeared altogether.

In all, we came across four whales, all of them sperm whales, which is a pretty good haul. It is curious to be so close to the world's largest creatures and to feel entirely unthreatened. Nor it seems did they feel threatened by us, for they basked quite happily not too far from the boat. The boats go no closer than about 90m, or 100yd, which is still close enough to see and hear the whales. The boats are careful not to position themselves head on to the whales as it seems that they have a blind spot, so that an unseen, but felt, presence can provoke panic. The boatsmen believe that the whales enjoy having the boats near by; perhaps they find the noise of the engines comforting, or even see the bulky vessels as travelling companions.

BANKS PENINSULA

Although part of the Canterbury region is a flat plain, to the southeast of Christchurch is the Banks Peninsula, a picturesque area of valleys, harbours, and bays. Diamond Harbour, Okains Bay, and Okuti Valley are particularly worth a visit, as is Akaroa. This town is the product by of attempt by French whalers to establish a colony on the peninsula in 1838. There are still many hallmarks of French life, including bakeries, restaurants, and street names. The leader of the colony, Jean Langlois, arrived back from France just too late to avert the Treaty of Waitangi (see page 173).

A SURFEIT OF WILDLIFE

After we had seen our four whales, the captain deemed that we'd had our fill and so we set off in search of other creatures. A school of dusky dolphins was sighted, and then we saw that great symbol of southern skies, the royal albatross, renowned for its huge wingspan. Two of these great birds were tussling with a fish head. On close inspection, an albatross looks like an extremely large and ungainly seagull, and all romantic connotations vanish when you see them struggling to take off. Their true glory is evident only when they are soaring in the air. Finally, we even saw a rare white great petrel bobbing on the water beside the boat. We had the full set and felt satisfied that we had seen more than we could possibly have hoped for.

Four sperm whales notwithstanding, we have not forgotten the excitement that awaited us as at the jetty. For the other passengers, this came as something of a surprise, and there was a palpable air of anxiety as the boat showed no sign of slowing, followed by a gasp as we slid up the shore like a seal deposited by a wave. And then Ken was there to take us back to the little town of Kaikoura, where we would be having lunch.

DOLPHINS

After lunch it was time to get afloat again, this time on a rather smaller vessel and in search of a smaller creature—the dolphin. That morning we had already seen a school of dusky dolphins, the smallest species, with a rather pale, mottled olive-green colouring, and we would be searching for them again that afternoon. We set off from the same quay (although regrettably there was no tractor and trailer on this occasion) and headed off along the coast. We had brought our swimming costumes, but despite the clear skies and the warmish air the water was still very cold indeed. However, if we did come across dolphins and if the conditions were favourable, wetsuits would be issued to those brave enough to enter the water. "Favourable conditions" mean no heavy swell that might prevent swimmers from getting back into the boat, and no mothers and young dolphins present as they might panic and even become aggressive.

The fine weather must have appealed to the dolphins as much as to human beings, for it was not long before a small school of them appeared close to the boat, their sleek bodies glistening just below the surface of the water. Sometimes they would rise a little higher and propel themselves forward in unison, their bodies arching gracefully and eagerly through the swell. Occasionally, they would break off to cross in front of us and then leap up into the air to crash

back into the water. Nobody knows why dolphins do this, but it is at the very least pleasant to imagine that it is just for the sheer hell of it. The dolphins, I was sure, wanted us to dive in and play with them, but a mother had been spotted with her young dolphin so we were forbidden to enter the water.

We saw an abundance of dolphins that afternoon and every encounter was a sheer delight, but on each occasion the presence of young dolphins meant that we could only watch. But this was no hardship. To be quite frank, it was a relief to see that New Zealanders, more than most, have learnt to treat the creatures seriously. At Kaikoura only one operator is permitted to take people out to the dolphins, one to the whales, and another to the seals.

SEAL WATCH

On the way back to Christchurch we were taken up to a lookout point for a last panoramic view of the mountains and sea, and then we stopped at the roadside to take a shoreline walk. Between the road and the sea, the shore was made up of substantial outcrops of grey rock, home to a colony of New Zealand fur seals. Not so long ago these seals were ruthlessly hunted, to the brink of extinction, for their skins, but they have survived to make what should be a lasting recovery. Looking for them against the rocks is akin to searching for a chameleon in dense undergrowth, but shortly we begin to notice some movement and before long more and more of them become visible, basking in the sun, or playing in rock pools. Like dolphins, seals appear to possess that gentle and trusting character that humans find so comforting and endearing. Perhaps, after all, it is only a false or misplaced judgement that attributes mute creatures with emotional qualities. But even if it is just a desire to disentangle oneself from the constraints and limitations of human existence, being close to these creatures certainly strikes a chord somewhere deep inside.

SOUTH ISLAND

GOING IT ALONE

INTERNAL TRAVEL

Christchurch is located on the east coast of South Island and can be reached by plane or by road. The airport, located 15 minutes from the city centre, is served by several domestic and international airlines, and is linked to all other major airports throughout the country. Buses and taxis are available to take you to the city centre.

If you wish to rent a car, this is easily done either in Christchurch itself or at the airport. Bus services operate daily between Christchurch and Kaikoura. There is a ferry service for passengers and cars between Wellington and Picton (about 140km, or 85 miles, to the north of Kaikoura), with departures at least twice a day. The crossing lasts about three hours and can be rough, although between November and April a fast ferry that takes half the time is in service.

WHEN TO GO

The best time for seeing whales is between October and April, and dolphins between October and May, but you stand a good chance of seeing them at any time.

PLANNING

Whale-watching and swimming with dolphins at Kaikoura can both be done in a single day, and excursions from Christchurch (four hours to the south) are readily available. Booking in advance (especially for the whale-watching) is essential. If you do not see a whale (it is probably as well to ask when you book what the chances of seeing them are), then a substantial part of your fare will be refunded. That said, heaven and earth are moved to make sure that this does not happen—a highly sophisticated network of watchers in boats and helicopters draws you inexorably into the whales' wake. Dolphins are more easily seen, although, of course, nothing is guaranteed. The opportunities for swimming with them depend very much on the weather conditions and on whether mothers with their young are present. New Zealand is becoming more and more conscious of the possible effects of tourism on the existence of these creatures, and so the rules are very strictly adhered to.

There is plenty of accommodation in Christchurch in all ranges and it should not be difficult to find a room at any time. In Kaikoura, there is less of a choice, although there are several bed-and-breakfast establishments that can be booked through Kaikoura Information and Tourism (see Contacts). If you intend to stay here, book your accommodation in advance.

TRAVELLERS' TIP

❑ The upper deck of the Whale Watch boat has only limited access, so if you have a place here you will be guaranteed space at the rail. The motion of the boat is greater, however, so those who suffer from seasickness may prefer to remain below. Some photographers maintain that the lower deck offers a better view of the whales as you are a little closer to them.

WHAT TO TAKE

❑ Swimming kit and towel.
❑ Warm clothing—it can get quite chilly out on deck.
❑ Binoculars, and camera with zoom lens.

HEALTH

The motion of the Whale Watch boat in a swell is significantly greater if you have a seat on the top deck, so those who suffer from seasickness are advised to remain below. You can also hire acupressure bracelets, which do seem to work provided that they are worn correctly.

Far left: *Bottlenose dolphins on the* Odyssea's *bow*
Inset: *Dolphins frolic around tour boats, and seem to be inviting you to join them*
Left: *Endearing fur seals enjoying the sunshine*

SOUTH ISLAND

21 High Country on Horseback

by Veronika Meduna and Andy Reisinger

Farming is a tough job in New Zealand, especially herding sheep and cattle, on horseback. in the rugged high country of the South Island. We spent three days riding powerful high country mounts to explore the harsh but beautiful landscapes and the romance of rural life in North Canterbury.

Canterbury is an essentially rural district, bounded by the Pacific Ocean, the alpine peaks of the South Island's main divide, and two mighty rivers. Pastures expand as far as the eye can see over the plains between the Waitaki River in the south and North Canterbury. From there to the Clarence River in the north, farmland rolls out over the contours at the foothills of the South Island's mountainous spine.

Land is Canterbury's most precious resource. Of New Zealand's 13 regions, Canterbury is the largest, and an aerial view illustrates the importance of agriculture. The patchwork of coloured, nearly perfect squares could be a page in a child's sketchbook, with bright green fields of crops, burnt sienna paddocks dotted with the white of grazing sheep, and the odd blob of deep purple lavender or bright yellow oilseed rape. The Southern Alps rise abruptly from the Canterbury Plains, the narrow, coastal ribbon that forms New Zealand's largest area of flat land. While the land between the wind-lashed eastern coastline and the first craggy hills is fertile pasture for the district's millions of sheep, the tussock-covered South Island high country is challenging farmland.

PASSION FOR HORSES

Our destination is the Hurunui region in North Canterbury, where we plan to explore the backcountry on horseback and experience the rural lifestyle of the high country stations for a few days. Some of New Zealand's largest farms are in this area, and none of them would get by without horses. In these remote highlands, farming still maintains the pioneering spirit and character of the old days and most of the farmers' machines have, literally, one horsepower. During the annual autumn muster sheep have to be brought back from the hills for shearing and drenching. At these times horses often outdo more modern means of transport such as quadbikes and all-terrain tractors. During the cold and harsh winters, they may also provide the farmer with his only means of getting off the farm.

It seems very appropriate to travel on

Multi-day treks involve about five hours of riding each day, but options range from half-day trips to eight-day cavalcades. Depending on the level of experience in the group, there will be opportunities to trot, canter, or jump. The horses are well trained and easy to ride even for novices, but groups can be split so that beginners can walk their horses.

★★ Accommodation is basic. Wool sheds or shearers' quarters serve as overnight shelters. Expect to sleep in a sleeping bag on a camp stretcher or bed with a spring mattress. Showers may be available only at some shelters. A luxury option is a farm-to-farm trek, which involves small groups stopping at a rural homestead every evening.

Temperatures can drop significantly so warm outdoor clothing is essential. Take a pair of comfortable trousers—riding or biking pants are ideal—and a pair of sturdy boots for the ride and the downhill walks. You will be provided with an oilcoat, a swag roll, and a riding helmet.

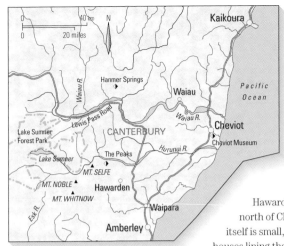

The extensive farming lands to the north of the Canterbury Plain

We meet our travel companions and guide, Jenny, at the farm gates of The Peaks. This rural property lies 20km (12 miles) along dust roads further inland from Hawarden, about 1½ hours north of Christchurch. Hawarden itself is small, no more than a few houses lining the road, with a dairy (convenience store) and a country pub, surrounded by paddock after paddock of grazing sheep, deer, cattle, and horses. Each of the townships along the road has its own character, represented by a historic building, a statue of a local hero, or some other relic from the days of the landed gentry. As we arrive, our horses are still happily cropping the grass in their paddock, and not exactly in the mood to be bridled and saddled up. We are told that horse care will be an integral part of the trip, so we walk off, halter in hand, to entice our mounts to follow us to the tack shed.

horseback in the Hurunui with its tiny country settlements and huge farms. The region is like a window into the heartland of country life, with many opportunities to connect with the history and culture of rural New Zealand. The craggy ruggedness of the land in particular seems to have left its mark on the people who work it. Historic accounts of early attempts to farm the high country are interwoven with tales of bravery and ingenuity in the face of utter isolation and exposure to harsh conditions. The high country folk we were to meet would confirm their reputation for unpolished charm and improvization.

SMALL COUNTRY TOWNS

Our journey starts in Christchurch, Canterbury's sprawling centre and—with a population of just over 300,000—the largest city in the South Island. Beyond the city's limits, grazed and farmed paddocks stretch out into the backcountry, interrupted only infrequently by small towns and villages. The road north along the eastern coastline is a main highway. However, most of the inland routes are country roads with many unsealed sections, the few road users ranging from pickup trucks with working dogs in the back to flocks of sheep with their horseriding shepherds.

MATCHING RIDER AND HORSE

Jenny has already chosen our horses with the help of details we had provided her about our size and riding experience. But the final selection is made in the field, once Jenny has met each of us in person: a jittery, young half-Connemara mare for the most experienced rider, who is keen to do some jumping; and an older thoroughbred "gentleman of a horse" for the least experienced participant. For Jenny, getting the best possible personality match between rider and mount is the first step to an enjoyable horse trek.

Most of our horses are crosses between thoroughbreds and Clydesdales. They are between 15 and 17 hands high, and all trained to be ridden in the English style. Clydesdales were originally used as workhorses on farms throughout New Zealand as their strong frame and docile nature make them ideal for being yoked to a wagon or plough. Thoroughbred horses frequently retire from the race-track to become trekking horses. Many high country farms breed their own horses, mixing the strength of the work-horse with the elegance of the racehorse.

Once we have bribed our horses off the paddocks we are briefed on the basics of horse care and introduced to the tack room. Each horse has its own bridle, blanket, saddle, and a set of cleaning tools. Good horse hygiene is essential before and after each ride—especially on multi-day treks—to prevent any chafing or bruising and to establish a bond of trust with our horses.

We are limited to a maximum load of 8kg (18 pounds) each – some of us struggle to separate essentials from luxury items. Soon, however, the unfurled swag rolls are filled, rolled up, and weighed to

Left: *Breakfast in the shearing shed*
Below: *Round Mount Selfe the hillsides are yellow with flowering broom, which, while attractive to the eye, is a pest for the high-country farmers*

make sure our luggage is distributed evenly over the sides of the packhorse that will carry the load. Once we are all geared up, we use an old tree stump to mount our steeds. We learn that this is more pleasant for the horses, and we will always try to find mounting blocks during the trek. We are also told that we will lead our horses on all downhill sections to protect their joints.

Our first day in the saddle starts with a slow ride along wide farm tracks skirting Mount Selfe, one of the lower peaks of the alpine foothills, which has been cleared for pasture. Once everybody is comfortable enough, we start climbing uphill on narrow paths through tussocky grass-

lands, past groups of ancient cabbage trees and thickets of the native spiky shrub, matagouri. It is difficult to imagine that these hills were once covered in temperate rainforests. It is even harder to fathom the determination of the early settlers who chose this harsh country to sustain their families.

CLEARING THE LAND

When European farmers arrived in the 1850s they found the fastest way to clear the land for stock was to take out the largest trees for timber and to burn the rest. Entire hillsides went up in blazing flames year after year, well into the 1930s. However, the real consequences of this burning were rapid erosion and loss of soil fertility. Today, stock roam vast areas in search of food, and can be found grazing on steep mountainsides between barren scree slopes and scars of naked earth, ripped open during landslides.

People who work the high country today recognize its ecological value and are often among the most ardent supporters of wildlife protection projects. As we circle Mount Selfe and turn towards Mount Noble Station, further uphill, a farmer passes us with a box full of broom beetles on the back seat of his pickup. Both broom and its prickly cousin, gorse, have conquered vast areas of the high country, smothering native vegetation and making the land virtually inaccessible for stock. Instead of using herbicides or

Below: After being briefed on the basics of horse care, we are introduced to the tack room

MAORI ROCK ART

There are 17 rock-art sites recorded in the Hurunui district, including one near Waipara, where pictures of fish, birds, dogs, and human forms can be seen on the walls of an overhanging limestone outcrop. Evidence of pre-European settlements can be found throughout the area, including the remains of Maori moa hunting sites at the mouths of the Hurunui, Waiau, Jed, and Conway rivers. The Cheviot Museum (in the town of the same name) is particularly renowned for its collection of Maori rock drawings. It also has a display of the bones of a moa, the giant flightless bird that used to roam the flat swamplands and river deltas of North Canterbury, and which was hunted to extinction by the Maori.

burning the annoying shrubs, the Mount Noble family has opted for biological pest control.

RIVER OF PLENTY

Further along the track, the view opens to reveal the steel-blue waters of the Hurunui River, the mighty braided waterway after which the region was named. Hurunui is the Maori term for "plentiful hair," and refers to the proliferation of plants along the river, which is still mostly untouched in its upper reaches. The main forest trees in valleys close to the main divide are beeches. Plants found in the damp valleys include New Zealand flax, cabbage trees, and toe toe, or red tussock, while mountain daisies, gentians, and buttercups thrive at higher levels.

The Hurunui River has its source in the Southern Alps, where its headwaters flow east to combine as a cascading, shaded river. The Hurunui soon spreads into its braided valley as the forests give way to tussock hill country. Lower down, the river crashes into a gorge renowned for its kayaking and then out onto the Canterbury Plains, before veering north to finish its journey in the Pacific. The river's upper reaches are a favourite haunt for recreational fishers, horse riders, and mountain bikers.

From the Hurunui's banks, our cavalcade turns inland onto the farmland of the Seven Hills Station, where we will spend the night in a wool shed. The track leads up to an open ridge, where we break into a trot. We have moved in single file for most of the way, so both riders and horses appreciate the opportunity to ride in a pack and as fast as we wish. On the flat farmland, we are told to trot or canter only if the paddocks carry no stock. Sheep and cattle are used to being mustered by riders, and are therefore easily set in motion by a group of fast-moving horses. The extra care taken near stock is part of the mutual agreement between the horse-trek operators and farmers, who are increasingly welcoming tourists onto their land.

EQUINE TRAINING

All farm gates are kept shut—even on empty paddocks—so the horses are unlikely to run off out of control. However, wire poses a more serious risk on high country farms. Throughout our ride, we come across bundles of unused wire, often overgrown by vegetation and hence invisible. Few things make a horse panic as easily as having a leg caught in wire, and therefore all of our trusty steeds have been trained to stand still on three legs. As we are negotiating some wire meshing during a single-file crossing of a small creek, one of the least experienced mares got caught. The terrified horse bolts once or twice—unfortunately enough to throw her rider—but then she stands still and lets our guide approach and cut the wire. Within minutes everyone is back in the saddle and we are on our way. Apart from minor scrapes and bruises, no one is injured.

Jenny tells us that horses bred to work the high country begin their training as foals. Most horses start out as packhorses, so they get used to carrying weight without the risk of injuring a rider. Next, they graduate to being ridden by experienced horsemen, and eventually they join the treks and follow the often confused commands of novice riders.

POLISHED BY HARD WORK

A few hundred metres before we reach our shelter for the night, we get off the horses and lead them through the last paddock. The short walk allows them to slow down gradually and to stop sweating before their saddle is removed. During the walk, we also loosen the girth by a notch or two to make sure that the blood flow returns to the horses' back muscles without any haemorrhaging.

At the wool shed, we go through the same routine as at the start of the ride: scrubbing and massaging the horses' skin, brushing their manes and tails, and cleaning their shoes. Jenny carries two separate first-aid kits, and any scrapes suffered by either horse or rider are treated immediately. Wool sheds are mostly used during the short shearing season (August–October), when gangs of shearers invade the high country, travelling from farm to farm in search of work. Outside the season, the sheds double as shelter for travellers. The aroma of lanolin permeates the entire building, and all the timber rails and floorboards reflect the shine of wool-fat polish. That evening, we sit on the porch with our barbecue meal, watching the horses as they rearrange their pecking order through playful fights and chases.

From the Seven Hills Station we ride around the foot of Mount Noble towards Mount Whitnow Station, travelling along the route first cut from east to west across the South Island. Initially established as a *pounamu* (greenstone) trail by Maori villagers, the track was later widened by European settlers. Today, it is a gravel road mostly used as access to Lake Sumner and other high country lakes renowned for their fishing.

Isolation marks life for the couple who

HERITAGE TRAIL

The Hurunui Heritage Trail connects 37 historic sites along a roughly triangular route north on Highway 1 from Amberley to Kaikoura, inland to Hanmer Springs, and then back to North Canterbury. The trail features historic farming homesteads, churches, hotels, museums, and the Weka Pass Railway. Maps are available from the Hurunui Visitors' Centre at Hanmer Springs.

---

farm Mount Whitnow. Their children travel nearly two hours to get to school, and at college age have to move to a boarding house because of the distances. Mount Whitnow supports 8,000 Merino wethers, which are free to roam 4,500ha (11,000 acres) for most of the year, until they are herded back to be shorn at the end of winter. These horned sheep are bred for the high country and can withstand the harsh conditions. However, to leave them some protection, they are still shorn with hand blades, which leave a thicker layer of wool on their skins. We stay in the shearers' quarters near the main homestead and are treated to an evening meal and a long talk about high country life. After a night at the station, nobody feels like a fast return to civilization, so we take our time to travel back and enjoy riding through refreshing rivers on the way.

SOAKING IN THE SPA

Nothing soothes sore muscles better than a bath in a hot pool. The South Island high country was formed by the combined forces of plate tectonics and successive glaciations and, as a reminder of the former, hot springs bubble out of the mountainsides along the various fault lines that created the main divide. The natural hot pools of the thermal reserve at Hanmer Springs, about half an hour from Hawarden, are a relaxing place to finish a long trek. Pity we couldn't bring the horses.

GOING IT ALONE

INTERNAL TRAVEL

The nearest international and domestic airport is at Christchurch. Direct flights are available from most international destinations, and the airport is the South Island's centre of domestic travel. Daily flights connect Christchurch with cities on the North Island, as well as Dunedin, Queenstown, and Invercargill.

Bus and shuttle services are available from Christchurch to other South Island destinations. Hawarden is on the Christchurch–Hanmer Springs route, which is serviced by a daily shuttle.

Major international and all national car- and campervan-hire companies have offices in downtown Christchurch, as well as at the airport.

WHEN TO GO

The seasons in the high country vary dramatically: summers can be searing (up to 35°C, or 95°F) and snow is common in the winter. Autumn is often mild and brings stunning seasonal colours, while green pastures and lambs dominate the spring landscape. Floods are common in spring, when the melting snow and rainstorms swell the rivers.

Northwesterly storms are common throughout the year in Canterbury. These are similar to the *föhn* of the European Alps, and bring warm winds that can parch the landscape. Some people suffer headaches during strong northwesterlies, which can last for several days.

PLANNING

The Hurunui district extends from Leithfield, 30 minutes north of Christchurch, to the Conway River (about halfway between Christchurch and the northern tip of the South Island). The most accessible high country farms lie between North Canterbury and the Clarence River near the Kaikoura Range. Essential services and accommodation to suit all budgets are dotted along the route.

TRAVELLERS' TIPS

❑ If you have never been in the saddle for more than a few hours, it pays to go on a few shorter treks before embarking on a multi-day journey. There are several operators in the Hurunui and around Christchurch who offer riding lessons and shorter excursions.

❑ Unless you are staying at a farmer's homestead, the trip is a team effort and you will be expected to help with food preparation, cooking, and washing the dishes. Even at a homestead, an offer to do the dishes will be appreciated.

❑ A good time to visit high country farms is during shearing and lambing (August–October); contact the farmers directly regarding extended farmstays. Note, however, that farmers may not want horse treks across their land at this time.

WHAT TO TAKE

❑ You can expect to be provided with all the gear necessary for horse riding, including a helmet and wet-weather gear. However, take your own boots, a pair of riding trousers, and clothing for all weather.

❑ You will need a sleeping bag if you plan to stay at wool sheds or shearers' quarters; check with farmers on this in advance if you are travelling independently.

HEALTH

Water supplies are drinkable throughout the Canterbury region. In the backcountry, stream water is clear, but because of the high number of stock, it is recommended that you boil or filter it before drinking it. Your horse-trekking guide will carry a first-aid kit to treat any injuries, but take any personal medical supplies you require.

Far Left: Our aim was to explore the harsh but beautiful landscape of the Hurunui region
Left: Rolling up the swags

22 Fly Fishing via the TranzAlpine

by Christopher Knowles

The TranzAlpine rail journey, linking the east and west coasts of South Island, is among the great train rides of the world. It crosses the Southern Alps, through some of New Zealand's finest scenery, to Westland, where I was introduced to the fine art of fly fishing.

I have always loved trains and train travel. A singular excitement attends the boarding of a train for a long journey, a mixture of pleasurable anticipation and an eager desire to be off. It is altogether one of the best means of transportation. However, as I hand my ticket over to the inspector at Christchurch station, mention is made, casually and almost inaudibly, of a slight delay. On the platform a largish crowd is milling around and I fall into conversation with some fellow travellers. Needless to say we end up airing our personal grievances about public transport around the world.

DEPARTURE AT LAST

And then finally, an hour after time, the TranzAlpine pulls into the station, a long line of pale blue carriages hauled by a pair of diesel locomotives. Everything

1 Fly fishing is difficult only in so far as there is much to learn and a certain knack to be acquired in order to cast the rod accurately.

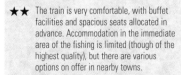

★★ The train is very comfortable, with buffet facilities and spacious seats allocated in advance. Accommodation in the immediate area of the fishing is limited (though of the highest quality), but there are various options on offer in nearby towns.

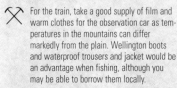

For the train, take a good supply of film and warm clothes for the observation car as temperatures in the mountains can differ markedly from the plain. Wellington boots and waterproof trousers and jacket would be an advantage when fishing, although you may be able to borrow them locally.

happens very quickly now, and as soon as all the passengers are aboard, the train pulls out. Announcements are made explaining the layout of the train. There is a snack bar (called, believe it or not, Snacks on Tracks) and a pair of observation cars. The seats are comfortable and the carriages pretty spacious. And then we are off. An air of excitement pervades the carriage, a mixture of relief after the delay and anticipation of what is to come.

The TranzAlpine has been ranked among the top five of the great railway journeys of the world. It takes its name from the fact that it leaves Christchurch in the east to traverse New Zealand's great mountain range, the Southern Alps, to arrive at Greymouth on the west coast. Not surprisingly, the railway follows the route of least resistance, but even so it rises to a considerable altitude (for a railway) and has to pass over some pretty inhospitable terrain. This terrain looks all the more intriguing for lying, that day, under a pall of low cloud and misty rain.

PLAIN RAILING AND MOUNTAIN SCALING

Now that we are finally under way, the spattering of rain against the window and the mist-draped landscape beyond convey a sense of adventure and accentuate the joy of travelling into the unknown. In the distance I can see the beginnings of the hills that mark the start of the Southern Alps. Before long we have emerged from the city confines to begin our amble along the Canterbury Plain, with its farms, vineyards, and huge wind-break hedges. A stop is made at a halt to pick up a few more passengers (who look very relieved to see us at long last), and then the journey continues towards the mountains, now incompletely visible, their contours taking on a blurred definition in the clinging mist. Soon we must gather ourselves for the slow, chugging ascent into them.

Even against the grey sky, it is scarcely difficult to imagine the monumental grandeur that is undoubtedly concealed behind the mist. Gradually, the villages peter out and we pass only the occasional homestead. We travel through tunnels (some 17 in all) and over bridges and viaducts that span gorges and rivers of frantic, icy blue water. Over the loudspeaker, there is a commentary explaining what we were passing, listing the names of the features, both natural and man-made, that commemorate the rugged people who explored the area in the 19th century and who went on to build the railway. The train, which is heaved along with dogged persistence by diesel locomotives, makes slow progress as we enter the mountain fastness. Sealed as we are from the brunt of the elements, and ensconced in the comfort of our upholstered seats, it is all too easy to overlook the determination and the extraordinary resilience and vision of the engineers and builders of this railway line. To construct it even now would be a feat worthy of admiration.

At the foot of the mountains there are tracts of gravel so vast that the great rivers in full flow across them seem to divide into mere trickles and streams, reminiscent of a high Himalayan plateau. There are lakes as still as mercury, but on this side of Arthur's Pass there is almost no vegetation, just acres of dried river grass, awaiting, I suppose, the summer sun to regenerate them.

TO THE OBSERVATION CAR

I make the journey through the neighbouring carriages (not too difficult, as we are travelling fairly slowly on this side of the pass) to emerge into a spartan affair that is a windowless wagon, where passengers can take photographs freely and without artificial barrier. It is a good place to lean out a little and photograph the curve of the train against the bleak landscape, and to savour the freezing mountain air. Although the mist is still with us, we can see the bases of the mountains curving away, one after the other, their forms evaporating gradually into a pale, opaque, blur. From time to time, the dim sunlight breaks through and illuminates a white peak in a brassy glow.

When we reach Arthur's Pass, the highest point of the journey, some passengers leave the train. They will spend some time up here, as there is good walking and climbing to be had, before resuming their journey.

FROM EAST TO WEST

Arthur's Pass, which is also the name of the area's national park, commemorates one Arthur Dudley Dobson, who in 1864 opened up what had been a Maori trading route to the settlers. Climatically, this place is quite remarkable as it marks exactly the boundary between Canterbury to the east and Westland. Often you can leave behind a set of weather conditions on one side of the pass, only to find yourself in exactly the opposite conditions on the other side. In wet weather as much as 250mm (10 inches) can fall on the pass in 24 hours, rendering conditions treacherous in the steep Otira Gorge on the western side.

Today, however, the conditions on both sides of the pass are pretty similar—cloud and rain. But the fundamental difference between the two sides of the pass is striking in another way. As soon as the train emerges on the western side of the pass, the landscape is transmuted from one of bleak mountain fastness, where water and rock dominate. Suddenly we are among dense, lusciously green rain forest, hanging in fronds over the railway track, so that we might almost

be in a botanical hothouse.

Now we make the long and steady descent to Greymouth. As the gradients flatten out towards the coast, the railway line divides into two, one branch heading north towards Westport, ours keeping west for Greymouth. New Zealand's best coal is still freighted across country by rail from the mines in Westport. Before long, we pull into Greymouth itself. Those passengers returning to Christchurch that afternoon have a short time to wander around the town before coming back to the station. Most of us are leaving the train to move on elsewhere. Many people head for the InterCity buses, parked at the ready alongside the platform, while I head for the station terminal to collect my car from the rental office.

ROAD SAFETY

As I produce my driving licence, the man behind the counter says, "Well, he won't be doing any more of that." "Of what?" "Cycling." "Cycling? Who won't be?" "The bloke who got killed at the railway crossing. Didn't you know? That was why the train was delayed." Only the day before I had scoffed somewhat flippantly at a new law that compels passenger vehicles to stop at railway crossings even when the warning lights are not flashing. Since I was about to take to the road myself, I would now make sure I was doubly

Above: *Rail bridge,
road bridge, and old
stanchions cross the
River grey at
Greymouth*
Left: *Wild lupins
carpet the meadows
of Arthur's Pass
National Park*

SOUTH ISLAND

attentive when it came to crossing railway lines myself.

Driving in New Zealand presents few problems. In fact, driving here, even for those who need to accustom themselves to driving on the left, should be a real pleasure as the roads are empty and well marked. There are one or local two idio-syncrasies. For example, on the main route through Westland you sometimes have to share bridges with the railway line—it really isn't used very often—but, on the whole, driving here is similar to what driving must have been like 40 years ago in more metropolitan places. The man at the car-hire office also recom-mends that I stick to Route 6 all the way to Queenstown, rather than be tempted off it onto seemingly shorter routes that could turn out to be treacherous for one reason or another.

TRAVELLING SOUTH

Very soon I am out of Greymouth and heading south on Route 6, which at this stage is also the coast road. Although my destination this evening, Kapitea Ridge Country Lodge, is not far away, I am not really sure what I am looking for. The instructions seem alarmingly vague, but then, as I drive out of Greymouth, I am reminded how almost any landmark tends to stand out in this unspoilt, sparsely pop-ulated country. On my right I catch glimpses of the surf rolling against a beach of black sand; to the left is a single railway track running along the base of the forested hills that rise above it. After half an hour I see a building high up above me. I turn left to cross the railway line very cautiously and follow the road up through the trees to arrive at a courtyard beside a new house of highly unusual design. It is an improbable piece of archi-tecture, a mixture of villa and Nissen hut, and yet one which, with its curved dark blue roof and its ochre walls, blends into the landscape. This is Kapitea Ridge, my home for the night, standing on a bluff at the edge of a forest plantation that over-looks the sea.

OVER THE TOP

Lying at an altitude of 924m (3,031ft), 154km (96 miles) west of Christchurch and on the eastern side of the Otira Tunnel, is Arthur's Pass, the only rail link through the Southern Alps. The Otira Tunnel itself is 8km (5 miles) long; it was completed in 1923 after 15 years of construction, and was the first electrified stretch of railway in the British Empire. There are plenty of opportunities for hiking in the area of Arthur's Pass, including half-day or full-day walks, or, if you prefer, more demand-ing treks that involve overnight stays in mountain lodges. This is New Zealand's speciality—raw nature, with waterfalls, gorges, and alpine flowers.

A WARM WELCOME

The door is answered by Hamish, the son of the house. Murray, Trixie, and Hamish, offer casual yet thoughtful hospitality, especially welcome on such a wild day. The large sitting room looks out over the sea, whilst in a corner there is a glowing wood fire. That evening I was to go fish-ing. Murray looks out of the window at the raging sea, driving rain, and battering wind. "Doesn't look too promising," he says. But he phones Dean, who, along with his father, organizes fishing expedi-tions. Dean says that he will come along anyway, so that he can at least give me an idea of what fishing is all about.

FISHING IN THE RAIN

Hamish drives us out into the rain in Kapitea's Toyota Landcruiser. We head back down to the coast road and then leave it again to enter a vale of rivers, nar-row roads, and lush pastures. In the distance we see a dredger that has recently been reintroduced into one of the rivers as part of an attempt to reacti-vate the gold-extraction industry. We drive along stony roads up into hills smothered in saturated forests, ploughing through pools of water and pausing, from time to time, at lookout points to peer vainly through the mist—on a clear day it is possible to see Mount Cook from up here. Eventually we stop at Harris Creek, and although the water is high, a lull in the rain allows us to trudge across the grass to the water's edge.

The fishing around here is excellent for fishermen of all levels of competence—the water is clean and the fish are abundant—but the great thing, from my point of view as a complete novice, is that Dean, a young, patient countryman, is willing to take me on. Other gillies may be less inclined to suffer beginners gladly, but Dean and his father are so passionate about fishing, and fishing in this area in particular, that they will take people like me on for a few hours without hesitation. And in good weather conditions there could be no better place to learn to catch fish. Like so many other places in New Zealand, and in South Island in particular, the scenery is incomparably breathtaking. Even in the teeming rain, beneath a lowering sky in the blackest of dusks, the overpowering beauty of the scenery is evident everywhere. In particular, it is all but empty of other people—indeed, there isn't a sign of habitation, not even a hint of a dwelling or of any sign of people in any direction. There's no noise, except for the stream and the sighing of a steady breeze; there are no garish colours, only the greens and browns of nature.

TEMPERAMENTAL TROUT

The appalling conditions notwithstanding, we wade out as far as is practicable. We are after brown trout, which would normally come close to the surface at this time of the evening, in search of insects. Dean prepares my carbon-fibre rod (a so-called "six weight" for beginners, which is lighter than usual), showing me how to attach the fly (an artificial imitation of an insect) and an almost invisible weight. There are numerous different flies, usually with colourful names (Royal Wolf and Pheasant Tail, to name but two) and the

one you choose depends on how the fish are behaving. Then Dean demonstrates how to cast the line. This is not as easy as it looks—witness the countless cartoons that feature hapless fishermen with their hooks embedded in anything except a fish—but it amounts to a slow, rhythmic flick, which comes good with practice. The aim is to get the fly to float on the surface, its colours and movement hopefully tricking the fish into thinking it's the real thing and bringing it onto the hook.

It is best, if possible, to be in the water and to stand behind the fish. Much, too, depends on how well you know the area and, of course, on the weather. The weather! We are not going to catch any brown trout today. The rain begins streaming down again, and the creek waters, already high, begin to rise still more. Under better circumstances, Dean tells me, it is practically impossible to come away empty-handed. I am sure he is right. The place feels as if it should teem with fish, but in any case just to be fishing in such glorious, virgin countryside is alone worth the effort.

THE ONES THAT GOT AWAY

Had we caught any trout, we may well have taken them back to the lodge to be cooked. On the way home we pass through a couple of small towns, and at the sight of a local pub we agree that we deserve a sharpener before dinner. The pub appears to be the domain of farmers, gathered here at the end of a grim and sodden day. I order a glass of Speights Old Dark as the landlady hands around some hot sausages. Back at Kapitea Ridge, it is time for a glass of local wine and a delicious dinner, which we eat all together around the table in the sitting room. The bedrooms are voluptuously comfortable, very well equipped, and yet completely unfussy. The rain is drumming against a window and the wind keening about the house. It has been a long day, and the weather has not been kind. The compensations, however, have been great for my introduction to Westland.

GOING IT ALONE

INTERNAL TRAVEL

The starting point for the TranzAlpine is Christchurch, which is located on the east coast of South Island and can be accessed by plane or road. The airport is served by several domestic and international airlines, and is located a 15-minute drive from the city centre. Buses and taxis are available to take you into the city centre.

The TranzAlpine leaves Christchurch at 9am, and departs Greymouth for the return trip in the early afternoon; the journey time is about four hours. It is essential to book your seat on the train in advance as the service is immensely popular.

You should also book car rental in advance, especially in Greymouth, where there is only one office. If you are not driving, the only other option is to continue your journey by bus. There are daily services between Christchurch and Dunedin, Mount Cook, Queenstown, and Nelson, as well as services between Christchurch and Greymouth, Hokitika, and Arthur's Pass.

If speed is vital, then it is also possible to reach or leave Greymouth by air, the nearest airport is at Hokitika, located about a half an hour's drive to the south. There are daily flights from Christchurch.

WHEN TO GO

The TranzAlpine runs all year round, but the spring and early summer is probably best avoided as the weather is highly unpredictable at this time and in this part of New Zealand. The same is true of the fishing, for which the most suitable time is between January and April.

PLANNING

Although New Zealand is relaxed by nature, much of its tourism is highly organized and it is therefore advisable to book ahead where possible. Operators will do their best to ensure that you get what you pay for, but the weather is out of their hands, and whilst it is possible to be flexible as to when you go fishing, you will have only one chance

at the train. In South Island it is always a good idea to allow yourself as much time as feasible, just in case the weather interferes too much with your plans.

There is a variety of accommodation in Greymouth. However, in the high season it may be hard to come by, so you are advised to book in advance, perhaps by contacting the Greymouth Visitor Information Centre (see Contacts). As a base for fishing Greymouth is fine as long as you have a car, but it is far better, if possible, to be in the countryside.

TRAVELLERS' TIP

❏ Don't turn your nose up at taking the TranzAlpine in the winter season, as this is probably the best chance you will have of enjoying clear skies and seeing snowy peaks (especially in May and June).

WHAT TO TAKE

❏ Camera and film.
❏ Warm clothing for the observation car on the train—it can get cold in the mountains, even in summer.
❏ Waterproof boots, waterproof trousers and jacket for fishing.

HEALTH

Clear streams and flourishing fish populations notwithstanding, you are not advised to drink stream water below the tree line. Giardia, a parasite that causes gastroenteritis, is present in the water.

Far left: *The fishing is excellent*
Left: *There is no noise except the gushing of the stream; there are no garish colours, only the greens and browns of nature*

227

23 High on Glaciers

by Christopher Knowles

In the glacier region of the Southern Alps I take a helicopter ride for a walk high on the ice and a skiplane to land on the mighty Tasman Glacier on Mount Cook, the highest mountain in New Zealand.

There is so little traffic in the region of Westland that the only real danger for motorists is falling asleep at the wheel. Frequently, however, the road will suddenly narrow to a single-lane bridge spanning a creek or river, and that is quite enough to whet the concentration. An hour or so after beginning my journey from Greymouth, the road started to curl and rise up into the mountains. It was still dull and intermittently wet, but the mist that had dogged the previous days had lifted quite considerably, so that, at last, it was at least possible to grasp the great scale of the scenery I was driving through. I was heading south to the glacier region of South Island and I was booked into a helicopter flight departing from Fox village.

After a long series of hairpin bends, passing through the township of Franz Joseph, I arrived at Fox village. The village, like Franz Joseph, is a small resort town, closely resembling the skiing centres that dot the mountain regions of Europe. Consisting of little more than a main street, its *raison d'être* is almost exclusively the organization of trips, be they walks, hikes, and flights of various kinds, to the glacier. Like the European ski resorts, it is a place of two contrasting moods: purposeful activity when the weather is good and impatient inactivity when the weather is lousy. My flight was due to take off at midday for Fox Glacier.

WEATHER AND WHETHER

I went straight to the office of Alpine Guides to see what the situation was regarding the helicopter flight. As expected, and as I had been warned, there would be no flight that afternoon. Would I like to rebook for the following day? I would. What time, the nine o'clock flight or the midday flight? It seemed to me that, as a general rule, bad weather the world over tends to worsen as the day progresses, so I plumped for the earlier flight and hoped for the best.

MORE REAL THAN THE REAL THING

I decided to spend the rest of the afternoon retracing my steps the 20km (12 miles) or so to Franz Joseph. There, you could watch a film of the helicopter flight on a wide screen—at least I would be able to see something of what I would miss

2 Walking on a glacier in the helihike trip requires only minimal fitness. You need to be able to walk slowly across slippery ground for about two hours, and to hoist yourself up and down a few ice steps. The skiplane excursion is easier still, since passengers only walk a little on powdery snow before re-embarking.

★★ Most of the accommodation in the area of the glaciers consists of comfortable, moderately priced motels (generally self-catering). In Mount Cook village there is a hotel, self-catering chalets, and a campsite. Since both the helihike and skiplane tours operate only in clear conditions, you can always expect it to be sunny when you alight on the glaciers.

 For the helihike nearly all the major equipment is provided: boots, thick socks, instep crampons, and a stick. For the skiplane landing you will need to take your own waterproof boots. For both trips you need sunglasses and several layers of warm clothes as you will probably get quite hot as you walk.

should the cloud fail to lift. The film is fairly short but intensely dramatic. It is shot mostly, I think, from a small helicopter but in such a way it seems as if Superman had been flying over the region, camera in hand. Sometimes the filming is so fast, the snow and water so close, and the crevices and gorges so precipitous, that you begin to flail inwardly and become overwhelmed with an alarming sensation of toppling over. But this lasts only a few seconds and you breathe more easily, relieved as if in a plane that has levelled out the last minute after a vertical dive.

After the film, I drove to the base of the Franz Joseph Glacier and walked to a lookout point. There was still very little to see, only an expanse of damp-looking snow and ice resembling sheets trying to dry in the rain. The nearby river was in full angry spate, its grey, glacial waters attacking the road bridge and drenching everything in a clammy mist. After my virtual airborne glacier experience I was looking forward to the real thing.

THE REAL THING

Come the morning, a miracle had occurred. The skies, though not yet cloudless, were fresh and clear. I made myself some breakfast (motels in New Zealand are often self-catering) and then walked over to the Alpine Guides office. Things were looking good, they said brightly, but they would not confirm the flight until the last moment.

Just before nine o'clock the flight was confirmed. There were nine of us going up onto the glacier. We were taken into the boot room behind reception, where pairs of tough hobnailed leather boots were handed out, tugged on over the two pairs of thick socks that we chose from a basket. We were invited to smear all exposed flesh with sunscreen, and after donning fleeces, hats, gloves, and sunglasses we headed out to the bus (a beautiful old Bedford that would have graced any transport museum) for the short journey to the helipad. There, our guide, Fiona, looking at our various builds and weights, organized us accordingly for the two flights it would take to get us up onto the glacier.

The first four were to go up with Fiona. They walked across the concrete to the waiting helicopter. The door was shut and then up they soared towards the glacier, behind which we could see the peak of Mount Cook, so limpid had the air become. Twenty minutes later the helicopter was back and it was our turn. It was a snug fit. Belts on, headphones on (through which we could strain to hear something of the comments made by the pilot), and immediate lift-off.

The sensation of flying in a helicopter is quite different from that of a plane, even a small one. Perhaps it is the absence of preparation that comes with vertical lift-off—no revving of engines, no gathering of speed, no undercarriage bedding into the fuselage. We headed up the mountain slopes, skirted the glacier to make a loop at the top, at the very highest of the snow fields, before swooping down the other side, passing close to what seemed at first to be a high, thin dribble of a waterfall. The so-called Victoria Falls are far from a dribble—it is only their great height that makes them seems so, but on closer inspection they are voluminous. Finally, we turned towards the glacier itself, aiming for a point about halfway up, opposite the falls, where black stones picked out from the moraine beneath the ice have been placed in a circle on a flattish ice shelf to create a landing spot for the helicopter.

ONE SMALL STEP

As the helicopter settled onto the ice, we could see our fellow hikers crouching together a few metres from us. We disembarked and made our way across the ice to join them. This was a bit unnerving, high up as we were on a slope of white, slippery ice. As always in such circumstances, fear holds everything together. Fiona rounded us into a group and handed out some instep crampons, which

SOUTH ISLAND

are not unlike a particularly severe dog collar to look at. These wrap around the boots in such a way that the metal teeth lie tight under the feet between toe and heel. We were also each given an alpenstock, a walking stick created for icy conditions.

Our confidence renewed, we looked around us, taking in the grandeur of our surroundings. On either side, at the margins of the glacier, were the high rocky slopes of neighbouring mountains. Below us, the glacier sloped down towards rainforest and beyond it the sea. Hanging over the sea in the far distance was a thick wad of cloud, inching towards us, although we were bathed in sunlight on an icy tongue of brilliant white. Where we stood resembled a rumpled platform of ice and snow, while above us there seemed to be at least two distinct areas,

Right: *Fox Glacier—an ever-changing phenomenon, where the ice resembles twists of blue meringue*
Inset: *Having the right kit is essential on the ice*
Left: *There is always a danger of avalanches*
Below: *Mount Cook towers above its neighbours; in the foreground is Lake Pukaki*

or shelves, where the ice had packed together to form peaks and troughs, all suffused with an icy, electric blue. Above them were those puffs of cloud that always brush mountain snowfields and, higher still, a sky of polar clarity. Fiona explained that we would be walking for about two hours, gradually making our way upwards in two stages. Pickaxe in hand, she started to hack away at the ice to form steps so that we could follow her in a train across the glacier.

GLACIER TECHNIQUE

The crampons certainly made the walking much easier. The crucial thing is to push down hard with your boots, feet facing forward, so that the crampons dig into the ice and give you support. Ideally, the alpenstock becomes no more than a prop, and therefore its metal tip is not pointed.

Although the air was still and cool, we soon worked up a sweat from the warmth of the reflected sunlight and the effort required to heave ourselves up the ice steps. But this was as nothing to the labours of Fiona, who had to carve out an

entirely new set of steps as the wet weather of recent days had all but washed away any trace of old routes. In any case, the glacier is a moving, ever-changing phenomenon, which means that the scenery is always shifting. The Fox, we were told, is the largest of the mighty west coast glaciers. Uniquely, it ends in temperate rainforest, 250m (820ft) above sea-level. The Fox has advanced 1km (½ mile) since 1986 and moves up to 5m (16ft) per day. And one final statistic: there are more 3,000m (9,800ft) peaks here than in any other valley in New Zealand.

We gingerly made our way upwards. Stops were made for photographs and we were advised to walk at our own pace, after all, there was no hurry and nowhere in particular to go. We had to cross narrow crevices, bypass blue grottoes, and avoid collapsing arches and caves, but as long as we followed in Fiona's footsteps all was well.

ICE DREAM

After an hour we were in the upper ice-fall, where the ice peaks cluster like twists of blue meringue. It was truly beautiful, so quiet, except for the crunch of our boots and our murmured conversation, and so calm, yet, in the wrong conditions, quite unforgiving. That is why the flights take place only when the conditions are approaching perfection.

We made our descent cautiously. Going down seemed to be harder than the ascent, but again, this was largely psychological. The temptation was to sidestep when in fact that is the last thing you should do. It is far better to do as you did going up—dig in and make the most of the crampons.

The helicopter returned on cue and we tipped headlong down the glacier towards the sea, just as in the film I had seen the previous day. The cloud that had, as if by magic, remained at bay at the head of the valley all morning, was now making its inevitable advance towards the mountains. We had indeed been lucky—

WALKING OPTIONS

Even in bad or indifferent weather, walks are still organized to the lower parts of both the Fox and the Franz Joseph glaciers. The walks are run from the townships both to the base of the glaciers and onto the glaciers themselves. Another popular walk is to Lake Matheson, just to the west of Fox village. One of New Zealand's classic sights, it is particularly famous for the reflection of the high peaks of the Southern Alps in its still waters. There is also an eight-hour return walk up through bush to alpine meadows with wonderful views of the mountains, the glacier, and the coast. If you have a car, there is a fascinating three-hour walk from Gillespies Beach, through a miners' tunnel, ending at a seal colony.

the midday flight had already been cancelled, and since the weather the following day was predicted to be even worse, I suspect that day's flights were also cancelled. The walk on the glacier had been an experience worth having, and the helicopter had enabled me to access its most enchanting and otherwise unattainable parts.

THE GREATEST DRIVE IN THE WORLD

That evening I was due to arrive in Queenstown, the home of bungee jumping. The journey south to Queenstown must surely qualify as one of the great drives of the world. Although the weather was closing in, I just managed to stay ahead of the worst of it. The brilliant sunshine had vanished, but the skies were still fairly clear, with enough light to give definition to the scenery around me. The initial stage is through an area similar to that prevailing in the vicinity of the glaciers, temperate rainforest and mountains. At intervals along the way (and this seems to be true of almost every route in New Zealand), there are plenty of stopping places. After an hour, I pulled into one of the frequent parking areas from where it is possible to follow waymarked walking tracks of various distances and degrees of difficulty. Beside a lake fringed by ferns and surrounded by dense forest, I ate my lunch. There were public lavatories which (like many things in this most environment-conscious of countries) were designed to work in conjunction with nature, as well as noticeboards detailing information about the lake and its wildlife.

THE MAGNIFICENT COASTLINE

Soon the scenery began to change. The road, which was completed only in 1965, rises high above a rocky coastline of inlets and small, unreachable beaches, where waves that have travelled thousands of uninterrupted kilometres across the Pacific finally crash to a splintering halt. Further on, where the road descends to sea-level, I stopped at Monro Beach, a stretch of ruffled sand and seaweed washed in by the foaming surf. Wild and remote though it was, duckboards crisscrossed the sand and a notice requested that visitors keep to these raised pathways. A small observation platform stands at the edge of the sand, from where, if you are lucky, you might catch sight of Fiordland crested penguins, which visit the beach between July and December.

As I continued south, still hugging the coast, the landscape became flatter and somehow saltier. It began to resemble a marshland, and the trees thinned out and became more gnarled, having keeled before the unbroken wind sweeping off the Tasman Sea. This is the Haast Beach area, a lonely delta of rivers and creeks teeming with fish. Once again I made a short stop, this time at the Haast Department of Conservation Visitor Centre, an unusual architectural creation built amid a maze of watercourses.

INTO THE ALPS

At Haast, I turned inland, still on Highway 6, to pass from one world into another. The road now took me into the heart of the Southern Alps. Here, heading up to Haast Pass at the foot of high and snowy peaks, shallow rivers tumble, like shards of crystal over rocks and pebbles, between alpine flower-filled meadows and spongy acres of peaty grassland. The forest is dense with moss- and lichen-covered trees, many of which lie fallen, ready to moulder into the earth. At one point I made another stop at the roadside to wander across the grass to the riverbank. I was there for a good half-hour and not a single car passed by. Gradually, the colours and contours of the land changed yet again. The road rose to a bluff, below which stretched the vast expanse of the wind-ruffled, blue water of Lake Wanaka. The wind was driving a lone windsurfer across the choppy water at great speed.

The landscape was so bare and unspoilt, as to be almost overwhelming.

In a way it was rather shocking to be so alone—I could quite easily imagine myself in the steppelands of Mongolia. But there was one final surprise. The road crested a rise to a view over another expanse of water, this one flat and still, out of which, on the far side, rose a huge

Left: *The 1920s steamer, the* TSS Earnslaw, *making a visit to Walter Peak Farm on Lake Wakatipu*
Below: *Lake Matheson, fringed by ferns and surrounded by dense forests*
Right: *The Remarkables flank Lake Wakatipu*

perpendicular wall of rock in the most dramatic fashion. This was Lake Hawea, drenched in the light of early evening.

THE HOME OF BUNGEE

Beautiful though it was, it was a relief to find myself driving through lower, gentler hills where there were farms and signs to settlements. I pulled into Queenstown on the shores of Lake Wakatipu. My room in the St. Moritz Suite Hotel had a fabulous view of the lake and the mountains (the delightfully named Remarkables) that flank it. A steamer, the *SS Earnslaw*, built in the 1920s and still going strong, gave a loud hoot and crossed the vista picturesquely before me, as it slid back to harbour at the end of the day.

Avoiding the bungee-jumping for which Queenstown is famous, I set off for Mount Cook, where I was hoping to take a plane ride up to the snowfields of the Tasman Glacier. Great Sights runs a double-decker bus service daily between Queenstown and Christchurch via Mount Cook, where you can either stop for a couple of hours or overnight if you prefer. Soon we were out of Queenstown, following Highway 8 towards the Lindis Pass. This is another spectacular mountain route, but the mountains here are lower, the hills are greener, and we passed more lakes and rivers teeming with fish. Although sparsely populated, much of the land is good for farming—fruit farms abound and a lot of the hill land is given

over to sheep grazing. On at least one occasion we had to inch our way through a flock that was being moved along the road to a new grazing area. The hillsides were ablaze with gorse and broom and dense with roses—introduced by settlers and gold prospectors for their hips, a rich source of vitamin C, but now a major headache for farmers.

TASMAN AND COOK

Just before we arrived at Mount Cook itself, clearly visible by now, we passed the unearthly, radiant blue Lake Pukaki. Empty of fish, its colour is caused by the presence of fragments of glacier. Then we turned off for the airfield. The weather was perfect for a mountain flight: a flawless blue sky, with the surrounding peaks (there are 140 peaks of at least 2,134m, or 7,000ft, in the Mount Cook National Park) glittering in the sunshine. The plane, a Cessna 185 equipped with both tyres and skis, seated four passengers. Before long we were in the air, aiming for one of the world's longest glaciers, the 27km (17-mile) Tasman, which grates along the rocky flank of Mount Cook. We flew the length of the glacier, a glistening finger of white ice, listening to the commentary provided by the pilot. The further we flew up it, the denser its snow covering, which in places has split apart into marshmallow-like cubes of delicate blue. At the uppermost reaches, which resemble a sort of snowfield, we banked and skimmed across it, sending up a cloud of white powder, before touching down and skidding gently to a halt. We all climbed out to wander about in the crisp, freezing air, taking in the profound quiet, and enjoying the sheer exhilaration of being up among mountains at the head of the glacier—perversely, a yearning came for a toboggan, to hurtle all the way down to the bottom. Once in the plane again, we set off down the slope through a mist of windblown snow. We then swung past the summit of Mount Cook before heading back to the little airfield at its foot for my return to Christchurch.

CLOUD-PIERCERS

In the summer of 1991 a large chunk of Mount Cook's summit fell away, reducing the mountain's height by about 20m (66ft). However, it remains the highest peak between Papua New Guinea and the Andes, standing at 3,754m (12,316ft). Mount Cook's Maori name, Aoraki, means "cloud-piercer," and it is surrounded by 18 peaks over 3,000m (9,842ft) high. It is challenging climbing terrain.

GOING IT ALONE

INTERNAL TRAVEL

Fox Glacier and Franz Josef are only 24km (15 miles) apart. Both are best reached by road. Cars can be hired at Greymouth, Hokitika Airport, or Queenstown. You sometimes share single-lane bridges with trains, and make sure that you know the whereabouts of the next petrol station. The driving time to the glaciers from Greymouth is about 3½ hours, and from Queenstown about six hours.

If you do not have a car, there are daily bus services along the west coast from Greymouth, Nelson, and Queenstown. Between Queenstown and Christchurch there is a daily double-decker service with commentary that travels via Mount Cook. Journey time is about five hours from Queenstown and four from Christchurch, and includes a couple of short refreshment stops *en route*.

The nearest airport to the glaciers is at Hokitika, about three hours' drive north of the glaciers. It is also possible to fly direct to Mount Cook; Air New Zealand operates regular flights from Christchurch and Queenstown.

WHEN TO GO

As always, the question of when to go is the key problem. Both the helihike and skiplane trips depend entirely on the clemency of the weather; if the weather prospects are not good they simply will not operate. Try to allow yourself time for cancellations as the operators will transfer your reservation to a later flight if possible. Theoretically, both activities are possible all year round, but the weather in South Island (and Westland in particular) is utterly unpredictable and safety is paramount.

PLANNING

There is no doubt that the best way to enjoy the visits to the glacier region and to Mount Cook is to go by road. If possible, hire a car for the stretch of countryside between Greymouth and Queenstown, or between the glaciers and Queenstown.

Most accommodation in Fox and Franz Joseph is in self-catering motels, and as the villages are both small, getting about on foot is not a problem if you have arrived by bus. There is a good supermarket on the main street and also a couple of restaurants serving reasonably priced food. There are limited accommodation options at Mount Cook village, from top-of-the-range Hermitage Hotel to self-catering chalets, each with two bedrooms.

The helihike and all the other glacier visits are run by Alpine Guides. The company operates every day except Christmas Day, although everything depends on the weather conditions. Various tours are on offer, including a half-day glacier walk (for which moderate fitness is required); a walk to the terminal of the glacier (almost any level of fitness), which operates only between November 1 and April 30; and the all-day glacier walk, for which a good level of fitness is required. Other options are available on request, including ice-climbing instruction. Advance booking is not necessarily essential for the glacier walks, although it is advisable, while booking ahead for the helihike is definitely recommended. Most of the equipment you will need is provided and what is not can be bought in the shop attached to the offices of Alpine Guides. Whilst walking on the glaciers is safe, at the very least you must be surefooted.

For the flight to Mount Cook with a landing on the Tasman Glacier a minimum of three passengers is required. Flights operate every hour on the half-hour, every day of the year, but again are dependent entirely on weather conditions and minimum numbers. Two options are available. The Grand Circle is a 55-minute flight including views of the west coast glaciers and a landing on the Tasman. The Glacier Highlights flight, lasts 40 minutes and also includes a landing. Reservations are recommended in the high season.

WHAT TO TAKE

- ❏ Sunglasses and sunscreen.
- ❏ Gloves and hat.
- ❏ A small rucksack to carry your essentials in.
- ❏ Warm clothes. Fleeces and thermal base layers are ideal.
- ❏ Waterproof footwear suitable for walking in snow and ice.

HEALTH

The sun can be especially fierce out on the ice, so apply plenty of high factor sunscreen and wear sunglasses that provide good U.V. protection. Cover up any exposed areas that are not used to the intense sun.

24 Thrills and Spills on the Shotover River

by Veronika Meduna and Andy Reisinger

Queenstown is New Zealand's undisputed adventure capital and the Shotover River the town's goldmine. You can swoop downriver in a raft, speed in a jetboat, take a gut-wrenching freefall and a hair-raising helicopter ride—all in just one day.

Nestled on the shores of Lake Wakatipu and framed by the majestic Southern Alps is Queenstown, within easy reach of some of New Zealand's most picturesque scenery. The town is the country's centre for adventure tourism and every year welcomes a million international visitors, most of whom come to challenge themselves mentally or physically. Others simply want to do something wild, the sort of experience that may take only seconds but lasts for a lifetime of memories. With more than 100 adventure activities on offer, the alpine resort buzzes all year round. Although Queenstown is only the size of a sprawling village, it has a cosmopolitan atmosphere and probably more cafés and restaurants per square metre downtown than any other New Zealand town. Its streets are lined with the shopfronts of tour operators who offer everything from sedate nature walks to the Crazy Kiwi package, which promises to zap visitors through the main attractions in just a few hours.

WHERE TO START

The sheer number of options is overwhelming, so we start our exploration with a gondola ride to Queenstown's Skyline restaurant. The panoramic view takes in the entire city and Lake Wakatipu, extending almost full circle from Coronet Peak to the Remarkables, two popular skiing destinations, and on to Cecil and Walter peaks on the other side of the lake. The restaurant and gondola are open well into the night, and we watch the sun set over the hills as we draw up a plan for the days ahead.

Our main destination is the Shotover River, which, with its rugged beauty, wild waters, and extravagant history, is one of Queenstown's main draws. We opt for a mountain-bike ride, followed by a four-wheel-drive trip, along the gravel road that leads upriver to the old Skippers township and beyond, so that we can enjoy several water-based activities on our way back downstream. The alternative is to fly in by helicopter or to drive all the way by jeep, but the road to Skippers Canyon is spectacular and worth a more leisurely exploration.

The gorges have been described as

---

3 Many of the activities around the Shotover River will challenge your courage more than your fitness. Most operators will have a range of options to suit the cautious, the fearless, and the just plain crazy. Both the Shotover and Kawarau rivers have rapids up to Class IV (Class I is easy, Class VI is unraftable).

 ★★★ Your accommodation will probably be in Queenstown, which offers a wide range, from exclusive lodges to budget backpackers' hostels. You can put up a tent at Skippers Canyon, but you will need to take your own gear.

 Whichever activity you choose, you are likely to get wet, so make sure you pack enough fast-drying, warm clothes. Rafting and river-surfing operators will provide wetsuits, but the water can be chilly even in summer.

Right: *The finale is a steep run straight into the refreshing shower of a gushing creek*
Inset: *Gold panning at Skippers Park Museum*

SOUTH ISLAND

LANDSCAPING THE CANYONLANDS

Bare rock, golden tufts of tussock, the thorny native shrub matagouri, and a few lonely beech trees was all the first miners found in the canyonlands of the Shotover River. To alleviate their frequent bouts of homesickness, many brought tree seedlings from their own countries, planting them haphazardly along the tracks and around the makeshift buildings. Over the years, this do-it-yourself landscaping added exotic shapes and hues to the weather-parched valley. Poplars, birches, larches, Douglas firs, and a whole range of fruit trees now line the road to Skippers Saddle and have spread throughout the river valley. In the valley itself, the diggers also planted roses to supplement their vitamin needs through rosehip jam. The Chinese miners, meanwhile, added medicinal herbs such as marjoram, which today fills entire hillsides with its fragrance.

the "Grand Canyon of the South," and although they are nowhere near the same scale, the landscapes are just as magnificent. The Wakatipu Glacier carved the first scar into the land during the last ice age. Over millions of years, Skippers Canyon was further eroded as the river cut a kilometre down into the glacial moraines, concentrating and exposing rich pockets of minerals in the walls. This striking geology is now visible in the coloured cliffs that rise high above the riverbed. Here, the golds and greens of the vegetation provide a counterpoint to the foaming blue of the river. The added attraction of the Shotover River is that gold-rush relics pop up in almost every corner.

THE WORLD'S RICHEST RIVER

In mid-November 1862, two shearers spent a Sunday off work fossicking for gold in the lower Shotover River,

equipped with a butcher's knife and a pan. Gold had already been discovered in other fields in Otago, but nobody had thought of the Shotover as a gold vein. Within hours the two mates heaped up 250g (9oz) of the precious metal.

By June of the following year, more than 4,000 men had arrived to scour the treacherous cliffs, deep gorges, gravel beds, and swift waters of the Shotover, and the river soon acquired a reputation as the world's richest. Those who pegged out a claim in the first two years reaped the rich rewards—some were taking out up to 300g (10oz) a day using only tin pans and sluice boxes.

MODERN QUEST FOR ADVENTURE

Today, the rush is on for adrenalin, although the goldmining days are still part of many modern adventures. Most operators specialize in one activity, so to explore the river we have to use several companies. The options differ in their fitness requirements rather than in their scenic appeal or thrill factor. The Shotover River is regarded as more difficult to raft than the Kawarau, the main river via which Lake Wakatipu drains into the Pacific Ocean, and its bungee bridges are significantly higher than the original bridge over the Kawarau.

Although both rivers have been mined for gold, the Shotover is the one with the more impressive and more visible history. Much of the goldminers' equipment has been left untouched in an open-air tribute to the bravery and sheer madness of the gold rush. The Shotover has also cut a much deeper canyon into the soft schist, so the views from both the tracks above and the river below are dramatic.

DOWNHILL ROLL

At Skippers Saddle, we are kitted out with full-suspension Iron Horse bikes and all the accessories necessary to look the part. Our guides are world-class bikers, who "retired" from competitive cycling to take tours along the old bridle paths leading into the Shotover canyonlands. They give us a brief pep talk about how to stay on the bike. All our biking is down-hill, and for the first hour follows a rutted single track with a few boulders thrown in for enjoyment. The path runs on the eastern side of the river, from where we can see the famously difficult gravel road—the only vehicle access route to Skippers Canyon—hugging the steep, rocky slopes of the other riverbank. But for now our challenge is mountain biking. We are told—and learn very quickly—that it is best to keep our feet on the pedals at an even level and to hold onto our brakes, at the same time standing on the bike and guiding the saddle with our knees. Anyone who is used to riding rigid or front-suspension bikes may find the fully suspended version like a precariously wobbly perch at first. But it doesn't take long to appreciate how gently these bikes roll over hurdles that would otherwise jar your spine or send you flying. After a few narrow S-bends and creek crossings, the finale is a steep run straight into the refreshing shower of a gushing creek near the ruins of the Welcome Home Inn.

HISTORIC PUB CRAWL

Locals say that at least 16 hotels sprang up as soon as the track between Queenstown and Skippers township was established in 1863. These wayside shanties provided drink, food, and accommodation for the first mob of miners and fortune seekers rushing to the newly discovered goldfields. Even at the time, the track was no more than a bridle path that led to the diggings, but in lieu of better access, it became the main highway to wealth until the road was cut into the bluffs on the opposite riverbank during the late 1880s.

Welcome Home Inn is the best-preserved historic pub, but even this ruin consists of just two tall chimneys. Most other houses were built from timber, which was so rare in the valley that it was continually recycled and reused for other purposes—often leaving no trace of the original buildings. Just before the hotel ruin, we meet our second guide, who has been following in the van along the road as a safety measure. Conveniently, he has now come to transport the bikes, and us, uphill for the next downhill ride.

THE ROAD TO SKIPPERS

The second lap of mountain biking follows Skippers Road from Bell's Hill, named after the last proprietor of the Welcome Home Inn, to Skippers Canyon and the site of the old township. From a cyclist's perspective, the gravel road is very pleasant and provides us with good views of the Shotover snaking through its narrow gorge. Mount Aurum, the snow-covered peak believed to be the source of the Shotover gold, provides a majestic backdrop. But for drivers, the road represents a major challenge. It is rarely wide enough for two-way traffic, so one vehicle will inevitably have to negotiate hairpin corners in reverse gear. Rental cars are usually not insured on Skippers Road, and most vehicles we meet belong to tour operators.

It took the miners and labourers six years to carve the nearly 30km (19 miles) of dirt road into the craggy hills. As we bike around Pincher's Bluff, the road is cut right into sheer rock, 105m (345ft) above the water and 90m (295ft) from the top of the steep cliff. Workers had to be lowered on ropes. The first shift would abseil equipped with hammers and chisels and, once they had scraped off enough of the rock face, the explosives crew would follow and ignite small charges of dynamite. The number of lives lost was never properly recorded.

PIONEERING HYDROPOWER

As we roll into Skippers Canyon, the gorge widens and both sides of the river flatten into terraces held in shape by rugged cliffs and crags. The old fortune hunters went to unbelievable lengths to tame the wild river and extract its wealth—and in the process they changed the landscape significantly. They dug

channels and water races into the terraced sections to divert creeks and collect their water in huge reservoirs high up in the hillsides. The water was then brought down to the river through gradually narrowing pipes, so the miners ended up with powerful sluice guns that reputedly cut through the gravel of the riverbanks like knives. The channels of the water races are still visible, crisscrossing the hillsides like the lines of a giant chessboard.

At Skippers Canyon the miners suspended a pipeline across the river to bring water from one side to holding dams on the other. Built in 1864, the Pipeline Bridge spans 150m (490ft), at a disquieting height of 102m (335ft) above the river. Even walking across the bridge makes us discover a new respect for heights, but this wouldn't be New Zealand if somebody hadn't spotted the structure's potential as a bungee platform. The Pipeline is the highest land-based bungee bridge, surpassed only by A.J. Hackett's latest highwire adventure from a gondola above the Nevis River. As you stand on the tiny ledge that juts out from the bridge, with your ankles tightly wrapped in a towel and a giant rubber band, the pickup boat below looks the size of a toy. The fact that the people in it seem to be waving does nothing to ease the tension. Letting go

Left: Bungee jumping off the Pipeline Bridge
Above: The Shotover Jet offers a high-speed thrill ride through the Shotover Gorge
Below: Wear tight-fitting clothing and remember to empty your pockets

simply defies all survival mechanisms in your brain.

MORE SPEED THRILLS

Very few people simply let themselves fall over the edge. Like most of the others, we jump into the air with arms outstretched, letting loose a primal scream. The fall is long enough to allow you time to think about what you have just done, and there is definitely a brief flash of stomach-churning fear—which quickly dissolves into absolute elation the moment you feel the elastic tug. The

243

rope has an 80 percent rebound, so there is plenty of yo-yoing before you can climb into the jetboat waiting at the bottom and hitch a horizontal speed thrill. The canyon's narrow walls make for an exciting ride, and the piles of historic junk in the river add a challenge for the driver.

Skippers Canyon was one of the busiest spots during the Shotover gold rush, and several miners stayed on after the madness of the first years receded. A few were still working the claims more than 100 years after the gold discovery. The last commercial dredge was pulled out in 1992; it extracted US$13 million worth of gold in 12 years. The last veteran to use the old-fashioned sluice guns and hydraulic suction machinery was Joe Scheib, who in the 1970s started what has now grown into Skippers Park, an outdoor museum and collection of memorabilia from the river's golden past.

BUNGEE LEGEND

Bungee-jumping veteran A.J. Hackett has left his mark all over the Queenstown area. Since he opened the first commercial jump site at the Kawarau Bridge in 1988, he has developed three more sites in the area, including the 134m (440ft) highwire thrill above the Nevis River. However, bungee jumping is no New Zealand invention. On Pentecost, one of the islands in Vanuatu, brave men have been jumping off high wooden towers for centuries. Their feet are attached to vines that have to be collected at just the right time to guarantee their elasticity. This ancient ritual inspired the Oxford University Dangerous Sports Club to try a few experimental jumps back in the 1970s; A.J. Hackett saw a video and was hooked. Extensive testing of latex rubber cords and a series of extreme jumps followed, first from a ski-field gondola 91m (300ft) above the snow, and then, in June 1987, from the Eiffel Tower and straight into the international spotlight.

SKIPPERS PARK

The weirdest exhibit is arguably an anonymous miner's boot, with the poor fellow's foot bones still inside. Also restored is the flying fox cable slide across the canyon.

Pumped up with adrenalin, we take a jeep ride further into the upper reaches of the river. The descendants of those who arrived here to make a fortune now farm the foothills of the Southern Alps, where the Shotover originates. The last stretch of Skippers Road, leading further upstream to the old township, is even narrower and windier, and offers spectacular views of Skippers Bridge. The suspension bridge, 72m (236ft) above the river, was opened in 1901, connecting the Shotover diggers with those who tried their luck along its many tributaries.

On our way to what is left of Skippers township, we pass the Blue Slip, an almost fluid-looking steep slope of schist that is particularly rich in silica. The fine silica dust covers everything with a greasy layer and acts as a lubricant for the mountain's frequent landslides.

GHOST TOWN

Skippers was once the largest settlement on the Shotover, but all that is left of it now is the school and the cemetery. Old photographs in the schoolhouse show a scattered cluster of cottages connected by a network of muddy tracks. Today, the remaining gravestones are framed by a mountainside covered in lush vegetation.

Despite the large number of Chinese diggers who lived in shelters and caves along the canyon, there is only one Chinese grave in the cemetery. The Chinese miners believed that their spirits would rest only if they returned to their homeland, so they spent a good part of their fortune on chartering ships to take their dead on the long journey to China. We stay the night in a tent on the terraces behind the Pipeline Bridge. There are no official campsites along the Shotover, but almost anything can be arranged as long as you ask first and take your own gear.

DOWNSTREAM JOYRIDE

The next morning sees us snatched back from tranquillity to the fizzing jostle of adventure sports—this time on the water. Rafting is one of the most popular activities on the Shotover, despite the fact that most people get chucked out of the rubber dinghy at least once. We meet our raft crew at Deep Creek, just a few minutes downriver from Skippers Canyon. About 50 people have either hitched a helicopter or a four-wheel-drive ride from Queenstown to swirl through rapids with such telling names a Shark Fins, Jaws, Toilet, and Cascade.

After a brief safety check and demonstration of paddling and rescue techniques, we climb into the rubber boat with six others. We are all first-time rafters, but prior experience is not a requirement. For the first few hundred metres, the river's gentle flow provides ample opportunity to paddle in unison, responding to military-style commands from the guide at the stern, not unlike slaves in a galley. Despite their unwieldy appearance, the rafts are easy to navigate, and a few strong paddle strokes turn ours easily. We sit on the tightly inflated outer rings of the pontoon, our feet tucked into rubber folds that keep us steady but won't trap us if we capsize. Where possible, we pull the raft into the calm bays that follow most rapids to wait until all the other boats have negotiated the cascading waves. Apart from giving us a chance to watch the spectacle, this is also important for safety reasons. In the likely scenario that one or more boats flip over, all other rafts will be needed to pick up people before they float too far down the river. There is only one spill during our trip, and it is reassuring to see that everybody manages to get into the floating position we had been taught and is back in the boat in less than five minutes.

SPILLS AND THRILLS

The highlight of our two-hour trip comes right at the end, when we steer the raft through the 170m (185yd) man-made Oxenbridge Tunnel. At the fading end of the gold rush, the miners carved this tunnel into the rock to divert the river so that they could get to the bottom of a long, swirling rapid in the vain hope of finding huge gold deposits there. Unwittingly, the miners created an added attraction for today's adventure seekers. The river now flows through both the tunnel and the rapid, so rafters have a choice, dependent on water levels, between bouncing down the Class III Mother in Law rapid or drifting through the surreal tunnel, which exits on the short Cascade rapid.

The rafting trip finishes at Arthur's Point, the site of the first gold find in the Shotover River, where a jetboat takes us further downriver through the Shotover Canyon. While this canyon is smaller than Skippers Canyon, its frame of vertical slabs of granite is impressive. A jetboat ride is the only way to see the canyon from the water, as no other boats are allowed along this stretch for safety reasons. The jetboats reach speeds of up to 70kmh (45mph) as they whizz past the canyon walls with no more than a few centimetres of leeway. Staying dry is impossible, as is ignoring the flush of adrenalin that gushes through the system. But despite the thrill, the ride remains a passive adventure compared to rafting the white waters of the Shotover, or throwing yourself straight into the rapids to surf the river on a body board.

GO WITH THE FLOW

Queenstown's most popular spot for river surfing is a sequence of rapids in the Kawarau River, not far from where it meets the Shotover. In contrast to the Shotover River, the Kawarau is a high-volume river with no exposed rocks in its rapids, and is therefore the safer option for body boarding. The fast-flowing water forms huge standing waves and whirls that sometimes break into each other and can make you feel like you are in a washing machine on full cycle. All you need to enjoy the trip is a degree of confidence in the water and a reasonable level of

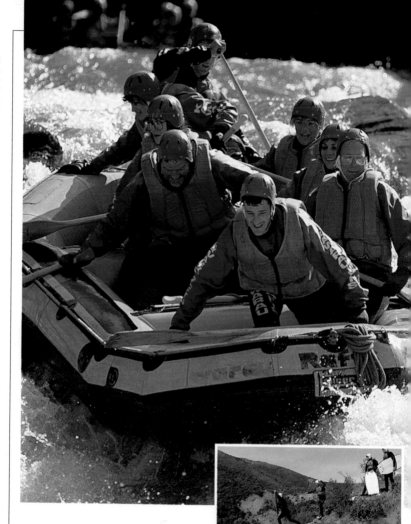

Above: *Negotiating the rapids requires teamwork to ensure that you stay in the boat and out of the water—although you'll still get wet!*
Right: *River surfing in the Kawarau*

fitness. The trip takes four hours, and even the stretches between rapids can be exhausting as you swirl in the eddies.

Our trip starts in a calm bay where our guides explain the basics of how a river flows around obstacles and how to ride the boards in calm or white water. The boards are fitted to each person's upper-body length, so that the legs are free to paddle. The river is swift enough to propel us along, so we need our fins (flippers) only to change direction or to swim against the current. The trip is designed to build up in difficulty gradually, so for the first half-hour we practise

riding in and out of eddies and "squirting," perhaps best described as flying under the surface along the wall of water that runs between two currents. The four rapids start at Class II, building up to Class IV by the last, a 400m (440yd) dog-leg of boiling water. It takes a minute to get through the rollercoaster ride of metre-high waves, but at the end nobody wants this trip to finish. To top it all off, we walk back along the river and jump straight back into the swirling rapid from a rock ledge 3m (10ft) above.

GOING IT ALONE

INTERNAL TRAVEL

Queenstown is served by flights from Sydney and Auckland all year round, and from Brisbane in winter. There are several daily connections with Auckland, Rotorua, Wellington, and Christchurch. A flight from Christchurch takes about 45 minutes.

Daily bus services are available from several destinations in the South Island. Major international and all national car- and campervan-hire companies have offices in Queenstown. Allow a full day for the very scenic drive from Christchurch.

WHEN TO GO

There is no wrong time to visit Queenstown. Most adventure activities—including whitewater rafting and jetboating—are possible throughout the year, although some trips may be shorter in winter to avoid exposure to the colder water. Summer temperatures can reach 30°C (90°F). The town lies just below the 45th parallel, so the sun does not set behind the Southern Alps until well into the evening. Horse riding, mountain biking, and walking are particularly popular in autumn, while in winter, Queenstown attracts huge numbers of skiers and snowboarders. Spring brings bursts of flowers and crisp mountain air, although the weather can be unstable—heavy rain and snowmelts can flood the rivers, making water-based adventures temporarily impossible. There is at least one special event every month, such as jazz in September, or wine and food in February.

PLANNING

During the main summer season, most visitors stay only one or two nights. In winter, the majority come for extended stints on the ski slopes. But anyone who enjoys outdoor activities could easily spend a week at any time of the year without getting bored.

Both Destination Queenstown and the Queenstown Visitors' Centre have a wide range of brochure material, which they will post out on request. For those with little time to spare, there are several combination packages available, including day packages that combine jetboating, bungee jumping, whitewater rafting, and helicopter flights. Apart from saving time, such package deals also save money.

TRAVELLERS' TIPS

- ❏ Book activities well ahead in summer.
- ❏ Don't be put off by bad weather; it can change quickly and you will get wet anyway.
- ❏ Don't try activities without a guide unless you are really experienced and know the rivers well—conditions can change rapidly and there can be unexpected dangers.
- ❏ Shop around for package deals that offer discounts on combinations of activities.
- ❏ If you are travelling by yourself, ask the operators if you can be buddied up with someone of similar fitness.
- ❏ If you plan to drive to Skippers Canyon, check with your car-rental company whether Skippers Road is covered by the insurance.
- ❏ If you feel the cold easily, wear thermal underwear and warm socks under your wetsuit.

WHAT TO TAKE

You can expect to be provided with all the gear necessary for the activities, including wetsuits, bike helmets, life jackets, and body boards. However, take swimwear and good outdoor clothing for all weather conditions.

If you plan to stay the night at Skippers Canyon you will need your own tent, sleeping bag, and food supplies. Good sun protection is essential even in winter, when snow reflection can cause bad sunburn.

HEALTH

Take a small personal first-aid kit with a general antiseptic, an insect repellent, and a cooling ointment against sandfly bites. The tap water is fresh and safe to drink. River water can be muddy after rain but is also generally safe.

Below: The bike trail follows old bridle paths, once the only access to the gold fields

SOUTH ISLAND

25 On the Routeburn Track

by Christopher Knowles

The three-day trek along the Routeburn through some of the loveliest scenery in the world is not particularly challenging, but provides spectacular panoramas of this pure and unspoilt mountain area.

There was something in the name that made me want to take on this walk above all the many other classic hikes available around Queenstown. The western part of New Zealand's South Island is infamous for the changeable, not to say capricious, nature of its climate. Grey skies, unstinting driving rain, and lowering mist had characterized the greater part of my stay over the past few days. Yet, out of nowhere and without warning, the skies would clear entirely to reveal the most breathtaking and varied scenery of anywhere in the world. Mountains, fjords, rainforest, beech forest, glaciers, lakes, waterfalls; it was all there, in abundance and on a grand scale.

PROSPECTING FOR GOLD

Although Queenstown is a tourism hub, a 20-minute drive in a Land Rover takes you into the inhospitable terrain known as Skippers Canyon. Among steep hills just below the local ski runs is an area that was once a centre for gold prospecting, but which is now home to a mere handful of hardy sheep farmers. The road, curving around the girth of the hills, high above a raging river, is still subject to landslides—even that day we had to pick our way across a fall of silty, brittle rock. Several thousand people used to live up here trying to make their fortunes. The old school has latterly been restored, and inside are displays of old photographs.

A GOLDEN PROSPECT

The pre-tour meeting is held in the offices of Routeburn Walk Ltd., situated at the corner of Queenstown's main street. There are to be eight of us in total. A film is screened to give us some idea of what lies ahead. Those of us who need them are provided with capacious rucksacks and good-quality waterproof jackets and trousers. Lightweight bedding is also distributed. Our hike is the first of this fickle season, but the weather forecast is good. My hotel, the St. Moritz Suites, overlooks Lake Wakatipu and, beyond it, the Remarkables, the uncompromisingly named range of mountains among which we would be trekking for the next three days. As the evening wears on, the rain stops and the sky reddens. The omens are indeed good.

A FINE START

There is no rain the next morning and the sky over the lake is clear. We meet at seven o'clock beside the Steamer Wharf, from where a bus will take us into the

 The Routeburn is clear and easy to follow, although some of it is uneven and strewn with boulders. There are a number of sustained ascents and descents, but these are infrequent and never severe. Though you need to be able to carry a backpack, you can walk at your own pace.

★★ The accommodation on the walk consists of lodges with comfortable bunk beds, warm duvets and no more than four to a room. There are hot-water showers, flushing toilets, gas lighting, drying rooms, a spacious dining room, and good food. The excellent guides are personable, fit, and responsible. The only possible irritants are sandflies.

 You will need good walking boots and both cold and wet weather gear. All can be purchased or hired locally.

mountains and our starting point. Eight hikers and three guides—what luxury! Our packs are loaded onto the bus, along with all sorts of packages and boxes. We pass alongside Lake Wakatipu until we reach the town of Te Anau, where we are served morning tea and scones. From Te Anau it is another couple of hours to the Divide, a day lodge located at an altitude of 530m (1,740ft) at the head of the Eglinton Valley, marking the start of the Routeburn Track. We disembark and claim our rucksacks, to which we add our packed lunches, provided for us by the guides. They are at great pains to assure us that each of us is to walk at the pace that suits us; they don't mind how slow we are.

Our introduction to the Routeburn is a steady ascent along a wide and well-formed track, rising through the so-called lower-altitude silver beech forest. The high rainfall here encourages the growth of a wide variety of ferns, mosses, and lichens. Many of the trees are covered in a thick green padding, and it is the wispy goblin moss that gives this part of the forest a certain eeriness, relieved by the sweet, distinctive song of a bellbird, perhaps feeding on red fuchsia. The pace is not hard, and there are frequent stops as the guides point out a flower or a fern. All is well.

GROUP DYNAMIC

Conversation at this stage is down to a minimum. We are getting used to our loads and establishing a rhythm for ourselves as individuals and as a group.

After three-quarters of an hour, at 790m (2,590ft), we come to a junction marking the turn-off for Key Summit. We can, if we wish, leave our packs here while we make a detour up to the 919m (3,015ft) mark to a lookout point at Key Summit. The path climbs to a flatter area of rocky pools, surrounded by patches of bogland interwoven with knots of small, delicate flowers. This is one of nature's viewing platforms. The views—which for me are the highlight of a hike in the

mountains—extend to three different valleys, the Eglinton, the Greenstone, and the Hollyford, which funnel water to three separate coastlines. A dense covering of green reaches up the sides of the valleys, merging into a white coverlet of snow that blazes across a great crowd of jostling peaks. The clear spring air brings limitless panoramas against a hazeless, summery blue sky.

BIRD FOOD

But lunchtime is approaching. Before we descend to take up our packs, we are assailed by two cheeky birds. They are keas. They have olive-green plumage, with orange underwings, and a loud braying call, usually transcribed as "kay-aa." They are known to use their curved beaks to lever rubber lining from around car windows and are practically fearless, perfectly content to waddle up to us and inspect our footwear.

We rejoin the track and continue for about 15 minutes to descend to our lunch stop at the public hut at Lake Howden, at 685m (2,247ft). In future we will be making up our own lunches, but on this occasion the guides have done us proud, with sandwiches, fruit, and chocolate. Apparently, the only potential problem is the presence of sandflies, but happily there are none to be seen or felt.

A WARM SHOWER

After lunch we climb again, for just over an hour, curving around the flank of the Humboldt Mountains, with the Hollyford Valley and the Hollyford River far below us to the left. Sometimes we can see small aircraft in silent motion, heading for one of the local airstrips that dot the country. The track has become rockier, but it is still good and easy to follow. By the time we reach 975m (3,200ft), the climb and the sun on our encumbered backs have made us all pretty hot. So the sound of rushing water is highly inviting, and as we turn a corner there, falling in a quaking curtain across the rockface, are the Earland Falls.

The guides are surprised to see the water so plentiful. We run the risk of getting wet if we carry on, but we all agree in the end to ignore the longer, drier diversion and instead to don our waterproofs, conceal our cameras, and take a shower. In the event, the path runs close to but not directly through the falls and so we, like the surrounding vegetation, merely get a light dousing of fine spray. To be so close to that thudding volume of water, falling in an unheralded gush right beside you from on high, is a liberating feeling.

WELL MET

The track now remains level for quite some time. Opposite us on the far side of the valley are the glaciated Darran Mountains, the highest peaks in the Fiordland National Park. We pass through patches of beech wood and sub-alpine scrub, where lichens, prickly shield ferns, and mountain ribbonwood trees predominate. The ribbonwoods have the appearance of fruit trees, and the track soon turns away from the valley to bring us to an area christened the Orchard, a

peaceful expanse of trees and grasses where we take a breather before setting off on the last stage of the day. Chocolate and biscuits make their appearances (once again the guides produce supplies from some corner of their packs), and we eat and drink in silence.

Leaving the Orchard, we climb one last time, for about a quarter of an hour, before starting our final half-hour descent to the lodge. This stage is fairly steep for our tired muscles, but doesn't prove to be too difficult.

ACCOMMODATING IN EVERY WAY

The Lake Mackenzie Lodge, which is used for the guided Routeburn groups only, is a roomy wooden building with a veranda, several bedrooms, a drying room, a bathroom with showers, lavatories, and washbasins, and a spacious sitting and dining room. The lake is encircled by mountains, some already in late-afternoon shadow, but others reflected in the perfectly still waters. We bathe our feet in the freezing water, but choose a hot shower in preference to an ice-cold swim! It has been a wonderful day.

OLD JOANNA

The Lodge manager, with the help of our tireless guides, prepares dinner. She is an excellent hostess—a great talker, with any number of opinions and quips, and also a pretty good cook. From time to time, while dinner is being made, she launches into a piano rendering of a familiar tune (which turns out to be something by the Bee Gees). Her hands dance over the keys in quite amazing fashion, and it is only when the routine of looking back and grinning over her shoulder starts to verge on the preposterous that we realize she is not playing at all. The piano turns out to be a pianola, the sheet music striking the keys as it turns. Dinner is hearty and delicious, and includes a glass or two of wine, rounded off by homemade chocolate cake and tea or coffee. By now it is dark, the air has cooled, and the sky is brimming with stars. We are looking forward to the next day.

SUBLIME CLIMB

The next day dawns clear. Porridge is available for breakfast, if required, and so are all the ingredients for a full cooked breakfast. We set off down to the lake, passing the public lodge on the way. At

Left: Breathtaking views all around us left everyone in awe of the sheer scale of our surroundings
Inset: Crossing the Routeburn on a wooden suspension bridge

SOUTH ISLAND

the lakeside, the path we shall be taking is pointed out to us—we can see it as it zigzags up the mountain, in long, shallow sections. But first we have to get around the lake. There are two paths, although the shorter is out of the question as it is waist deep in water. The second, longer one takes us through a patch of dense, mossy silver beech woodland, which necessitates a bit of clambering over fallen trees before we join the main path and the beginning of our ascent.

Soon the track rises out of the woodland to enter once again the realm of alpine flowers, although at this time (early November) we would be lucky to see any in bloom. None the less, a few are just beginning to open and others are not far behind. The path rises through a marvellous natural garden where snow marguerites, daisies, Haast's carrot, Maori golden onions, avens, and gentians grow in profusion.

After some 1½ hours of leisurely though constant climbing, we reach Ocean Peak Corner at 1,175m (3,855ft), which marks the boundary between the Mackenzie and Hollyford valleys. After our exertions up the zigzag track we will literally turn a corner to enter a long stretch of undulating path along the Hollyford Face. Before embarking on the next section of the walk, however, we have ample time to linger on this natural platform at the junction of the two valleys, replenishing our stomachs and, once again, just staring at the magnificence of our surroundings. We can gaze back to Key Summit, where we were the day before, scan the entire length of the Darran Mountains until they vanish into Lake McKerrow, and see beyond to Martins Bay, where the Hollyford River meets the Tasman Sea.

VALLEYSIDE WALK

For the next two hours we walk along a shelf above the valley, with the Darran Mountains on our left. On such a warm, clear day as we have the good fortune to enjoy (this is the most exposed section of

the entire route), this is walking at its very best. Little bridges take us over miniature canyons where cut-glass streams hurtle beneath us, and the sun has wrought another small miracle in that the so-called Mount Cook lilies, the world's largest buttercups, have already shown their faces.

The track now edges inland in a series of scalloped curves, and with every corner you expect to come upon the shelter. Just as exasperation is reaching its peak, there it is, a small, raised hut at 1,277m (4,190ft), where we can stop for a well deserved lunch.

THE PEAK OF OUR EFFORTS

The kettle is boiling and before long we are all seated in the sun, eating our sandwiches and listening to the keas as they wheel about the hills. After lunch there is the opportunity to make the optional climb up to the summit of Conical Hill, and any thoughts of giving it a miss are shattered by the sight of a party of 60-year-olds striking out for the top. Just below the summit there are still a few patches of lingering snow to wade through, after which we clamber up to yet another of those natural platforms, from where we see the most spectacular panorama yet. This time we are all but surrounded on all sides by snow-capped peaks, but through a gap looking north it is possible to see, shimmering in the far distance, the waves breaking on the beach at Martins Bay.

ANOTHER HIGH POINT

Having taken our fill of these wonders, we return to the hut at Harris Saddle, collect our things and head out for the last part of the day's walking. We climb once again for a short distance up to 1,310m (4,298ft)—this is the highest point of the track, not including the optional excursions—to walk along a shelf on a bluff overlooking the blue-green waters of Lake Harris. And then it is a long descent, lasting 1–1½ hours, along rocky but quite manageable paths all the way to the

Routeburn Falls, where we shall spend the night.

The landscape changes in character as we make the descent. It is more akin to walking among hills, since the mountains have crowded in on us and we are no longer gazing at the whole, gigantic range, with its fields of snow and glaciated valleys. Here, sheltered from the worst onslaughts of wind and weather, a different flora flourishes. There are tree daisies, snow tussocks, snowberries, pygmy pines (the world's smallest conifer) and the notorious Spaniard, an unpleasantly prickly plant whose name reflects the antipathies of the early settlers.

FIRST, YOU MUST CATCH YOUR PANCAKE

The path levels out to a junction where the waters of the Routeburn River begin to gather momentum towards the falls below. Here there is the opportunity to take a second optional walk up to Paddy's Point, from where there are fine views of the Routeburn Falls about 500m (1,640ft) below and the Routeburn Valley beyond. One or two decide to take it on, while the rest of us choose to call it a day.

The lodge is perched dramatically on boulders and rocks practically alongside the falls, which tumble down in a series of cascades. The accommodation is even more spacious than that the previous night, although at this early stage in the season there is not yet a manager, and so our guides—who we have increasingly come to admire—will be taking on that role as well. We are allowed a couple of pre-dinner beers tonight, having come through the most demanding part of the route unscathed, and dinner is excellent yet again, although part of it is served in an unusual way. The chef stands with a pancake in the pan, his back to the recipient, who stands in readiness with a plate. On the signal, the pancake is flipped blindly through the air in the vague hope that it will land on the plate. Somehow, it does, almost every time.

LAST DAY

In the morning, before breakfast, several of us visit the falls independently to photograph them in the vivid morning light. A helicopter lands among us, one of a succession of flights bringing in supplies. After another excellent breakfast, and with our sandwiches made up, we are outside the hut lacing up our boots, watching New Zealand's smallest bird, the rifleman, a member of the wren family, chirruping on a bush a few feet away.

Today, we have to keep to some sort of schedule, since at the end of the walk, after lunch, we are to be met by a bus that will take us back to Queenstown. The route starts with a descent through mixed beech forest along a rocky track, which requires a little concentration but is perfectly manageable. After no more than one hour we arrive at the Routeburn Flats Hut, at an altitude of 700m (2,300ft), where we are able to have a welcome cup of tea or coffee. The Routeburn River, which is quite wide here, bubbles along a few metres away,

ROUTEBURN WILDLIFE

There is a considerable amount of wildlife to be found along the Routeburn. Apart from keas and riflemen, look for the long-tailed bat, various grasshoppers, and other birds such as the yellowhead, or mohua, the yellow-crowned parakeet, and the tui. An interesting book about the singular birdlife of New Zealand is *Kea—Bird of Paradox: The Evolution and Behaviour of a New Zealand Parrot*, by Judy Diamond and Alan B. Bond (University of California Press, 1999). The authors have traced the role of the kea, the world's only alpine parrot, in New Zealand's unique, prehistoric ecology, and discuss how it—as opposed to the moa, the giant bird that is now extinct—has survived the changes wrought by man in its environment.

whilst beyond it a flat expanse of marshy grassland extends all the way to the foot of the mountains.

FINALLY ON THE ROUTEBURN TRACK

The forest here is filled with stately red beech trees, taking advantage of the sun that falls across the flats onto the north-facing slopes. Where the cold air collects in the winter, around the edge of the grassy flats on the poorer and more exposed areas, then silver beech tend to grow. The kea's forest-dwelling cousin, the kaka, is often seen here and may even nest close to the track.

After our break, it is time to set out on the final stretch of the walk. It is as if we are being levered gently back into the everyday world, for the trek is refreshingly flat through woodland alongside the Routeburn. The river intermittently becomes a torrent seething among boulders, or swirling along the bottom of small gorges, or transforming itself into a series of deep green pools. A whole sequence of rope and wood suspension bridges, trembling and undulating at our footfall, has to be crossed. Each bridge responds to the step of the first walker, sending a bouncy wave along its length that will almost certainly not coincide with the rhythm of the person behind.

Our final lunch is taken at a shingle beach beside the river. It is a quiet affair, everyone absorbed in the commotion of the water and in a sentimental contemplation of the surroundings we are soon to leave. From here it is but a short stroll to the road where we are to meet the bus.

On the way home we make a stop at a pub at Glenorchy, where we pose for a photograph. By four o'clock we are back at Queenstown, giving us time to prepare for a farewell dinner that evening. There our photographs and certificate are presented to us. It has been a short, intense, euphoric experience with a small group of likeable, enthusiastic people, led by a trio of exceptional guides. We have had unexpectedly perfect weather. We could not have asked for more.

Left: *Earland Falls*
Below: *View of the glaciated Darren Mountains, the highest peaks in the Fiordland National Park*

SOUTH ISLAND

GOING IT ALONE

INTERNAL TRAVEL

The base and starting point for the Routeburn is Queenstown in South Island, which is served by flights from Mount Cook, Auckland, Christchurch, Rotorua, and Wellington.

There are daily bus services from Mount Cook, Christchurch, the glacier regions, Nelson, Greymouth, and Dunedin. If you are coming from the west coast by car the scenery is some of the finest anywhere in the world, but you are advised to stick to Highway 6. You may find that your insurance does not cover you for some of the other roads. Journey time from Fox Glacier is about six or seven hours, or from Christchurch (via Mount Cook) about eight.

WHEN TO GO

The best time of year to undertake the Routeburn is the beginning of summer, perhaps in early December. The weather will be fairly settled (although nothing is guaranteed in South Island), the route should not yet have become too crowded, and many of the flowers will be in bloom. However, if you are lucky with the weather, spring and autumn provide clear air and so the best views, and no crowds.

PLANNING

There is a variety of accommodation in Queenstown. You are advised to book in advance, especially in the busy season. The Queenstown Visitor Information Centre will be able to help.

The Routeburn is perhaps the best of several classic walks available in the region. The trip comprises three days of walking with two nights' accommodation in the mountains.

Everything is included in the price. A sleeping sheet, pillowcase, towel, and plastic pack liner at the briefing, while soap, shampoo, and conditioner are provided at the lodges. The ratio of guide to walker is such that you really can walk at your own pace. You need to be able to walk about 16km (10 miles) a day and be able to cope with steady ascents that may last an hour, all with a pack on your back.

TRAVELLERS' TIPS

- ❑ A walking stick might be seen as an unnecessary encumbrance, but a good one is very useful and can be bought locally. Choose one of the modern, lightweight, telescopic sticks rather than a traditional wooden one.
- ❑ Leave everything you don't need in your hotel in Queenstown. Make sure it is clearly labelled.

WHAT TO TAKE

The following items are considered essential, and can be hired or bought locally.

- ❑ Walking boots. Make sure they are worn in and you are comfortable walking in them over rough terrain.
- ❑ Woollen socks or their modern technical fibre equivalent.
- ❑ Warm hat and gloves.
- ❑ Sweater or fleece top.
- ❑ Swimwear.
- ❑ Thermal underwear, whatever the season.
- ❑ Wind and waterproof jacket with a hood. You will feel the benefits if it is made of a "breathable" fabric.
- ❑ Waterproof leggings
- ❑ Rucksack sufficient to carry the items you will need along the route.
- ❑ Sunglasses.
- ❑ Insect repellent.
- ❑ Water bottles sufficient to carry at least two litres.

HEALTH

The main hazard walkers may encounter is the sandfly. Cover yourself in insect repellent as the bites can itch for several days. Drink river water only above the treeline, and always seek local advice before you do so. If in doubt, boil it first.

WALKING WITHOUT A GUIDE

It is possible to walk the Routeburn on a self-guided basis. This has to be booked through the Department of Conservation (DOC) for a given date in order to prevent overcrowding in the lodges. Instructions and maps can be purchased locally. You will have to carry all your own food and gear. Use a large rucksack with a liner, and take clothes that are warm and that dry out easily. Remember that everything you take with you must be carried out, including all rubbish.

INTRODUCTION

Contained in the first section of these "Blue Pages" are lists of selected contacts relevant to the 25 adventures related on pages 18–256. Because the adventures are personal accounts, the information provided here will reflect each author's own experience, and therefore details will vary accordingly. Remember also that some contacts are in remote places, so be sure to call or write in advance before setting out. None of the places in the Contacts or the A–Z have been vetted in any way by the publishers and, although some of the companies were used by our writers, this is no guarantee they will still be run by the same people or to the same standard of proficiency.

The Contacts section gives details of companies used by our authors and complements the Activities A–Z in the second part. Below is some general information to help you plan your own adventures.

INTERNATIONAL DIALLING CODES

Telephone and fax numbers given in this section of the book begin with a modified area code. When dialling from outside the country, prefix this number with the international network access code of the country you are in, followed by the country code. When dialling from within the country prefix this number with a 0 e.g. (02) 6257 5837.

International Network Access Codes

For calls from the U.K. 00
For calls from the U.S. 011

Country Codes

Australia 61
New Zealand 64

EMBASSIES AND CONSULATES

British Embassies

For details of United Kingdom Government offices in Adelaide, Brisbane, Melbourne and Perth (and opening times of those listed below) visit the Foreign and Commonwealth Office website at www.fco.gov.uk

Australia
British High Commission
Commonwealth Avenue
Yarralumla
Canberra, ACT 2600
☎ (2) 6270 6666 **fax:**
(2) 6270 6653 (Chancery);
(2) 6270 6606 (Information)
website: www.uk.emb.gov.au
Consular Section
(passports/visas):
Level 10, S A P House
Crnr Akuna and Bunda Streets
Canberra, ACT 2601
☎ 1902 941 555 (premium
rate call) **fax:** (2) 6257 5857

British Consulate-General
Level 16, The Gateway
1 Macquarie Place
Sydney Cove
Sydney, NSW 2000
☎ (2) 9247 7521
fax: (2) 9251 6201

New Zealand
British High Commission
44 Hill Street
Wellington 1
Mailing address:
P O Box 1812
Wellington
☎ (4) 472 6049
fax: (4) 471 1974 (Consular);
(4) 495 0831 (Chancery)
email: bhc.wel@xtra.co.nz
website: www.brithigh
comm.org.nz
Office hours: 8:45–5

British Consulate-General
17th Floor
Fay Richwhite Building
151 Queen Street
Auckland 1
Mailing Address:
Private Bag 92014
Auckland 1
☎ (9) 303 2973
fax: (9) 303 1836
Office hours: 8:45–5

British Trade Office & Consulate
PO Box 13292
Christchurch 8031
☎ (3) 332 0668
fax: (3) 337 9938
Office hours: 9–5

U.S. Embassies

For details of United States Government offices visit www.americanembassy.com or www.webofculture.com

The U.S. State Department website, www.state.gov, is a useful source of background information on a particular destination. The official U.S. information site for Australia, www.usis-australia.gov/embassy/ gives information on safety and immigration. For New Zealand look up http://usembassy.state.gov/wellington/

PRACTICAL MATTERS

Embassy Addresses

Australia
Moonah Pl
Canberra, ACT 2600
Mailing Address: APO AP 96549
☎ (6) 270 5000 **after hours** ☎ (6) 270 5900
fax: (6) 270 5970
Telex: 62104 USAEMB

59th Floor, MLC Centre
19-29 Martin Place
Sydney, NSW 2000
Mailing Address: PSC 280, Unit 11026,
APO AP 96554-0002
☎ (2) 373 9200 **fax:** (2) 373 9125

13th Floor
16 St. George's Terrace
Perth, WA 6000
Mailing Address: APO AP 96530
☎ (9) 231 9400 **fax:** (9) 231 9444

New Zealand
29 Fitzherbert Terrace
Thorndon
Wellington
Mailing Address: P.O. Box 1190, Wellington
PSC 467, Box 1
FPO AP 96531-1001
☎ (4) 472 2068 **fax:** (4) 471 2380

4th Floor, Yorkshire General Bldg
Corner of Shortland and O'Connell Sts.
Private Bag 92022
Auckland
Mailing Address: PSC 467, Box 99,
FPO AP 96531-1099
☎ (9) 303 2724 **fax:** (9) 366 0870

ACCOMMODATION PRICES

Hotels listed in the Contacts
and A–Z sections have been
split into three price cate-
gories. Some parts of the world
are generally cheaper than
others but a rough guide is as
follows:

$ = under $40
$$ = $40–$85
$$$ = over $85

---

1 UP A CAPE, DOWN AN OCEAN ► 20–29

OPERATORS

Exmouth Dive Club Centre
P.O. Box 798
Payne Street
Exmouth, WA 6707
☎ (8) 9949 1201 **toll free** ☎ 1800 655 156
fax: (8) 9949 1680
email: whaleshark@exmouthdiving.com.au
website: www.exmouthdiving.com.au
Runs a full range of dive tours, a Muiron
Islands' day trip with 2 dives and P.A.D.I. dive
courses, including a 5-day P.A.D.I. Open Water
course. A full-day whale shark interaction tour
operates Mar–Jun.

Ningaloo Ecology Cruises
P.O. Box 572
Exmouth, WA 6707
☎ (8) 9949 2255 **fax:** (8) 9949 2255
The shallow draft boat of Ningaloo Ecology
Cruises operates daily, Jun–Dec, from
Tantabiddi Beach. A 1-hour coral viewing and
marine life cruise leaves at 10am sharp. The
2-hour tour the author took, with the
snorkelling option, leaves at 11:30am. The
Ningaloo Reef bus to Tantabiddi leaves
Exmouth daily at 9am, returning at 2:15pm.

Ocean Quest Charters
Ningaloo Reef
Exmouth, WA 6707
☎ (8) 9949 1111 **mobile** ☎ 0419 968 042
fax: (8) 9949 1116
The 14m (40ft) *Ocean Quest* departs on whale
watching tours daily (minimum 6 passengers),
1:30–5:30pm. They have an excellent record of
spotting whales.

Village Dive
Exmouth Cape Tourist Village
P.O. Box 19
Exmouth, WA 6707
☎ (8) 9949 1101 **toll free** ☎ 1800 621 101
fax: (8) 9949 1402
email: diving@exmouthvillage.com
website: www.exmouthvillage.com/
diving.html
Impressive dive operation offering a comprehensive range of P.A.D.I. dive courses and
recreational dive tours. Departure time of the
half-day Navy Pier dive depends on the tides.
P.A.D.I. Open Water courses last 4–5 days.

Yardie Creek Tours

P.O. Box 687
Exmouth, WA 6707
☎ (8) 9949 2659 **fax:** (8) 9949 2659
email: yct@nwc.net.au
website: www.nwc.net.au/yardiecreektours
Neil and Rhondda McGregor's multi-award-winning Yardie Creek boat cruise operates year round (except in adverse weather conditions). This tour often forms part of larger tour packages run by several Exmouth-based tour operators.

GETTING THERE
Skywest Airlines

Perth Domestic Airport
Belmont, WA 6104
☎ (8) 9478 9999 **toll free** ☎ 1800 642 225
fax: (8) 9478 9955
email: info@skywest.com.au
website: www.skywest.com.au
This subsidiary of Ansett operates an extensive network of routes around West Australia, including daily flights to Learmonth/Exmouth. Book ahead—a sliding scale of fare discounts (21, 14, 7 and 2 days ahead of the flight date) applies.

INFORMATION
Exmouth Tourist Bureau

P.O. Box 149
Murat Road
Exmouth, WA 6707
☎ (8) 9949 1176 **fax:** (8) 9949 1441
email: exmouth-tour@nwc.net.au
website: www.exmouth-australia.com
Located in modern offices near the football oval, friendly staff provide a comprehensive service, including booking tours and accommodation on your behalf. Regional books and souvenirs are also on sale.

Western Australian Tourist Centre

Forrest Place
Corner Wellington Street
Perth, WA 6000
☎ (8) 9483 1111 **fax:** (8) 9481 0190
email: travel@westernaustralia.net
website: www.westernaustralia.net
This centre has a comprehensive range of information and can make bookings for tours and hotels on your behalf.

West Australian Tourism Commission (WATC)

Australia Centre
Strand
London WC2B 4LG
U.K.
☎ (020) 7240 2881 **fax:** (020) 7379 9826
email: westozuk@tourism.wa.gov.au
This office provides a wide range of information and literature on adventure travel options.

ACCOMMODATION
Potshot Hotel Resort $–$$

P.O. Box 82
Murat Road
Exmouth, WA 6707
☎ (8) 9949 1200 **fax:** (8) 9949 1486
A modern hotel located right in the centre of town. A range of accommodation from backpacker communal style to executive 3-bed apartments. The Potshot Bar, next to the swimming pool, has a very good restaurant.

Sea Breeze Resort $

116 North C Street
Inside Harold E. Holt Naval Base
P.O. Box 766
Exmouth, WA 6707
☎ (8) 9949 1800 **fax:** (8) 9949 1300
email: seabreeze@nwc.net.au
This unique resort, 5km (3 miles) north of Exmouth town, has been transformed from the old navy officers' accommodation into a very comfortable hotel. Two bars, a cafeteria, and an excellent restaurant on site.

---

2 BREATHLESS DOWN SOUTH
► 30–37

OPERATORS
Adventure In

Lot 9, Yates Road
Margaret River, WA 6285
☎ (8) 9757 2104 **mobile** ☎ 0419 927 160
fax: (8) 9757 9123
email: abseil@yahoo.com.au
website: http://users.highway1.com.au/~abseil
Trevor McGowan has been running excellent tailor-made courses for climbers, abseilers and cavers throughout the Margaret River region for many years. Courses are charged per half day and per full day, and include all the necessary specialist equipment and qualified instructors, but exclude food and drinks, which should be arranged independently.

Bay Dive & Adventures (Diving Ventures)

26 Dunn Bay Road
Dunsborough, WA 6281
☎ (8) 9756 8846 **fax:** (8) 9756 8806
email: diving@dventures.com.au
website: www.dventures.com.au
Now part of the Perth-based Diving Ventures group, and the store is part of the Dunsborough Bay Village Resort. Offers a 2-dive trip to the HMAS *Swan* wreck (discounts for having some or all of your own equipment). All the diving instructors and dive masters are fully qualified (P.A.D.I., S.S.I., etc). Courses cater for all abilities. Recreational dive tours can be organized to any of Western Australia's major diving destinations.

Bikewest

Ground Floor
441 Murray Street
Perth
Postal address:
P.O. Box 7272
Cloisters Square, WA 6850
☎ (8) 9320 9305 **fax:** (8) 9320 9315
email: jkrynen@transport.wa.gov.uk
Bikewest is a government-run organization that offers a wide range of cycling maps and information for Perth and the south west region. Personal visitors are welcome and there is a map shop at reception.

Cave & Canoe Bushtucker Tours

Rivermouth
P.O. Box 479
Margaret River, WA 6285
☎ (8) 9757 9084 **mobile** ☎ 0419 911 971
fax: (8) 9757 9084
email: btt@netserv.com.au
Helen Lee's award-winning canoeing and cultural tours are run on a daily basis (regardless of weather conditions), Sep-May, and daily, except Tue and Thu, during the winter months. The 4-hour tour, which includes all specialist canoeing equipment, a bushtucker lunch and torches for the cave visit, departs at 10am from the Margaret River mouth at Prevelly Park (10 minutes' drive from Margaret River town centre; take an unsigned right turn before reaching the main ocean car park).

Escape Tours

11 Susan Court
Albany, WA 6330
☎ (8) 9844 1945 **fax:** (8) 9844 1946

email: escape@rainbowis.com.au
John Healy's company specializes in bus tours of the southern region, including the Porongorup and Stirling Range parks. On the bus tours there is no time for actually climbing the mountains—if you really want to get the high view, John can organize tailor-made trips to suit your requirements.

Josh Palmateer's Surf Academy

P.O. Box 856
Margaret River, WA 6285
☎ (8) 9757 3850 **mobile** ☎ 0418 958 264
Josh Palmateer offers expert, fun-filled coaching to suit surfers of all abilities, from absolute beginner to upcoming champions. The location depends on surf conditions so can change at short notice to ensure catching the best waves. He caters for individuals and groups (2–15 people), and will pick up and drop off at your hotel. All the coaches, including Josh, are fully qualified lifesavers and Australian Surfing Association accredited. Advance booking is recommended.

Ngilgi Cave

Caves Road
Yallingup, WA
☎ (8) 9755 2152 **fax:** (8) 9755 2022
email: ngilgi@netserv.net.au
website: www.capeweb.com.au/escape
Whilst the main Ngilgi showcave is open 7 days a week, 9:30–3:30, with guided tours leaving every half hour, the adventure caving tours run just once a day, starting at 9:30am. Advance booking is essential. The tour lasts 2–3 hours, depending on the clients' ability and desires. Take old, comfortable clothes, including full-length trousers such as jeans, and closed footwear—sneakers are fine.

GETTING THERE
AIRLINES
Qantas
website: www.qantas.com

CAR HIRE
Budget Rent A Car
960 Hay Street
Perth, WA 6000
☎ (8) 9322 1100 **fax:** (8) 9481 1392
email: cars@budgetwa.com.au
website: www.budget.com.au
This office is open Mon-Fri, 8–6, but they have offices at both the domestic and international airports too. Costs include unlimited kilometres

and insurance (with an option to reduce the insurance excess with a further payment). There are often deals offered for weekend or longer rental periods. Availability of 4WD vehicles from Perth is limited. Advance booking is recommended.

BIKE HIRE
About Bike Hire
No. 4 Car Park
Riverside Drive (nr. Causeway)
Perth, WA 6000
☎ (8) 9221 2665
Open 7 days a week, Mon-Fri 10–4, Sat 10–5, Sun 9–5. Conveniently situated near the Causeway Bridge, in mobile units alongside the Swan River foreshore cycle path. Apart from a range of bikes—from mountain bikes to tandems—they also hire out accessories.

INFORMATION
Travellers Club
499 Wellington Street
Perth, WA 6000
☎ (8) 9226 0660 **fax:** (8) 9226 0661
email: pstravel@git.com.au
website: www.travellersclub.com.au
Owned and run by experienced backpacker travellers, this travel advice centre/agency offers free, unbiased and knowledgeable information for travellers looking for adventure holidays in Western Australia. They have links with many of the best adventure tour operators and can book trips for you.

Western Australian Tourist Centre
See p. 259.

West Australian Tourism Commission (WATC)
See p. 259.

ACCOMMODATION
Best Western Emerald Colonial Lodge $$
Corner Walcliffe & Mansfield Avenue
Margaret River, WA 6285
☎ (8) 9757 2633 **fax:** (8) 9757 9001
email: mr@emeraldhotel.com.au
website: www.emeraldhotel.com.au
Located just close to Margaret River town centre, the Emerald Colonial Lodge offers a range of high quality accommodation. There is a good restaurant, small bar, and parking for guests.

Dunsborough Bay Village Resort $–$$
26 Dunn Bay Road
Dunsborough, WA 6281
☎ (8) 9755 3397 **fax:** (8) 9755 3790
email: dunnbay@netserv.net.au
website: http://capeweb.com.au/dbayresort
In central Dunsborough, this resort has accommodation to suit most budgets, from backpacker to luxury traveller: chalets offer spacious, apartment-style accommodation complete with everything for an extended stay; executive villas have ocean-view balconies; and multi-share rooms serve the backpacker. The resort boasts three on-site restaurants (the Golden Bay Chinese Restaurant is recommended), an indoor heated pool, and sauna. The Cape Dive operation is also on-site for scuba diving on the HMAS *Swan* wreck.

Flinders Park Lodge $$
Corner Lower King & Harbour Road
Albany, WA 6330
☎ (8) 9844 7062 **fax:** (8) 9844 7062
email: doug@parklodge.com.au
website: www.parklodge.com.au
This charming, luxurious lodge has R.A.C. 4-star-plus status. It combines the homely warmth of an English cottage with Mediterranean architecture. Accommodation is on a bed and breakfast basis. All rooms have polished jarrah floors, en-suite or private facilities, and most have views over Oyster Harbour. The beautiful garden, complete with a unique "retirement" pond for old boats, is a lovely place to relax after an active day.

Karri Valley Resort $$–$$$
Vasse Highway
Pemberton, WA 6260
☎ (8) 9776 2020 **fax:** (8) 9776 2012
website: www.oztravel.com.au/travel_mall/hotels/Karri_Valley_RePembert.html
Set in a breathtaking location, on the edge of Lake Beedelup and surrounded by forest, this is one of Western Australia's premier places to stay—pricey but well worth the indulgence. It has a range of en-suite motel and chalet-style accommodation, an excellent lakeside *a la carte* restaurant with a cocktail bar. The resort is very suitable for families. Activities and courses on offer include canoeing, hiking, horse riding, mountainbiking, fishing, birdwatching, woodcraft, and landscape photography.

Surf Point Lodge $

P.O. Box 1093
Riedle Drive
Gnarabup Beach
Margaret River, WA 6285
☎ (8) 9757 1777 **toll free** ☎ 1800 071 777
fax: (8) 9757 1077
email: surfpoint@iinet.net.com
website: www.surfpoint.com.au

A modern, comfortable hotel, on the coast at the southern end of Prevelly (15 minutes drive from Margaret River town centre), ideal for beach and watersports lovers. Accommodation ranges from 4-bunk rooms to standard doubles and deluxe doubles. Spacious dining room with kitchen facilities for preparing your own meals, and a games room. The lodge offers a bus service to the town of Margaret River.

3 HEART OF THE LAST FRONTIER ➤ 38–45

OPERATORS
Drysdale River Station

See Accommodation, below, for details.
Run a bush explorer and Bradshaw ancient rock art tour, minimum of 2 days and 2 people. Also run the wetland day trip, to see native flora and fauna and to taste bushtucker food.

El Questro Station & Wilderness Park

See Accommodation, below, for details.
Organizes the Chamberlain Gorge boat trip, horse riding and scenic helicopter flights.

Old Mornington Bush Camp $

See Accommodation, below, for details.
Arranges half-day canoe tours through Dimond Gorge and tours out to the art sites.

GETTING THERE
Ansett Australia

c/o Air New Zealand
Elsinore House
77 Fulham Palace Road
Hammersmith
London W6 8JA
U.K.
☎ (020) 8741 2299 **fax:** (020) 8741 4645
website: www.ansett.com

Ansett Australia operates 3 direct flights a day (2 at weekends) to Broome from Perth. All flights depart before midday. It pays to book in advance: book your flight 21 days prior to pay half the standard cost.

Budget Rent A Car

P.O. Box 1295
Broome Airport
Broome, WA 6725
☎ (8) 9193 5355 **fax:** (8) 9193 5325
email: broome@budgetwa.com.au
website: www.budget.com.au

It is essential to hire a 4WD vehicle to tackle the Gibb River Road. There are often deals on offer. You must pay an additional one-way fee if you want to leave the vehicle in Kununurra.

INFORMATION
West Australian Tourism Commission

See p. 259.

Western Australian Tourist Centre

See p. 259.

ACCOMMODATION
Cable Beach Inter-Continental Resort $$–$$$

P.O. Box 1544
Cable Beach Road
Broome, WA 6725
☎ (8) 9192 0400 **toll free** ☎ 1800 199 099
fax: (8) 9192 2249
email: cablebeach@interconti.com
website: www.interconti.com (listed under 'Asia Pacific')

One of the country's premier hotel resorts and genuinely worth the price. Opposite the pristine and lengthy Cable Beach, and set amongst beautifully landscaped tropical gardens, it is built to have minimal visual impact on the natural locatio., All of its 260 well-equipped en-suite rooms have a minibar and a balcony overlooking the garden and/or the large swimming pool.

Drysdale River Station $

P.O. Box 9
Via Wyndham, WA 6740
☎ (8) (8) 9161 4326 **fax:** (8) 9161 4326
email: drysdaleriver@bigpond.com
website: www.drysdaleriver.com.au

Ann and John Koeyers offer comfortable twin or double rooms with full kitchen facilities, toilets and showers, and laundry room. The station has fuel, including diesel, a small shop selling food and drink, and a public phone (in the fridge!). You can self-cater or enjoy the home-cooked food in the restaurant. Access to Drysdale River is subject to road conditions, so phone ahead to check, particularly in the wet season.

El Questro Station & Wilderness Park $–$$$

Gibb River Road
P.O. Box 909
Kununurra, WA 6743
☎ (8) 9161 4318 **fax:** (8) 9161 4355
email: sales@elquestro.com.au
website: www.elquestro.com.au

This extensive and popular wilderness resort really does offer choices for every budget, from the outstanding luxury of the magnificent Chamberlain suite in the homestead, which is cantilevered high over the Chamberlain River, to basic camping areas in isolated riverside spots. Between these extremes are other homestead rooms, en-suite bungalows with air conditioning in the main El Questro complex and tented cabins at the lovely Emma Gorge. Restaurants and bars on site.

Kununurra Lakeside Resort $$

P.O. Box 1129
Casuarina Way
Kununurra, WA 6743
☎ (8) 9169 1092 **toll free** ☎ 1800 786 692
fax: (8) 9168 2741
email: lakeside@comswest.net.au

Comfortable, modern accommodation in motel-style bungalows on the bank of beautiful Lake Kununurra. En-suite rooms with air conditioning, T.V., fridge, and telephone. Laundry service, swimming pool, and free airport pick-up. Sit in the excellent lakeside restaurant, open a bottle of good-quality wine, and watch the spectacular sunset.

Mount Hart $

P.O. Box 653
Derby, WA 6728
☎ (8) 9191 4645 **fax:** (8) 9191 4645
email: taffyabbotts@bigpond.com
website: http://holiday-wa.net/mthart.htm

Mount Hart is a lovely place for getting away from the pressures of the modern world. Taffy Abbotts offers comfortable accommodation in the main homestead. The rooms are not en suite but there are 3 bathrooms nearby. Excellent meals, in a spacious dining room, are topped off with Taffy's own freshly baked bread and fruits from the garden. Canoeing on the homestead waterhole is free. Add to these books, tea and coffee facilities, and large verandas, for a great way to taste outback life.

Old Mornington Bush Camp $

Mornington Station
P.O. Box 925
Derby, WA 6728
☎ (8) 9191 7035 **toll free** ☎ 1800 631 946
fax: (8) 9191 7037
email: oldmornington@bigpond.com
website: http://holiday-wa.net/omornington.htm

The owner, Michael Kerr, offers luxury camping with 3 hearty home-cooked meals, or camp in your own tent for a rate that includes a farewell picnic lunch. Bar and toilet on site.

4 WILDERNESS WAYS ► 48–57

OPERATORS
Odyssey Safaris

P.O. Box 3012
Darwin, NT 0801
☎ (8) 8948 0091 **fax:** (8) 8948 0646
email: info@odysaf.com.au
website: www.odysaf.com.au

Odyssey Safaris have been operating small-group, high-quality trips around the Northern Territory's wilderness regions for over 12 years. They will also tailor-make itineraries. Tours are very well run by knowledgeable, fun guides; comfortable camping and delicious food cooked fresh in the bush. The 5-day "Top End Experience" tour includes 3 days in Kakadu National Park, a visit to Manyallaluk Aboriginal community and Nitmiluk National Park (home to Katherine Gorge). The 7-day "Top End Experience" includes one day and night in Lichfield National Park, visits to Manyallaluk and Katherine Gorge and 3 days in Kakadu. Also available are a 3-day Kakadu Adventure, a 5-day Kakadu Experience, a 2-day Lichfield's Hidden Secrets tour, and lodge-based tours.

INFORMATION
Northern Territory Tourism Commission

Head Office
3rd Floor, 43 Mitchell Street
Darwin, NT 0800
NT Holiday Centre Information Line toll free ☎ 1800 808 244 ☎ (8) 8999 3900
fax: (8) 8999 3847
email: nttc@nt.gov.au
website: www.nttc.com.au

The Northern Territory Holiday Centre provides a complete range of tour information and can book tours and accommodation for you.

Australia's Northern Territory (NTTC London)

1st Floor, Beaumont House
Lambton Road
London SW20 0LW
U.K.
Brochure Line ☎ 0906 479 9994 ☎(020) 8944 2992 **fax:** (020) 8944 2993
email: nttc@rha-lon.co.uk
website: www.nttc.com.au
Call the brochure line for a complete range of very useful and well-produced brochures covering all types of activities and accommodation.

ACCOMMODATION
Best Western Emerald Hotel $$

81 Cavenagh Street
Darwin, NT 0800
☎ (8) 8981 7771 **fax:** (8) 8981 7760
email: emeraldhoteldarwin@octa4.com.au
website: www.emeraldhotel.com.au
This modern hotel, in the heart of Darwin, offers very comfortable and well-appointed apartment-style rooms, with separate living room/kitchen area and en-suite double bedroom. It has a small pool, shop, and undercover parking. A great base for exploring the region.

5 A DREAM ENCOUNTER
► 58–65

OPERATORS
Odyssey Safaris

See entry above
The overnight visit to Manyallaluk is included as part of its longer trips, the 5-day or 7-day "Top End Experience," to Katherine Gorge and Kakadu National Park (see p. 48–57).

Tiwi Tours

Nguiu
Bathurst Island, NT 0822
☎ (8) 8978 3630 **toll free** ☎ 1800 183 630
fax: (8) 8941 1016
email: aussieadventure@attglobal.net
website: www.aussieadventure.com.au
Run 1- and 2-day trips to Bathurst Island—prices include return flight from Darwin. The 1-day tour operates Mon–Fri; the 2-day camping tour departs on Tue and Thur, May–Nov.

INFORMATION
Northern Territory Tourism Commission

See p. 263.

Australia's Northern Territory (NTTC London)

See above.

ACCOMMODATION
Best Western Emerald Hotel

See above.

6 SAILING ACROSS THE RED CENTRE
► 66–75

OPERATORS
Alice Springs Camel Outback Safaris NT

P.O. Box 74
Stuarts Well
☎ (8) 8956 0925 **fax:** (8) 8956 0909
Ride your own camel for anything from half a day to 14 days. These excellent safaris include all meals and basic accommodation in tents at a base camp.

Anangu Tours

Yulara
☎ (8) 8956 2123 **fax:** (8) 8956 3136
email: LBANANGU@bigpond.com, **website:** wwww.users.bigpond.com/LBANANGU
Fascinating Aboriginal-guided walking tours around Uluru. Learn about bush survival skills as well as the Dreamtime legends.

A.A.T. Kings

74 Todd St
Alice Springs
☎ (08) 8952 1700
Touring & Information Centre, Ayers Rock Resort ☎ (08) 8956 2171
Reservations **free call** ☎ 1800 334 009
National company, offering an extensive range of good-value guided bus tours around the Red Centre, including programmes linking Uluru, Kings Canyon and Alice Springs.

Norm's Gold & Scenic Tours

Tennant Creek
☎ (8) 8962 1500 **mobile** ☎ 0418 897711
email: norm@swtch.com.au
Arranges fossicking tours in the Tennant Creek area.

Outback Ballooning

35 Kennett Court
Alice Springs, NT 0870
☎ (8) 8952 8723 **fax:** (8) 8952 3869
email: balloons@topend.com.au
website: www.balloons.in.australia.as

Alice Spring's original ballooning company. Two others now offer pretty much the same deals.

Professional Helicopter Services

Yulara

☎ (8) 8956 2003 **fax:** (8) 8956 2788

email: ho@phs.com.au

website: www.phs.com.au

Cheaper of the two helicopter operations flying over Uluru: 15-min flights to the Rock start at $65, a half-hour Uluru and Kata Tjuta flight $130. They also run the flights at Kings Canyon.

Steve's Mountain Bike Tours

P.O. Box 8670

Alice Springs, NT 0871

☎/**fax:** (8) 8952 1542 **mobile** ☎ 0417 863 800

Rugged off-road tours in the foothills of McDonnell Ranges on full-suspension mountain bikes. From a challenging 1-hour ride to 4–5 hours for experienced and fit riders only.

GETTING THERE

Both Alice Springs and Uluru have airports served by daily Ansett and Qantas flights. Alice Springs' airport is 14km (9 miles) south of town; an airport shuttle bus to the local hotels is $9, a taxi around $18. Free transfers from Uluru airport to the Ayers Rock Resort hotels.

Uluru Express

☎ (8) 8956 2152

Provides shuttlebuses throughout the day from Ayers Rock Resort to the Uluru National Park.

ACCOMMODATION
Alice Springs Resort ($$$)

34 Stott Terrace

Alice Springs, NT 0870

☎ (8) 8952 6699 **fax:** (8) 8953 0995

Reservations **toll free** ☎ (in Australia) 1800 805 055 **website:** www.alicespgsres.aust.com

Part of the same group that runs the Ayers Rock and Kings Canyon resorts. Large comfortable rooms, plenty of facilities and within easy walking distance of the town centre.

Todd Tavern ($)

Wills Terrace

Alice Springs

☎ (8) 8952 1255

Reasonable mid-range en-suite rooms. Good value since they include breakfast. Beneath is Alice's main pub, with live music some nights. Cheaper rooms are available if you don't mind using the communal bathrooms.

Melanka Lodge ($)

94 Todd St, Alice Springs

☎ (8) 8952 2233 **fax:** (8) 8952 3819.

If you can't get into the Pioneer YHA ☎ (8) 8952 8855 **fax:** 8952 4144), this is a decent alternative, although some dorms are cramped.

Ayers Rock Resort

free call ☎ 1800 089 622 or (2) 9360 9099

website: www.ayersrockresort.com.au

One management company runs each of the accommodation options here. At the top end is the elegant Sails in the Desert ($$$), followed by the equally appealing Desert Gardens Hotel ($$$). If you're in a group or a family, consider the self-contained Emu Walk Apartments ($$$), rather than the Spinifex Lodge budget hotel ($$$), where facilities are shared. The Outback Pioneer Hotel is where you'll find the dorms ($) as well as good-value motel rooms. The campground ($) also has cabins for rent.

Kings Canyon Resort

Watarrka National Park

P.O. Box 136, Alice Springs

☎ (8) 8956 7442 **fax:** (8) 8956 7410,

Reservations **free call** ☎ 1800 089 622

☎ (2) 9360 9099

website: www.ayersrockresort.com.au

Fine luxury ($$$) accommodation, a budget hostel ($/$$) and a pleasant campground ($) are available, but space is limited, so book.

INFORMATION

The **Visitor Centre of the Central Australian Tourism Industry Association** (C.A.T.I.A.) is at the Todd River end of Gregory Terrace, opposite Todd Mall ☎ (8) 8952 5800, **fax** (8) 8953 0295 **email:** visinfo@catia. asn.au. Bookings for accommodation, trains and buses can be made here as well as for most local tours. Maps, fact sheets and information on road conditions are also available from the very helpful staff. At **Yulara**, the **Visitors Centre** ☎ (8) 8957 7377 is next to the Desert Gardens Hotel, and the **Touring & Information Centre**, where you can book all tours in and around the national park, is in the shopping centre. The **Uluru-Kata Tjuta Cultural Centre** ☎ (8) 8956 3138 is within the park, 1km (¾ mile) from the Rock. Register with the **National Parks and Wildlife Service in** Darwin ☎ 1300 650 730 before you depart on the Larapinta Trail. The **Northern Territory Department of Mines and Energy** ☎ (8) 8956 9770 supplies fossicking permits for the Arltunga Fossicking Reserve, 110km (68 miles) east of Alice Springs. The **Tennant Creek Visitor Centre** is in the Battery Hill Regional Centre on Peko Road in Tennant Creek ☎ (8) 8962 3388

email: trcrta@topend.com.au

Contact the park rangers at the **Watarrka National Park** ☎ (8) 8956 7488 for Giles Track details and to register before you set off.

FOOD AND DRINK

Bar Doppio (Fan Arcade, Alice Springs) is a cool BYO (bring your own alcohol) café, serving Mediterranean inspired nibbles. **Outback Pioneer Hotel BBQ** (Ayers Rock Resort) is a fun, good-value DIY barbecue. **Red Ochre** (Todd Mall, Alice Springs) offers fine dining in a sophisticated atmosphere. **Sounds of Silence** (Ayers Rock Resort) is an evening desert experience. Held alfresco after you've watched sunset over Uluru.

7 WALKING IN THE FLINDERS RANGES
► 76–85

INFORMATION
Department of Transport

☎ 1300 361 033

Call for daily updates on road conditions.

Flinders Ranges National Park

☎ (8) 8648 0048.

Flinders Ranges and Outback SA Tourism

toll free ☎ 1800 633 060

For maps and guides on the Flinders Ranges.

Gammon Ranges National Park

☎ (8) 8648 4829.

Mount Remarkable National Park

☎ (8) 8634 7068.

South Australian Department of Sport and Recreation

P.O. Box 219

Brooklyn Park, SA 5025

☎ (8) 8416 6705

For information on the Heysen Trail walking track and the Mawson Trail cycling track.

8 EXPLORING QUEENSLAND'S OUTBACK
► 88–97

OPERATORS
Jungle Tours and Trekking Australia

P.O. Box 179

Westcourt, QLD 4870

☎ (7) 4032 5600 **toll free** ☎ 1800 81 7234

fax: (7) 4032 5611

email: reservations@jungletours.com.au

website: www.jungletours.com.au

Outback tours combined with rainforest and the Great Barrier Reef. See also p. 267.

Springmount Station

Mareeba, QLD

☎ (7) 93 4493

Run by Gracie Gargan, this cattle station that grows passion fruit offers rides through the bush, boomerang throwing, swimming and 2-day camp-out trail rides.

The Adventure Company, Australia

Clauson House

1st Floor, 13 Shields Street

City Place

Cairns, QLD 4870

☎ (7) 4051 4777 **fax:** (7) 4051 4888

email: adventures@adventures.com.au

website: www.adventures.com.au

From U.S.A:

☎ 1800 388 7333 **fax:** 303 823 6654

email: adventures@aussieventures.com.au

European office: Pacific Downunder Föhrenweg 10, CH-8500 Frauenfeld Switzerland ☎ (52) 722 3003 **fax:** (52) 720 1005 **email:** pacific@bluewin.ch

Outback art discovery tours and safaris, plus Cape York safari from May to Nov.

GETTING THERE
Undara Experience

P.O. Box 6268

Cairns, QLD 4870

☎ (7) 4097 1411 **fax:** (7) 4097 1450

email: info@undara-experience.com.au

website: www.undara-experience.com.au

Organizes day coach tours to Undara from Cairns, 2- and 3-day tours, and a 3-day rail experience on *The Savannahlander* outback train. They can also fly you in to Undara, should you not wish to make the road journey.

RAIL TRAVEL

The Savannahlander:
Cairns Travel Centre
☎ (7) 052 6211
Mt Surprise Railway Station ☎ (7) 062 3108
Forsayth ☎ (7) 062 5374
The Gulflander:
☎ (7) 7451 391 **fax:** (7) 7451 222

4WD HIRE
Cairns 4WD hire

55 Mulgrave Roa
 Cairns, QLD 4870
☎ (7) 4051 0822 **fax:** (7) 4051 0557
Minimum 3 days hire; rates include 250km (155 miles) per day and insurance.

INFORMATION
Department of Environment and Heritage

P.O. Box 38
Queen Street
Chillagoe, QLD 4871
☎ (7) 4094 7163 **fax:** (7) 4094 7213
For information about the Chillagoe-Mungana Caves National Park.

Far North Queensland Promotion Bureau

Corner Grafton and Hartley Street
Cairns, QLD 4870
☎ (7) 051 3588.

The Gulf Savannah Tourist Organisation

P.O. Box 2312
Cairns, QLD 4870
☎ (7) 051 4658 **fax:** (7) 031 3340

ACCOMMODATION
Undara

Gulf Savannah (see also p. 266)
P.O. Box 6268
Cairns, QLD 4870
☎ (7) 4097 1411 **toll free** ☎ 1800 990 992;
fax: (7) 4097 1450
email: res@undara-experience.com.au
website: www.undara-experience.com.au
Offers accommodation to suit most budgets:
Lava Lodge in restored Queensland rail carriages; Swag tented village with lights and beds; caravan and campsite. Facilities include a restaurant, meal packages, linen hire, swimming pool, showers, and bush breakfast. Short, half- and full-day tours and self-guiding bushwalks.

Mount Surprise Roadhouse and Caravan Park

Mount Surprise
☎ (7) 4062 3153
Facilities include caravan site, camping, restaurant, take away, fuel, and bookings for Undara Lava Tubes, *The Savannahlander* train, and fossicking.

Tallaroo Hot Springs

☎ (7) 4062 1221
40km (25 miles) from Mt Surprise, towards Georgetown, this basic camping ground has toilets, shower, and a pool fed by hot springs.

FOOD AND DRINK

Towns in the outback usually have at least one pub or a service station selling hot meals, ice creams, and cold drinks. For the real bush experience, take a camping stove, plenty of fuel, and cook your own food in the open.

9 DIVING THE GREAT BARRIER REEF ► 98–107

OPERATORS (DIVING)
Hayes and Jarvis Diving Worldwide

Hayes House
152 King Street
London W6 0QU
U.K.
☎ (020) 8222 7840 **fax:** (020) 8741 0299
Offers live-aboard diving expeditions on the Great Barrier Reef, including the outer edge of the Reef, Cod Hole and Yongala wreck.

Jungle Tours and Trekking Australia

See p. 266 for details.
Diving and snorkelling on the outer Great Barrier Reef off the coast of Cape Tribulation, by high-speed power boat.

Pro Dive

Tropical Arcade
P.O. Box 5551
Corner Abbott & Shields Street
Cairns, QLD
☎ (7) 4031 5255 **fax:** (7) 4051 9955
email: info@prodive-cairns.com.au
website: www.prodive-cairns.com.au
One-day dive adventures, introductory dives, live-aboard diving cruises, and higher education courses.

OPERATORS (SAILING AND DIVING)
Anaconda II and Anaconda III

toll free ☎ 1800 466 444

Three-day, 2-night sailing around the Whitsunday Islands, with snorkelling on the island's fringing reefs and bushwalking on the islands. Includes full board and snorkelling equipment for young, fun adventurers. Also sailings on the mega yacht *Anaconda III*, more luxurious and offering up to six dives.

GETTING THERE
Ansett Australia

See p. 262 for details.

McCafferty's

28-30 Neil St
Toowoomba, Qld 4350
☎ (7) 4690 9888 **fax:** (7) 4638 3815
email: infomcc@mccaffertys.com.au
website: www.mccaffertys.com.au
Coach travel on networks throughout Australia.

Oz Experience

Corner of Kings Cross Road and
Darlinghurst Road
Kings Cross
Sydney, NSW 2011
☎ (2) 9368 1766 **toll free** ☎ 1300 300028
email: enquiries@ozex.com.au
website: www.ozexperience.com.au

INFORMATION
Brisbane Tourism

City Hall
King George Square
P.O. Box 12260
Elizabeth Street
Brisbane, QLD 4002
☎ (7) 3221 8411 **fax:** (7) 3229 5126
email: enquiries@brisbanetourism.com.au
website: www.visitbrisbane.com.au

Reef Wonderland Information Centre

Environmental Protection Agency
Shop 22
Great Barrier Reef Wonderland
2-86 Flinders Street
Townsville
☎ (7) 4721 2399 **fax:** (7) 4771 5578
Everything you need to know about the Great Barrier Reef and its inhabitants.

Tourism Tropical North Queensland

51 The Esplanade
P.O. Box 865
Cairns, QLD 4870
☎ (7) 4051 3588 **fax:** (7) 4051 0127
email: information@tnq.org.au
website: www.tnq.org.au

COACH TRAVEL
Greyhound Pioneer Australia

A 24-hour national reservations hotline within Australia ☎ 13 20 30
Brisbane office: ☎ (7) 3258 1600
Cairns office: ☎ (7) 4051 3388
website: www.greyhound.com.au
U.K. (London) office: ☎ (020) 7291 4590
U.S.A. (Los Angeles) office: ☎ (310) 578 5455

ACCOMMODATION
Cairns Backpackers Inn $

242–248 Grafton Street
Cairns, QLD 4870
☎ (7) 4051 9166 **toll free** ☎ 1800 681 889
fax: (7) 4051 8377
website: www.cairnsbackpackers.com.au
Great hospitality. Facilities include bar and restaurant, pool, laundry, free safe and store-room, fax, email, and internet access. Here you can book all activities, diving, and tours.

Koala Beach Resort $

408 Esplanade
Hervey Bay, QLD 4655
☎ (7) 4125 3601 **toll free** ☎ 1800 354 535
website: www.koalaresort.com.au
Beachfront, self-contained units or dorm beds, bar serving barbecues and evening meals, pool, laundry, T.V. room and courtesy bus.
Discounted rates for those with a V.I.P. pass.
Organizes 4x4 Fraser Island safaris and whale watching.

Koala Beach Resort $

Shute Harbour Road
Airlie Beach, QLD 4802
☎ (7) 4946 6001 **toll free** ☎ 1800 800 421
email: koala@whitsunday.net.au
website: www.koalaresort.com.au
Dorms and rooms with en suite, T.V., air condi-tioning, pool, spa, bistro, and bar. It also has a campsite. Organizes overnight sailing trips, dive courses, and other activities.

Tangalooma Wild Dolphin Resort $–$$

P.O. Box 1102
Eagle Farm, QLD 4009
☎ 1300 652 250 **fax:** (7) 3268 6299
website: www.tangalooma.com

VIP Backpackers Resorts $

P.O. Box 600
Cannon Hill, QLD 4170
☎ (7) 3268 5733 **fax:** (7) 3268 4066
email: backpack@backpackers.com.au
website: www.backpackers.com.au
Scores of hostels in good locations, discounts
on bus passes, tours, and activities.

FOOD AND DRINK
Cock & Bull

6 Grove Street
Cairns, QLD
☎ (7) 4031 1160
Designed as a traditional English pub with dark
wood panelling and "olde English" memorabilia
collected by the owner, Graham. Grills, Cajun
fish, steaks, puddings, and real ales.

Morocco's

Airlie Beach, QLD
Happy hour drinks, big portions of pasta,
nachos, potato wedges, salads, and steaks.

> **10 ON SAFARI THROUGH THE WET TROPICS ► 108–117**

OPERATORS
Jungle Tours and Trekking Australia

See p. 266.
Offers short and longer tours into the rainforest, which can be combined with days spent in
the outback, and diving/snorkelling on the
Great Barrier Reef.

Raft 'n' Rainforest Company

48 Abbott Street
P.O. Box 1938
Cairns, QLD4870
☎ (7) 051 7777 **toll free** ☎ 1 800 079 039
fax: (7) 031 4777
Offers 2- and 5-day rafting expeditions, flying
in by helicopter and rafting out, as well as half-
and full-day rafting trips on the Barron and
Tully Rivers. Also rainforest camping and
walks, and rafting combined with ballooning,
bungee jumping, and 4WD safari.

Raging Thunder PTY Ltd

P.O. Box 1109
Cairns, QLD 4870
☎ (7) 4030 7900 (24-hour reservations)
fax: (7) 4030 7911
email: sales@ragingthunder.com.au
website: www.ragingthunder.com.au
Full-day rafting on Tully River, with barbecue
lunch, light evening meal, optional video, and
photos. Also half-day Barron River rafting and
North Johnstone heli raft, including helicopter
flight to remote rainforest river site and camping tours along the North Johnstone River
(in season). Also offers kayaking, ballooning,
tandem skydive and horse riding.

The Adventure Company, Australia

See p. 266 for details.
Offers 1- to 5-day rafting trips along North
Johnstone River, with a choice of bus, rainfor-
est track or helicopter.

INFORMATION
Environmental Protection Agency

Northern Regional Centre
2–4 McLeod Street
Cairns, QLD
☎ (7) 4046 6602 **fax:** (7) 4052 3080
website: www.qld.gov.au/environment
Information on Queensland's national parks
and rainforest.

Naturally Queensland Information Centre

Environmental Protection Agency
Ground Floor
160 Ann Street
Brisbane, QLD
☎ (7) 3227 8187 **fax:** (7) 3227 8197
Information on Queensland's national parks
and rainforest.

Tourism Tropical North Queensland

See p. 268 for details.

ACCOMMODATION
On the Wallaby Backpackers' Lodge $

34 Eacham Road
Yungoburra, QLD 4594
☎ (7) 4095 2031 **fax:** (7) 4031 6566
email: dreamtime@iig.com.au
website: www.dreamtimetravel.com.au

An excellent backpackers' forest lodge, offering a range of activities to adventure travellers including wildlife safaris, cycling, and canoeing on the tropical tablelands.

Crocodylus Village $

☎ (7) 4098 9166 **fax:** (7) 4098 9131
Located between the Daintree River and Cape Tribulation, it offers safari-style dormitories and en-suite huts, built within the rainforest. Swimming pool and restaurant with own-cooked food. Activities include sea kayaking, guided night forest walks and horse riding. Discounts for YHA members.

FOOD AND DRINK
Nap's Nest Crafts and Coffee

Yungaburra
☎ (7) 4095 3139
Serves Devonshire-style tea and coffee and homemade jam, amidst pottery, and postcards for sale.

Nick's Swiss-Italian Restaurant and Yodeller's Bar

Yungaburra
☎ (7) 40 953 330
website: www.nicksrestaurant.com.au
A la carte food served in an Alpine chalet-style atmosphere; the menu includes crocodile, barramundi fish, pastas, and homemade strudel.

---

11 CYCLING THE SHIPWRECK COAST
► 120–127

OPERATORS
Boomerang Bicycle Tours

P.O. Box 6543
Parramatta, NSW 2150
☎ (2) 9630 0587 **fax:** (2) 9630 3436
email: ozbike@ozemail.com.au,
website: www.ozemail.com.au/~ozbike
Currently the only fully supported bike tour along the Great Ocean Road. All accommodation, meals, and equipment needed during the 7-day/6-night tour, including excellent bikes, are included in the price.

Tiger Moth World

Blackheath Road
Torquay, VIC
☎ (3) 5261 5100 **fax:** (3) 5261 5797
Offers a range of scenic flights above the Great Ocean Road.They also have a branch at Telford Street in Apollo Bay ☎ (3) 5237 7370.

GETTING THERE
V/Line Passenger

Marketing Dept.
P.O. Box 5343BB
Melbourne, VIC 3001
☎ 136 196
website: www.victrip.com.au
Public bus service along the Great Ocean Road.

Wayward Bus Touring Co.

P.O. Box 7067
Hutt Street
Adelaide, SA 5000
☎ (8) 8232 6646 **toll free** ☎ 1800 882823
fax: (8) 8232 1455
email: wayward@waywardbus.com.au
website: www.waywardbus.com.au
Backpacker tours along the Great Ocean Road.

West Coast Railway

P.O. Box 1936
Geelong, VIC 322
☎ (3) 5226 6500
email: wcrl@pipeline.com.au
Public rail services between Geelong and Warrnambool and Melbourne.

ACCOMODATION
Cape Otway Lighthouse ($$-$$$)

Otway Lighthouse Road,
Cape Otway, VIC 3233,
☎ (3) 5237 9249 **fax:** (03) 5237 9245,
email: keeper@lighthouse.com
website: www.lightstation.com
Two renovated former lighthouse keeper's cottages let as holiday accommodation.

King Parrot Holiday Cabins ($$$)

Dunce Track
Pennyroyal, VIC 3235
☎ (3) 5236 3372 or 015 519 567.
Self-catering luxury cabins hidden away in the foothills of the Otway Ranges. Set in over 81ha (200 acres) of bushland. A good base for biking and hiking in the Otways, but 25km (16 miles) from Lorne.

Sandridge Motel ($$-$$$)

128 Mountjoy Parade
Lorne, VIC 3232
☎ (3) 5289 2180 **fax:** (3) 5289 2722
website: www.sandridgemotel.com.au
Classy modern motel accommodation.
Attached Marks restaurant is worth trying.

Southern Ocean Motor Inn ($$-$$$)
Great Ocean Road
Port Campbell, VIC 3269
☎ (3) 5598 6231 **fax:** (3) 5598 6471
Port Campbell's most upmarket option is comfortable enough but has a dated atmosphere.

INFORMATION
A useful tourist office to contact is **Geelong Tourist Information** ☎ /**fax:** (3) 5222 2900, at the Wool Museum in Geelong, open daily 9am–5pm; they have plenty of information sheets, brochures, and maps covering this section of the Victorian Coast. Along the route, the tourist offices in **Apollo Bay** ☎ (3) 5237 6529 and **Warrnambool** ☎ (3) 5564 7837 are also helpful and good sources of information.

12 RIDING THE HIGH COUNTRY ► 128–135

OPERATORS
Cochran Family Tradition Horse Treks
Yaouk
☎ (2) 6454 2336 **fax:** (2) 6454 2936
email: riverman@snowy.net.au
website: www.cochranhorsetreks.com.au
Offers all-inclusive, adventurous rides lasting 3, 4 or 5 days for generally small groups. Peter Cochran, his family and guides know this country like the back of their hands and have worked hard to provide a truly authentic pioneer experience.

Paddy Pallin
Thredbo Turnoff Jindabyne
PMB 5
Jindabyne, NSW 2627
☎ (2) 6456 2922 **toll free** ☎ 1800 623 459
fax: (2) 6456 2836
email: paddys@jindabyne.snowy.net.au
website: www.snowy.net.au/~paljin
A full programme of adventures packages. Winter season: alpine touring, snowboarding, cross-country skiing, snowcamping, and telemark skiing. Summer season: mountainbiking, white-water rafting, canoeing and kayaking, trekking, and horse riding.

Raw NRG Mountain Bicycle Centre
P.O. Box 131
Thredbo Village, NSW 2625
☎ (2) 6457 6990

email: info@rawnrg.com.au
website: www.rawnrg.com.au

GETTING THERE
Greyhound Pioneer Australia
Has offices in all major Australian cities—see entry on p. 268.

Impulse Airlines
Eleventh St.
Sydney Kingsford Smith Airport
Mascot, NSW 2020
☎ (2) 9317 5400 **fax:** (2) 9317 3440
website: www.impulseairlines.com.au

Murrays
P.O. Box 60
Red Hill, ACT 2503
☎ 13 22 51 **fax:** (2) 6274 8118

Wayward Bus Touring Co.
See p. 270.

INFORMATION
Snowy Region Visitors Centre
Kosciuszko Road
Jindabyne
☎ (2) 6450 5600
email: srvc@npws.nsw.gov.au
Open daily 8–7. An excellent source of leaflets and information on just about every adventure option in the national parks and the surrounding countryside. It's also a good place to buy maps, books, and souvenirs.

The Cooma Visitors Centre
119 Sharp St
Cooma
☎ (2) 6450 1742 **toll free** ☎ 1800 636 525
Open daily Jun–Oct 7–6, Nov–May 9–5. The assistants here are very helpful.

Thredbo Tourist Information
toll free ☎ 1800 020 589
website: thredbo.com.au
Has details of skiing, walking, mountainbiking and fishing packages. Website gives daily skiing information.

Perisher Blue
website: www.perisherblue.com.au
This comprehensive website gives daily skiing information for the whole of the Perisher Blue ski area, including the resorts of Perisher, Blue Cow, Smiggins, and Guthega

ACCOMMODATION

To check on general availability (and for information about the resorts) call Thredbo on **free call** ☎ 1800 020 589 or 1800 801 982, and Perisher Blue on **freecall** ☎1300 655 822.

Currango Homestead and Cottages $–$$$

c/o Tumut Region Visitors Centre
The Old Butter Factory
5 Adelong Road
Tumut, NSW 2720
☎ (2) 6947 1849 **fax:** (2) 6947 3752
email: tumutrvc@npws.nsw.gov.au
You'll need a 4WD or sturdy car to reach this charming homestead and couple of rustic log cottages in the far north of Kosciuszko National Park. Facilities are basic, but the location is stunning. Prices rise at weekends and over holiday periods.

The Kosciusko Accommodation Centre

toll free ☎ 1800 026 354
email: kfnsales@acr.net.au
website: www.firstnational.com.au/kosciusko
They can also make bookings for apartments and lodges in Jindabyne, Thredbo and Perisher.

Thredbo YHA Lodge $

8 Jack Adams Path
Thredbo Village, NSW 2627
☎ (2) 6457 6376 **fax:** (2) 6457 6043
email: thredbo@yhansw.org.au
website: www.yha.org.au
Excellent budget accommodation, run by a friendly manager, with kitchen, comfortable lounge, and internet facilities. Rates are double from Jun 19 to Oct 5—this is a heavily booked period, so for the peak weeks there's a lottery system for bookings.

Thredbo Alpine Hotel

Thredbo Village
☎ (2) 6459 4200 **fax:** (2) 6459 4201
The resort's top hotel is a comfortable, convivial place, but, like much of the rest of Thredbo, is distinctly overpriced during the ski season. Visit in the rest of the year for a more relaxed, better-value stay. The Lounge Bar's copper-topped open fireplace conveys the right level of alpine style for sipping warming *après ski* drinks.

FOOD AND DRINK

The prime time for dining is the winter season, when a multitude of cafés and restaurants open to feed the hungry appetites of the ski crowd.

Thredbo

On the main shopping strip, **Altitude 1380** is a good budget choice, serving a range of snacks and light meals as well as good coffee. Nearby, but only open for dinner, is the excellent **T-Bar**, for hearty main courses; booking is essential. Year round, the **Cascades Café and Bar** in the Thredbo Alpine Hotel (above) is a fine choice, with surprisingly tasty food for a hotel operation, including some fancy but not overpriced fish dishes.

Perisher Blue

The best bet for a mid-downhill pick me up or lunch is the funky, relaxed café, **Cowpaccino**, at the Blue Cow Ski Tube terminal.

13 ADVENTURES IN THE
BLUE MOUNTAINS
► 136–145

OPERATORS
Australian School of Mountaineering

166b Katoomba Street
Katoomba, NSW 2780
☎ (2) 4782 2014 **fax:** (2) 4782 5787
email: asm@pnc.com.au
The Blue Mountains' original outdoor adventure company, established in 1985, and still one of the best. Abseiling, rock climbing, ice-climbing and mountaineering, canyoning, bushcraft, survival, and navigation are among the courses they offer.

Fantastic Aussie Tours

283 Main St
Katoomba, NSW 2780
☎ (2) 4782 1866 **fax:** (2) 4782 1860
Offer guaranteed daily transfers to or from Jenolan Caves if you're walking the Six Foot Track, as well as all-inclusive trips to the caves for the show caves or the plug-hole adventure caving tour. To get off the beaten track take their 4WD trips into the Grose Valley or to the Kanangra Walls canyon in the Kanangra-Boyd National Park.

Great Australian Walks

Suite 2
637 Darling Street
Rozelle
Sydney, NSW 2039
☎ (2) 9555 7580 **fax:** (2) 9810 6459
email: gowalkaus@rivernet.com.au
website: www.walkaustralia.com
Sydney-based outfitter with a range of short-break tours in NSW, including the Six Foot Track, longer tours including to the Snowy Mountains, Warrumbungles, Flinders Ranges and Fraser Island, and adventure treks in far north Queensland (Hinchinbrook), and Tasmania (Overland Track).

Jenolan Caves Reserve Trust

Jenolan Caves
☎ (2) 6359 3311 **fax:** (2) 6359 3307
email: jencaves@jenolan.org.au
Guided tours around the show caves last between 1 and 2 hours; on Saturday night there's a ghost tour. Full-day and shorter adventure caving tours are available. Also has details of accommodation in cabins and at the campsite.

GETTING THERE
Wayward Bus Touring Co.

See p. 270.

INFORMATION

Blue Mountains Tourism publishes the free brochure *The Blue Mountains Holiday Book*, which has lots of useful information, including self-drive itineraries, a bushwalking guide, and comprehensive accommodation lists.

Blue Mountains Visitor Information Centre

Great Western Highway
Glenbrook
☎ (2) 4739 6266
Open 8:30–5 (8:30–4:30 Sun).

Katoomba Visitor Information Centre

Echo Point
Katoomba
freecall ☎ 1300 653 408
email: bmta@lisp.com.au
website: www.lisp.com.au/~bmta.
Open daily 9–5.

The New South Wales National Parks and Wildlife Service Heritage Centre

Govetts Leap Road
☎ (2) 4787 8877
Open daily 9–4:30. Near the Govetts Leap Lookout.

ACCOMMODATION
Balmoral House $$–$$$

196 Bathurst Road
Katoomba, NSW 2780
☎ (2) 4782 2264 **fax:** (2) 4782 6008.
Built in 1876, this Victorian-style guesthouse has a highly convivial atmosphere. Log fires, antique brass beds and pretty gardens are part of the appealing mix. Bed and breakfast Sun to Thu; Dinner, bed and breakfast Fri and Sat.

Hydro-Majestic Hotel $$$

Great Western Highway
Medlow Bath, NSW 2780
☎ (2) 4788 1002 **fax:** (2) 4788 1063
A multi-million-dollar restoration has really put this Blue Mountains institution back on the map. Its view across the Megalong Valley is unparalleled. Drop by for a drink if nothing else.

Jenolan Caves Resort $–$$$

Jenolan Caves, NSW 2790
☎ (2) 6359 3322 **fax:** (2) 6359 3388
email: bookings@jenolancaves.com
Besides the Jenolan Caves is Caves House, a rambling, mock-Tudor mansion with considerable old-world charm. The resort also includes the Mountain Lodge, Gatehouse—the only budget, dormitory option—and Binoomea Cottage. Rates rise significantly at weekends.

Katoomba YHA Hostel $

66 Waratah Street
Katoomba
☎ (2) 4782 1416 **fax:** (2) 4782 6203
email: bluemountains@yhansw.org.au
website: www.yha.com.au
Dormitory accommodation, starting from 4 beds to a room, at this conveniently sited hostel in a charming old guesthouse. Plenty of facilities, including a large kitchen, laundry, internet, T.V. lounge and abundant information on what's going on in the mountains. Book well ahead for weekends and holiday periods.

The Carrington $$$

15-47 Katoomba Street
Katoomba, NSW 2780
☎ (2) 4782 1111 **fax:** (2) 4782 1421
email: carrington@thecarrington.com.au
website: www.thecarrington.com.au
Dating from 1882, this Katoomba landmark has
been recently restored to its former glory, providing a glamorous step back in time to a
gentler age of mountain vacations. The Grand
Dining Room and cocktail bars are sumptuous.
A great place for afternoon tea.

FOOD AND DRINK

Katoomba, Leura and Blackheath all have very
healthy restaurant and café scenes—a good
reason to linger in the mountains rather than
rush back to Sydney.

Café Niagra

92 Main Street
Katoomba
☎ (2) 4782 4001
Open Mon-Fri 10am till late, Sat & Sun 8am till
late. Stylish, recently renovated deco café serving a tasty range of modern Australian dishes as
well as snacks and delicious cakes. On Sat at
8pm there's a cabaret drag show in the upstairs
dining rooms.

Parakeet Café

195b Katoomba Street
Katoomba
☎ (2) 4782 1815
Open Mon–Wed 8am–9pm, Thu-Sun
7am–10pm. Funky, inexpensive café does
big breakfasts, blockbuster sandwiches and
live music.

Silks Brasserie

128 The Mall
Leura
☎ (2) 4784 2534
Daily 12–3.30 and 6–10. Hearty, slow-cooked
dishes, such as oxtail on mash with sautéed
grapes, and an excellent wine list, make this
one of the local, upmarket favourites.

The Paragon Café

65 Katoomba Street
Katoomba
☎ (2) 4782 2928
Open Tue–Sun 10:30–4:30. Taking tea in this
art deco beauty, a National Trust treasure, will
whisk you back several decades. The cakes and
homemade chocolates are irresistible.

14 TRAMPING THROUGH TASMANIA'S SOUTHWEST ► 148–155

OPERATORS
Par Avion Wilderness Tours

P.O. Box 324
Rosny Park, TAS 7018
☎ (3) 6248 5390 **fax:** (3) 6248 5117
email: flights@paravion.com.au
website: www.tassie.net.au/~paravion
This company provides set-down flights to
Melaleuca, scenic flights, a boat trip up to
Bathurst Harbour, a 2-day/1-night Forest
Lagoon camp, and a 2-day/2-night Southern
Explorer cruise. Par Avion also offers free
transfers to and from Hobart hotels to
Cambridge Airport.

Roaring 40s Ocean Kayaking

Oyster Cove
Marina Ferry Road
Kettering, TAS 7155
☎ (3) 6267 5000 **fax:** (3) 6267 5004
email: rfok@ozemail.com.au
website: www.roaring40s kayaking.com.au
Take 5-day guided trips from late Nov–Easter,
using folding double kayaks. Rates include a
night's accommodation before the trip, flights,
and food. Participants must have a reasonable
degree of fitness, but experience is not necessary. Also hire out folding double kayaks.

Tasair

Cambridge Aerodrome
Kennedy Drive
Cambridge, TAS 7170
☎ (3) 6248 5088 **fax:** (3) 6248 5528
email: flights@tasair.com.au
Operates "on demand." Flies all-year-round
into Cox Bight or Melaleuca; also offers set-
down flights to Melaleuca and scenic flights.

Tasmanian Expeditions

110 George Street
Launceston, TAS 7250
☎ (3) 6334 3477 **toll free** ☎1800 030 230
fax: (3) 6334 3463
email: tazzie@tassie.net.au
website: www.tassie.net.au/tas_ex
Established in 1989, this is an extremely professional operation with friendly, knowledgable
guides. Offers a 9-day trek on the remote South
Coast Track, Melaleuca–Cockle Creek: fly into
Melaleuca and walk out, participants carry
packs of about 20kg (44lb)—for fit walkers

only, preferably experienced. Also offers walking trips in the Freycinet Peninsula, the Walls of Jerusalem National Park, and Cradle Mountain (see below). Cycling, rafting, rock-climbing, and abseiling adventures are also part of their extensive programme.

World Expeditions

(Booking agent for Tasmanian Expeditions)
Head Office:
Level 3
441 Kent Street
Sydney 2000
☎ (2) 9264 3366 **fax:** (2) 9261 1974
email: enquiries@worldexpeditions.com.au
website: worldexpeditions.com.au
Melbourne office ☎ (3) 9670 8400
Brisbane office ☎ (7) 3216 0823
New Zealand office:
21 Remuera Road
Newmarket
Auckland
New Zealand
☎ (9) 522 9161 **fax:** (9) 522 9162
email: enquiries@worldexpeditions.co.nz
U.K. office:
3 Northfields Prospect
Putney Bridge Road
London SW18 1PE
U.K.
☎ (020) 8870 2600 **fax:** (020) 8870 2615
email: worldex@dircon.co.uk
U.S.A. office:
Level 6
580 Market Street
San Francisco
CA 94104
U.S.A.
☎ (415) 989 2212 **fax:** (415) 989 2112
email: contactus@weadventures.com

INFORMATION
Parks and Wildlife Service

134 Macquarie Street
Hobart
Mailing address:
P.O. Box 44A
Hobart, TAS 7001
☎ (3) 6233 6191
email: tracks@dpiwe.tas.gov.au
website: www.parks.tas.gov.au

---

15 THE LAND TIME ALMOST FORGOT
► 156–165

OPERATORS
Cradle Huts

22 Brisbane Street
Launceston, TAS 7250
☎ (3) 6331 2006 **fax:** (3) 6331 5525
email: cradle@tassie.net.au
website: www.cradlehuts.com.au
This 6-day/5-night trip is the most upmarket option for covering the Overland Track. The guides are excellent and the standards of accommodation and catering are high—extremely popular, so book well in advance. The company also offers a 4-day walk through the Mt William National Park on Tasmania's east coast, taking in the spectacular white sand beaches of the Bay of Fires.

Paddy Palin

110 George Street
Launceston, TAS
☎ (3) 6331 4240
Hire out camping gear.

Peregrine Adventures

Level 5
38 York Street
Sydney, NSW 2000
☎ (2) 9290 2770 **fax:** (2) 9290 2155
email: travelcentre@peregrine.net.au
website: www.peregrine.net.au
Arrange rafting on the Franklin River.

Tasmanian Expeditions

See p. 274 for details.
This company runs an 8-day/7-night Cradle Mountain Trek and a 3-day trip based at the Cradle Mountain end of the track.

World Expeditions

See above for details.
Rafting trips on the Franklin River.

OTHER OPERATORS

For information on other adventure tour operators on the island, check out this **website:** www.tasmanianadventures.co.au.

GETTING THERE
Kendell Airlines

118 Queen Street
Level 3
Melbourne, VIC 3000

toll free ☎ 1800 338 894 (reservations)
fax: (3) 9670 3218
email: kendell@kendell.demon.net.au
website: www.kendell.com.au
Operates flights to some of the smaller towns in Tasmania.

Maxwell Coaches

45 Narrawa Road.
Wilmot, TAS
☎/**fax:** (3) 6492 1431
Buses to the parks' access points and transfer services.

Tassielink

P.O. Box 292
Moonah, TAS 7009
☎ 1300 300 520 **fax:** (3) 6272 7555
website: www.tassie.net.au/wildtour
Previously known as Tasmanian Wilderness Travel, the now more trendily named carrier runs buses to the parks' access points and transfer services.

INFORMATION
Cradle Mountain Visitor Centre

☎ (3) 6492 1110 **fax:** (3) 6492 1120

Lake St Clair Visitor Centre

☎ (3) 6289 1172
These are excellent National Parks and Wildlife Service information centres, with informative displays. Both open daily 8–5.

Parks and Wildlife Service

See p. 275.

Tasmanian Travel and Information Centre

Paterson and St John Streets
Launceston
☎ (3) 6336 3133
Open Mon–Fri 9–5; Sat 9–3; Sun 9–noon.You can book accommodation and travel tickets here. Also has useful information sheets on things to do in the area.

ACCOMMODATION
Ashton Gate $$–$$$

32 High Street
Launceston
☎ (3) 6331 6180 **fax:** (3) 6334 2232
Highly recommended B&B in National Trust-classified Victorian house. All the well-appointed bedrooms are ensuite. Extra charge for a cooked breakfast.

Cradle Mountain Lodge $$$

Cradle Mountain
☎ (3) 6492 1303 **fax:** (3) 6492 1309
These upmarket, self-catering log cabins are set in the forest on the edge of the national park. The central lodge has plenty of facilities including a restaurant, bar, sauna, free movies each night, and an activities desk that offers a range of day trips within the park.

Fiona's B&B $$

141 George Street
Launceston
☎ (3) 6334 5965 **fax:** (3) 6331 6455
Pleasant, mid-range accommodation in a complex of 12 rooms set back from main road.

Launceston City Backpackers $

173 George Street
Launceston
☎ (3) 6334 2327
Based mainly in a house built c1900, this is the best of the budget options; facilities include T.V. lounge, kitchen, and laundry. It's popular, so book ahead.

Waldheim Cabins $

Cradle Mountain Visitor Centre
P.O. Box 20
Sheffield, TAS 7306
☎ (3) 6492 1110 **fax:** (3) 6492 1120
Eight comfortable, self-catering cabins on the edge of the World Heritage Area. All have heating, bunk beds and cooking equipment. Hot showers and composting toilets in a separate block. Minimum charges depend on the size of cabin you take (discounts Jun–Sep).

FOOD AND DRINK
Gourmet on Brisbane

86 Brisbane Street
Launceston
Come here for hearty breakfasts in the attached café, a packed-lunch from the sandwich bar or to stock up for your camping trip.

Manfredi

106 George Street
Launceston
☎ (3) 6334 2490
Delicious cakes and biscuits at this German-style *konditorei*, which also does fine sandwiches, salads, and light meals. Open for dinner at weekends. Try to grab a table on the outdoor terrace upstairs. Mon–Fri 9–5:30, Fri and Sat 9–10.

Pepper Berry

91 George Street
Launceston
☎ (3) 6334 4589
Relaxed, café atmosphere at this award-winning place to sample modern-Australian dishes using Tasmania's top-class produce. Mon–Sat 8:30am till late.

Ripples Café

Ritchies Mill Arts Centre
Paterson Street
Launceston
☎ (3) 6331 4153
Enjoy a drink or meal with a view of the Tamar River. Has outdoor tables and serves a good range of sandwiches, salads, pasta, and polenta dishes. Open daily 9:30am till late. Book for dinner.

PUB FOOD IN LAUNCESTON

Cheap pub meals are available at **The Royal Oak** on Brisbane Street (opposite the City Park), **Irish Murphy's** at 211 Brisbane Street, and **The Star Bar Café** at 113 Charles Street.

16 KAYAKING THROUGH THE BAY OF ISLANDS ➤ 168–175

OPERATORS
Coastal Kayakers

P.O. Box 325
Paihia
Bay of Islands
☎ (9) 402 8105 **fax:** (9) 403 8550
website: http://destinatio-nz.com/nz/members/coastalkayak

Salt Air

Amphibian Ramp
Paihia Waterfront
P.O. Box 293
Paihia
Bay of Islands
☎ (9) 402 8338 **fax:** (9) 402 8302
email:saltair@xtra.co.nz
Run sea plane flights.

Watea

P.O. Box 6
Paihia
Bay of Islands
☎ (25) 858 557
Operate tours with all-terrain vehicles.

GETTING THERE
Budget Rent A Car

83 Parnell Road
Auckland
☎ (9) 375 2220 **fax:** (9) 375 2221

Great Sights

☎ (9) 375 4700 **fax**: (9) 379 6649
email: gsinfo@greatsights.co.nz
Operate a guided bus tour that includes stops en route and an informative commentary from the driver. They also operate various packages to include sightseeing and stopovers.

ACCOMMODATION
The Copthorne Resort

Box 150
Paihia
☎ (9) 402 7411 **fax:** (9) 402 8200

The Novotel

8 Customs Street
Auckland
☎ (9) 377 8920 **fax:** (9) 377 8992

17 GOING UNDERGROUND ➤ 176–183

CAR HIRE
Avis New Zealand

P.O. Box 92809
Penrose
Auckland
☎ (9) 525 2510 **freecall** ☎ 0800 655 111
fax: (9) 525 0324

Brits NZ Rentals

P.O. Box 59-235
Mangere
Auckland
☎ (9) 275 9090 **fax:** (9) 275 1834
email: info@brits.com.au
Recreational vehicles, campervans, motorhomes, and 4WDs.

Budget Rent A Car

☎ (9) 375 2222 **freecall** ☎ 0800 652 227

Maui New Zealand

26 Richard Pearse Drive
Mangere
Auckland
☎ (9) 275 3529 **fax:** (9) 275 9019
email: nzinfo@maui-rentals.com
Offer a complete range of modern and well-equipped 2-, 4-, or 6-berth motorhomes, as well

as a full range of late model rental cars, from compact hatchbacks to 4WDs.

OPERATORS
Black Water Rafting
P.O.Box 13 Waitomo Caves
New Zealand
☎ (7) 878 6219 **fax:** (7) 878 5190
email: www.blackwaterrafting.co.nz

Waitomo Adventures Ltd
P.O.Box 29 Waitomo Caves
New Zealand
☎ (7) 878 7788 **freecall** ☎ 0800 924 866
fax: (7) 878 6266
email: bookings@waitomo.co.nz
website: www.waitomo.co.nz
Used for the abseiling part of the underground trip.

18 MUD ON YOUR WHEELS ► 184–193

ACCOMMODATION
Howard's Lodge
Sylvia and Peter Guy
Carroll Street
National Park
P.O.Box 9 National Park
New Zealand
☎ / **fax** (7) 892 2827
email : howards.nat.park@xtra.co.nz
Can arrange equpment hire for you and has a number of cheaper tent sites available.

19 HORSE TREKKING ALONG ANCIENT MAORI TRAILS ► 194–201

OPERATORS
Tamaki Tours
P.O. Box 1492
Rotorua
☎ (7) 346 2823 **fax:** (7) 347 2913
email: tamaki@wave.co.nz
Guided tours of a small, traditional Maori settlement are available several times a day and, as the village comes alive with tribal songs and dances, the guides explain Maori protocol and custom. Short, guided walks through the villages can be combined with a traditional concert and a *hangi* (see Food and Drink, p. 279) in the evening.

Te Urewera Adventures of New Zealand
Private Bag 3001
Rotorua
☎ (7) 366 3969 **fax:** (7) 366 3333
email: biddlemarg@clear.net.nz
Makere and Whare Biddle have been taking visitors on guided walks and horse treks through the heartland of the Tuhoe people since 1975. Whare was born in the area and is of Tuhoe descent. Makere was raised by a tribe living in the Waikato and, although she has been married to Whare since 1959, she is still acutely aware of being a "newcomer" to her husband's traditions, which makes her a good guide to Tuhoe culture. The couple offer homestays and guided horse treks and walks (from one to five days) as well as fishing trips along the Whakatane River and its many tributaries.

Waimangu Volcanic Valley
P.O. Box 6141
Rotorua
☎ (7) 366 6137 **fax:** (7) 366 6137
The craters and steaming pools of this valley are the legacy of the 1886 eruption of Mount Tarawera. Wheelchair accessible walkways connect several craters, huge, hot pools and sinter terraces. Boat cruises are available on Lake Rotomahana, which was created by the eruption, to volcanic features visible only from the boat. Allow half a day for the valley walks and boat cruise. From here you can explore Mount Tarawera and the buried village, which disappeared under the volcano's hot ashes and lava flows.

GETTING THERE
Air New Zealand
Rotorua Travel Centre
Corner Fenton and Hinemoa Streets
Rotorua
☎ (7) 343 1100 **fax:** (7) 343 1101
website: www.airnz.co.nz
You can book your flights online.

Ansett New Zealand
69 Boulcott Street
P.O. Box 2994
Wellington
☎ (4) 471 1051 **freecall** ☎ 0800 267 388
fax: (4) 471 1158

TranzRail
Passenger Services
Wellington Railway Station

Bunny Street
Wellington
☎ (4) 498 3000 **freecall** ☎ 0800 801 070;
fax: (4) 498 3259
email: Info@tranzrail.co.nz
or passengerservices@tranzrail.co.nz
website: www.tranzrail.co.nz
TranzRail operates all train connections and
the ferry services across Cook Strait.

INFORMATION
Department of Conservation (DOC)

Aniwaniwa Visitor Centre
Private Bag 2213
Wairoa
☎ (6) 837 3803 **fax:** (6) 837 3722
website: www.doc.govt.nz
The D.O.C.'s regional centres are a good source
of information, with a wide selection of regional
books. They also issue permits for the use of
D.O.C. huts. Its website has information about
all national parks, including the Te Urewera
National Park, as well as New Zealand's Great
Walks, conservation initiatives, and community
activities.

Eastland First Light Tourism

186 Grey Street
P.O. Box 2000
Gisborne
☎ (6) 867 2000 **fax:** (6) 868 1368
email: info@firstlight.co.nz
Contact for all information and bookings for the
East Cape.

Tourism Rotorua

1106 Arawa Street
Private Bag 3007
Rotorua
☎ (7) 348 4133 **fax:** (7) 349 4133
email: marketing@tourism.rdc.govt.nz
website: www.rotoruanz.com
Contact for all information and bookings for the
Rotorua area.

ACCOMMODATION
Ruatahuna

Ruatahuna has just one, small motel.

Te Urewera Adventures of New Zealand

See above, under Operators, for details.
Offer homestays, using a number of guest
rooms (doubles or twins) in the main house or
a separate spacious sleepout.

Rotorua

Rotorua offers a range of options, from budget
backpackers to exclusive lodges. The town has
more than 12,500 visitor lodgings, with 4-star
hotels, motels, and backpacker hostels all
within walking distance from the city centre.

Around Rotorua

Rotorua is surrounded by sprawling farmland
and pine plantations; many people offer farm
and homestays. Camping grounds are close to
town and near the lake areas; most offer a
range from fully self-contained motels and
tourist flats to family cabins and budget cabins,
as well as tent sites. A local Maori family offers
overnight accommodation at a *marae*.

FOOD AND DRINK

Dining options range from inexpensive meals at
local bars to family restaurants and gourmet
establishments. A specialty is the *hangi*, a traditional feast of lamb, kumara (sweet potato),
chicken, wild game, potato, pork, and beef
steam-cooked over hot boulders in an earth
oven. Rotorua's lakes also deliver fresh trout.

Fishpot Restaurant and Takeaways

Eruera Street
Rotorua
☎/**fax:** (7) 349 3494
A good choice for seafood.

> ### 20 WATCHING WHALES, DOLPHINS AND SEALS
> ► 202–211

OPERATORS
Dolphin Encounter

58 West End
Kaikoura
☎ (3) 319 6777
email: info@dolphin.co.nz
Organize dolphin swimming.

Graeme & Matt's Seal Swimming Team

202 Esplanade
Kaikoura
☎ (3) 319 6182
Can introduce you to the seals. Wetsuits provided.

Royale Tours

189A Clyde Road
Christchurch

☎ (3) 351 8625 **fax:** (3) 351 9638
email: royale.tours@xtra.co.uk
Can coordinate both whale watching and dolphin swimming, as well as arranging scenic flights in search of whales. They specialize in small groups.

Whale Watch
The Whaleway Station
P.O. Box 89
Kaikoura
☎ (3) 319 5045 **fax:** (3) 319 5160
email: wally@whalewatch.co.nz
Operate whale watching exclusively.

GETTING THERE
FLIGHTS
Christchurch is located on the east coast of South Island and can be reached by plane or by road. The airport, located a 15-minute drive from the city centre, is served by **Air New Zealand**, **Ansett New Zealand**, **Korean Air**, **Quantas**, **Singapore Airlines**, **Japan Airlines** and **Mount Cook Airlines.** It is linked to all other major airports throughout the country. Buses and taxis are available to reach the city centre.

BUSES
There are daily bus services between Christchurch and Dunedin, Mount Cook, Queenstown, and Nelson. These are run by **Mount Cook Landline** (☎ (3) 343 8085), **Intercity** (☎ (3) 377 0951) and **Great Sights** (☎ (9) 375 4700). Services between Christchurch and Greymouth, Hokitika, and Arthur's Pass are run by **Alpine Coaches** (**freecall** ☎ 0800 274 888) or **Coast to Coast** (**freecall** ☎ 0800 800 847).

CAR HIRE
Budget Rent A Car
Corner of Oxford Terrace & Lichfield Street
Christchurch
☎ (3) 366 0072
They also have an office at the airport.

ACCOMMODATION
CHRISTCHURCH
The Chateau on the Park
189 Deans Avenue
P.O. Box 8161
Riccarton
Christchurch
☎ (3) 348 8999 **fax:** (3) 348 8990
email: res@chateau-park.co.nz

KAIKOURA
There is less choice of accommodation here but there are several bed and breakfast establishments.

INFORMATION
Kaikoura Information and Tourism
☎ (3) 319 5641 **fax:** (3) 319 6819
Bus services operate daily between Christchurch and Kaikoura run by **Intercity** and **Mount Cook Landline**.

FOOD AND DRINK
Highly recommended is a seafood lunch, to include a crayfish, mussel chowder, and passion fruit pavlova.

The Craypot
70 Westend
Kaikoura
☎ (3) 319 6027 **fax:** (3) 319 6041

21 HIGH COUNTRY ON HORSEBACK ► 212–219

OPERATORS
Hanmer Springs Thermal Reserve
Amuri Road
P.O. Box 30
☎ (3) 315 7511 **fax:** (3) 315 7528
email: lee@hotfun.co.nz
website: www.hotfun.co.nz
The thermal reserve has been offering a range of therapeutic hot pools, a freshwater swimming pool and saunas since 1859. It is in the centre of the alpine village of Hanmer Springs, which offers other outdoor activities, including skiing, mountainbiking, forest walks, river rafting, and bungee jumping. (View the website for details of opening hours, which vary with the seasons.)

Hurunui Horse Treks
23 Hewitts Road
Hawarden
North Canterbury
☎ (3) 314 4204 **fax:** (3) 314 4204
email: stanleyR@xtra.co.nz
website: www.horseback.co.nz
Since first offering horse treks in 1987, Rob Stanley has pioneered treks through some very remote country, widening his repertoire to include anything from half-day treks to an 8-day ride from North Canterbury to Kaikoura.

The shorter rides explore the Lake Sumner Forest Park and the Hurunui River, while longer trips take riders through Molesworth Station, the largest high country station in New Zealand. Homestays are also possible.

GETTING THERE
Air New Zealand
Christchurch Travel Centre
702 Colombo Street
Christchurch
☎ (3) 353 2800 **fax:** (3) 353 2801
website: www.airnz.co.nz
You can book your flights online.

Ansett New Zealand
69 Boulcott Street
P.O. Box 2994
Wellington
☎ (4) 471 1051 **freecall** ☎ 0800 267 388
fax: (4) 471 1158

TranzRail
See p. 278.

INFORMATION
Christchurch Visitor Information Centre
Corner of Worcester Boulevard & Oxford Terrace
P.O. Box 2600
Christchurch
☎ (3) 379 9629 **fax:** (3) 377 2424
email: info@christchurchnz.net
website: www.christchurchnz.net

Department of Conservation
South Marlborough Area Office
Gee Street
P.O. Box 51
Renwick
Marlborough
☎ (3) 572 9100 **fax:** (3) 572 8824
website: www.doc.govt.nz
This D.O.C. office is in charge of opening Molesworth Station to the public. Generally, the station is open during January and part of February, but the times can change due to weather conditions or fire risk.

Hurunui Tourism Board
Hurunui District Council
66 Carters Road
P.O. Box 13
Amberley 8251
North Canterbury
☎ (3) 314 8816 **fax:** (3) 3 314 9181
email: infor@hurunui.govt.nz
website: www.hurunui.com

Hurunui Visitors Centre
Reservations and Information
Main Road
Hanmer Springs
☎ (3) 315 7128 **freecall** ☎ 0800 733 426
fax: (3) 315 7658
email: hanvin@nzhost.co.nz
website: www.hurunui.com

Merino New Zealand
P.O. Box 25 160
Christchurch
☎ (3) 377 7990 **fax:** (3) 377 7991
email: john.brakenridge@merinonz.com
website: www.merinonz.com/
This organization has developed a Merino Trail, which takes visitors on a tour of Merino farms throughout the country. While most farmers provide overnight accommodation and meals, many will be happy to take visitors on a tour of their land and introduce them to their lifestyle. Merino New Zealand provides information about Merino farming, from details about the wool to maps of Merino farms in New Zealand.

ACCOMMODATION
Hurunui Tourism Board
See above, under Information, for details. Several farms in the Hurunui offer accommodation, and most facilities are listed with the board. There is also a range of other options, from campgrounds and backpackers' hostels to bed & breakfasts and exclusive lodges (such as **Braemar Lodge** in Hanmer Springs).

Mt Whitnow Homestead
2018 Virginia Road
Hawarden
☎ (3) 314 4020 **fax:** (3) 314 4664
Doug and Dawn Kirk farm this 4,451ha (11,000-acre) property, running mostly Merino wethers. The farm is on the Merino Trail as well as providing overnight accommodation for travellers visiting the area on horseback.

FOOD AND DRINK

Christchurch provides the full range of cuisine you would expect from a metropolitan centre, but the Hurunui area also has some culinary delights on offer. Country lodges often employ gourmet chefs and open their restaurants to casual diners. These restaurants are drawing in local people as well as visitors. Country pubs offer more affordable traditional fare and take-outs.

**22 FLY FISHING VIA THE
TRANZALPINE
► 238–247**

OPERATORS
Naturally New Zealand

☎ (9) 480 0580 **fax:** (9) 480 0282
email: info@nzholidays.co.nz
Seats on the *TranzAlpine* (which operates throughout the year) can be difficult to obtain—book well in advance. Naturally New Zealand can book it for you, and can also book the fishing safari.

CAR HIRE
Budget Rent A Car

Railway Station
Mackay Street
Greymouth
☎ (3) 768 4343 **fax:** (3) 768 9098.
See p. 280 for Christchurch details.

ACCOMMODATION

See p. 280 for accommodation in Christchurch.

Kapitea Lodge

☎ (3) 755 6805 **fax:** (3) 755 6895
email: kapitea@minidata.co.nz
Ideal for the fishing, or simply as a base for the area.

Naturally New Zealand

See operators above.

**23 HIGH ON GLACIERS
► 228–237**

OPERATORS
Alpine Guides

P.O. Box 38
Fox Glacier
☎ (3) 751 0825 **fax:** (3) 751 0857
email: foxguides@minidata.co.nz
Operate the heli hike, and all the other glacier visits. They operate every day except Christmas Day although everything depends on the weather conditions. Other tours on offer include: a walk to the terminal of the glacier (almost any level of fitness will suffice), which only operates Nov–Apr; a half-day glacier walk (moderate fitness required); and a full-day glacier walk (good fitness level required). Other options are available on request, including ice-climbing instruction.

Mount Cook Ski Planes

P.O. Box 12
Mount Cook
☎ (3) 4351 026/027 **fax:** (3) 4351 886
email: mtcook@skiplanes.co.nz
Operate the flight to Mount Cook with the landing on the Tasman Glacier—the only operator able to land a plane there. Choose from the "Grand Circle," a 55-minute flight to include views of the west coast glaciers and a landing on the Tasman, and the 40-minute "Glacier Highlights" flight, which also includes a landing. The airline also runs a shuttle-service between the airport and Mount Cook Village.

INFORMATION
Fox Glacier Visitor Information

☎ (3) 751 0807

GETTING THERE

Fox and Franz Josef glaciers are just 24km (15 miles) apart. Both are best reached by road. It is also possible to fly to Mount Cook. **InterCity** run daily bus services along the west coast from Greymouth (☎ (3) 768 1435), Nelson (☎ (3) 548 1539) and Queenstown (☎ (3) 442 8238).

Air New Zealand

See p. 281 for details.
Operate regular flights from Christchurch and Queenstown.

Budget Rent A Car

Queenstown office:
☎ (3) 442 9274 **fax:** (3) 442 6480
Queenstown Airport office:
☎ (3) 442 9274
See p. 282 for Greymouth office.

Great Sights

See p. 277 for details.
Run daily buses between Queenstown and Christchurch, via Mount Cook.

ACCOMMODATION
FOX GLACIER
Rainforest Motel

Cook Flat Road
Fox Glacier

☎ (3) 751 0140 **fax:** (3) 751 0141

The rooms in this self-catering motel are spacious and clean, and have commendable kitchen facilities. It is located within walking distance of the pubs and Alpine Guides offices. There is a good supermarket on the main street and also a couple of restaurants serving reasonably priced food.

MOUNT COOK VILLAGE

There are limited accommodation options at Mount Cook village.

Hermitage Hotel

☎ (3) 435 1809 **fax:** (3) 435 1879

This top-of-the-range option is a large, rambling affair that has something of a Scottish country hotel about it. It has wonderful views.

Mount Cook Chalets

☎ (3) 627 1809 **fax:** (3) 435 1879

Self-catering chalets, each with 2 bedrooms.

---

24 THRILLS AND SPILLS ON THE
SHOTOVER RIVER
► 238–247

OPERATORS
Gravity Action

c/o Queenstown Backpacking Specialist
35 Shotover Street
P.O. Box 482
Queenstown

☎ (3) 441 1021 **mobile** ☎ (25) 226 3124
email: graction@ihug.co.nz

Run by two brothers—former competitive bikers—who are very competent riders and guides. All riding is on downhill sections and varies between rutted single track, gravel road, and sealed road, depending on the groups' skill level. No prior mountainbiking experience required. They offer packages combining biking and bungee.

Helicopter Line

The Station Building
Corner Shotover and Camp Streets
Queenstown

☎ (3) 442 7318 **freecall** ☎ 0800 423 836
fax: (3) 442 6749
email: combos@new-zealand.com

website: www.new-zealand.com/combos

The helicopter line offers various combinations with other adventures, such as the Shotover Trio (jetboat-helicopter-raft) or the Awesome Foursome (jetboat-bungee-helicopter-raft).

Pipeline Bungy

27 Shotover Street
Queenstown

☎ (3) 442 5455 **fax:** (3) 442 4029
email: bungy@pipeline.co.nz
website: www.bungy.co.nz

The bungee bridge was built on top of an old pipeline from the days of the gold rush. A flying fox operates near the bridge, also at 102m (340ft) above the Shotover River in Skippers Canyon. The company also offers 4WD trips into the upstream reaches of the Shotover River.

Queenstown Rafting

35 Shotover Street
Queenstown

☎ (3) 442 9792 **freecall** ☎ 0800 723 8464
fax: (3) 442 4609
email: qtn.raft@xtra.co.nz
website: www.nzcom.co.nz/Queenstown/Rafting

The company offers rafting trips on the Shotover and Kawarau rivers. Also offers package deals for combined trips with helicopter flight, jetboat ride, and bungee jump. Operates all year, with shorter trips during winter.

Serious Fun River Surfing

P.O. Box 564
Queenstown

☎ (3) 442 5262 **fax:** (3) 442 5265
email: sfun@voyager.co.nz
website: www.riversurfing.com

Owner/operator Jon Imhoof has pioneered river surfing in New Zealand since arriving with his body board in 1989. In the southern hemisphere summers he takes clients down Queenstown's Kawarau River, and in winter he surfs the Zambezi River in Africa. Guides are selected for their people skills and undergo long training. They teach you the techniques of river surfing gradually as the water becomes more challenging, so you come away feeling that you have done something and learned something.

Shotover Jet

Shotover Jet Beach
Arthurs Point
P.O. Box 189
Queenstown
☎ (3) 442 8570 **freecall** ☎ 0800 746 868
fax: (3) 442 7467
email: reservations@shotoverjet.co.nz
website: www.shotoverjet.co.nz
The company is the only one with a permit to
cruise through the lower Shotover Canyon. It is
also one of the longest established (since 1970)
and with the best safety record so far. Jetboats
leave every 15 minutes and there are always
3 boats on the water. It's a very polished operation, but can lack a personal feel as hundreds of
tourists go for a ride on a busy summer day.
Operates all year.

Skippers Canyon Jet

P.O. Box 522
Queenstown
☎**/fax:** (3) 442 9434
email: winkys@skipperscanyon.co.nz
website: www.skipperscanyon.co.nz
The jet boat ride is through Skippers Canyon,
part of Skippers Park, which also includes
Winky Scheib's museum and a collection of gold
rush relics. Winky's family is also involved with
the Pipeline Bungy. She plans to restore even
more artefacts from the goldfields and to
develop the area into an open-air museum.

GETTING THERE
Air New Zealand

See p. 281.

Ansett New Zealand

See p. 281.

TranzRail

See p. 278.

ACCOMMODATION

Queenstown offers the entire range of accommodation facilities for all budgets and
preferences, from backpackers and camping
grounds to exclusive lodges and luxury hotels.

The Dairy Guesthouse $$$

10 Isle Street
Queenstown
☎ (3) 442 5164 **fax:** (3) 442 5166
email: TheDairy@xtra.co.nz
website: www.thedairy.co.nz
Australians Brian and Sarah Holding bought

this former dairy in 1996 and have turned the
building into a luxury bed & breakfast in
European chalet-style, with a friendly atmosphere. In the heart of Queenstown, within
walking distance of the gondola.

FOOD AND DRINK

Dining options range from take-outs from a
hole-in-the-wall fast-food kitchen to gourmet
meals prepared by celebrity chefs at restaurants in historic buildings. Queenstown's ethnic
restaurants include Chinese, Thai, Mexican,
and Italian. Some suggestions:

Gantley's Restaurant

Malaghans Road
Queenstown
☎ (3) 442 8999 **fax:** (3) 442 7007
Based in a building constructed in 1863 at the
height of the gold rush, Gantley's offers cosmopolitan cuisine, and is the country's only
multiple winner of the *Wine Spectator* magazine's Award of Excellence.

Gibbston Winery

Gibbston
Road Delivery 1
Queenstown
☎ (3) 442 6910 **fax:** (3) 442 6909
email: gvwltd@gibbston-valley-wines.co.nz
website: www.gibbston-valley-wines.co.nz
Wine tastings and matchings at vineyard
restaurant. Mediterranean influences in cuisine, based on fresh New Zealand produce.

Moa Bar and Café

5 The Mall
Queenstown
☎ (3) 442 8372
Breakfast, lunch and dinner, alfresco dining,
cosmopolitan cuisine.

Skyline Gondola Restaurant

Skyline Gondola
Offers a "Taste of New Zealand" buffet with
South Island venison, Akaroa salmon, Bluff oys-
ters (in season), and New Zealand cheeses.
Nice salad bar.

Sombreros

Upstairs in the Beech Tree Arcade
Beach Street
Queenstown
☎ (3) 442 8240
Mexican cuisine and drinks. Slightly tacky
interior but very friendly staff.

Vudu Café

23 Beach Street
Queenstown
☎ (3) 442 5357
website: www.vudu.co.nz
Gourmet coffee and fresh healthy fare—a good vegetarian choice. Vudu Café roasts its own special blend of Arabica coffee beans daily.

INFORMATION
Destination Queenstown

P.O. Box 353 39
Ballarat Street
Queenstown
☎ (3) 442 7440 **fax:** (3) 442 7441
email: info@queenstown-nz.co.nz
website: www.queenstown-nz.co.nz

Queenstown Visitors Centre

The Station Building
Corner Shotover and Camp Streets
P.O. Box 1014
Queenstown
☎ (3) 442 5252 **fax:** (3) 442 5384

**25 ON THE ROUTEBURN TRACK
► 248–256**

OPERATORS
Nomad Safaris

P.O. Box 531
Queenstown
☎ (3) 442 6699 **fax:** (3) 442 8074
Organize the landrover 4WD visit to Skipper Canyon.

Routeburn Walk Ltd

P.O. Box 568
Queenstown
☎ (3) 442 8200 **fax:** (3) 442 6072
email: routeburn@xtra.co.nz
Operate the guided Routeburn trek, on an all-inclusive basis, from an office located at Top Floor, The Station, a modern building on the corner of Shotover and Camp Streets. The Routeburn lasts for 3 days—3 days' hiking with 2 nights' accommodation in the mountains. It is also possible to combine the Routeburn with the Greenstone—the "Grand Traverse."
The Routeburn can be undertaken without a guide. In this case, different lodges are used and walkers have to carry many of their own supplies. Permission needs to be gained from:
Department of Conservation (D.O.C.)
37 Shotover Street
☎ (3) 442 7933

GETTING THERE
FLIGHTS

Queenstown Airport, only a short distance from the city (linked by a shuttle service bus), is served by flights from Mount Cook, Auckland, Christchurch, Rotorua, and Wellington.

BUSES

Daily bus services connect Queenstown with Mount Cook, Christchurch, the glacier regions, Nelson, Greymouth, and Dunedin. These are operated by **InterCity** (see p. 280) and **Great Sights** (see p. 277).

CAR HIRE
Budget Rent A Car

See p. 282.

ACCOMMODATION
The Novotel

St Moritz Suites
10-18 Brunswick Street
☎ (3) 442 4990 **fax:** (3) 442 4667
email: stmoritz@novotel.co.nz
This hotel has an excellent location on a rise close to the shore of the lake, with wonderful views.

Queenstown Visitor Information Centre

☎ (3) 442 4100
The centre will be able to help with finding accommodation.

INTRODUCTION

This book has, we hope, whetted your appetite for adventure, and the Activities A–Z is intended to supply a useful, if not comprehensive, list of as many adventurous activities as the authors could discover within an area. The activities vary from volunteer work, cultural, and language opportunities to really intrepid sports. Most of the experiences call for interaction with local people and many are directly connected to ecotourism—where strict controls are applied to guarantee the benefits to the environment and to minimize the damage caused by the impact of increasing numbers of visitors to sensitive areas. We have supplied the names and addresses of organizations that can help the traveller to achieve these challenging pastimes, but they have not been inspected or vetted by us in any way. Even where the authors have used a company to organize their own trip, this is no guarantee that any company is still run by the same people or to the same degree of efficiency. Bear in mind that, although politically stable, many of the regions covered can be climatically volatile. Weigh up all the factors first, get a feel for your chosen destination, and let us guide you towards the outfits that can help.

WEBSITES

Some of the more useful websites for planning an adventure trip are:

www.oztravel.com.au

http://kiwiadv.co.nz

www.nelson.co.nz

ABSEILING, CLIMBING, AND MOUNTAINEERING

You can go climbing and abseiling in both Australia and New Zealand— although the rocky regions of New Zealand offer the widest range of opportunities. If abseiling seems a bit tame for you, then there is always rap jumping, offered by some operators in New Zealand. Essentially this involves lowering yourself down cliffs head first, instead of feet first. You can even rap jump down a skyscraper in Auckland. In Australia the best climbing site is considered to be Mount Arapiles in New South Wales, which has more than 2,000 different climbs, ranging from basic to advanced. You can also climb in the glorious Blue Mountains. New Zealand could have been specially made for climbers. It has some of the highest peaks in the southern hemisphere— as you might expect for the home and training ground of Everest pioneer Sir Edmund Hillary. You should have some experience before you set off and should make sure that you go with a qualified guide.

NEW SOUTH WALES & VICTORIA
Arapiles Climbing Guides
P.O. Box 142, Natimuk, VIC 3409
☎/fax: (3) 5387 1284
email: climbacg@netconnect.com.au
Arapiles Climbing Guides offer instruction in rock-climbing at Mount Arapiles and the Grampians National Park.

Adventure Guides Australia
38 Victoria Road, Beechworth, VIC 3747
☎ (3) 5728 1804 fax: (3) 5728 2933
email: agati@netc.net.au
website: www.vtoa.asn.au/adventureguides
Professionally conducted abseiling and rock climbing excursions in various locations.

Bushsports Adventures
P.O. Box 6543, Parramatta, NSW 2150
☎ (2) 9630 0587 fax: (2) 9630 3436
email: info@bushsports.com.au
website: www.bushsports.com.au
This operation also run Boomerang Bicycle Tours. Offers a variety of adventure activity courses in the Blue Mountains and around New South Wales.

High'n'Wild Mountain Adventures
3/5 Katoomba Street, Katoomba, NSW 2780
☎ (2) 4782 6224 fax: (2) 4782 6143
email: highwild@pnc.com.au
Offer abseiling, mountaineering (in the Snowy Mountains) and bush skills courses. Their 55m (180ft) abseil is the highest in the Blue Mountains. Also offer canyoning trips.

Outland Expeditions

P.O. Box 6, Mt Victoria, NSW 2786
☎ (2) 4787 1777 **fax:** (2) 4787 1766
email: base@outland.com.au
website: www.outland.com.au
Professional guides take small groups on a range of adventure trips. Abseiling activities range from 1-day beginner's course to a weekend trip to the Blue Mountains.

TASMANIA
Aardvark Adventures

toll free ☎ 1800 649514
mobile ☎ 040 812 7714
email: aardvark@southcom.com.au
website:www.southcom.com.au/~aardvark/
Organize trips to the world's highest commercial abseil at Strathgordon dam in south west Tasmania.

Summit Sports

444 Huon Road, South Hobart, TAS 7004
mobile ☎ 0418 362 210 **fax:** (3) 6223 1741
email: summit@southcom.com.au
website:
www.summitsports.southcom.com.au
Run by Stephen Cameron, an experienced climber, this company specializes in abseiling and climbing adventure tours. Half-day abseiling tours, suitable for first-timers and the more experienced, in Tasmania.

NORTH ISLAND

Popular climbing areas in the North Island are Mount Eden Quarry in Auckland, Whanganui Bay and Motuoapa near Lake Taupo. You can also try the Wharepapa climbing field, near Te Awamutu, with has over 40 climbs to choose from.

Cliffhanger Adventure Tours

P.O. Box 91596, A.M.S.C. Auckland
☎ (9) 815 1851 **fax:** (9)815 1832
email: Philpott@PI.Net
Abseiling from 10m (33ft) to 110m (361ft), including the world's highest tourist abseil. Also offer rock climbing and sea kayaking.

Plateau Adventure Guides

P.O. Box 29, National Park, Tongariro 2653
☎ (7) 892 2740 **fax:** (7) 892 2740
email: PlateauGuides@kiwiadv.co.nz
Established since 1984 and offering an extensive range of activities in the Tongariro and Whangunui National Parks. Activities include abseiling, caving, and mountaineering.

Wanderwomen

P.O. Box 68 058, Newton, Auckland
☎ (9) 360 7330 **fax:** (9)7332
email: Lizzie@wanderwomen.co.nz
Offers abseiling and rock-climbing for women, as well as a challenge high ropes course.

SOUTH ISLAND

Experienced climbers head for the extreme routes of the Darrans, while there are a number of good friction climbs around Castle Hill.

Franz Josef Glacier Guides

Main Road, P.O. Box 4, Franz Josef
☎ (3) 752 0763 **fax:** (3) 752 0102
Full and half-day guided trips of the Franz Josef Glacier, plus ice-climbing and heli hiking.

Independent Mountain Guides

28 Shotover Street, Queenstown
☎ (3) 442 3381 **fax:** (3) 442 3381
Moderate to challenging adventures with qualified guides. As well as abseiling, they offer mountaineering, climbing, and snow-shoeing.

Peak Experience

38 Wakatu Avenue, Christchurch
☎/**fax:** (3) 384 3262
email: peakx@clear.net.nz
website: http://kiwiadv.co.nz/Canterbury/PeakExperience.htm
A small team of professional mountaineers (members of N.Z. Mountain Guides Association) offering mountaineering instruction courses at all levels, and 5 days' guided climbing at Arthurs Pass. Also offer more advanced and alpine-climbing.

BALLOONING

Ballooning trips give you a unique view of the landscape, whether flying over the parched lands of Australia or over New Zealand's mountain regions.

NORTHERN TERRITORY & SOUTH AUSTRALIA
Outback Ballooning

35 Kennett Court, Alice Springs, NT 0870
☎ (8) 8952 8723 **fax:**(8) 8952 3869
email: balloons@topend.com.au
website: www.balloons.in.australia.as
Alice Spring's original ballooning company—choose a 30-minute or 1-hour flight. Packages with camel rides are also available.

Queensland

Hot Air, P.O. Box 5115, Cairns, QLD 4870
☎ (7) 4054 4488 **toll-free** ☎ 1800 800 829
fax: (7) 4054 4433
email: hotair@hotair.com.au
website: www.hotair.com.au
Hot-air ballooning over the Queensland landscape in the flying Koala.

NEW SOUTH WALES & VICTORIA
Peregrine Tours

258 Lonsdale Street, Melbourne, VIC 3000
☎ (3) 9662 2700 **fax:** (3) 9662 2422
website: www.peregrine.net.au
Peregrine Tours offers a dawn hot air ballooning trip over the Yarra Valley wine growing region. The flight lasts about 1 hour and ends with a champagne breakfast.

NORTH ISLAND
Balloon Expedition Co of NZ Ltd

150 Moire Road, Royal Heights, Auckland
☎ (9) 416 8590 **fax:** (9)416 8590
Dawn balloon flights over Auckland with a champagne breakfast to follow.

SOUTH ISLAND
Aoraki Balloon Safaris

P.O. Box 75, Methven 8353
☎ (3) 302 8172 **fax:** (3) 302 8162
email: calm@voyager.co.nz
website: http://kiwiadv.co.nz/Canterbury/AorakiBalloon.htm
Operate a range of balloon flights from Christchurch and Methven. As well as standard 1-hour flights they can arrange mountain flights, a Rakaia Gorge Safari, high-altitude flights to 7,000m (23,000ft), and an extended, cross-country flight lasting 3 hours.

Up Up and Away

P.O. Box 14160, Christchurch
☎ (3) 358 9859 **mobile** ☎ 025 325 611
fax: (3) 358 9829
email: upupandaway@xtra.co.nz
Experienced ballooning company offering a dawn balloon flight over Christchurch.

BIRDWATCHING

The unique birdlife of Australia and New Zealand makes for a twitcher's paradise. Tours available range from specialized ones that cater for dedicated birdwatchers, to those that mix birdwatching with activities such as hiking.

Australian birdlife is rich and colourful. Perhaps the most famous bird is the kookaburra, but you should also watch out for bellbirds, black swans, brilliantly coloured parrots, and budgerigars. Little penguins and albatrosses live along the south coast, while the cassowary lives in the tropical rainforest. Emus live in the dry areas of the west. The kiwi is New Zealand's national bird. On Stewart Island you'll find the brown kiwi, while the little spottedkiwi is confined to offshore islands. The North Island has blue duck and the kokako.

GENERAL TOURS
Emu Tours

P.O. Box 4, Jamberoo, NSW 2533
☎ (2) 4236 0542 **fax:** (2) 4236 0176
Tours for birdwatchers throughout Australia, run by Richard Jordan, an expert birder. Tours can last from a week to a month.

Naturetrek

Cheriton Mill, Cheriton, Nr Alresford, Hampshire SO24 ONG, U.K.
☎ (01962) 733051 **fax:** (01962) 736426
email: info@naturetrek.co.uk
website: www.naturetrek.co.uk
Run 2- to 3-week escorted birdwatching and botanical trips to Queensland, Western Australia and the Kimberleys. You'll walk each day and be interested in birds and wildlife.

Ornitholidays

29 Straight Mile, Romsey
Hampshire SO51 9BB, U.K.
☎ (01794) 523500 **fax:** (01794) 523544
email: ornitholidays @compuserve.com
website: www.ornitholidays.co.uk
Run escorted birdwatching tours throughout Australia and New Zealand.

NORTHERN TERRITORY & SOUTH AUSTRALIA
Denise Goodfellow

P.O. Box 39373, Winnellie, NT 0821
☎ (8) 8981 8492
Denise is the author of a number of books on the birds and wildlife of the Northern Territory. She offers specialized, guided tours, mainly for birdwatchers in its unique landscape.

Yellow Water Cruises

Kakadu Highway, Jim Jim, NT 0886
☎ (8) 8979 0145 **fax:** (8) 8979 0148
Offers 1–2 hour cruises on Yellow Water, a landlocked billabong that floods during the wet

season to become part of the Jim Jim Creek and South Alligator River systems. Gives you a chance to see the spectacular birdlife of the wetlands.

NEW SOUTH WALES & VICTORIA
Australian Eco Tours

2 Drysdale Place, Mooroolbark, VIC 3138
☎ (3) 9726 8471 **fax:** (3) 9727 1545
Specialize in nature tours from Sydney, but also offer extended tours led by ornithologist Chris Doughty in other parts of Australia, giving you the opportunity to see unique species.

NORTH ISLAND
Kiwi Wildlife Tours

24 Polkinghorne Drive, Whangaparaoa
☎ (9) 424 2505 **fax:** (9)428 0347
email: karenbd@clear.net.nz
website: www.kiwi-wildlife.co.nz
Although based in North Island, knowledgeable guides take small groups on birdwatching tours throughout New Zealand. Tours range from 12 to 18 days and include a liveaboard boat tour.

SOUTH ISLAND

Species you might spot on the South Island include the kaka, the banded dotterel, and the rare black stilt.

Ocean Wings

58 West End, Kaikoura
☎ (3) 319 6777 **fax:** (3) 319 6534
email: info@oceanwings.co.nz
Birdwatching ocean trips to observe the birds of the Kaikoura coast; mollymawks, petrels, terns, and albatross.

BUNGEE JUMPING

New Zealand is the home of modern bungee (or bungy or bungi) jumping and you can be assured that you will get the full bungee, adrenalin-pumping experience here. All you have to do is throw yourself off a high bridge or ledge—with your feet attached to a springy "cord" or bungee. Then, just as you're about to hit the ground or the water you are catapulted back into the air. Nothing to it. Not an activity for those with back or neck problems.

NORTH ISLAND
Taupo Bungy

202 Spa Road, P.O. Box 919, Taupo
☎ (7) 377 1135 **freecall** ☎ 0800 888 408
fax: (7) 377 1136
email: jump@taupobungy.co.nz
Offers scenic bungee jumps 46m (151ft) above the Waikato River. Specialize in water touches.

SOUTH ISLAND

This is where you will find the original bungee jumping site, as well as the "bungee with a twist" experience, known as the bungee rocket.

AJ Hackett Bungy

The Bungy Centre, The Station Building
P.O. Box 488, Queenstown
☎ (3) 442 4007 **fax:** (3) 442 7121
email: bungyjump@ajhackett.co.nz
website: www.AJHackett.com
These are the original bungee people. AJ Hackett developed modern bungee jumping, jumping from the Eiffel Tower in 1987. The company offers jumps at Kawarau Bridge (43m/141ft) the world's first official bungee site and at 3 other sites in the Queenstown area.

Bungee Rocket

New Brighton Pier, Marine Parade
Christchurch
☎ (3) 388 8295 **fax:** (3) 388 8356
email: bungeerocket@xtra.co.nz
website: www.newzealandnz.co.nz
/bungeerocket
This is bungee with a difference. You are first fired into the air—where you will experience a G force of 5, followed by weightlessness—and then fly towards the ground, bouncing 10 times before the experience ends.

Pipeline Bungy

See p. 283.

BUSHWALKING

Bushwalking is a term that was once used to distinguish serious walkers from casual hikers. Today it tends to mean anything from a stroll in the bush to a backpacking expedition. Although the term is used in New Zealand, it is most common in Australia. If you go bushwalking you should make sure that you are well-equipped with maps, wide-brimmed hats, food, water, and the correct footwear. Let someone know where you intend to go so that, should you get lost, someone knows to come looking for you. Also see below, under Trekking. There are opportunities for bushwalking throughout Australia, with plenty of long-distance tracks, most of which are in the south of the country. Given the risk from bush-fires, do be extremely careful if lighting a fire, and check before you go whether a fire ban is in operation.

WESTERN AUSTRALIA

The southwestern corner is the best place for bushwalking. It is where you will find the Bibulman Track, an old Aboriginal trail, which passes through eucalyptus forests.

Sirius Adventures Bushwalks

20 Archer Street, Derby, WA 6728
☎ (8) 9193 2064 **fax:** (8) 9168 2110
Customized bushwalks tailored to your requirements, in Western Australia and Northern Territory. Tours include bush camping, bird-watching and remote wilderness experiences.

NORTHERN TERRITORY

The most popular bushwalking areas are in Litchfield Park, during the dry season, and the Larapinta Trail, west of Alice Springs.

Trek Larapinta

22 Chewings Street, Alice Springs, NT 0870
☎ (8) 8953 2933 **toll free** ☎ 1800 803 174
fax: (8) 8953 2913
email: charlie@treklarapinta.com.au
Offer 1- and 2-day bushwalking tours on the Larapinta Trail through the West MacDonnell Ranges. You only have to carry a daypack as overnight camp is brought to you.

Willis's Walkabouts

12 Carrington Street, Millner, NT 0810
☎ (8) 8985 2134 **fax:** (8) 8985 2355
email: walkabout@ais.com.au
Nine different off-trail wilderness walks in the Red Centre. Suitable for fit people able to carry full packs for 5 days or longer.

NEW SOUTH WALES & VICTORIA

Most of the best bushwalking in southeast Australia takes place in the Blue Mountains and the Grampian Mountains.

Bunyip Tours

C/o Backpacker Adventure Tours, 8 Grey Street
St Kilda, VIC 3182
☎ (3) 9534 8866 **fax:** (3) 9534 9904
email: woosh@battours.com.au
Tailor-made bushwalking tours of Wilsons Promontory—a coastal national park with abundant native flora and fauna.

Echidna Walkabout

P.O. Box 370, Port Melbourne, VIC 3207
☎ (3) 9646 8249 **fax:** (3) 9681 9177
Tailor-made bushwalking and nature tours to various regions around Victoria, including the Croajingolong National Park, Grampians National Park and the Buchan Caves.

Mountain Escapes

P.O. Box 590, Katoomba, NSW 2780
toll free ☎ 1800 357 577
email: escapes@mountains.net.au
website: www.bluemts.com.au/escapes
Family business combining small group bus tours in the Blue Mountains with activities. Bushwalking trip is 3 days.

Otway Ocean Tours

6 Hull Court, Grovedale, VIC 3216
☎/**fax:** (3) 5244 0944
email: otwayocean@profit.com.au
A range of wildlife and bushwalking tours led by a naturalist guide. Areas covered include the Great Ocean Road and Wilsons Promontory.

TASMANIA

A great bushwalking destination, home to the 80km (49 mile)-long Overland Track, which runs from Cradle Mountain to Lake St. Clair.

Club Tarkine

174 Charles Street, Launceston, TAS 7250
☎ (3) 6334 4455 **fax:** (3) 6334 1297
email: tark@tassie.net.au
website: www.tased.edu.au/tasonline/tarkine/
Ecotourism outfit offering day tours and extended bushwalks in the Tarkine Wilderness.

Tasmanian Highland Tours

P.O. Box 29, Latrobe, TAS 7307
☎ (3) 6426 9312 **fax:** (3) 6426 9350
email: pweeks@tassie.net.au
website: www.tassie.net.au/~pweeks/tht.html
Offer 8-day lightweight, guided backpacking tours along the Overland Track; gear, food, and transport provided. Suitable for beginners.

CAMPING SAFARIS

These trips give you a taste of the outdoors, often combined with some adventure activities. The trips on offer range from soft adventure tours to those that require you to "rough it." You can find trips that offer you just 1 or 2 nights or ones that last for several days.

WESTERN AUSTRALIA
All Terrain Safaris

Lot 26, Wandeara Crescent, Mundaring,
WA 6073

☎ (8) 9295 6680 **toll free** ☎ 1800 633 456
mobile ☎ 0419 709 053 **fax:** (8) 9295 6681
website: www.allterrain.com.au/

Camping safaris from 3 to 35 days, to Ayers
Rock, Kakadu, Monkey Mia, and the Valley of
the Giants.

Snappy Gum Safaris

P.O. Box 881, Karratha, WA 6714
☎ (8) 9185 1278 **toll free** ☎ 1800 09 4811
fax: (8) 9144 2597
email: snappygum@kisser.net.au
website: www.kisser.net.au/snappygum or
holiday-wa.net/snappy.htm

Two-day camping safari in the Karijini National
Park with spectacular cliff faces and gorges.

NORTHERN TERRITORY & SOUTH AUSTRALIA
Billy Can Tours

P.O. Box 4407, Darwin, NT 0801
☎ (8) 8981 9813 **toll free** ☎ 1800 813 484
fax:(8) 8941 0803
email: billycan@ozemail.com.au

Soft adventure camping tours of 2-5 days in the
Kakadu, Katherine Gorge and Litchfield
National Parks.

CAMEL TOURS

Camels are not native to Australia but are
admirably equipped to cope with the continent's expansive deserts. It is possible to go
camel trekking in most regions and it gives you
an unusual way of seeing the country.

WESTERN AUSTRALIA
Cameleer Park Camel Farm

300 Neaves Road, Wanneroo, WA
☎ (8) 9405 3558 **fax:** (8) 9306 1448
email: wolfgang@cameleer.com.au
website: www.cameleer.com.au

Take a short ride (up to 2 hours) or try a 1- or
2-day camel safari.

NORTHERN TERRITORY & SOUTH AUSTRALIA
Frontier Camel Tours

Frontier Camel Farm, Ross Highway
Alice Springs, NT 0871
☎ (8) 8953 0444 **fax:** (8) 8955 5015

email: camelfrom@ozemail.com.au
website: www.cameltours.com.au
Also: P.O. Box 275, Ayers Rock Resort, NT 0872
☎ (8) 8956 2444 **fax:** (8) 8956 2251

Short camel rides can be taken from the Camel
Farm or Ayers Rock Resort. They are usually
combined with breakfast, dinner or other activities, such as hot air ballooning in Alice Springs.

Outback Camel Company

132 Wickham Street, Fortitude Valley
QLD 4006
☎ (7) 3854 1022 **fax:** (7) 3854 1079
email: peregrin@eis.net.au
website: www.outbackcamel.com.au

This company pioneered the first commercial
camel expeditions in Australia. Organizes
camel safaris and expeditions, from 12 to 30
days, across the Great Victoria, Simpson, and
Strzelecki Deserts. No back-up vehicles.

NEW SOUTH WALES & VICTORIA
Silverton Camel Farm

P.O. Box 751, Broken Hill, NSW 2880
☎ (8) 8088 5316

Camel treks ranging from a 15-minute ride to a
5-day safari, beginners to advanced.

CANOEING

Canoeing trips can vary from a gentle paddle
(many companies offer training for beginners),
to an extreme white-water canoeing experience. Despite its image as a dry, parched
country, there are a number of good places in
Australia to canoe and plenty in New Zealand.

NORTHERN TERRITORY
Gecko Canoeing

P.O. Box 2072, Katherine, NT 0851
☎ (8) 8972 2224 **fax:** (8) 8972 2294
email: gecko@topend.com.au
website: www.geckocanoeing.com.au/

Experienced guides take you on 3- to 6-day
tours along the Katherine and other river systems in the Northern Territory.

QUEENSLAND
The Adventure Company, Australia

See p. 266 for details.

Wide range of adventure and nature tours for
individuals and groups. Offer 1-day canoeing in
tropical rainforest. Can also combine canoeing
with longer biking, rafting, hiking and reef trips.

TASMANIA
Rafting Tasmania
☎ (3) 6239 1080 **fax:** (3) 6239 1090
email: raftingtas@tasadventures.com
Canoeing tours in Tasmania.

NORTH ISLAND
Canoe Safaris
P.O. Box 180, Ohakune
☎ (6)385 9237 **fax:** (6)385 8758
email: canoe@voyager.co.nz
Five-day canoe and kayak trips exploring the
Whanganui National Park, including the Bridge
to Nowhere.

SOUTH ISLAND
Funyaks
P.O. Box 1241, Queenstown
☎ (3) 442 7374 **fax:** (3) 442 6536
email: funyaks@inc.co.nz
website: www.funyaks.com
This company, run by a former kayak champion, operates full-day trips down the Dart
River using inflatable canoes called "funyaks."

CANYONING

Canyoning is for those who love a challenge. A
tour may involve anything from abseiling down
a gushing waterfall to swimming through narrow passages of foaming water. It is an activity
that takes you to places you might previously
have thought of as inaccessible. There are
plenty of opportunities for canyoning in
Australia. A number of operators offer this
activity together with caving, climbing, and
abseiling. New Zealand makes wonderful
canyoning country, and there are operators in
both the North and the South Islands.

NEW SOUTH WALES & VICTORIA
Bushsports, **High'n'Wild Mountain
Adventures** and **Outland Expeditions** offer
canyoning—their details can be found above
under Abseiling, Climbing and Mountaineering.

Mountain Escapes
See Bushwalking, for details.

NORTH ISLAND
AWOL Canyoning Adventures
Ltd
P.O. Box 56 207, Dominion Road, Auckland
☎ (9) 630 7100 **fax:** (9)623 0505
email: info@awoladventures.co.nz

website: www.awoladventures.co.nz
Canyoning and abseiling adventures. Tours
include 2 hours canyoning in the Waitakere
Ranges, as well as a short bush walk and a visit
to the black sand of Piha surf beach.

SOUTH ISLAND
Deep Canyon Experience
P.O. Box 101, Wanaka
☎ (3) 443 7922 **fax:** (3) 443 7922
Offer canyoning in the Matukituki Valley, with
abseils down a 400m (1,312ft) waterfall.

X11 Mile Delta Canyoning
C/-NZ Post, Wakatipu
☎/**fax:** (3) 442 3315 **mobile** ☎ 025 507 67
email: canyoning@xiimile.co.nz
website: www.xiimile.co.nz
Professionally qualified guides take you on
canyoning adventures that include abseiling
down waterfalls and swimming narrow passage-
way. Heli canyoning is also available.

CAVING

Experience the thrill of exploring underground
on an organized tour—or if you are experienced, by going with a local club. A popular
activity, particularly in New Zealand, is cave
rafting, also known as cave tubing or black-
water rafting. This involves floating through
caves on a custom-made tyre tube. You'll be kitted out with a wetsuit and hard hat.

NORTH ISLAND
The most popular caving spot on North Island is
at the Waitomo Caves.

Black Water Rafting Ltd
See p. 278.

Kawiti Glow-worm and
Limestone Caves
P.O. Box 21, Kawakawa
☎ (9) 404 1256
Maori guided tours of 300-year-old caves with
glow-worms and limestone formations.

Plateau Adventure Guides
See Abseiling, Climbing and Mountaineering.

Waitomo Down Under
Waitomo Caves, P.O. Box 24, Waitomo
freecall ☎ 0800 102 605 **fax:** (7) 878 6565
Float, abseil or pothole through Waitomo Caves.

SOUTH ISLAND

For caving experiences on South Island make for the caves near Westport and Greymouth.

Norwest Adventures-Underworld Rafting

41 Dommett Street, Westport
☎ (3) 789 6686 **fax:** (3) 789 8922
email: norwest@xtra.co.nz
Cave tours, cave rafting and adventure caving tours, from easy to challenging.

CRUISING

The coastlines of both Australia and New Zealand offer restful cruising and active sailing. Experienced sailors will find plenty of places where you can hire vessels.(See also p. 303).

WESTERN AUSTRALIA
Buccaneer Sea Safaris

36 Knowsley Street East, Derby, WA
☎/**fax:** (8) 9191 1991
email: derbytb@comswest.net.au
Sea safaris in the Buccaneer Archipelago. Trips last 4–10 days and provide opportunities for fishing, snorkelling, and whale-watching.

QUEENSLAND
The Cruise People Ltd

88 York Street, London W1H 1DP, U.K.
☎ (020) 7723 2450 **freephone** ☎ 0800 526 313 **fax:** (020) 7723 2486
email: cruise@dial.pipex.com
website: www.cruisepeople.co.uk
Operate 3- and 4-night cruises to the Great Barrier Reef and the islands, including Fitzroy, Lizard and Ribbon islands.

The Cruise People Ltd

1252 Lawrence Avenue East, Don Mills, Ontario, M3A 1C3, Canada
toll free ☎ 1800 268 6523
email: cruise@tcpltd.com

NORTH ISLAND
Adventure Cruises

51 Anzac Street, Takapuna
☎ (9) 488 0762 **mobile** ☎ 025 924 191
fax: (9)488 0762
email: sails@ihug.co.nz
Sail on the *Spirit of Musick*, a 47ft ketch. Full- and half-day trips available in Auckland Harbour and Islands, as well as longer trips to the Hauraki Gulf and Bay of Islands.

MV Waipa Delta

Memorial Park Jetty, Memorial Drive
P.O. Box 4301, Hamilton
☎ (7) 854 7813 **fax:** (7) 854 9819
email: waipadelta@xtra.co.nz
website: www.waipadelta.co.nz
Cruise on the Waikato River on a paddle steamer.

Sail on *Snow Cloud* 11.2m

Te Ngaere Bay, RD1, Kaeo
☎ (9) 405 0523 **mobile** ☎ 025 903 861
fax: (9)405 0604
Offer a skippered day trip to the Cavalli Islands or take an extended coastal cruise.

Soren Larsen, Squaresail Pacific Ltd

P.O. Box 310, Kumeu
☎ (9) 411 8755 **fax:** (9)411 8484
email: sorenlarsen@voyager.co.nz
Help sail the classic tall ship, the *Soren Larsen*. Day sails available as well as 3-, 5- and 10-day explorations of New Zealand.

CULTURAL TRIPS

Not an active adventure, but you may see aspects of the country that you would otherwise miss. Such trips may involve anything from staying in someone's home—which could be an isolated sheep station in Australia—to a tour led by a native Aboriginal or Maori. Learn about native art or bush medicines, or be introduced to the rich history of indigenous people.

WESTERN AUSTRALIA
Wooleen Station

Via Mullewa, Murchison
☎ (8) 9963 7973 **fax:** (8) 9963 7684
Stay on this enormous (½ million acres) station with Brett and Helen Pollock. Get involved with station life, watch the remarkable birdlife, and see the kangaroos, emus, and 14,000 sheep.

NORTHERN TERRITORY & SOUTH AUSTRALIA
Aboriginal Desert Discovery Tours

P.O. Box 130, Alice Springs, NT 0871
email: aborart@ozemail.com.au
This Aboriginal-owned and operated company run half-day tours in the Alice Springs Desert Park, and to a homeland to learn about Aboriginal culture. They also run a 6-day safari to Ayers Rock and the Simpson Desert.

Anangu Tours

P.O. Box 435, Yulara, NT 0872
☎ (8) 8956 2123 **fax:** (8) 8956 3136
email: lbanangu@bigpond.com
website: www.users.bigpond.com/lbanangu
Fascinating Aboriginal guided hiking tours
around Ayers Rock. Learn about bush survival
skills as well as the Dreamtime legends.

Umorrduk Aboriginal Safaris

P.O. Box 41086, Casuarina, NT 0811
☎ (8) 8948 1306 **fax:** (8) 8948 1305
Small group discovery tours specializing in
Aboriginal rock art and culture in the wilderness areas at the top end of Northern Territory.

QUEENSLAND
Dele Rule's Ecole/Homes Across the Sea

11 Murphy Street, Ipswich, QLD 4305
☎ (7) 3812 0211 **fax:** (7) 3812 2188
Live like a local and stay with an Australian
family. 250 host families picked to suit your
interests from the outback to the tropics.

The Adventure Company, Australia

See p. 266 for details.

NEW SOUTH WALES & VICTORIA
Harry Nanya Tours

Shop 10, Sandwych Street, Wentworth
NSW 2648
☎ (3) 5027 2076 **fax:** (3) 5027 3697
Aboriginal-guided tours to Mungo National
Park, Perry Sandhill's, and Thegoa Lagoon.

Ponde Tours

162 Seventh Street, Mildura, VIC 3502
☎ (3) 5023 2488
Aboriginal-guided tours to Mungo National
Park. Day trips or overnight visits available.

NORTH ISLAND
E.C.O. Tours Ltd

Whangaruru North Road, RD4, Hikurangi
☎ (9) 433 6682 **fax:** (9)433 6594
Maori-owned and operated company specializing in cultural immersion adventure tours.

Kaitoki Bush Camp

Motatau off SH1, Prime Holdings Ltd,
Motatau, RD1, Kawakawa
☎ (9) 404 0651 **fax:** (9)404 1727
Educational experience with a Maori family.
Learn about culture and forest medicines.

Manaia Hostel and Treks

Mitimiti, RD2, Kohukohu, North Hokianga
☎ (9) 409 5347 **fax:** (9)409 5347
Maori-guided tour of the North Head sand
dunes at the mouth of the Hokianga harbour.

CYCLING

You don't have to be a cycling fanatic to enjoy a
cycling tour. You can choose to take a trip that
takes you on modest distances each day, giving
you plenty of chance to stop and take photographs, explore villages or watch wildlife.
Operators will provide up to date bikes and
many offer guided tours.

NORTHERN TERRITORY & SOUTH AUSTRALIA
Bogong Jack Adventures

P.O. Box 4, Kangarilla, SA 5157
☎ (8) 8383 7198 **fax:** (8) 8383 7377
email: ecotrek@ozemail.com.au
Operating since 1981, this company run a variety of easy to moderate cycling tours in South
Australia. Lengths vary from 2 to 10 days.

NEW SOUTH WALES & VICTORIA
Boomerang Bicycle Tours

P.O. Box 6543, Parramatta B/C, NSW 2151
☎ (2) 9630 0587 **fax:** (2) 9630 3436
email: ozbike@ozemail.com.au
website: www.ozemail.com.au/~ozbike
Inclusive small group bicycle tours.

NORTH ISLAND
Coromandel Four Wheel Bike Safaris

20 Blackjack Road, Kuaotunu, RD 2, Whitianga
☎ (7) 866 2034
Guided bush safaris on a remote coastal property with secluded coves and native forests.

New Zealand Pedaltours

P.O. Box 37 575, Parnell, Auckland
☎ (9) 302 0968 **fax:** (9)302 0967
email: pedaltours@xtra.co.nz
Operate 12 different cycling tours, lasting from
3 to 19 days, in North and South Island.

SOUTH ISLAND
Adventure South Backroad Cycle Tours and Backcountry Walks.

P.O. Box 33 153, Christchurch
☎ (3) 332 1222 **fax:** (3) 332 4030

email: cycle@advsouth.co.nz
website: www.advsouth.co.nz
Small group cycle tours of scenic parks and reserves throughout the South Island.

Naturally New Zealand Holidays

P.O. Box 34703, Auckland 1330
fax: (9) 480 0282
email: info@nzholidays.co.nz
website: http://nzholidays.co.nz
Operate 5- to 10-day backroad cycling tours, suitable for all levels of fitness and experience.

Pacific Cycle Tours

13 Trent Street, Avonside, Christchurch
☎ (3) 389 0583 **fax:** (3) 389 0498
email: pct@xtra.co.nz
website: www.pacificcycletours.co.nz
Specializes in tailor-made tours and off-the-beaten track trips for cyclists.

DIVING

The waters around Australia and New Zealand offer some of the world's best diving. You do not have to be an experienced diver, as there are plenty of places offering training courses. Make sure that the instructors are qualified—P.A.D.I. (Professional Association of Diving Instructors) is the internationally recognized diving qualification. P.A.D.I. Open Water courses typically last 4–5 days and enable you to go on and dive anywhere you want in the world. Obviously the Great Barrier Reef is a big draw, but the warm seas of New Zealand's North Island are also good. A number of companies offer wreck diving—the Greenpeace ship, *Rainbow Warrior*, being a particularly popular site.

WESTERN AUSTRALIA
Bay Dive and Adventures

26 Dunn Bay Road, Dunsborough, WA
☎ (8) 9756 8846 **fax:** (8) 9756 8806
email: dive@capeweb.com.au
website: http://capeweb.com.au/baydive
Full and half-day diving and snorkelling trips, wreck diving and night dives.

Beagle Island Dive

Tamarisk Street, Leeman, WA
☎ (8) 9953 1190 **fax:** (8) 9953 1185
email: beagleislanddive@bigpond.com.au
Dive charters, scuba instruction, and snorkelling available in the waters off Leeman.

Diving Ventures

384 South Terrace, South Fremantle, WA
☎ (8) 9430 5130 **fax:** (8) 9430 5641
email: diving@dventures.com.au
website: www.dventures.com.au
Various diving tours run by P.A.D.I. divers. Trips include a 3-day cruise to the Abrolhos Islands, wreck diving, and diving on the Ningaloo Reef.

Eco Abrolhos

61 Reg Clarke Road, Geraldton, WA
☎ (8) 9964 7887 **fax:** (8) 9964 7848
email: abrolhosbookings@wn.com.au
website: www.com.au/abrolhosbookings/ecotour.htm
The *Eco Abrolhos* is a charter boat that operates diving tours around the Abrolhos Islands.

QUEENSLAND

It just doesn't get any better than this. In Queensland you'll find the World Heritage-listed Great Barrier Reef, which extends over 2,550km (1,584 miles), home to over 6,600 species of flora and fauna. Some of the Reef's most beautiful islands are easily accessible from tropical North Queensland, and there are loads of diving options to choose from, catering for everyone from beginners to advanced.

Compass Outer Barrier Reef Trips

P.O. Box 2488, Grafton Street, Cairns QLD 4870
☎ (7) 4050 0666 **toll free** ☎ 1800 815 811
email: reeftrip@reeftrip.com
website: www.reeftrip.com
Day and overnight trips, snorkelling and diving on the Great Barrier Reef.

Diversion Dive Travel

P.O. Box 7026, Cairns, QLD 4870
☎ (7) 4039 0200 **fax:** (7) 4039 0300
email: info@diversionoz.com
website: www.diversionoz.com/ozmail.htm
Dive travel and training specialist in Queensland.

Oceania Dive

257 Shute Harbour Road, P.O. Box 1060 Airlie Beach, QLD 4802
☎ (7) 4946 6032 **toll free** ☎ 1800 075 035
email: oceania@whitsunday.net.au
Diving and snorkelling the outer Great Barrier Reef, dive adventure cruises, P.A.D.I. beginners and advanced diving courses.

Quicksilver Connections Ltd

P.O. Box 171, Marina Mirage, Port Douglas
QLD 4871
☎ (7) 4099 5455 **fax:** (7) 4099 5525
email: or quick3@ozemail.com.au
website: www.ozemail.com.au/~quick3
Diving and cruising in outer Great Barrier Reef
and Great Barrier Reef. Includes guided
snorkelling trips led by marine biologists.

Reef Encounters

P.O. Box 2488, Cairns, QLD 4870
☎/**fax:** (7) 4031 7217
toll free ☎1800 815 811
Cruises to the outer Great Barrier Reef, diving
and snorkelling.

The Adventure Company, Australia

See p. 266 for details.
Discovery and research dive expeditions in
Great Barrier Reef Marine Park.

Tusa Dive

Cnr The Esplanade and Aplin Street
Cairns, OLD 4870
☎ (7) 4031 1248 **fax:** (7) 4031 5221
email: tusa@c130.aone.net.au
website: www.tusadive.com
Dives for certified divers and introductory
dives. Also offer guided snorkelling tour of the
outer Great Barrier Reef.

NORTH ISLAND
Aqua Action

Marina Road, Tutukaka, RD 3, Whangerei
freecall ☎ 0800 689 222 **fax:** (9)434 3884
email: aquaaction@xtra.co.nz
Diving and snorkelling trips to the Poor Knights
Islands.

Matauri Bay Holiday Park

P.O. Box 5, Kerikeri
☎ (9) 405 0525 **fax:** (9)405 0525
Specialize in guided scuba diving on *Rainbow
Warrior*, submerged offshore of Matauri Bay.
Maximum of 4 divers.

Pacific Hideaway

13 Moody Avenue, Whangarei
☎ (9) 437 3632 **fax:** (9)437 2469
email: rees@dive.nz.co.nz
website: www.divenz.co.nz
Operate snorkelling and diving trips from a
catamaran, which takes you out to the Poor
Knights Islands.

Paihia Dive Hire and Charter

Williams Road, P.O. Box 210, Paihia, Northland
☎ (9) 402 7551 **fax:** (9)402 7110
email: tim.barke@xtra.co.nz
P.A.D.I. dive schools, dive hire and dive charters to the *Rainbow Warrior* wreck and the
Bay of Islands reef.

Wellington Dive Adventures

Owhiro Bay
☎ (4) 934 5473
email: wda@dive.net.nz
website: www.dive.net.nz
Professional charter company offering trips off
the southwestern corner of North Island.

SOUTH ISLAND
Slipper Island Resort

P.O. Box 897, Pukekohe, Auckland
☎/**fax:** (9)238 7558
email: slipper@clear.net.nz
website: www.marrserv.com/slipper
This weekend retreat has P.A.D.I. instructors
and offers tours, courses, and night diving.

EXPLORATION AND ADVENTURE TOURS

These tours are ideal if you want to experience
a bit of everything. They generally combine
some sightseeing with a range of adventure
activities, so you may find yourself snorkelling
one day and mountainbiking the next. They are
a great way of squeezing a lot into a short time.

GENERAL TOURS
Australian Tour Experience

5 Dorchap Court, Hoppers Crossing, VIC 3029
☎ (3) 9748 9652 **fax:** (3) 9748 0489
Soft adventure accommodated and camping
tours for small groups to all areas of Australia.

Australian Tracks and Trails

School Road, Yorketown, SA 5576
☎ (8) 8852 1385 **fax:**(8) 8885 2135
Nature and adventure touring for independent
travellers and special interest groups.

Outback Stations of Australia

750 Piedmont Ave, NE Atlanta, GA 30308
U.S.A.
☎ (404) 888 0909 **fax:** (404) 888 0081
email: outback@bushhomes.com
Tours designed to enable you to experience the
very best of Australia. You can help muster

cattle or sheep on isolated stations, swim with dolphins or perhaps go diving on the Great Barrier Reef.

Travelbag Adventures

15 Turk Street, Alton, Hampshire GU34 1AG U.K.
☎ (01420) 541007 **fax:** (01420) 541002
email: info@travelbag-adventures.co.uk
website: www.travelbag-adventures.co.uk
Run a 15-day adventure tour in Queensland, including canoeing, rainforest hiking, mountainbiking, and sea kayaking. Also run 13- and 25-day tours on the West Coast and Gibb River Road. There are 3 varied adventure tours in New Zealand, both North and South Islands, which take you into wilderness areas.

Travel Deals

70 North End Road, London W14 OSJ U.K.
☎ (020) 7371 6300 **fax:** (020) 7371 1953
email: travel.deals@virgin.net
This agency represent a whole range of operators running adventure travel holidays in both Australia and New Zealand.

WESTERN AUSTRALIA
Australian Adventure Travel

Unit 3, 33 Oxleigh Drive, Malaga, WA
☎ (8) 9248 2355 **fax:** (8) 9248 2366
email: email@safaris.net.au
website: www.safaris.net.au
Operate a wide range of 4WD and camping safaris. Their 15-day Kimberley Explorer gives you the chance to aboriginal art, view wildlife, and take a helicopter flight. They also run a 6-day camping safari to Ayers Rock.

Design A Tour

P.O. Box 627, Albany WA 6331
☎ (8) 9841 7778 **fax:** (8) 9842 2809
email: info@dat.com.au
website: www.dat.com.au
Family owned company offering tours to National Parks, boat trips or wildlife watching.

West Kimberley Tours

Lot 180 Bell Creek Way, Derby, WA
☎ (8) 9193 1442 **toll free** ☎ 1800 621 426
fax:(8) 9193 1590
email: derbytb@comswest.net.au
website: www.comswest.net.au/~derbytb
Small group tours of the Kimberley, including a full day tour of Windjana Gorge and Tunnel Creek, an exposed fossil reef complex.

Western Travel Bug

11a Hutt Court, Two Rocks, WA 6037
☎ (8) 9561 5236 **toll free** ☎ 1800 627 488
fax:(8) 9561 6021
Run inclusive eco activity tours for budget travellers, travelling in small coaches and staying in hostels or forest cottages.

QUEENSLAND
Raging Thunder PTY Ltd

See p.269 for details.
Adventure packages in Cairns including sea kayaking, white-water rafting, and ballooning.

NEW SOUTH WALES & VICTORIA
Frontier Photographic Safaris

36 Thomas Street, Chippendale, NSW 2008
☎ (2) 9319 3458 **fax:** (2) 9698 7661
Day tours and extended outback safaris for both small and large groups.

TASMANIA

www.tasmanianadventures.com.au
Has information on many adventure tour operators on the island.

NEW ZEALAND
New Zealand Encounters

P.O. Box 273, Whitianga 2856
☎ (7) 866 2250 **fax:** (7) 866 2650
email: Gina@NZEncounters.co.nz
website: www.nzenounters.co.nz
Run by American Gina Ratcliffe, this company operates a range of inclusive tours, adventure activities, and guided trips.

Uniquely New Zealand

P.O. Box 131, Salida, Colorado 81201, U.S.A.
email: uniquenz@rmi.net
website: www.adventuresports.com/travel/zealand/welcome.htm
Operate small group exploration and adventure tours lasting from 8 to 21 days. Include hiking, 4WD, helicopter trips, rafting and sea kayaking.

NORTH ISLAND
Auckland Adventures

P.O. Box 87-023, Meadowbank, Auckland
☎ (9) 379 4545 **mobile** ☎ 025 855 856
fax: (9)379 4543
email: auckland-adventures@acb.co.nz
website: www.acb.co.nz/adventure
Operate a full-day Wilderness Adventure tour. This soft adventure includes wine tasting, swimming, and hiking, including the a walk down into the crater of Mt Eden volcano.

Wilderness Escapes

7A Ward Place, Taupo
☎ (7) 378 3413 **mobile** ☎ 025 776 066
fax: (7) 378 3493
email: wildesc@reap.org.nz
website: www.reap.org.nz/~wildesc
Run by Brian Neville, who offers lots of activities, from caving to microlight flying. Trips include a hiking tour in the Pureora Forest Park, famous for the endangered kokako bird.

SOUTH ISLAND
Canterbury Trails Ltd

5 Dannys Lane, Cashmere, Christchurch 2
☎ (3) 337 1185 **fax:** (3) 337 5085
email: trails@xtra.co.nz
Variety of small group tours including a 9-day wilderness expedition and explorer tours of Mount Cook and Mackenzie Country.

Edgewater Adventures Ltd

59a Brownston Street, Wanaka
☎/**fax:** (3) 443 8422
email: ewa@clear.net.nz
Small group discovery and adventure tours of the South Island. Trips include heritage, trekking and camping.

Glacier Discoveries

P.O. Box 32, Mount Cook National Park
☎ (3) 435 1890 **fax:** (3) 435 0893
email: charles@outside.z.com
Take a glacial lake boat trip in Mount Cook National Park. The trip explores Mueller Glacier Lake and includes a short trek on the Mueller Glacier.

High Country Explorer

6 Fraser Place, Rangiora
☎/**fax:** (3) 377 1391 **freecall** ☎ 0800 863 975
email: High-Country@xtra.co.nz
website: www.high-country.co.nz
This half-day tour takes you into the Southern Alps by coach, where you then take a 4WD safari followed by a jet boat river cruise. You can also take a full-day tour that includes a TranzAlpine train journey as well.

FOSSICKING

Fossicking means searching or rummaging for gems, minerals or fossils. It is particularly popular in Australia, which is rich in mineral deposits. You won't get rich but it's great fun.

NORTHERN TERRITORY & SOUTH AUSTRALIA

In Northern Territory you can fossick for garnets, aquamarine, quartz, amethyst, and gold.

AAT King's Tours

P.O. Box 696, Alice Springs, NT 0871
☎ (8) 8952 1700 **toll free** ☎ 1800 334 009
fax: (8) 8952 8028
email: austour@aatkings.com.au
Operate a 4WD journey to the old gold town of Arltunga, then take you to the gemfields where you can try your hand at fossicking.

The Gemtree

Plenty Hwy, P.O. Box 8895, Alice Springs
☎ (8)8956 9855
Self-drive fossicking trips from roadhouse.

QUEENSLAND
North Queensland Miner's Den

55 McLeod Street, Cairns, QLD 4870
or P.O. Box 7429, Cairns, QLD 4870
☎ (7) 4051 4413 **fax:** (7) 4031 2056
email: goldmine@ozemail.com.au
George Mayer is the manager of this specialist fossicking shop. Detector hire, jewellery and lapidary, gold pans, and sieves.

FOUR-WHEEL-DRIVE TOURS

A 4WD tour can vary from a half-day's sightseeing trip to a 3-week safari. The trips give you the chance to see remote and otherwise inaccessible landscapes. They are often combined with other adventure activities and are particularly suited to the vast landscape of Australia.

WESTERN AUSTRALIA
Global Gypsies PTY. Ltd

P.O. Box 123, Scarborough, Perth, WA 6922
☎ (8) 9341 6727 **fax:** (8) 9205 1330
email: info@globalgypsies.com.au
website: www.globalgypsies.com.au
Drive yourself on fully escorted 4WD safaris—tuition is part of the package. Trips include Perth to Alice Springs safari or Sydney.

Gold 'n' Valley Tours

91 Mullaloo Drive, Mullaloo, WA
☎ (8) 9401 1505 **fax:** (8) 9401 1507
email: gnvt@iinet.net.au
website: www.iinet.net.au/~gnvt
Their outback discovery tour includes a night at a sheep station and lots of wildflowers.

Safari Treks
Unit 1, 11 Foundry Street, Maylands, WA
☎ (8) 9271 1271 **fax:** (8) 9271 9901
email: info@safaritreks.com.au
website: www.safaritreks.com.au
Operate day and extended 4WD tours all over
Australia, specializing in wildflowers, wildlife
and photographic safaris. Run an 8-day tour to
Mount Augustus, the largest rock in the world.

Travelabout
88 Guthrie Street, Osborne Park, WA 6017
☎ (8) 9244 1200 **toll free** ☎ 1800 621 200
fax: (8) 9445 2284
email: travel@travelabout.au.com
website: www.travelabout.au.com
Various 4WD inclusive adventure tours on offer,
lasting anything from 4 to 24 days. Trips may
include hiking, swimming or dolphin watching.

West Coast Explorer
33 Lucich Street, Kelmscott, Perth, WA 6111
☎ (8) 9495 1210 **fax:** (8) 9495 1640
email: westcoast@highway1.com.au
website: www.highway1.com.au/westcoast
4WD camping tours of 7 or 15 days, operating
between Perth, Broome, and Darwin. Tours
include hiking, swimming, and climbing.

NORTHERN TERRITORY & SOUTH AUSTRALIA
Billy Can Tours
See Camping Safaris for details.

Sahara Outback Tours
P.O. Box 3891, Alice Springs, NT 0871
☎ (8) 8953 0881 **toll free** ☎ 1800 806 240
fax:(8) 8953 2414
email: sahara@saharatours.com.au
website: www.saharatours.com.au
Established for over 10 years, this outfit runs
small group 4WD camping safaris to Ayers
Rock, Kings Canyon, and Kakadu.

Wilderness Challenge Safaris
15 Panguna Street, Trinity Beach, QLD 4879
☎ (7) 4055 6504 **fax:** (7) 4057 7226
Wide variety of 4WD tours from day trips to
accommodated or camping safaris such as 5
days in Cape York, or 16 days in the Kimberley.

Wilpena Pound Resort
Wilpena Pound, SA 5434
☎ (8) 8648 0004 **toll free** ☎ for bookings only
1800 805 802 **fax:** (8) 8648 0028
email: wilpena@adelaide.on.net
website: www.wilpenapound.on.net
4WD tours through the Flinders Ranges and
the Outback. Half and full-day tours available,
and you can "tag along" in your own vehicle.

QUEENSLAND
Top Tours
P.O. Box 224, Torquay, QLD 4655
☎ (7) 4125 3933 **fax:** (7) 4125 4199
email: toptours@bigpond.com.au
website: www.fraserislandtours.com.au
4WD tours of Fraser Island, a World Heritage
site. Optional scenic flight.

NEW SOUTH WALES & VICTORIA
Cox's River Escapes
P.O. Box 81, Leura, NSW 2780
☎ (2) 4784 1621 **fax:** (2) 4784 2450
email: coxrivesc@autralis.net.au
Run small group 4WD tours to more remote
parts of the Blue Mountains as well as Six Foot
Track camping expeditions.

Mountain Top Experience
45 McLean Street, Morwell, VIC 3840
☎ (3) 5134 6876 **fax:** (3) 5133 0975
email: camier@latrobe.net.au
website: www.latrobe.net.au/camier
4WD tours through the wild mountains and
rivers of Gippsland, led by Ron and Andrea
Camier, who have over 25 years' experience in
4WD tours. Personalized passenger and "tag-
along" tours available.

6WD Bushmobile Tours and Expeditions
26 Paxton Crescent, Cherrybrook, NSW 2126
☎ (2) 9680 4664 **fax:** (2) 9634 1863
Not 4 but 6 wheeled vehicles are used for 1-, 2-
and 8-day tours throughout New South Wales,
between Sep and Apr. From May to Sep the
company operates expeditions across the
deserts of Australia.

NORTH ISLAND
Coromandel Four Wheel Bike Safaris
1 Blackjack Road, Kuaotunu, Rd 2, Whitianga
☎ (7) 866 2034 **fax:** (7) 866 2034
email: C4bikes@kiwiadv.co.nz
website: http://kiwiadv.co.nz/Coromandel/
CFWBSafari.htm
Guided bush safaris on quad-bikes. Trips last
around 4 hours and no experience is necessary.
Experienced quad bikers can join a Glow Worm
Safari to a cave, including night riding.

FOUR-WHEEL-DRIVE TOURS

Cross Country Tours
P.O. Box 10224, Te Rapa, Hamilton
☎ (7) 849 3949 **fax:** (7) 849 3320
email: CCR@thenet.co.nz
Specialize in small-group 4WD adventures.

Mount Tarawera 4WD Tours
P.O. Box 3252, Hawkes Bay Mail Centre, Napier
☎ (6) 843 2510 **mobile** ☎ 21 648 486
fax: 21 785 486
email: mttarawera@xtra.co.nz
website: http://kiwiadv.co.nz/Volcanic
/MtTarawera4WD.htm
Tours to the crater rim of the Mt Tarawera,
include Waiotapu geothermal area, where you
can swim in a hot thermal mineral stream.

SOUTH ISLAND
Unimog 4WD Adventure Tours
Clifton Road, Greymouth
☎ (3) 768 6649 **fax:** (3) 768 9149
email: Paul@newzealandholiday.co.nz
Serious 4WD touring adventures that take you
right off the road.

NORTH ISLAND
Marine Helicopters Ltd
The Agrodome Leisure Park, P.O. Box 291
Rotorua
☎ (7) 357 2512 **fax:** (7) 357 2502
email: mhinz@xtra.co.nz
Choose from a variety of helicopter sightseeing
trips, including a landing on White Island, New
Zealand's most active volcano. Heli jet boating
and heli fishing also available.

Tarawera Helicopters
Te Whakarewarewa Thermal Valley
Hemo Road, P.O. Box 6104, Rotorua
☎ (7) 348 1223 **fax:** (7) 349 3709
Scenic flights over the thermal pools and lakes
of the Rotorua region.

Volcanic Air Safaris
P.O. Box 640, Rotorua
☎ (7) 348 9984 **fax:** (7) 348 4069
email: volcanicair@xtra.co.nz
Helicopter and small aircraft tours over Mount
Tarawera and thermal area.

HELICOPTER FLIGHTS

Helicopter flights give you the feeling of adventure without the effort. They give you a great
view of the landscape and are the perfect way
of viewing sights such as Uluru (Ayers Rock) in
Northern Territory.

NORTHERN TERRITORY & SOUTH AUSTRALIA
Professional Helicopter Services
Yulara
☎ (8) 8956 2003 **fax:** (8) 8956 2788
email: or phsrock@topend.com.au
website: www.phs.com.au
Headquarters: Bundora Pde, Moorabbin
Airport, Mentone, VIC
☎ (3) 9580 7433
Cheaper of the 2 helicopter operations flying
over Ayers Rock and Kings Canyon.

QUEENSLAND
Heli-Adventures
Hangar 10, General Aviation, Cairns
International Airport, QLD
☎ (7) 4034 9066 **fax:** (7) 4034 9077
email: info@heliadventures.com.au
website: www.heliadventures.com.au
Helicopter trips over the rainforest, that can be
combined with rafting and diving adventures.

HORSE RIDING/TREKKING

You get two adventures in one here: a ride on a
strange horse through unspoilt countryside and
a chance to see remote areas that would be
inaccessible to vehicles. There are plenty of
treks for experienced riders—but several operators also cater for beginners.

NORTHERN TERRITORY & SOUTH AUSTRALIA
Ossie's Outback Horse Treks
33 Cavenagh Crescent, Alice Springs, NT 0870
☎ (8) 8952 2308 **toll free** ☎ 1800 628 211
fax: (8) 8952 2211
email: ossies@topend.com.au
Operate various day and overnight horse trails
around Alice Springs.

QUEENSLAND
Ride World Wide
Staddon Farm, North Tawton, Devon
EX20 2BX, U.K.
☎ (01837) 82544 **fax:** (01837) 82170
email: rideww@aol.com
website: www.rideworldwide.co.uk
Specialist operator running 7-night riding
holidays based at a stud farm in Queensland.
Not suitable for beginners. Also offer a number
of riding holidays in New Zealand.

NEW SOUTH WALES & VICTORIA
Dinner Plain Trail Rides

P.O. Box 31 Dinner Plain, VIC 3898

☎ (3) 5159 6445 **fax:** (3) 5159 6515

This company offers stunning horse trail rides in the Alpine High Country. Half-day, full-day and extended tours are available.

Mountain Escapes

See Bushwalking for details.

Pack Saddlers

Green Gully, Megalong Valley, NSW 2785

☎ (2) 4787 9150 **fax:** (2) 4787 9158

Trail rides from 1 hour to a full day, through forest and along riverbanks in the Blue Mountains.

Reynella Kosciuszko Rides

Reynella, Adaminaby, NSW 2630

☎ (2) 6454 2469 **toll free** ☎ 1800 029 909

fax: (2) 6454 2530

email: reynella@snowy.net.au

website: www.snowy.net.au/~reynella

Roslyn and John Rudd have been running horse treks in the Snowies for over 25 years.

Stoney's Bluff and Beyond Trail Rides

P.O. Box 287, Mansfield, VIC 3722

☎ (3) 5775 2212 **fax:** (3) 5775 2598

email: stoneys@mansfield.net.au

website: www.stoneys.com.au

Various horse riding trips led by mountain horsemen. Trips vary from 2 hour rides, to full-day excursions and 7- to 18-day rides.

NORTH ISLAND
Jakes Horse Trekking

Mitimiti, RD 2 Kohukohu, North Hokianga

☎ (9) 409 5003

Horse treks especially designed to lead to historical Maori sites. All levels of experience catered for.

North River Treks

Helmsdale Road, RD 2 Waipu, Northland

☎ (9) 432 0565 **toll free** ☎ 0800 743 344

fax: (9)432 0562

email: northrvr@igrin.co.nz

website: http://kiwiadv.co.nz/Northland /NorthRiverTrek.htm

Operate a range of trips from 1 hour to 2 days, through the native bush and river trails of Northland. Some trips take you to a working sheep and cattle station, as well as the caverns and glow-worm grottoes of Waipu Caves.

Te Urewera Adventures of NZ

P.O. Box 102-081, North Shore Mail Centre Rororua

☎ (9) 486 5494 **fax:** 21 785 486

email: biddlemarg@clear.net.nz

website: http://kiwiadv.co.nz/Bayof Plenty/TeUrewera.htm

Trek through ancient Maori lands of mountain and bush. Choose from treks of 3, 5 and 7 days.

SOUTH ISLAND
Alpine Horse Safaris

Waitohi Downs, Hawarden, North Canterbury

☎ (3) 314 4293 **fax:** (3) 314 4293

email: alpinehorse@kiwiadv.co.nz

Lawrie and Jenny O'Carroll offer moderate to challenging horse treks through the rugged alpine landscapes of North Canterbury.

Huruni Horse Treks

Taihoa Downs, RD, Hawarden

North Canterbury

☎**/fax:** (3) 314 4204

email: StanleyR@xtra.co.nz

Horse trekking tours around Lake Sumner Forest Park and the Huruni River. Trips last from 2 to 8 days.

Kowhai Equestrian Farm Stay

Island Road, View Hill, Oxford

North Canterbury

☎ (3) 312 4309 **fax:** (3) 312 3079

email: kowhai@caverock.net.nz

Chris Thomas specializes in professional horse riding instruction and shorter treks of up to 2 days. Riding lessons include dressage, showjumping and cross country.

Nic Kagan Guiding

2 RD Cromwell, Central Otago

☎ (3) 445 1444

email: nic.kagan@xtra.co.nz

website: www.nzsouth.co.nz/kagan/

Nic Kagan offers pack horse treks lasting from 2 to 10 days, retracing old gold miners and settlers routes. You usually spend up to 6 hours a day in the saddle and should be fit enough to walk downhill for up to an hour.

JET BOATING

Wet, wild, and extremely exciting. Jet boating trips power you along at incredible speeds—and you don't have to move a muscle. You won't see much of the landscape but you'll certainly get your adrenalin flowing. Jet boats were invented to operate on the often shallow and difficult rivers of New Zealand's South Island and the most famous locations are still the Shotover, Kawarau, and Dart rivers.

TASMANIA
Huon River Jet Boats
P.O. Box 159, Huonville, TAS 7116
☎ (3) 6264 1838 **fax:** (3) 6264 1031
Year round 35-minute jet boat trips, with commentary, on the Huon River.

NORTH ISLAND
Eastern Bay Jet Tours
P.O. Box 566, Opotiki
☎/**fax:** (7) 315 4632 **mobile** ☎ 025 761 158
Operate jet boat rides up the Motu River, lasting 1 or 2 hours. Shorter trips also available.

River Spirit Jetboat Tours
Campbell Road, RD1, Whanganui
☎ (6)342 1718 **fax:** (6)342 1748
Operate a range of tours on the scenic Whanganui River. Tours last from 1 to 2 hours.

SOUTH ISLAND
Jet Thrills River Tours
P.O. Box 102 081, North Shore Mail Centre, Canterbury
☎ (9) 486 5494 **fax:** 21 785 486
email: JetThrills@kiwiadv.co.nz
website: http://kiwiadv.co.nz/Canterbury/JetThrill.htm
A 35-minute trip on the Waimakariri River can also be combined with a helicopter ride.

Shotover Jet
See p. 284 for details.
Exciting experience includes 360-degree spin.

MOTORCYCLE TOURS

This is one for those who love the thrill of the open road. Plenty of places hire motorcycles in both Australia and New Zealand and you can join one of the many motorcycle guided tours.

NORTHERN TERRITORY & SOUTH AUSTRALIA
Uluru Motorcycle Tours
P.O. Box 75, Yulara, NT 0872
☎ (8) 8956 2019 **fax:** (8) 8956 2196
email: harleys@topend.com.au
website: www.topend.com.au/~harleys

Passenger tours on the back of a Harley Davidson, will take you to Uluru (Ayers Rock) and back. Longer tours to the Olgas or Kings Canyon are also available, as are self-ride tours.

QUEENSLAND
Australian Motorcycle Adventures
C/o Metro Yamaha, 424 Samford Road Enoggera, QLD 4051
Offer self-guided tours and guided group tours, both on- and off-road. Tours include the Bush Biker Tour of Australia, where clients can travel and camp in small groups throughout Queensland, fully supported by 4WD and experienced guides.

NEW SOUTH WALES & VICTORIA
Easyrider Motorbike Tours
P.O. Box 2654
Sydney, NSW 2001
☎ (2) 9247 2477 **fax:** (2) 9221 4348
email: ride@easyrider.com.au
website: www.easyrider.com.au
Operate short tours of Sydney, riding as a pillion passenger. Also offer night tours and adventure trips.

NORTH ISLAND
New Zealand Motorcycle Rentals
31 Beach Road, Downtown, Auckland
☎ (9) 377 2005 **fax:** (9)377 2006
email: info@nzbike.com
and 166 Gloucester Street, Christchurch
☎ (3) 377 0663 **fax:** (3) 377 0623
email: chch@nzbike.com
website: www.nzbikes.com/tours.htm
Motorcycle hire shops offering fully and semi-guided tours, lasting from 5 to 18 days. They also offer an outback riding adventure tour.

SOUTH ISLAND
GoTourNZ.com
P.O. Box 674, 82 Achilles Avenue, Nelson 7015
mobile ☎ 21 969 071 **fax:** 021 218 0394
email: mctours@gotournz.com
website: www.gotournz.com
Run inclusive bike tours with an "off the beaten track" theme to places usually missed off the standard tourist itinerary. You will also have the opportunity to participate in various other adventure activities, such as bungee jumping, and whale watching. Bikes are valeted every day and they even lay on a support coach for non-riding partners.

MOUNTAINBIKING

Cycling with a harder edge, mountainbike tours generally require you to be fairly fit as the bikes allow you to cover some rough country. Guided tours are widely available and you can choose from trips lasting just a few hours to a few days. (See also Cycling, above.)

NORTHERN TERRITORY & SOUTH AUSTRALIA
Rolling On Mountain Bike Tours
P.O. Box 19, Hove, SA 5048
☎/fax: (8) 8358 2401
email: rolling@dove.net.au
website: rolling.mtx.net/tours.htm
Run cycle tours throughout the year in South Australia. Tours vary from 2-week wine and wildlife trips to 1- and 2-day adventures in the Barossa Valley or Southern Vales.

Steve's Mountain Bike Tours
P.O. Box 8670, Alice Springs, NT 0871
☎/fax: (8) 8952 1542 mobile ☎ 0417 863 800
Rugged off-road tours in the foothills of McDonnell Ranges.

QUEENSLAND
The Adventure Company, Australia
See p. 266 for details.
Two-day mountainbike tour in Atherton Tablelands. Chance to see duck-billed platypus.

NEW SOUTH WALES & VICTORIA
Bushsports Adventures
See Abseiling, Climbing and Mountaineering.

NORTH ISLAND
Auckland Adventures
See Exploration and Adventure Tours, for details.
Operate a full-day mountainbike adventure around Auckland, with experienced guides.

SOUTH ISLAND
Alpine and Heli
P.O. Box 257, Wanaka
☎ (3) 443 8943 mobile ☎ 025 331 714
Heli biking and alpine biking. Ridge ride the highest mountainbike track in New Zealand.

Heli Bike
P.O. Box 56, Twizel
freecall ☎ 0800 435 424 fax: (3) 435 0626
email: A.Shearer@xtra.co.nz

Heli bike trips combine a helicopter flight in the Mount Cook region with a guided mountainbike ride down high country farm tracks.

SAILING

The coastline of Australia offers some great sailing—and you don't have to be experienced as there are plenty of companies offering skippered trips to neighbouring islands and wildlife sites.

QUEENSLAND
Sunvil Activity Holidays
Sunvil House, Upper Square, Old Isleworth
Middlesex TW7 7BJ, U.K.
☎ (020) 8232 9779 fax: (020) 8758 4788
email: activity@sunvil.co.uk
Bareboat sailing around the Whitsunday Islands including tuition, liveaboard and shore-based options.

The Adventure Company, Australia
See p. 266 for details.

NEW SOUTH WALES & VICTORIA
Sail Australia
P.O. Box 417, Cremorne, NSW 2090
☎ (2) 9960 6111 fax: (2) 9960 7009
email: aka@iinet.net.au
website: sailaustralia.com.au
Sailing tours of Sydney Harbour, either with an experienced skipper or sailing yourself.

SCENIC FLIGHTS AND ADVENTURE FLIGHTS

Have a passive adventure and admire the mountains and deserts from above. If you're more adventurous you can take an aerobatic flight, where the view will be the last thing on your mind. As you might expect in a country that prides itself on its adventure activities, New Zealand offers flights with a difference. You can loop-the-loop in an aerobatic flight or pilot yourself in a tethered plane—the closest you can come to flying without a pilot's licence.

WESTERN AUSTRALIA
Kookaburra Air
105 Corinthian Road, Shelley
☎ (8) 9354 1158 fax: (8) 9354 5898
email: aka@iinet.net.au

ACTIVITIES A–Z

SCENIC FLIGHTS AND ADVENTURE FLIGHTS

website: kookaburra.iinet.net.au
Run a range of air safaris, combining flights with ground tours. They also offer a flight around Perth, or a short introduction to flying with a chance to fly the plane yourself.

NORTHERN TERRITORY & SOUTH AUSTRALIA
Aboriginal Air Services
P.O. Box 1238, Alice Springs, NT 0871
☎ (8) 8953 5000 **fax:** (8) 8953 4410
Join an Outback flight delivering mail and passengers to remote Aboriginal communities.

NEW SOUTH WALES & VICTORIA
Dakota National Air
Office 3, Building 483, Airport Avenue, Bankstown, NSW 2200
☎ (2) 9791 9900 **fax:** (2) 9791 9285
This company has a fleet of DC-3 aircraft and offers scenic flights over Sydney, and full-day winery tours to the Hunter Valley.

TASMANIA
Tasair Pty Ltd
Cambridge Aerodrome, P.O. Box 451E
Hobart, TAS
☎ (3) 6248 5088
email: herit@southcom.com.au
website: www.view.com.au/tasair
Scenic flights to Tasmania and coastal areas.

NORTH ISLAND
Fly by Wire
11 St Mary Street, Wellington
mobile ☎ 025 300 300 **fax:** (4) 499 8383
email: neilharrap@hotmail.com
website: www.flybywire.co.nz
Not flying as such. You control a high-speed, tethered plane.

SOUTH ISLAND
Air Fiordland
Queenstown Airport, P.O. Box 2055
Queenstown
☎ (3) 442 3404 **fax:** (3) 442 3526
email: airfiord@airfiordland.co.nz
Scenic flights from Queenstown or Te Anau, over Fiordland and Milford Sound.

Air Tours Kaikoura
P.O. Box 40, Kaikoura
☎ (3) 319 5986 **fax:** (3) 319 6262
email: AirKra@kiwiadv.co.nz
Operate a range of sperm whale-watching flights, lasting from 30 minutes.

Alpine Scenic Flights
P.O. Box 71, Lake Tekapo
☎ (3) 680 6880 **fax:** (3) 680 6740
email: sales@airsafaris.co.nz
website: www.airsafaris.co.nz
A variety of air safaris are available, taking you over New Zealand's highest mountains. Flights last from 30 to 50 minutes and trips include a Grand Traverse of Mount Cook and Westland National Parks.

Biplane Adventures
P.O. Box 121, Wanaka
☎ (3) 443 1000 **fax:** (3) 443 1006
email: biplane@skyshow.co.nz
website: www.biplane-adventures.co.nz
Hold on to your stomach for a scenic flight with a difference. Take a spectacular aerobatic flight in a purpose built biplane and experience the loops, rolls, G-force, and even scary upside-down flying.

Southern Air
Invercargill Airport, P.O. Box 860, Invercargill
☎ (3) 218 9129 **fax:** (3) 214 4681
email: sthnair@xtra.co.nz
This company offers a scenic flight landing at Mason's Bay, where you can do a 4-hour bush walk with the opportunity of spotting kiwis.

SEA KAYAKING

Sea kayaking is becoming more and more popular and allows you to explore the coastline at a leisurely pace. It also gives you the chance to get up close to marine mammals and birds. You do not have to be experienced as most operators have courses and trips suited to beginners as well as seasoned kayakers. In Australia there are excellent coastal waters off Queensland, Tasmania, Victoria, and New South Wales. New Zealand's best spots for sea kayaking are the Bay of Islands, Stewart Island, and Abel Tasman National Park. The nationally recognized industry association is S.K.O.A.N.Z. (Sea Kayak Operators Association of New Zealand).

QUEENSLAND
The Adventure Company, Australia
See p. 266 for details.
Three-day sea kayaking trip around the Barnard Islands. A chance to see lots of varied sealife, including spectacular sea eagles overhead.

New South Wales & Victoria
Central Coast Kayak Tours
2/227 The Round Drive, Avoca Beach
NSW 2251
☎/fax: (2) 4381 0342
email: wayne@kayaktours.com
website: www.kayaktours.com
Choose from a range of guided kayak adventures graded according to your abilities.

Meridian Kayak Adventures
12 Clonard Avenue, Elsternwick, VIC 3185
☎/fax: (3) 9596 8876
email: meridian@ocean.com.au
website: www.meridiankayak.com.au
Explore Victoria's coastline with ACF qualified guides and instructors.

Outland Expeditions
See Abseiling, Climbing and Mountaineering.

Tasmania
Coastal Kayaks
P.O. Box 403, Sandy Bay, TAS 7006
☎ (3) 6257 0500 **fax:** (3) 6257 0447
email: coastalkayak@vision.net.au
website: www.view.com.au/coastalkayak
One-, 3- and 5-day trips on Freycinet
Peninsular, staying in a wilderness camp.

Rafting Tasmania
See Canoeing for details.

South Island
Abel Tasman Kayaks
Marahau Beach, RD 2, Motueka, Nelson
toll free ☎ 0800 527 8022 **fax:** (3) 527 8032
email: outside@kayaktours.co.nz
website: www.travelmedia.co.nz/level3/kayak
Experienced company operating 1-, 3- and 4-day tours in the Abel Tasman National Park.

Abel Tasman National Park
P.O. Box 351, Motueka, Nelson
☎ (3) 528 7675 **fax:** (3) 528 0297
email: ate@abeltasman.co.nz
website: www.abeltasman.co.nz
Operate 3- and 5-day sea kayaking and trekking trips including the seal colony at Tonga Island.

Cable Bay Kayaks
Cable Bay Road, RD 1, Nelson
☎/fax: (3) 545 0332
email: rapidriver@xtra.co.nz
Guided sea kayaking trips exploring the intricate coastline of the Pepin Islands.

Naturally New Zealand Holidays
See Cycling, for details

Ocean River Adventure Co.
Marahau Beach, RD 2, Motueka
☎ (3) 527 8266 **freecall** ☎ 0800 732 529
email: ocean.river@xtra.co.nz
Offering guided tours and rentals from 1 to 3 days.

Stewart Island Sea Kayaking Adventures
Innes' Backpackers, Argyle Street, P.O. Box 32, Stewart Island
☎/fax: (3) 219 1080
email: InnesBackpack@kiwiadv.co.nz
Operate a week-long sea kayaking trip around the coast of Paterson Inlet.

North Island
Auckland Wilderness Kayaking Ltd
P.O. Box 20 467, Glen Eden, Auckland
☎/fax: (9) 813 3369 or ☎ (9) 813 3399 (bookings only)
email: gowild@nzkayak.co.nz
website: www.nzkayak.co.nz
Operate a range of sea kayaking trips including a full day to Rangitoto, twilight and moonlight kayaking, and an overnight trip to Mahurangi.

The Little Adventure Company
P.O. Box 32384, Devonport, Auckland
☎ (9) 446 6335
email: littleadventure@paradise.net.nz
website: www.littleadventure.co.nz
Tours along the Auckland shore, lasting from 1 hour to a full day.

SKIING

You can ski from Jun to Oct in the Southern Hemisphere. The best skiing in Australia is in the **Snowy Mountains** (see p. 271) and **Victoria**, but there is also some skiing, particularly cross-country, in **Tasmania**. New Zealand, too, has some fine ski areas. The main areas on North Island are **Whakapapa** and **Turoa**, while on South Island they are centred on **Queenstown** and **Wanaka**. Many operators offer heli skiing, where helicopters take you to areas of deep powder snow. For a good overview of all skiing opportunities in the Southern Hemisphere check the website **www.goski.com**.

NEW SOUTH WALES

See p. 271.

VICTORIA
Mount Buller Ski Area
☎ (57) 776 052 **fax:** (57) 776 027
website: www.skibuller.com.au
The largest lift system and the most marked runs in the state. Has a big ski school and is home to the Australian Ski Institute.

Falls Creek Ski Area
PO Box 55
Falls Creek, VIC 3699
☎ (57) 583 3100 **fax:** (57) 583 337
website: www.fallscreek.net
With expansion planned, Falls Creek is already a world class resort with 22 lifts and 14km (9 miles) of cross country trails.

NORTH ISLAND
Whakapapa Ski Area
Private Bag, Mount Ruapehu
☎ (7) 892 3738 **fax:** (7) 892 3732
email: ski.whakapapa@xtra.co.nz
New Zealand's largest developed ski area. There is a stand along the beginner's area, trails for intermediate and expert skiers, and off-piste skiing. Snowboarding is also available.

SOUTH ISLAND
Alpine Guides Fox Glacier
Main Road, P.O. Box 38, Fox Glacier
☎ (3) 751 0825 **fax:** (3) 751 0857
email: foxguides@minidata.co.nz
Operate moderate to challenging adventures including glacier skiing, full- and half-day glacier walks, heli hikes, and ice-climbing.

Southern Alps Guiding
P.O. Box 15, Twizel, Mt Cook Region
☎ (3) 435 0890 **fax:** (3) 435 0893
email: harles@outside.nz.com
Internationally qualified guides offer guiding service for heli skiing, as well as heli trekking and mountaineering.

SKYDIVING

Jumping out of a plane would count as an adventure in most people's book. To do so over the unique landscapes of Australia or New Zealand is particularly special. There are plenty of qualified outfits able to take you skydiving, and training courses are available.

QUEENSLAND
Skydive Cairns
Unit 1/6 Tom McDonald Drive, General Aviation Cairns Airport, QLD 4870
☎ (7) 4035 9662 **fax:** (7) 4035 9658
email: admin@skydive.net.au
website: www.skydive.net.au
Take a half-day tandem skydive from 2400m (8,000 ft). No experience is necessary and the company are members of the Australian Parachute Federation.

NEW SOUTH WALES & VICTORIA
Total Control Skydivers
P.O. Box 13162, Lawcourts Post Office
Melbourne 8010
☎ (4) 1854 5154 **fax:** (3) 9383 2846
email: skydive@totalcontrol.com.au
website: www.totalcontrol.com.au/skydive
Skydiving from several locations north of Melbourne. First jump courses for beginners are available.

NORTH ISLAND
Volcanic Wunderflites
Rotorua Airport, Te Ngae Road, P.O. Box 118 Rotorua
☎/**fax:** (7) 345 6077
email: volwunflt@kiwiadv.co.nz
website: kiwiadv.co.nz/Volcanic/VolcWunderflite.htm
Operate flights over spectacular volcanic scenery. Trips include Mt Ruapehu volcano; Waimangu Thermal Valley; and White Island volcano, one of the most active in the world, with continual eruptions of steam and ash.

Wairarapa Pilot and Parachute Centre
Hood Aerodrome, South Road RD 5, Masterton
mobile ☎ 025 428 805 **fax:** (6)378 8143
email: flight-training@contact.net.nz
website: kiwiadv.co.nz/Wairarapa/WPCintro.htm
Offer tandem skydiving adventures (no experience needed) and accelerated free fall courses. Accelerated free fall covers 9 graduated skydives—stage 1 involves 6 hours training, followed by a jump the next day.

SOUTH ISLAND
Tandem Skydive Nelson Ltd
19 Tamaki Street, Nelson
☎ (3) 548 7652 or (3) 546 4444
fax: (3) 546 4242
email: tandem@skydive.co.nz

website: www.nelson.co.nz/skydive/index.html
Small company owned by skydive enthusiasts.
No experience is needed and you can choose
from skydives at 2,133m, 2,743m, and 3,658m
(7,000, 9,000, and 12,000 ft respectively).

SNORKELLING

Even if you don't fancy scuba diving you will be
able to go snorkelling. It is a great way of seeing
the rich marine life without having to undergo a
long training session. Many operators who offer
diving trips also offer snorkelling.

QUEENSLAND
The following companies all offer diving and
snorkelling trips—for their details see above,
under Diving: **Compass Outer Barrier Reef
Trips; Oceania Dive; Quicksilver
Connections Ltd, Reef Encounters** and
Tusa Dive.

NORTH ISLAND
Palliser Dive and Safari
Kahutara Road, RD2, Featherston, Wellington
☎ (6)308 8362 **mobile** ☎ 025 440 690
Small-group, guided snorkelling and 4WD tours
of Wairarapa's southern and eastern coastlines.
Holders of approved Marine Mammals Licence
for swimming with seals.

SURFING

Australia and New Zealand are just full of surf-
ing possiblities and there are even surf schools
so you don't have to make a fool of yourself.
Some of the best known surfing areas in New
Zealand are Raglan, the Mahia Peninsular,
Palliser Bay, Greymouth, and Kaikoura.

NEW SOUTH WALES & VICTORIA
Sydney Safe Surf School
102 Austral Street, Malabar, NSW 2036
☎ (2) 9311 2834 **fax:** (2) 9349 2602
Individual or group surfing lessons at Maroubra
and Coogee beaches.

Westcoast Adventure and
Westcoast Surf School
Miranda Close, Torquay, VIC 3228
☎/fax: (3) 5261 2241
This outfit offers surfing lessons at some of
Australia's best surf beaches. There are classes
suitable for all abilities, from beginners to

experienced. They can also arrange other
adventure activities such as rock climbing,
abseiling, and trail bike tours.

TREKKING

Walking, trekking, hiking or tramping, whatever
you call it, this has to be the best possible way
to see a country. You'll get great exercise, you
will see wildlife and meet people. It's much the
same thing as bushwalking. If you aren't fit, or
haven't done much hiking before, choose a day
trip or one that does not involve many hours of
hiking each day. Check too whether you have to
carry a pack or not, and wear in your boots
before you go.

QUEENSLAND
**The Adventure Company,
Australia**
See p. 266 for details.

NEW SOUTH WALES & VICTORIA
Auswalk
P.O. Box 516, Jindabyne, NSW 2627
☎ (2) 6457 2220 **fax:** (2) 6457 2206
email: monica@auswalk.com.au
website: www.auswalk.com.au
Based in the Snowy Mountains, this specialist
offers inn-to-inn and centre-based holidays.

Walks Worldwide
25 Mount Carmel Street, Derby DE23 6TB, U.K.
☎ (01332) 230883 **fax:** (01332) 360851
email: sales@walksworldwide.com
website: www.walksworldwide.com
Inclusive, self-guided hiking tours in New
South Wales. Hiking is from inn to inn, with
your baggage sent on ahead. Tours range from
mountain treks to bushwalking and are available to suit all abilities.

TASMANIA
Craclair Tours
P.O. Box 516, Devonport 7310
☎/fax: (3) 6424 7833
email: craclair@southcom.com.au
website: craclair@southcom.com.au/~craclair
Long-running tour operator, offering an 8- to
10-day camping trip along the Overland Track.

Walks Worldwide
See New South Wales/Victoria, above.
Offer an escorted 6-day tour along the
Overland Track.

NORTH ISLAND

New Zealand Nature Safaris
52 Holborn Drive, Stokes Valley 6008
☎ 025 360 268 **fax:** (4) 563 7324
email: mail@nzsafaris.co.nz
website: www.nzsafaris.co.nz
Operate small group, off-the-beaten-track
guided hiking holidays. Tours in both North and
South Islands last from 4 to 10 days.

The Walking Connection
4722 W. Continental Drive, Glendale
AZ85308-3440, U.S.A.
☎ (602) 978 1887 **fax:** (602) 978 5500
email: info@walkingconnection.com
website: www.walkingconnection.com
Offer an inclusive hiking tour covering the
North and South Islands of New Zealand.

SOUTH ISLAND

Abel Tasman National Park
See Sea Kayaking.

Adventure South Backroad Cycle Tours and Backcountry Walks
See Cycling for details. Small-group hiking
tours ranging from 5 to 10 days in length.

Banks Peninsular Track
Akaroa
☎ (3) 304 7612
email: bankstrack@xtra.co.nz
website: http://nz.com/webnz/bbnz/
bankstrk.htm
This 35km (22-mile) track is privately owned
and managed by local families in this remote
area.

Bush and Beyond
P.O. Box 376, Motueka
☎ (3) 528 9054 **fax:** (3) 526 6093
email: glenavon@xtra.co.nz
Easy to challenging guided hikes in Kahurangi
National Park. Trips last from 1 to 8 days.

Kahurangi Guided Walks
Dodson Road, RD 1, Takaka, Golden Bay
☎/fax: (3) 525 7177
email: CROXFORDS@xtra.co.nz;
Easy to challenging guided hikes in Kahurangi
National Park. Trips last from 1 to 8 days.

Kiwi Wilderness Walks
136 Palmerston Street, Riverton
☎ (3) 234 8886 **freecall** ☎ 0800 248 886
fax: (3) 234 8816
email: KIWIwalks@riverton.co.nz
Tours of Stewart Island and The Waitutu Track.

Mountain Recreation Ltd
P.O. Box 204, Wanaka
☎/fax: (3) 443 7330
email: geoffmtnrec@xtra.co.nz
Small-group guided treks on Mount Aspiring.
Treks and guided climb to the Bonar Glacier
and Mount French.

Routeburn Walk Ltd
P.O. Box 568, Queenstown
☎ (3) 442 8200 **fax:** (3) 442 6072
email: routeburn@xtra.co.nz
website: http://nz.com/SouthIs/Routeburn
Guided hikes through Fiordland and Mt
Aspiring National Parks.

Staveley Outdoor Experience
Flynns Road, Staveley, Mid Canterbury, RD 1
Ashburton
☎/fax: (3) 303 0862
email: Staveley@xtra.co.nz
Guided Mount Somers Walk with native bush,
historic sites, and unusual rock formations.

Upland Journeys
Milford Road, RD 1, Te Anau
☎ (3) 249 7492
email: upland@teanau.co.nz
website: http://webnz.com/upland/
Guided hikes in the Fiordland National Park.

WHALE (AND DOLPHIN) WATCHING

Whale watching is the ultimate passive adventure for many people and in the southern
hemisphere you will observe sperm whales, as
well as playful dolphins and rare whale sharks.
Some trips allow you to swim with dolphins.

WESTERN AUSTRALIA

Diving Ventures
See Diving, above, for details.

Dolphin Encounters Mandurah
4 Picaroon Place, Mandurah
mobile ☎ 0407 090 284 **fax:** (8) 9581 3679
email: kirbyhs@southwest.com.au
website: www.southwest.com.au/~kirby/
swims.html
Run a 2½ hour cruise to swim with dolphins.

QUEENSLAND

Top Tours

See Four-Wheel-Drive Tours for details.

NEW SOUTH WALES & VICTORIA

Coffs Harbour Marina

Booking Office, Coffs Harbour Marina, Coffs
Harbour, NSW 2450

☎/fax: (2) 6651 4612

Booking facilities for "parawhaling" trips during
whale migration season. Spot whales on a
cruise, includes a short parasailing experience.

Moonraker Dolphin Swims

2 St Aubins Way, Sorrento, VIC 3943

☎ (3) 5984 4211 fax: (3) 5984 4044

email: moonraker@surf.net.au

website: www.sx.com.au.moonraker.mondol

Trips to the southernmost point of Port Phillip
Bay, where you can swim with wild dolphins.

Moonshadow Charters

P.O. Box 192, Nelson Bay, NSW 2315

☎ (2) 4982 0666 fax: (2) 4984 6814

Operate whale watching cruises off the coast of
Nelson Bay. Cruises take place during the
migration season, between Jun to Jul and Sep
to Nov.

NORTH ISLAND

Bay of Islands Heritage Tours

Maritime Building, Marsden Road, P.O. Box 96
Paihia, Bay of Islands

☎ (9) 402 6288 fax: (9) 402 6808

Get a traditional Maori welcome as you board
the boat that will take you dolphin spotting. You
will have the chance to swim with dolphins.

Fullers Bay of Islands

Level 17, Westplaza, Custom Street, Auckland

☎ (9) 358 0260 fax: (9)303 0254

email: marketing@fullers-bay-of-islands.co.nz

website: www.fullers-bay-of-islands.co.nz

Cruises include a 4-hour catamaran trip to see
and swim with dolphins. Also run a "Cream
Trip" cruise, delivering mail to islands, with
plenty of wildlife spotting available enroute.

Quest for Nature

29 Straight Mile, Romsey, Hampshire SO51 9BB
U.K.

☎ (01794) 523500 fax: (01794) 523544

email: questfornature@compuserve.com

website: www.ornitholidays.co.uk

Run a 20-day escorted whale watching and natural history tour to New Zealand.

SOUTH ISLAND

Dolphin Encounter

58 West End, Kaikoura

☎ (3) 319 6777 fax: (3) 319 6534

email: info@dolphin.co.nz

website: www.dolphin.co.nz

New Zealand's first dolphin swimming and
watching operator runs trips 3 times a day.

Dolphin Watch

1 Hinton Road, Greymouth

☎ (3) 768 9770 fax: (3) 768 7538

Philip Low is a specialist on the rare Hector's
dolphin.

Dolphin Watch Marlborough

Next to Railway Station, Picton

☎ (3) 573 8040 fax: (3) 573 7906

Comprehensive eco tour that includes landing
on Motuara Island. Opportunity to see four different species of dolphin, seals, and seabirds.

Dolphin Experience Akaroa

32 Rue Balguerie, Akaroa

☎/fax: (3) 304 7866

email: dolphin.experience.@clear.net.nz

Swim with the fabulous wild Hector's dolphins.

Kaikoura Wildlife Centre

Westend Kaikoura, P.O. Box 85, Kaikoura

☎ (3) 319 6622 fax: (3) 319 6808

email: nzsz@southern.co.nz

Where you can swim with dolphins, snorkel
with fur seals, and watch sperm whales.

WHITE-WATER RAFTING AND ECO RAFTING

White-water rafting is popular in both Australia
and New Zealand, and is anything but a tame
paddle up a river. You don't have to be experienced, but make sure that your guides are
qualified before you set off and choose a trip
that is suited to beginners. Trips can last from
an hour to a few days. The high mountains of
New Zealand produce fast rivers that are ideal
for white-water rafting, with plenty of lively
rapids. Many operators are members of the
New Zealand River Guides Association, a volun-
tary body with high safety standards. In New
Zealand you may also see river sledding or surfing, which is essentially white-water
rafting—but without the raft. You ride down
the river holding a polystyrene board, wearing a
wetsuit and helmet.

QUEENSLAND
Foaming Fury
P.O. Box 460, Cairns, QLD 4870
☎ (7) 4031 3460 **toll free** ☎ 1800 801 540
fax: (7) 4031 7460
email: info@foamingfury.com.au
website: www.foamingfury.com.au
White-water rafting on the Russell, Barron and Johnstone rivers. Can be combined with a trip in a hot-air balloon.

Raft 'n' Rainforest Company
See p. 269.

NEW SOUTH WALES & VICTORIA
Peregrine Tours
See Ballooning for details.

Rapid Descents Whitewater Rafting
P.O. Box 65, Khancoban, NSW 2642
☎ (2) 6076 9111 **toll free** ☎ 1800 637 486 for bookings **fax:** (2) 6076 9112
email: rafting@rapiddescents.com.au
website: www.rapiddescents.com.au
Inclusive 1- and 2-day trips on the Upper Murray, Mitta Mitta, and Snowy rivers. Some trips can be combined with abseiling.

Upper Murray Whitewater Rafting
P.O. Box 63, Jindabyne, NSW 2627
☎**/fax:** (2) 6457 2002 **toll free** ☎ 1800 677 179 for bookings
email: rafting@snowy.net.au
White-water rafting on the Upper Murray River.

TASMANIA
Aardvark Adventures
See Abseiling, Climbing and Mountaineering.

Rafting Tasmania
See Canoeing for details. Owner/manager Graham Mitchell, among the first to raft the Franklin, has been down it over 100 times since. Also offer rafting trips on the Upper Gordon, Derwent, Mersey, and Picton rivers.

Tasmanian Wild River Adventures
P.O. Box 90, Sandy Bay, TAS 7006
mobile ☎ 0409 977 506
email: enquiries@wildrivers.com.au
website: www.wildrivers.com.au
Inclusive 5-, 7- or 11-day rafting trips on the Franklin River. Regular Grade IV rafting.

NORTH ISLAND
Great Kiwi Whitewater Co
122 Devon Street, Rotorua
☎ (7) 348 2144 **mobile** ☎ 025 872 910
fax: (7) 348 2144
email: sarathom@wave.co.nz
Experienced company offering challenging white-water experiences. They raft the Kaituna, Rangitaiki, and Wairoa rivers.

Wet n Wild
P.O. Box 601, Rotorua
☎ (7) 348 3191 **fax:** (7) 349 6567
email: wetnwild@wave.co.nz
website: www.wave.co.nz/pages/wetnwild
Operate a range of half-day rafting excursions and longer expeditions. The longer trips are on the Motu, Mohaka, and Clarence rivers. You can also combine rafting and jet boating.

SOUTH ISLAND
Alpine Rafts
47 Ogilvie Road, Gladstone, Westland
☎ (3) 755 8156 **freecall** ☎ 0800 223 456
fax: (3) 762 6152
email: newzealand.holidays@xtra.co.nz
Heli rafting specialists operate rafting trips in remote canyons, gorges, and natural hot springs. Water ranges from Grade III to V.

Pioneer Rafting
P.O. Box 102 081, NSMC, Otago
☎ (9) 486 5494
email: pioneeraft@kiwiadv.co.nz
http://kiwiadv.co.nz/Otago/PioneerRafting.htm
Eco adventures on the Clutha River. Trips range from half-a-day to 8-day Alps to Pacific expeditions. Their full-day excursion includes the chance to fossick for gold.

Rangitata Rafts
RD 20, Peel Forest, Geraldine
South Canterbury
☎ (3) 696 3534 **freecall** ☎ 0800 251 251
fax: (3) 696 3534
email: rangitatarafts@xtra.co.nz
website: www.rangitata.rafts.co.nz
NZRGA registered guides will take you on a 3-hour trip on the Rangitata River. Grade V water and a chance for some white-water swimming.

Ultimate Descents NZ
Lodder Lane, Riwaka, P.O. Box 208, Motueka
☎**/fax:** (3) 528 6363
email: info@rivers.co.nz
website: www.cyberskink.co.nz/rivers

White-water rafting trips lasting from 2 hours to 9 days. Destinations include Clarence River and Buller Gorge. Also offer heli rafting.

WILDLIFE

The unique wildlife found in Australia and New Zealand makes these ideal destinations for those who love getting out into the wilderness and being close to nature. Where else could you see kangaroos, kiwis, and koalas, as well as whales, dingos, and possums? If you want to see some of everything your best bet is to take a wildlife safari run by specialists.

Earthwatch

57 Woodstock Road, Oxford OX2 6HJ, U.K.
☎ (01865) 311600 **fax:** (01865) 311383
email: info@earthwatch.org
website: www.earthwatch.org
or 126 Bank Street, South Melbourne
VIC 3205, ☎ (3) 9682 6828
email: earth@earthwatch.org
Work as a paying volunteer alongside field scientists and researchers. Projects vary, but may include studying Australian forest marsupials, vanishing frogs or Queensland dolphins. There are also projects in New Zealand.

Falcon Tours

7/342 South Terrace, South Fremantle
WA 6162
☎ (8) 9336 3882 **fax:** (8) 9336 3930
This company specialize in inclusive, wilderness wildlife tours throughout Australia. Tours are guided by Simon Nevill, a professional wildlife guide and ornithologist.

Wildlife Worldwide

170 Selsdon Road, South Croydon, Surrey
CR2 6PJ, U.K.
☎ (020) 8667 9158 **fax:** (020) 8667 1960
email: sales@wildlifeworldwide.com
website: www.wildlifeworldwide.com
Tailor-made wildlife tours throughout Australia.

WESTERN AUSTRALIA
Coate's Wildlife Tours

P.O. Box 64, Bullcreek, WA 6149
☎ (8) 9455 6611 **fax:** (8) 9455 6621
Small-group, inclusive tours lasting from 6 to 17 days, to various parts of Western Australia, including the Christmas and Cocos Islands. The Christmas Island tour gives you the chance to view seasonal wildlife such as dolphins, whale sharks, and the famous annual march of the land crabs. Tour guides are natural historians, ornithologists or botanists.

Eco Bush Tours

P.O. Box 183, North Fremantle, WA 6159
☎ (8) 9336 3050 **fax:** (8) 9335 6757
email: frank@bushecotours.com.au
website: www.bushecotours.com.au or
www.webpag.com/ecotours
Small-group, inclusive eco tours lasting from 1 to 4 days, giving good opportunities to view wildlife. Chance to participate in activities such as bushwalking, swimming or canoeing.

Landscope Expeditions UWA Extension

The University of Western Australia, Nedlands
WA 6907
☎ (8) 9380 2433 **fax:** (8) 9380 1066
email: extension@uwa.edu.au
For research and project details contact:
Kevin Kenneally
☎ (8) 9334 0561 **fax:** (8) 9334 0498
email: kevink@calm.wa.gov.au
Become a paying volunteer in a University field research project. Can take you to remote places and often gives you a chance to see wildlife at close quarters. You'll work alongside scientists but experience is not necessary. Past expeditions have included documenting plants in the little known Purnululu National Park and surveying the fauna of the ancient Pilbara area.

Snappy Gum Safaris

See Camping Safaris for details. Can provide special interest tours in the Pilbara region, noted for its geological formations and diverse range of plants and animals.

Western Geographic Eco Tours

31 Marmion Street, Fremantle, WA
☎ (8) 9336 4992 **fax:** (8) 9336 4485
email: ecotours@starwon.com.au
website: www.starwon.com.au/~ecotours
Offer various 4WD tours, including some that specialize in wildflowers. Also run a 15-day eco tour that takes in Ayers Rock.

NORTHERN TERRITORY & SOUTH AUSTRALIA
Umorrduk Aboriginal Safaris

See Cultural Trips for details. Birdwatching and wildlife tours in the wilderness areas of the Northern Territory.

New South Wales & Victoria
Australian Eco Tours

See Birdwatching for details.

North Island
New Zealand Nature Safaris

52 Holborn Drive, Stokes Valley 6008
mobile ☎ 025 360 268 **freecall** ☎ 0800 697
232 **fax:** (4) 563 7324
email: nzns@globe.co.nz
website: www.nzsafaris.co.nz
Small-group nature safaris all over New
Zealand. There are 4 different tours lasting
from 4 to 10 days.

South Island
Catlins Wildlife Trackers

Papatowai, RD 2, Owaka, Sth Otago
☎/**fax:** (3) 415 8613
email: catlin@es.co.nz
website: www.es.co.nz/~catlinw/home.htm
Stay in the home of your hosts who offer 2- and
4-day eco tours of the Catlins Coast. You will
have the chance to see Hooker's sealions, ele-
phant seals, and fernbirds.

Graeme's Seal Adventures Kaikoura

202 Esplanade, Kaikoura
☎ (3) 319 6182 **fax:** (3) 319 6241
email: sws/graeme@clear.net.nz
Two-hour trips that give you the chance to
snorkel with fur seals in their natural habitat.

Monarch Wildlife Cruises

Corner Wharf and Fryatt Streets, P.O. Box 102,
Dunedin
☎ (3) 477 4276 **freecall** ☎ 0800 666 272
Operate wildlife cruises with the chance to
observe albatross, penguins, seals, and shags.

Nature Quest New Zealand

P.O. Box 6314, Dunedin, South Island
☎/**fax:** (3) 489 8444
email: naturequest@compuserve.com
website: www.naturequest.co.nz
Specialists in tailor-made environmental education tours, particularly birding and botany.

Royal Albatross Centre

Taiaroa Head, Otago Peninsular, P.O. Box 492
Dunedin
☎ (3) 478 0499 **fax:** (3) 478 0575
email: albatross@es.co.nz
Guided tours of the world's only mainland
albatross colony.

Safari Excursion

41 Glencarron St, Alexandria, Central Otago
☎/**fax:** (3) 448 7474
Guided wildflower walks through valley floors
and on the mountains of Otago.

St Arnaud—Eco Activities and Adventures

Cnr Bridge and Holland Street, St Arnaud 7150
☎ (3) 521 1028 **fax:** (3) 521 1028
email: c-clarke@st-arnaud.co.nz
Botanist-guided 4WD tours and walks in alpine
environment with unique native flora.

The Oamaru Blue Penguin Colony

Breakwater Road, Oamaru Harbour
Private Bag 50058, Oamaru
☎/**fax:** (3) 434 1718
email: oamvin@nzhost.co.nz
Early evening viewing of the world's smallest
penguin returning home to socialize and play.

White Heron Sanctuary Tours

P.O. Box 19, Whataroa
☎ (3) 753 4120 **fax:** (3) 753 4087
Trips to New Zealand's only White Heron
(Kotuku) breeding colony. The trip lasts 2-
hours and includes a jet boat trip.

Yellow Eyed Penguin Conservation Reserve

Penguin Place, RD 2, Harrington, Point Road
P.O. Box 963, Dunedin
☎/**fax:** (3) 478 0286
This is a conservation programme for the
world's rarest penguin. There is a 90-minute
tour during which you can observe the penguins from a hide system.

ZORBING

Zorbing is the latest craze in New Zealand and
involves being strapped into a large PVC ball
surrounded by a bubble of air. You are then
hurled down a hill or onto water, snow or ice.

North Island
Zorb Rotorua

P.O. Box 586, Rotorua
☎ (7) 332 2768 **mobile** ☎ 025 850 628
email: zorb@zorb.com
website: www.zorb.com/zorbnz.htm
Roll downhill or bounce around on the water in
an enormous PVC ball.

GENERAL INDEX

GAZETTEER

GAZETTEER

ACKNOWLEDGEMENTS

Anna Carter: Thanks to Margaret, still speaking to me after I understated our subterranean adventure because I couldn't face it on my own. Also to fellow traveller Graeme Johnson, who shared his experience and good humour with me, and to Sylvia and Peter Guy, owners of Howard's Lodge, for encouragement, kindness and inviting me to their home for a cold beer and a brag.

Matt Cawood: Thanks to Lorraine Edmunds, SA Department for Environment & Heritage; Keith & Lynette Rasheed, Wilpena Pound Resort; Tourism Tasmania, Albert Thompson and Tasmanian Department of Conservation & Land Management for help in South West Tasmania.

Christopher Knowles: Thanks to Trish at Naturally New Zealand Holidays for making my trip to New Zealand possible despite inclement weather conditions.

Andy Reisinger and Veronika Meduna: Thanks to Makere and Whare Biddle for their hospitality and generosity; Winky, the daughter of the last gold digger on the Shotover River, and our Skipper's Canyon guide Pete, and Jenny, our horse trekking guide in the Hurunui. Further thanks to Graeme Ching and Mike Kelly for help with logistics. Veronika is also grateful to the crowd on the Pipeline bungee bridge for counting her down, and to Gentleman Jim for not galloping off with her. Many thanks also to all other operators whose adventure activities we shared and to Chris Bagshaw. Andy values the advice from guide Brad, on cold water and certain body parts.

Simon Richmond: Thanks to Ayres Rock Resort, Alice Springs Camel Outback Safaris, Peter Cochran at Cochran Family Tradition Horsetreks, Kosciuszko Thredbo, Cradle Huts, Tasmanian Expeditions, Great Australian Walks, Fantastic Aussie Tours and Jenolan Caves Reserve Trust.

Lee Karen Stow: Thanks to Kate Clarke at Brisbane Tourism; Delvene Bee at Greyhound Pioneer Australia; Bastien and Danny at Jungle Tours Rainforest and Outback Adventures; Sarah Carter at Raging Thunder; Undara Lodge in the Gulf Savannah; Tangalooma Wild Dolphin Resort; Rod Austin at VIP Backpackers Resorts and all the staff; Brett Claxton at Cairns Backpackers Inns. Finally, Todd Willis, roller-skating champion at Blade Sensations, Brisbane, for curing my jet lag.

Steve Watkins: In Western Australia: Stephanie Lang at the London office of the Western Australia Tourism Commission and Marina Grant at the Perth office, Qantas, Simon Fitzclarence for providing a bed and entertainment in Perth, Kirsty Hunt at the Exmouth Tourist Bureau, Peter Turner at Exmouth Cape Tourist Village, Kristin Anderson at Exmouth Diving Centre, Jeff Bubb at Ocean Quest Charters, Neil and Rhondda McGregor at Yardie Creek Cruises, Richard Wain at Ningaloo Ecology Cruises, Axel and Eske at the Sea Breeze Resort and the Potshot Hotel Resort. In the South West: Budget Rent A Car, About Bike Hire in Perth, Kim Hancock at Dunsborough Bay Village Resort, Greg and Gaby at Cape Dive, Helen Lee at Cave and Canoe Bushtucker Tours, Trevor McGowan at Adventure In, Mark at Ngilgi Cave, Josh Palmateer and the girls from Margaret River High School, the Karri Valley Resort, Doug at Flinders Park Lodge in Albany, John Healy at Escape Tours. Gibb River Road: Ansett Airlines, Sam Lovell, Taffy Abbotts at Mount Hart, Michael Kerr at Old Mornington, Anne and John Koeyers at Drysdale River, El Questro Wilderness Park, Cable Beach Inter-Continental Resort in Broome and Kununurra Lakeside Resort. In Northern Territory: Carolyn Brown and Jovanka Ristich at the Northern Territory Tourism Commission office in London and Claire George in the Darwin office, Best Western Emerald Hotel in Darwin, Odyssey Safaris and their guide Annette Cook and Tiwi Tours.

Copy editors: Susi Bailey, Nick Reynolds **Paste-up:** Steve Pitcher **Proofreading:** Hilary Weston, Jackie Staddon **Indexer:** Marie Lorimer **Editorial management:** Outcrop Publishing Services, Cumbria

Abbreviations for terms appearing below: (t) top; (b) bottom; (l) left; (r) right; (c) centre

Cover acknowledgements

Front cover (t): **Robert Harding Picture Library** Front cover main picture: **Images Colour Library** Front cover inset: **AA Photo Library/Paul Kenward** Spine: **Robert Harding Picture Library** Back cover (t): **AA Photo Library /Andy Reisinger & Veronika Meduna** Back cover (c): **AA Photo Library/Simon Richmond** Back cover (b): **AA Photo Library/Simon Richmond** Back cover (br): **AA Photo Library/Paul Kenward** Inside flaps: (t): **AA Photo Library/Steve Watkins**; (ct): **AA Photo Library/Steve Watkins**; (cb): **AA Photo Library/Simon Richmond**; (b): **AA Photo Library/Andy Reisinger & Veronika Meduna**

The Automobile Association wishes to thank the following photographers and libraries for their assistance in the preparation of this book:

Australian Tourist Commission Inside cover: Fish, 102(b); **Andy Belcher** Inside cover: Blackwater rafters, 7, 86/87, 99(t), 106(main), 106(inset), 174(main), 174(inset), 178, 179, 182, 183, 186, 186/187, 210(main), 210(inset), 211, 227, 230/231, 231, 234/235, 243(b); **Bruce Coleman Collection** 95(t), 114, 203; **Focus New Zealand Photo Library** 190/191, 222/223, 223; **Christopher Knowles** 175, 206, 250/251

The remaining photographs are held in the Association's own library (**AA PHOTO LIBRARY**) with contributions from the following photographers:

Adrian Baker 46/47; **Matthew Cawood** 78/79, 79, 82/83, 82(t), 82(b), 83, 150(main), 150(inset), 151, 154(t), 154(b); **Nick Hanna** 199(t), 254, 255; **Paul Kenward** Inside cover: Harran's Sky Tower, Auckland, 6/7, 138, 166/167, 167, 170/171, 170, 171, 187, 190, 191, 194, 195(b), 199(b), 202/203, 206/207, 207, 226, 230(t), 230(b), 234, 235, 246(t), 250; **Andy Reisinger & Veronika Meduna** Inside cover: Kaka beak flower, 195(t), 198(t), 198(b), 214, 214/215, 215, 218, 219, 239(main), 239(inset), 242, 243(t), 246(b), 247; **Simon Richmond** Inside cover: Uluru at sunrise, 15, 66, 67, 70/71, 71, 74(main), 74(inset), 78, 118/119, 119, 122, 123(t), 123(b), 126, 127, 130/131, 130, 131, 134(main), 134(inset), 138/139, 139, 142(t), 142(b), 142/143, 146/147, 147, 158/159, 158(l), 158(r), 159, 162, 163(main), 163(inset); **Lee Karen Stow** 3, 87, 90(t), 90(b), 91, 94/95, 94, 95(c), 95(b), 98, 99(t), 102(t), 102/103, 103, 110/111, 110, 111, 114/115, 115; **Steve Watkins** Inside cover: Manyallaluk Aboriginal Tour, 2/3, 18/19, 19, 22/23, 22, 23(tl), 23(tr), 26/27, 26, 27(t), 27(b), 31(main), 31(inset), 34, 35(t), 35(b), 39(t), 39(b), 42/43, 42, 43, 47, 50(t), 50(b), 51, 54/55, 55, 58, 59(t), 59(b), 62(t), 62(b), 63(t), 63(b)

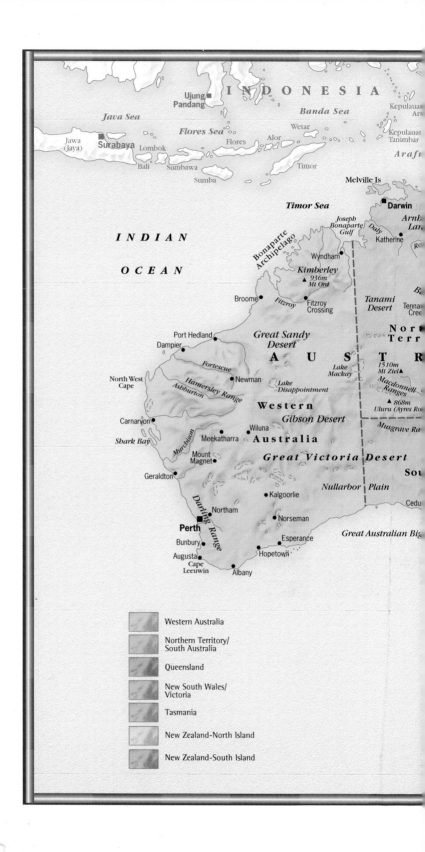

INDONESIA

Java Sea

Banda Sea

Kepulauaı
Arı

Ujung
Pandang

Flores Sea

Wetar

Jawa
(Jaya) **Surabaya** Lombok

Alor

Kepulauaı
Tanimbar

Bali Sumbawa

Flores

Aiafı

Sumba

Timor

Melville Is

Timor Sea ■ **Darwin**

INDIAN

Joseph
Bonaparte
Gulf

Daly

Aml
Laı

Katherine

Rᴏ

OCEAN

Wyndham

Kimberley
▲ 936m
Mt Ord

*Tanami
Desert* Tennaı
Creε

Broome *Fitzroy* Fitzroy
Crossing

*Great Sandy
Desert*

N o r ᴛ
T e r r

Port Hedland
Dampier ●

A U S   T   R

Fortescue

Lake
Mackay

1510m
Mt Ziel▲

Hamersley Range ● Newman

*Lake
Disappointment*

*Macdonnell
Ranges*

North West
Cape

Ashburton

Western

▲ 868m
Uluru (Ayres Rɔ

Carnarvon ●

Gibson Desert

Wiluna ●

Musgrave Rai

Shark Bay

Murchison

Meekatharra *Australia*

Great Victoria Desert

Mount
Magnet ●

Geraldton ●

Nullarbor Plain

Sou

● Kalgoorlie

Cedu

Darling Range

Northam

Great Australian Big

● Norseman

Perth

Bunbury ●

Esperance

Augusta ●
Cape
Leeuwin Albany

Hopetown

	Western Australia
	Northern Territory/ South Australia
	Queensland
	New South Wales/ Victoria
	Tasmania
	New Zealand-North Island
	New Zealand-South Island